People in Places

PEOPLE IN PLACES
THE SOCIOLOGY OF THE FAMILIAR

EDITED BY

ARNOLD BIRENBAUM
Rose F. Kennedy Center
Albert Einstein College of Medicine

AND

EDWARD SAGARIN
The City College
City University of New York

PRAEGER PUBLISHERS
New York • Washington

PRAEGER PUBLISHERS
111 Fourth Avenue, New York, N.Y. 10003, U.S.A.

Published in the United States of America in 1973
by Praeger Publishers, Inc.

Library of Congress Cataloging in Publication Data

Birenbaum, Arnold, comp.
  People in places.
  CONTENTS: Birenbaum, A. and Sagarin, E. A. Introduction: Understanding
the familiar.—Schwartz, B. Notes on the sociology of sleep.—Wolfe, M. Notes on
the behavior of pedestrians. [etc.]
    1. Social interaction. 2. Social role. 3. Role playing. I. Sagarin, Edward,
1913–   joint comp. II. Title.
HM291.B48   301.11   73–1913

Printed in the United States of America

the sociology of the familiar. edited by
Arnold Birenbaum and Edward Sagarin.
New York, Praeger Pub. [1973]

301 p.

Contents

People in Places

Introduction:
Understanding the Familiar

ARNOLD BIRENBAUM AND EDWARD SAGARIN

The 1970's appear to be a time when people are learning new ways of relating to each other. Men and women, blacks and whites, Chinese and Americans, all are going through a painful process of finding out who they are and what they might become, without the support of the traditional myths of sexism, racism, and nationalism. In recent years, these older ways of thinking have been questioned and generally found inadequate for understanding a pluralistic world, but no new ways of thinking have emerged. To examine the activities of everyday living is to engage in an effort to discover a new way of interpreting how we relate to each other, building on some of the most sensitive and insightful thinking in sociology.

The most difficult things to study scientifically are the familiar, the stuff out of which our everyday experiences are constituted. These taken-for-granted occurrences and relationships are elusive and slippery things, providing no vantage point, no "strategic research site," no outside perspective or scaffolding on which to stand. Notice how uncomfortable people get when they think they are being observed or when they are asked to focus on something they normally do routinely and unself-consciously, such as walking down the street. Indeed, people usually take their own routine actions and the actions of others for granted; even when they do subject these activities to close scrutiny, they often do so in the language of everyday life, so that the result is an endless circle of conversation rather than analysis. Breaking through this circle is certainly difficult unless an alternative model of social reality is employed, one that subjects actions as well as words to analysis.

The distinguished American sociologist Erving Goffman has developed such a framework for looking at social relationships by employing the metaphor of the theater and examining the underlying, shared assumptions that members of society utilize when they come into one another's presence. Goffman reminds us of no other social thinker so much as he does of great men of letters, perhaps Marcel Proust or Franz Kafka (we draw the analogy to novelists from Marshall

Berman, 1972). Despite his capacity to discern and point out the deeper significance of apparently insignificant human endeavors, in the great tradition of these artists, he is as precise an observer as any ethnologist or student of animal behavior in natural settings. Unlike those sociologists who study human beings removed from their environments, Goffman always looks at his subjects in the field: in bus stations, on beaches, in living rooms, in elevators, in parks. Moreover, he observes them as social creatures, interacting with others.

Goffman published his first book in 1959, under the revelatory title *The Presentation of Self in Everyday Life*. Thus, he indicated that his concern was with ordinary events in the lives of ordinary people. In everyday life one encounters Everyman, Mr. Nobody, Ms. Anybody, committing no major crimes and creating no great works of art, just managing to survive from morning till night, not in the sense of struggling for food or warding off enemies but in the sense of getting through the day—knowing what to do when he sees a neighbor or a stranger on the street, how to board a bus and find a place to sit, the rules that govern transactions in a store or in a restaurant, gesturing, smiling, hurrying, loitering, greeting, ignoring, each in an apparently unstudied yet highly structured manner.

Goffman's title took account not only of the ordinary and everyday character of behavior but also of how man presents himself to others, the masks he wears, the self he projects. Goffman thus was concerned with man's attempt to give off the best impressions of himself and to do this in such a way that situations are sustained. Central to Goffman's image of people is how their social character is revealed in face-to-face interaction. Alone, a person is hardly human except in the biological sense. He is shaped and emerges as a human being in contact with social institutions and with an entire culture, always mediated through individual relations, one-to-one, one-to-two, one-to-a-group, as the case may be. He reveals himself in these interactions, and others are revealed to him, but the revelations are clouded by the fact that each actor is attempting to dictate how others see him and is at the same time receiving both the image and the attempt to project it from others. The "real" self, the "true" self, is buried in this mutual projection of identities.

Goffman's task, delineated in his first book and followed assiduously in a half-dozen works thereafter, was to demonstrate how the self is constructed in face-to-face interaction and, accordingly, to discern the man behind the mask, although only the mask is there to examine. In a sense, his approach is that of social behaviorism, for he has only the behavior to go by, but he delves far deeper than behaviorists ever dreamed of, for the action is only the starting point, not the symbolic end point, of analysis. His technique involves, first and as a very foundation, naturalistic observation: to determine what human beings do, how they live, who behaves in a given manner and who does not, and what the areas of similarity are between behaviors in dissimilar situations.

The moment the sociologist steps into this role as observer, he becomes reflective about himself, about those he is interacting with, or about those he is watching in interaction. At this time, he has created a special vantage point, and from this position he questions things; the familiar is no longer taken for granted. The sociologist can then consider routine events as being problematic: To the extent that he can raise questions about what occurs, he can also ask questions about how and why such events take place. Then he can move toward asking questions about the conditions under which these behaviors occur or how these behaviors can be grouped with other, seemingly different phenomena.

What is convincing about this method of analysis is the manner in which it depends upon our own experiences as members of society. In this sense, the dramaturgical model of society is far more successful in offering full explanations than are the models of sociologists who study institutions abstractly. This is particularly true if we are to understand how we relate to each other, how we please each other and hurt each other. For example, in "The Insanity of Place" (part of *Relations in Public*, 1971), Goffman depicts the breakdown of family relations when two warring yet collusive factions emerge in the home. "The home, where wounds were meant to be licked, becomes precisely the place where they are inflicted. . . . Offender and offended are locked together screaming, their fury and discomfort socially impacted, a case of organized disorganization." Quoting this passage, Berman (1972) writes: "This is the way more and more of us have come to live now."

Have we? And if we have come to live that way, with what consequences? Berman addresses himself to this question:

> If this is so, it forces us to face some disturbing questions about the breakthroughs of the sixties. For so many Americans these were years of unprecedented personal expression and political confrontation. In every sphere, we "refused to keep our place," we broke boundaries, tore down walls, acted out what we felt, encouraged others to do the same. And where are we now? Goffman's final vision seems unrelievedly bleak. Life in the streets appears as a Hobbesian nightmare, life in the family an existential battleground. It seems terrifying both to go out and to stay in. And social life turns out to be far more fragile, more vulnerable than we thought.

In using Goffman's work to show how we live in today's world, Berman implicitly raises questions about many of the things we regard as "sacred" and unalterable in society. How necessary are many of the social forms and relationships for the maintenance of social order? Don't these forms and relationships inhibit the full expression of our selves? How much of their own lives can human beings create,

and how much must they accept as given from the previous generation? The study of the familiar can shed light on these questions
in several ways, focusing on the self, others, and institutions.

First, the examination of the markedly different ways in which
different people perform the same role reveals much about the range
of behaviors that are permissible in our society and how much of our
selves can be expressed and developed. Secondly, the fully interdependent relationship between conforming and deviant behavior can be
examined in face-to-face interaction, as when people say and do things
whose moral rightness others question, when people fail to respond
to threats and warnings, or when they respond more strongly than
was expected. Accordingly, if we wish to avoid being objectified and
treated as things, awareness of the basic processes of conformity,
deviance, and social control becomes crucial in avoiding the application of labels and categories that may be turned into characteristics
of the person. Such a discovery would be tremendously liberating for
people faced with the problem of avoiding or redefining an unacceptable identity, as in the current effort to decriminalize the deviant life
styles of drug users, homosexuals, political radicals, and prostitutes.
Finally, if we can discover how human beings create and re-create
institutions in face-to-face interaction, it would not only give us
greater respect for the impact of social institutions on our lives but
also suggest new ways of controlling them; by mastering and controlling
their sources—our own behavior—we can receive immediate responses
to our efforts to change institutions.

The Classical Tradition

It is our view that sociology is at its best when it is sensitive to
the problems that confuse and divide the members of society, providing
an alternative vision of reality to those views created by the mass
media and other supposedly official sources. The naturalistic perspective on society, referred to earlier as social behaviorism, has its diverse
roots in the classical tradition of sociology.

The study of situations and their actors began with men who
analyzed their own thoughts and actions rather than directly observing
other people in interaction. In the United States, the philosophers
John Dewey and William James (and to a lesser extent James Mark
Baldwin) provided brilliant speculations on the nature of self and
society, while sociologists George Herbert Mead and Charles Horton
Cooley theorized about the social development of the mind and self.
The University of Chicago produced a school of sociology known as
symbolic interactionism; its later members were noted for their studies
of people playing roles in a variety of situations: occupational, criminal,
sexual, ethnic, and urban. Much of this work was inspired by the
immediate experiences of scholars who had lived through the transition
of America from a homogeneous nation of small-town and farming

communities to a pluralistic nation of large cities with major industries (Stein, 1960).

At the same time, there were four European thinkers who, in one way or another, contributed to the development of sociological perspectives on everyday and commonplace behavior. They were Sigmund Freud, Georg Simmel, Max Weber, and Alfred Schutz. Even earlier, we might trace the thread of this perspective, unexpectedly enough, to Karl Marx.

Marx advanced many useful theoretical assumptions about human beings and the humanly constructed nature of society: as makers of the social world through concrete practical activity, as capable of realizing their selves only through social interaction, as both subject and object at the same time. Further, he showed what happened when men were not fully aware of their capabilities, when they regarded the world as given, when they were forced to debase themselves in false social relationships, and when they turned themselves into objects rather than achieving actualization. This complex view, articulated by Marx in his early works (for example, *The Economic and Philosophical Manuscripts of 1844* [Fromm, 1962]) was later demonstrated in *Capital: A Critique of Political Economy*. This work provides a solid foundation for later efforts to interpret society according to the social relationships made and unmade by its members. However, it suggests that sociology should undertake to deal with what society might be as well as with what it is.

Freud (1965), undoubtedly the best known and to the public the most influential of these thinkers (except for Marx), saw in the everyday life of everyday persons—normal persons, to use the psychological term—certain manifestations that he characterized as psychopathology: for example, forgetting the name of a very familiar person, making a slip of the tongue that proves embarrassing if not humiliating, leaving a hat or an umbrella in a place to which, on a conscious level, one never intends to return. In these actions, Freud found meaning to the actor, the one committing the act. Essentially, Freud utilized everyday experiences to show that his theories of human development and behavior were relevant to persons who were not regarded as mad as well as to those who were. Freud was interested in the unconscious meaning and motivations of what might be termed the pathological acts of everyday man; later thinkers placed their emphases on the social meanings and social bases of the non-pathological or familiar behavior of the same everyday anybody. By pointing out the situationally induced way in which normal persons could perform pathological acts, Freud showed others how to search for meanings in the usual and recurrent acts of human beings as well as in their aberrations.

From Max Weber, the new sociology drew the concept of *verstehen*, a procedure by which the investigator was able to understand the actions of others by taking their role and seeing the world of acts and actions through their eyes. A fundamental aspect of *verstehen*, writes one of Weber's American interpreters (Parsons, 1937:485), "is its reference to 'subjective' phenomena. In so far as 'meanings' may be said to have an empirical spatiotemporal 'existence' at all it is 'in the mind.' There is unquestionably an exceedingly close connection between the apprehension of meaningful relations as such, on the one hand, and the study of the subjective aspect of action, on the other." Weber believed that one could not study social events without taking into account the meaning these acts had to the actors involved. Sociology was the study not merely of "social forces" but of human endeavor as well.

Georg Simmel (1964), a prominent German sociologist and a contemporary of Weber, developed, in what came to be called formal sociology, a forerunner of the modern study of social situations. Formal sociology does not describe an attribute of the discipline but its subject: It is a study of the *forms* of social relationships and associations, including deference, competition, conflict, affection, envy, and subordination, among others. These forms have a similarity and continuity that override the substantive areas in which they manifest themselves; thus, conflict found in a marital situation is, in some respects, not unlike the conflict in an employer-employee or nation-to-nation relationship. Identification of the forms of sociability in the study of large groups of people, their institutions, and their gross departures from expected behavior can contribute to an understanding of the most ordinary and obvious. More important, the reverse is also true.

Finally, and later than the others, there was Alfred Schutz (1967), a refugee from Nazi Germany who came to the United States in the 1930's. Although he is little known to the public, he is now exerting a tremendous influence on American sociology. He emphasized the tenet that reality itself, as we perceive and experience it, is a social construct; that there are different or multiple visions of that reality, each fully valid for those experiencing it; and that the universe through which each of us moves in carrying out our daily tasks is the taken-for-granted world that we create from our surroundings.

By closely following the seminal work of Weber and Mead, Schutz attempted to answer the essential question: If there are multiple realities, how is social order possible? Other theorists, particularly Émile Durkheim, the founder of French academic sociology, answered this question by assuming that people were motivated to comply with the rules of society because they acquired these values early in life, when they were dependent and plastic creatures. Schutz shifted the focus to the active qualities of mind possessed by every individual. He claimed that people make assumptions about one another that overcome the problem of multiple realities; that they share a belief in the "reciprocity of perspectives" (meaning that they regard their own actions objectively to some extent and can take the role of others in reference to themselves); that one's commonsense view of things is a result of one's social position, and that an exchange of positions would produce an exchange of perspectives; that, despite different personal conceptions of reality, language and speech are collective and social mechanisms that make a congruence of relevances possible; and, finally, that knowledge is socially distributed, with each person limited in his understanding of the world but aware of his interdependence with others from whom he might find out things he needs to know. Clearly, then, human beings are not merely subject to the social order but are the makers (and unmakers) of it.

A Way of Seeing

The men whose ideas we have sketched have taught us new ways of looking at the familiar. Are these familiar scenes uninteresting and unimportant? Anyone can see that people more often speak to strangers sitting at a bar than to those seated next to them on subways. A child learns early that he may look but not stare if he sees a midget, that he must walk on the right side on a crowded sidewalk but make sure that he does not bump into anyone else, that there are people whom he addresses as "mister" and other whom he calls by their first names. So what? It is not a recent discovery that these examples of folkways and etiquette make society possible. They are the simple norms that guide everyday activities, the things we all do all through the day and all through our lives. If we had to ask ourselves each moment what the appropriate act is in a given situation and what the probable response to such an act would be, we would be virtually paralyzed.

One may be tempted to reject as unworthy of concern, much less of scholarly study, such unreflecting actions as drinking in a bar, saying "excuse me," riding to and from work, giving gifts, and even getting ready to go to sleep. But it is such nonevents that provide the casualness that everyday life requires for its continuance. Commonplace experience has a substantial part in social life, supplying it with certainty and security. People know that the everyday world is there all the time as a background without ever having to think about it.

In this sense, one need not be concerned with or anxious about the familiar world; nevertheless, it buttresses all human projects, real or imagined. In fact, it is often initially observed, and its importance for sustaining self-concepts and identities is brought into consciousness only when failure to do or say something has made its continuance as an unquestioned background doubtful. At those times, one must grope to recapture that easeful and mindless certainty and security, that orderliness that human beings create and on which they depend for making sense out of the comings and goings and doings of others and of themselves.

The study of man in his most familiar settings can be called situational sociology. It makes social life into a drama, but one in which there is no clear line between actors and audience. People are actors improvising and ad-libbing, almost invariably within programmed limits. And they have been programmed to expect and to desire these limits. When they step outside them, a new situation is created that will again draw forth programmed responses. Or will it create a new drama altogether?

Adolescents laugh as they swing around on a merry-go-round. Like all laughter, theirs is an expression of delight. But it also has a special meaning: The youth are projecting an image of themselves as unlike the people who typically ride on carousels. They are not small children. They define themselves apart from the role they are apparently playing, and a concept arises out of the description, a term, a key to an understanding of a familiar experience. The concept is called role distance, and the remarkable aspect of it is that it illuminates the behavior of people as they go shopping, attend a football game, teach a college class, or cavort with their peers. In such situations people may play roles half-heartedly but still play them. The implications for understanding human society are enormous. It is by looking at these actions and interpreting them that we begin to perceive what Berman has described as "deep tensions and absurdities" in the structure of our social lives. Perhaps, once they are recognized, we can call them into question and change them.

This book is organized according to some traditional but important sociological concepts: culture, conformity and deviance, sociability and solidarity, social control, and, finally, institutions. Starting with the symbols that human beings create, the models they use in interpreting the responses of others, the essays and articles presented here move through the complex social processes that constitute the familiar, here expressed in their most generalizable forms. The end point is the study of institutions—organized ways of doing things—presented in such a way that the reader can see himself as a person who acts within such a complex web of affiliations (to use Simmel's term) and is also acted upon by their structures.

We present here some classic statements by long-established sociologists as well as some less well-known but equally interesting recent efforts. We hope to make the reader simultaneously more familiar with the sociological way of seeing and more appreciative of his own extraordinary capacity to navigate his way through the modern world. In so doing, we seek to share our enthusiasm for *doing* sociology, not just studying it, and the endless fascination that can result from being reflective about what often has been designated the commonplace and the trivial. Perhaps a new language has to be created to refer to the astonishing world of the familiar. Perhaps one will be.

References

BERMAN, MARSHALL
  1972 Review of "Relations in Public." *New York Times,* February 27, 1972.
FREUD, SIGMUND
  1965 *The Psychopathology of Everyday Life.* Translated by ALAN TYSON. New
      York: Norton.
FROMM, ERICH, ed.
  1962 *Marx's Concept of Man.* New York: Frederick Ungar.
GOFFMAN, ERVING
  1971 *Relations in Public.* New York: Basic Books.
  1959 *The Presentation of Self in Everyday Life.* Garden City: Doubleday
      Anchor Books.
MARX, KARL
  1936 *Capital: A Critique of Political Economy.* New York: Modern Library-
      Random House.
PARSONS, TALCOTT
  1937 *The Structure of Social Action.* New York: McGraw-Hill.
SCHUTZ, ALFRED
  1967 *Collected Papers.* Edited by MAURICE NATANSON. The Hague: Martinus
      Nijhoff.
SIMMEL, GEORG
  1964 *The Sociology of Georg Simmel.* Edited by KURT H. WOLFF. New
      York: Free Press.
STEIN, MAURICE R.
  1960 *The Eclipse of Community: An Interpretation of American Studies.*
      Princeton: Princeton University Press.

I. Being Human: The Pervasiveness of Culture

I. Being Human:
The Pervasiveness of Culture

We human beings are strange creatures; while our personalities are very much influenced by our environments, we are nevertheless biological entities—the products of millions of years of evolutionary development. No matter how far along we are in the cultivation of intelligence and creativity, we remain men rather than angels. In fact, cultural evolution and our social natures have made us even more aware of our physiological needs and the great amount of attention they require if the species is to survive. Still, when these biological needs are met, as anthropologists and sociologists have often observed, this is accomplished in culturally defined and socially approved ways.

Culture is the set of symbols people create as members of society, as a way of making sense out of the world. Culture provides a set of recipes for living as well as for sustaining life. Eating, for example, involves not merely filling one's stomach but tacitly complying with a number of conventions, which transforms this simple act of consumption into an occasion, into dining. Moreover, these rules are generally informally enforced by others, often by ridicule, sarcasm, or threats to end social interaction. We are also careful (at least in some sectors of American society) to demonstrate approval or disapproval, in both words and gestures, of the person who prepared the food, to refrain from starting our meal until all who are expected to share it arrive, and to begin dining at the proper place and at the proper pace.

Meeting the basic need for an adequate nutritional and caloric intake is, in general, fraught with cultural restrictions. Anthropologists and historians tell us that hungry people have starved rather than eat a forbidden food. Others have suffered the same fate when they would not sacrifice their honor by begging or stealing food. Thus, consuming the appropriate food and drink is a sign of membership in one's community. Much less dramatic, but of equal import for understanding how human beings develop a sense that the world may be taken for granted, is the way in which these simple social acts related to sheer human existence help to establish social and temporal certainty. The consumption of food, the elimination of wastes, and rest become ways of regularly marking the beginning, middle, and end of our days, ways of knowing that all's right with the world and that we can continue to believe in its existence and our own existence as well. Similarly, they signify the development of a social relationship as it moves toward greater intimacy or from intimacy to alienation. Dining together may cement a relationship or end one, as the Last Supper did.

It is interesting to observe what happens to people when these routine activities become problematic. People become disoriented when they have not been able to sleep, eat, or eliminate at their own will. Reports from concentration camps, prisons, and mental institutions often note regressive behavior as a result of loss of control over when and where to conduct these sustaining activities. Novels about human survival in closed societies, such as Alexander Solzhenitsyn's *The First Circle*, describe how authorities deliberately disorient new prisoners by making their control over their own bodies unpredictable. In turn, these circumstances can become the basis for acquiring a new way of looking at reality; thus Malcolm X, in his autobiography, movingly describes his acceptance among non–English speaking Muslim pilgrims at an impromptu meal in an airport on the way to Mecca.

It is useful to begin this excursion into the sociology of everyday life by examining sleep—simultaneously important as a restorer of our energies and as a way of knowing that one day has ended and another begun. Moreover, even a supposedly private and biological act such as sleeping is socially organized to blend in with the rhythms of society while providing its members with a period of psychic and physical remission. Barry Schwartz, an acutely sensitive analyst of the social aspects of such common activities, contributes a revealing account of the sociological implications of this seemingly nonsocial act.

Similarly, the biologically given ability to walk provides the observer of human interaction with the opportunity to show how organized and controlled such an activity can become, with its implicit rules and its sanctions for upholding and violating those rules. Walking in the presence of others is not just a culturally influenced activity but also a form of social display in which people express the selves they would like others to regard them as being. The bop-walk of the teenage gang member tells that he is looking for action. In traditional Western societies, taking a turn around the town square is an event; it is more than getting from one place to another. Indeed, in many languages the expression "to take a walk" is quite different from the word used to express the act of walking. The Sunday family walk as depicted in the Czech film *The Shop on Main Street* was a social occasion in which the respectable segment of society reaffirmed its respectability. Michael Wolff, in his essay on pedestrian behavior, analyzes the complex social behavior of people on one of the world's most famous streets.

Finally, what appears to be a private entertainment, without great significance, sometimes reveals people who are trying to live up to implicit rules for behavior while ostensibly killing time—as in playing pinball machines. When people create such rules, William B. Sanders shows, they are not only making possible the complex management of many activities in a given territory; they are also making it possible for people to express their solidarity with one another. Perhaps a large part of being human is not just learning the recipes for living but being willing to seek out others for mutual support and reinforcement of these recipes, even in the most unexpected places.

1. Notes on the Sociology of Sleep [*]

BARRY SCHWARTZ

Sleep as a Periodic Remission

Every social organization exhibits structural features which both guarantee the regular performance of duties and insure release from such performances. As Philip Rieff (1966:232–33) points out, all groups must "(1) organize the moral demands men make upon themselves . . . [and] (2) organize the expressive remissions by which men release themselves, in some degree, from the strain of conforming to the controlling symbolic. . . ." As the term implies, "expressive remissions" have two functions: (1) to insulate the individual from the pressure of normative demands and (2) to enable him to express such aspects of his nature and character as would be inhibited in the absence of such insulation. By providing relief from the discipline of social life, remissions make that life more bearable and are for this reason important modes of social control.

Two modes of "expressive remissions" are distinguishable. First, there exist such "bands of remission" as surround or give latitude to the role prescriptions governing current activities. The scope of such latitude is quite variable, ranging from mildly remissive "side involvements" (Goffman, 1963a:43) [1] to the outrightly deviant "institutionalized *evasions* of institutional rules" (Merton, 1957:343). [2]

---

[*] Reprinted from *The Sociological Quarterly*, Vol. 11, No. 4 (Fall 1970), pp. 485–99. Copyright 1970 by the Midwest Sociological Society. Reprinted by permission of the Midwest Sociological Society and the author.

[1] For Goffman, "A main involvement is one that absorbs the major part of an individual's attention and interest, visibly forming the principal current determinant of his actions. A side involvement is an activity that an individual can carry on in an abstracted fashion without threatening or confusing simultaneous maintenance of a main involvement. Whether momentary or continuous, simple or complicated, these side activities appear to constitute a kind of fuguelike dissociation of minor muscular activity from the main line of an individual's action. Humming while working and knitting while listening are examples" (1963a:43).

[2] Merton writes: "*Some* measure of leeway in conforming to role expectations is presupposed in all groups. To have to meet the strict requirements of a role at all times, without some degree of deviation, is to experience insufficient allowances for individual differences in capacity and training and for situational exigencies which make strict conformity extremely difficult. This is one of the sources of what has been elsewhere noted in this book as socially patterned, or even institutionalized, evasions of institutional rules" (1957:343).

Secondly, we may designate as "periodic remissions" those which admit of total emancipation from the imperatives which are merely mitigated by the permissiveness that is built into them. Among the periodic remissions we find holidays, vacations, weekends, and nights-out, as well as orgies, debaucheries, and binges of varied sort. Less dramatic remissions of this type include coffee breaks, lunch hours, lavatory visits, and similar "role releases" or (what Goffman would call) "subordinate involvements." [3]

Sleep is perhaps the most important form of periodic remission. If it were not forced upon us by nature, we would be obliged to find some functional equivalent for it, for social coexistence would cease to be gratifying—or even bearable—if men could not regularly renounce their consciousness of it. It would be difficult to imagine anyone with the capacity to abandon himself to an incessant wakefulness without becoming overwhelmed by the cumulative demands and irritations to which he would then be subject.[4] Parsons (1951:396), for example, writes:

It is inherent in the view of social action taken here that all such action involves tensions and the necessity of the imposition of frustrations and disciplines of the most various sorts. This fact underlies the occurrence of a variety of rhythmic cycles of effort and rest, of discipline and permissive release and the like. Sleep is clearly one of the most fundamental of these tension release phenomena, which though it has

[3] Intermittent "subordinate involvements" (Goffman, 1963a:44) are sustained by an individual "only to the degree, and during the time, that his attention is patently not required by the involvement that dominates him. Subordinate involvements express . . . in their style a continuous regard and deference for the official, dominating activity at hand." Thus, while side involvements may accompany dominant involvements, subordinate ones are periodic remissions from them. As such, subordinate involvements, unlike side involvements, may be engrossing. "Thus, while waiting to see an official," writes Goffman, "an individual may converse with a friend, read a magazine, or doodle with a pencil, sustaining these engrossing claims on attention only until his turn is called, when he is obliged to put aside his time-passing activity even though it is unfinished." As we have seen, however, periodic remissions may also constitute dominant involvements, as in the case of sleep.

[4] Thomas Mann (1933:270; 275) made the same point when he wrote: "I know what it was that . . . fanned my latent fondness [for sleep] to a conscious love. It was the tale of a man who did not sleep, who was so abandonedly committed to time and affairs that he invoked a curse on sleep, and an angel granted him the awful boon of sleeplessness, breathing on his eyes till they became like grey stones in their sockets, and their lids never closed again. Now this man came to rue his wish; what he had to bear as a sleepless solitary among men, dragging out his doomed and tragic life, until at last death released him and night, that had stood inaccessible before his stony eyeballs, took him to and unto herself. . . . [Thus], precisely as morals function to correct and discipline the free possible into the limited and actual, so perhaps morals in their turn need a corrective, a ceaseless admonition, never quite to go unheeded, a call to withdrawal and communion. If this be wisdom, then its opposite will be the folly of the man who cursed sleep and clung with blind eagerness to time and day."

biological foundations is nevertheless profoundly influenced by interaction on sociocultural levels.

We would amend Parsons by designating sleep as *the* fundamental
tension release phenomenon, for it is emancipating not merely with
respect to the social world outside of us but also (as Cooley would
put it) with respect to the "society within" (1964:119–22); it admits
of withdrawal from all that is subjectively as well as objectively social.
Because it circumvents consciousness itself, sleep is a total [5] release
from the frustrations and disciplines to which Parsons refers. Sleep
thus achieves its sociological significance as the most radical form
of institutionalized periodic withdrawal.

The Institutionalization of Sleep

Sleep is such an important aspect of life, so socially and biologically
necessary, that social organizations must see to its protection. Indeed,
one of the most important questions facing the sociology of sleep is,
"How do groups insure the sleep of their members when sleep is itself
so unstable, so vulnerable to immediate external stimuli?"

For Freud, also, sleep was problematical. However, his conception
of the problem differs from our own. Freud sought to clarify the
dilemma posed to sleep by its *internal* adversaries. His solution illumi-
nated the manner in which personality defended sleep against the
menace of forbidden wishes pressing for conscious recognition. The
dream, as we all know, plays the key part in this process. For Freud
(1950:424–26; 430–32), the dream protects sleep.

Addressing ourselves as we do to the *external* threats to sleep, we
are concerned with the social arrangements by which it is regulated
and defended. This involves us in the problem of how sleep is
institutionalized as a role within social systems. Institutionalization
thus plays the same part in the sociology of sleep that the dream
plays in its psychology.

[5] There is some question as to whether dreams violate the totality of sleep's
remission. One function of the dream is to provide symbolic fulfillment of desires
whose very existence is prohibited in waking life (Freud, 1950:33–69. See especially
67–68). The dream is thus remissive with respect to normative constraints. It may
therefore be argued that while dreamless sleep denies the discipline of wakefulness
by closing off consciousness of it, the dream-filled sleep achieves this same objective
by neutralizing the *content* of such discipline. Even the nightmare may perform
a remissive function. Viktor Frankl (1963:45), for example, describes the following
concentration camp experience: "I shall never forget how I was roused one night
by the groans of a fellow prisoner, who threw himself about in his sleep obviously
having a horrible nightmare. Since I had always been especially sorry for people
who suffered from fearful dreams or deliria, I wanted to wake the poor man. Suddenly I drew back the hand which was ready to shake him, frightened about the
thing I was about to do. At that moment I became intensely conscious of the fact
that no dream, no matter how horrible, could be as bad as the reality of the camp
which surrounded us, and to which I was about to recall him."

Schedules and Their Default

"One of the primary functions of institutionalization," writes Parsons (1951:302), "is to help order . . . different activities and relationships so that they constitute a sufficiently coordinated system, to be manageable by the actor and to minimize conflicts on the social level." One aspect of such ordering is the "time schedule" whereby certain times are set aside for specific activities (see, e.g., Moore, 1963). The coordination within a collectivity of the timing of sleep is one of the most important senses in which it is institutionalized. It is because persons must have one another at their disposal in waking life that they sleep simultaneously.[6] But simultaneity serves an additional function. Because most of us engage in sleep during approximately the same hours, we are—within generally tolerable limits—automatically insulated against sleeplessness and/or premature awakening caused by the activities of others.

The coordination of sleep becomes more imperative as the possibilities for its disruption increase. The mere number of individuals in a social unit has a direct bearing upon this probability. Among married couples, for example, the arrival of a new child so compromises their sleeping schedule (and, thereby, the order of their daily lives) as to make the earliest possible synchronization of his sleep with theirs an imperative. This feat requires such tactics as keeping the child awake late enough so that sleep throughout the night becomes necessary for him. In this way, the prerequisite of sleep synchronization hastens and insures the youngster's integration into the family's pattern of activity. Individuals therefore sleep simultaneously not only to have one another at their disposal in waking life, but they may also interact with one another in order to synchronize their sleep.

In urban life, where the density of population heightens the possibility of collisions between the sleeping and the wakeful, the phenomenon of the sleep-schedule is of greater moment as a condition of life-in-common than it is in the more sparsely populated areas. Especially in apartment living, where neighbors reside in very close proximity to one another, any de-synchronization of activity schedules is liable to be disruptive to the sleep of neighbors. Apartment landlords make provision for such difficulties in their leases, which generally prohibit the use of radios, TV's, and phonographs before and after

---

[6] It is true that sleep scheduling is more dependent upon such cosmic variations as night and day in non-industrial communities than in industrial ones, for many activities, including agriculture and hunting, can only be carried out in daylight. Similarly, sleep patterns must adjust themselves to climate. Siestas, for example, are a routine part of the daily activity structure of many societies situated in hot climates. However, cosmic factors affect the *timing* of sleep more than they do its *functions*. Even where cosmic limitations are overcome by artificial light and temperature controls, people continue to tend to sleep simultaneously. But these artificial resources do admit of more flexibility in the scheduling of sleep and wakefulness. Such flexibility raises problems to which we shall attend later.

certain hours. This specific rule is an instance of a general principle set down by Simmel (1950:413): "the technique of metropolitan life is unimaginable without the most punctual integration of all activities and mutual relations into a stable and impersonal time schedule."

The effective scheduling of sleep requires the regulation of not only those activities which *inhibit* sleep but also of activities which *facilitate* it. Endeavors which promote drowsiness must be fitted into those parts of the day during which the individual is unengaged in work or serious activity. Eating is one example. In modern societies, for instance, "dieticians seem unanimous that the last should be the big meal of the day. It is thought to be the only time of day when sleepiness would not hinder important activity" (de Grazia, 1962:171).

The Sleep Role and Its Transition Phase

If every member of a community retired and awoke at precisely the same time the question "How is sleep brought under institutional control?" would be satisfactorily answered. But the most interesting aspect of schedules is their inability to coordinate social life *perfectly*. We need not go into the many individual differences which compel one to begin or terminate sleep a little early or late to recognize the problems which such variability present to the social unit. Because of this variability, the sleeper must be placed in a socially categorized or institutionally defined framework which evokes the deference and support of the wakeful. Were those first awake not inhibited by a set of institutionalized expectations (and therefore subject to certain evaluations and sanctions) the repose of the group would much more frequently end for all because it had ended for one. The body of rights and obligations that surround the sleeper thus *supplement* the controlling function of schedular integration.

The fundamental right of the sleeper is obviously that which forbids his awakening within a specific time period.[7] In our society this interval is of course far more ambiguous on weekends than it is on weekdays. However, an individual need not give up the rights of the sleep role, even if he is physically awake, until its (variably defined) limits are reached. He who chooses to remain awake in bed is, up to a certain point, *socially* asleep and entitled to all the benefits attending such a status.

Deference to the sleeper is not required merely of those in his intimate circle; outsiders must show the same consideration. They must refrain, for example, from making social calls or even telephone calls at a late hour in respect for his desire not to be bothered by anything that might disturb the state of mind or mood necessary for sleep. The reason for this convention is that the sleep role, like

[7] One of the most radical definitions of this right is to be found among the Navaho, for whom misfortune flows from the act of even stepping over a sleeping person (see Kluckhohn, 1946:47).

all roles that require substantial physical and/or mental preparation, cannot be abruptly taken on and cast off; its assumption must be preceded by an institutionalized "transition phase" wherein the individual may gradually adapt himself to it. Because the transition phase hardens the boundaries between the prospective sleeper and a potentially disruptive outer-world, the sleeper is able to easily disattend or suppress this world. He is thus protected by an "interaction membrane" (Goffman, 1966:121) [8] which reliably filters out disturbing communications.

The transition phase which lessens the difficulty of moving into the sleep role also facilitates its abandonment. This function is indispensable to the just-awakened, who must be protected from public demand until he is capable of responding to it. He must warm up, so to speak, by first attending to the self-imposed rituals of leaving bed, bathing, and dressing before he confronts the demands of his family. These rituals mediate his transition from unconsciousness to interaction. Such a difficult passage is facilitated architecturally. "When asleep in bed," writes Goffman (1959:121), "the individual is also immobilized, expressively speaking, and may not be able to bring himself into an appropriate position for interaction or bring a sociable expression to his face until some moments after being awakened, thus providing one explanation of the tendency to remove the bedroom from the active part of the house." Moreover, the sleeper may not only be *unable* to immediately assume the obligations of waking life; he may also be *unwilling* to do so. The principle laid down by Becker and Strauss (1956:259) in reference to *status passages* may therefore be relevant to *role passages* as well. "Transition periods are a necessity," they write, "for a man often invests heavily of himself in a position, comes to possess it as it possesses him, and suffers in leaving it. If the full ritual of leavetaking is not allowed, the man may not pass fully into his new status." [9]

The just-awakened is thus confronted by a reality with which his ego has not yet made complete contact and which his unconscious impulses might therefore offend, for the ego, upon awakening, does not immediately reassert its control over them, but does so only gradually (Bettelheim, 1950:95). Thus, among emotionally disturbed children, notes Bettelheim (1950:95), the reestablishment of ego control requires that social contact after awakening be mediated by a pleasant representative of the reality to be confronted. In helping such children to engage an heretofore painful world, then, the world must be made as congenial as possible. "Therefore, first and foremost,

[8] This concept was introduced by Erving Goffman (1966:65). It is also possible to find individuals who take advantage of the interaction membrane by doing work that might be disturbed during other parts of the day.

[9] The similarity of the terms "transition phase" and "transition period" is coincidental. Similar to both is Bettelheim's (1950:115–32) concept of "in-between time."

the counselor must be there when the children awake, and he must not try to waken them before they are ready." Thus, in this special setting—and in this particular sense—the individual is spared some of the burden of adjusting to the world; to a degree, the world adjusts itself to him. (For a concrete instance of this process, see Bettelheim, 1950:93–94. For a discussion of class differences in modes of awakening, see Bossard and Boll, 1950:113.)

In some total institutions, however, such transition mechanisms as those which we have described are conspicuously absent. Very much unlike the civilian, or Bettelheim's patients, the newly-awakened prisoner is subject to sudden and uninsulated external demands, as Hassler (1954:155) shows:

> At 5:30 we were awakened and had to jump out of bed and stand at attention. When the guard shouted 'One!' you removed your nightshirt; at 'Two' you folded it; at 'Three' you made your bed. (Only two minutes to make the bed in a difficult and complicated manner.) All the while three monitors would shout at us: 'Hurry it up!' and 'Make it snappy!'

It is perhaps the default of protection against sudden shifts in or impositions of normative demand that best sensitizes us to the benefits of such insulatory modes as the transition phase. It also appears that the transition phase serves the same function in respect of *role shifts* that anticipatory socialization (Merton, 1957:165) does with reference to *status shifts*. Whereas the former mechanism eases passage from one role to another during movement through the daily activity cycle, the latter lubricates the passage from one status to another in movement across the life cycle. Both mechanisms, then, facilitate movement to new social "locations" and ease adjustment once the shift has been made; in their absence, shifts in roles and statuses become, in effect, social shocks.

The Reciprocity of Motive and Action in the Sleep Role

In considering the successful assumption or abandonment of the sleep role it would be misleading to overemphasize the functions of the transition period. This is because many roles possess an internal compulsion which helps insure proper conduct by setting up predefined and self-sustaining grooves for it. This process is conspicuous in the bedtime preparation ritual.

The bedtime ritual is generally initiated by a familiar cue such as the face of a clock or the end of a TV program. This cue sets into motion the ceremony of undressing, putting aside the clothes in a certain way, washing, donning the sleeping costume, and so forth. These habituations [or obsessions (Freud, 1963:18), as the case may be] are not only carried out in response to sleepiness, but they also produce it. This paradox reveals an interesting convergence of role theory and conditioning theory. As is known, the natural stimulus of fatigue almost always becomes associated with a particular mode of preparation, a certain time, a familiar bed, darkness, and quiet. The individual may be so well conditioned by these stimuli that he will fall asleep when they are operative even though he is not particularly tired. "Exactly in the same manner," writes Pavlov (1960:263), "extra stimuli and conditioned stimuli which upon repetition bring about a state of sleep, with practice bring about this state more and more easily." Thus, the more the bedtime ritual is repeated the more inexorable it becomes as a conditioning stimulus. Note that what is conditioned is motive. The individual, as we have seen, does not simply prepare for bed because he is tired; he also grows tired *because* he prepares for bed. While the motive to assume the sleep role may exist before it is assumed, the assumption itself acts back upon the motive and strengthens it. This reciprocal effect between motive and action, between, let us say, "inside" and "outside" constitutes the control dynamic that, according to Berger (1963:98), is inherent in all roles. As Berger notes, "Each role has its inner discipline. . . . The role forms, shapes, patterns both action and actor. It is very difficult to pretend in this world. Normally, one becomes what one plays at."

The ritualized movements which condition sleep take place during the nightly transition phase; another set of movements conditions wakefulness in the morning. Note, however, that different functions are served in the two cases. At bedtime the transition phase, via insulation from external demand and ritualized, conditioning actions, helps to relax ego control and diminish its watchfulness so as to permit sleep; in the morning, however, the transition phase helps to re-establish ego control (Bettelheim, 1950:350).

Anomic Sleep Roles

We have seen that sleep is facilitated by institutionalized transition periods and a built-in dynamic that strengthens the motive of the role incumbent; but, we have also observed that sanctions are required in order to deter those who might interfere with either the preparation for or the actual undertaking of sleep. The sleep role may therefore be designated as anomic when sanctions fail to correspond to abuses of its expectation system. Such a condition, which renders the sleep role oppressive, is exemplified by the night-shift worker.

We know that sanctions regarding sleep include, in their negative forms, (1) formal punishments for disturbance of the (public) peace and (2) informal household punishments. Both forms of sanction happen to be less binding during daylight hours than they are at night. This is because the sleep role is "missituated" (or imperfectly institutionalized) during the day and therefore evokes less deference. Since almost the entire community must be active (and often disrup-

tively so) during the day, it is unlikely to back up a complaint that
particular expectations of sleep-deference have been violated. This fact
presents a problem for those who routinely sleep during the day and
who lack the sleep-protection nightly afforded by political authority
to the more conventional folk.

Even within the home, the controls of the sleep role may fail to
operate. Children of the night-shift worker often have difficulty
defining the daylight hours as a time for the self-restraint elsewhere
reserved for the night. Therefore, "the demand for daytime sleep,"
writes Mott (1965:12),[10] "can generate friction in the family. Very
often the husband's sleep, the children's play, and the wife's housework
must be carried out at the same time. If the worker cannot adapt to
the noise level created by these activities, he may become irritable
with both wife and children, or they with him, and family relations
may become strained." The case of the daytime sleeper thus highlights
for us the contagiousness of marginality. Those whose activities fail
to "fit in" with the interests of those around them in one sphere
soon find themselves to be misfits with respect to others as well.

The Obligations of the Sleep Role

Through his own inability to fulfill them and by way of the problems
with which he is thus confronted, the night worker introduces us to
the *obligations* of the sleep role in the more conventional life. The
presence of the sleeper, as we have seen, opens up and closes off
certain possibilities of action among the wakeful; therefore, specific
rules must defend individuals against the impositions to which the
sleeper might otherwise subject them.

The central obligation of the sleeper is not to demand more
deference than he is due. Above all, he must segregate himself physically
so as not to needlessly intrude upon the conscious world, lest his relation to this world lose the respect that it requires. Family members,
for example, justly resent another's napping in such public areas as
the parlor insofar as they are deprived of their right to undertake the
social relations which require access to this room. Moreover, many
individuals feel that they have the right *not* to be exposed to the
"creature release behavior" of the sleeper. For Goffman (1963a:68),
"creature releases . . . consist of fleeting acts that slip through the
individual's self-control and momentarily assert his 'animal nature'."
Among sleepers these acts may include grunting, scratching, squirming,
snoring, flatulence, and the like. Such behavior may compromise the
dignity of not only the sleeper but of the wakeful as well. A slight
amendment must therefore be made to the well-known term "information control" which, as used by Goffman (1963b:41–104), refers to

[10] "All of the 'worker-oriented' studies to date," explains Mott (1965:10), "have
cited difficulties in sleep as a frequent source of complaint, and two studies single
this out as the central problem of shift work."

the manner in which individuals (by the selective granting and with-holding of data about themselves) supervise the impressions they make upon others. We have found this usage to be too restricted, for the individual must also shield himself against "noxious information" *emitted* by others; one may contaminate oneself by the receipt as well as the transmission of demeaning information. Thus, to keep oneself uninstructed is an important aspect of information control. This point bears directly upon Goffman's correlative concept of "back region." The "back region" refers to a physical area within an establishment, bounded by barriers to perception, wherein individuals and groups prepare themselves for or relieve themselves from public display in "front regions" (1959:106–40). But we have observed the back region being used as a quarantine device by which members of a social unit preserve its dignity by temporarily isolating other members who are engaged in such creature release behavior as sleep. The back region may thus be imposed as well as appropriated; it may be employed to close in as well as to close out.

Sleep, Residence, and Identity

The sleeper has also an obligation to do his sleeping within (rather than outside of) the home. This rule is obvious but not trivial and has certain implications for identity. As Aubert and White (1959:1) point out, "The component of a person's status known as residence, which identifies the person with a definite spatial location, is given by the normal sleeping location. A person 'lives' where he sleeps." Even more, a person *belongs* where he sleeps; sleep establishes where the person is in social as well as spatial terms; it situates him in accordance with membership rather than mere presence and, thereby, generates an identity for him. Furthermore, residential membership is solidified when an individual is officially assigned to the same sleeping place that he emotionally "appropriates" for his own. This coincidence of assignment and appropriation is carefully supervised. A crisis exists when it breaks down. Aubert and White (1959:13–14) write:

> What needs to be emphasized here is that a very rigid system of social control operates to enforce the norms of sleep location. It is dramatically demonstrated when the question of 'alibi' is being put, and the suspect fails to show that he slept at the proper time at the proper place. Viewed from an entirely different angle: for a youngster to stay out overnight without parental approval of alternative sleeping place is a kind of deviance which may lead to extensive control measures. These are intimately related to other norms, against sexual activities and against gang delinquency. But whatever the motives behind the invoked sanctions are, they function so as to emphasize the strict normative rule governing sleep location. They may be viewed as a countermeasure against a threat to family solidarity, an attempt to eliminate a disturbance of its most sacred ritual.

Clearly, to sleep "under another roof" is one of the most powerful denials of intimacy. However, the disintegration of social bonds is perhaps nowhere seen or felt more vividly than in the practice among failing marriages of sleeping in the same house but in separate rooms. This is because the *physical* intimacy of common life under a single roof sets in bold relief the *emotional* distance separating the couple, making such distance all the more striking precisely because it is concealed in the physical, i.e., residential sense.

As regards extra-residential sleeping, it might be useful to distinguish between sleeping in private and public places. The former mode of deviation is exemplified in extra-marital sexual arrangements. These unions are often referred to by the expression "sleeping with another woman (or man)." Such terminology suggests that the sexual intercourse which precedes sleep constitutes only one aspect of marital infidelity. The second element is given in the lovers' decision to share a single sleep location, a decision which (particularly when repeated) lifts the relationship beyond a purely physical basis and stamps it with an intimacy that cannot be claimed when the termination of the *social* relationship coincides with the termination of its *sexual* component. Whereas the strictly erotic union subtracts from the sexual aspect of marriage, the act of sleeping together undermines the status and identity embodied in the common residence of a married couple. Purely lustful relations are therefore more likely to leave the performers' visible status and identity intact. These relations may eventually lead to the breakdown of a marital status, but they do not symbolize it as well as when a common sleep residence is superimposed upon them.

Extra-residential sleep is designated as a private matter as long as it is practiced in private places. Those who make use of public places (e.g., parks, transportation facilities, alleys, etc.) for sleeping, however, offend the collectivity and bring down upon themselves the stigma of public condemnation. Like conventional folk, then, "the bum" is recognized and labelled in terms of his sleep location. It follows that one of his problems is to avoid being assessed as such and to thereby retain his sleeping place. Techniques of so doing have been sampled by Edmund G. Love (1957:17-33).[11]

The Vulnerability of Sleep

During the hours of sleep the members of a social unit share not only a common residence and activity but also a common vulnerability. Thus, the solution to the question, "How is sleep protected and brought under society's control?" creates a new question: "How does the sleeping society cope with its absence of control?"

[11] These techniques may be subsumed under Goffman's (1969:12-17) concept of "control moves."

The situation of sleep places the group in perhaps the most marginal position conceivable. A collective separation from consciousness strips the social unit of its orientation in experience and, thereby, of its reality and identity. As Simmel (1959:338) suggests, the very principle of society negates itself when it relinquishes self-consciousness, for "the consciousness of constituting with . . . others a unity is actually all there is to this unity." It is in this particular sense that a society whose entire membership is asleep is, at that moment, no society at all.[12]

The unconscious collectivity lacks not only a *sense* of location in but also an effective control over its social and physical environment. Therefore, no society could afford to permit sleep to overtake its entire membership. Thus, at night, wakefulness itself becomes a scarce and therefore marketable commodity. The phenomenon of "the night watch" introduces itself as the most important mechanism for coping with the vulnerability created by collective unconsciousness. Aubert and White (1959:14) explain that "society must know, from its registers, who and where a person is, when he is incapable of knowing it himself. When people sleep some of the responsibility they have for taking care of their own and society's interests is transferred to others. Watchmen and guards who stay awake when others sleep symbolize this transfer of protective functions."

The insecurity of sleep applies to individuals as well as groups. Nightly, the individual must face the possibility that, because of predatory contingencies, his world may appear altogether differently on the morrow. He needs therefore to find some method of sufficiently mitigating his apprehension so as to be able to willingly give himself up to unconsciousness. It is well known that obsessive, ritualistic preparations for sleep (or any other activity) is a widely-used technique of coping with anxiety (Freud, 1963:18).

During sleep, of course, the individual not only reduces his control over external predators but also relaxes his control over himself. According to Bettelheim (1950:341–74), the default of ego control results in a breakthrough of impulses which were hitherto repressed leading, in turn, to anxiety in the person about what he might do while he is asleep. A moderate amount of such anxiety seems to be quite general. In public places or conveyances, for example, individuals are reluctant to give themselves over totally to unconsciousness for long periods of time, fearing always the compromise of the public bearing that has come to be expected of them. The unsegregated sleeper may commit acts having biographical or reputational consequence precisely at that point where his control over such acts is at a minimum. Even in the privacy of the bedroom, however, there exists the possibility that uncontrolled utterances will betray some secret

[12] Cooley (1964:119–22) makes this same point in his implication that society is dead when individuals cease to serve one another as objects of imagination.

aspect of self and make what was hitherto private information food for thought for at least a public of one.

In some total institutions the bedroom is a public place whose occupants must make themselves available for constant monitoring and inspection. For example, Rule 42 of the Iowa State Penitentiary (1962:89) reads: "When the lights go out at the designated hour go to bed at once and remain quiet. . . . Sleep with the head uncovered to enable the officer to see you." Thus, while the institutionalized sleeper may be minimally vulnerable to external predators, he is maximally subject to the mortification of giving *public* vent to his lower physical and psychological impulses. In general, sleep locations may be characterized in terms of their position on the two dimensions of vulnerability to which we have just drawn attention.

Incidentally, it is precisely because of the vulnerability of sleep that the feigning of sleep places the wakeful in the defenseless position that might otherwise be attributed to the sleeping person. Such modes of impression management as "playing possum" reverse the great difference that normally exists between the power of those sleeping and those awake.

Sleep and Social Rank

In the first section of this paper I tried to indicate the manner in which sleep subserves "horizontal order" by providing a total release from social relations when they have accumulated to such an extent as to be irritating. I have also tried to show how the sleep remission is institutionalized as a role within social systems. Several aspects of this role have been considered. I shall now treat briefly of one further aspect of the sleep role, namely, the manner in which its regulations reflect and, in reflecting, stabilize the "vertical" or hierarchical order. (For further discussion of "horizontal" and "vertical" order see Schwartz, 1968:774.)

In family life, individuals are normally associated with a sleeping place that corresponds to their authority. Among the Yakut of Siberia, for example, sleeping alcoves are uniformly assigned to family members with a clear prestige value attached to each particular alcove (Aubert and White, 1959:15). Similarly, in America, the authority of the parents is affirmed by their appropriation of the "master" bedroom. Sleeping arrangements may also be employed to *level* status differences. In total institutions, for example, the assignment of diverse inmates to identical wards, dormitories, cell blocks, etc. accentuate (from the official point of view) their equality with respect to one another as well as the equivalent inferiority of their status *vis à vis* their caretakers.

There is much evidence to show that high occupational status and social honor are related to later bedtimes and awakenings (for a brief summary see Aubert and White, 1959:12). Indeed, temporal and spatial sleep patterns may be employed as an index of life style.[13] Moreover, even within the family, it is generally true that older children, by dint of their age, are ascribed with the privilege of remaining awake longer than younger ones. This particular practice has implications which merit extended comment. Aubert and White (1959:12–13) note:

> The permission to stay up longer and longer with increasing age, and also as rewards for meritorious behavior, links bedtime to prestige. For children there is a 'career line' within the family; and one of the most significant rewards in this career line is the promotion to a later sleep time. This is, of course, also one of the main reasons why parents' decisions on what is the proper bedtime often are so hotly contested by the children, usually with references to playmates enjoying a more privileged position in this respect.

Sleep patterns do not only reflect the status arrangements within a social unit, but they are also part of a network of power and are employed or imposed (within certain physiological limits) in accordance with an individual's position in this network. At the edge of every power relationship, of course, hangs the possibility of exploitation. Instead of going to sleep themselves, for example, parents may attain some relief from public demand by commanding their public to sleep. Children may therefore be put to bed at an early hour not only by reason of their age and need for sleep but also because they must be gotten rid of. (For a case history in which this practice is routine see Senn and Hartford, 1968:29–83.)

Sleep is also frequently used in early childhood as a mode of control. In many places, children are sent to bed early for misbehavior and rewarded for virtuous conduct by being allowed to stay up a little longer. Either the stratification of bedtime in accordance with status or its delay as a mode of reward may induce children to (correctly) perceive in it many pejorative connotations. So far as they define the sleep role in negative terms, as either status-degrading or punitive, instrumental uses of sleep schedules perhaps contribute (along with the anxieties of which Bettelheim [1950:341–74] has much to say) to the reluctance with which children go to bed. The child is understandably hesitant to retire when he has learned to define his bedtime as a status degradation ceremony.[14] Relatively early bedtimes are there-

[13] By spatial sleep patterns we refer, of course, to variations in privacy during sleep; whether the individual has his "own room" or is a member of a sleeping unit composed of two or more people.

[14] On the other hand, status degradation is by definition an inherent feature of all processes which contribute to hierarchy. Because differential rank is indispensible to social order we are forced to recognize degradation as an inevitable component of all social life; therefore, its acceptance by the child must be inculcated not only through the socialization of his sleep but of his other drives as well. The reference of status degradation, then, cannot be limited, as Garfinkel (1956) suggests, to formal *shaming* ceremonies. It would be more correct to view the latter as a particular instance of the former.

fore unpleasant because they entail not only a separation from a protective social circle but also because they symbolize an inferior status within it.

Summary

If sleep is to serve as an effective periodic remission, the sleeper must be placed in a socially categorized framework. Such categorization, embodied in the sleep role, is scheduled in order to avoid conflicts with other (waking) activities; this role is further insulated from those which precede and follow it by a transition phase and is rendered more compelling by an internal control dynamic that is based on the conditioning process. I have tried to emphasize that the sleep role must be part of a fairly stable authority structure, for it remains institutionalized only so far as sanctions exist to protect the sleeping and the wakeful from one another. When this sanction system breaks down, the remissive opportunity structure is endangered. As was seen in the case of the night-shift worker, such breakdown acts back to further undermine the authority structure of the social unit in which it occurs. Put differently, authority and remission from it are instrumental with respect to one another: remissions reinforce authority by making it more bearable; on the other hand, the remissive opportunity structure is protected by the very authority against which it provides intermission.

Finally, although sleep provides periodic release from the demands and irritations of social life, it also creates problems for the individual who, in temporarily taking leave of the world, relinquishes his control of it and of himself. On the other hand, that aspect of sleep which pertains to its location and timing helps define the individual's identity by symbolizing his position in the world. The individual thus takes leave of society in a framework that defines his relation to it.

References

AUBERT, V., AND H. WHITE
    1959   "Sleep: A sociological interpretation." *Acta Sociologica* 4 (Fasc. 1):46–54; (Fasc. 2):1–16.
BECKER, H. S., AND A. STRAUSS
    1956   "Careers, personality, and adult socialization." *American Journal of Sociology* 61 (November):253–63.
BERGER, PETER
    1963   *Invitation to Sociology.* Garden City: Doubleday.
BETTELHEIM, BRUNO
    1950   *Love Is Not Enough.* Glencoe: Free Press.
BOSSARD, J. H. S., AND E. S. BOLL
    1950   *Ritual in Family Living.* Philadelphia: University of Pennsylvania Press.

COOLEY, CHARLES HORTON
    1964   *Human Nature and the Social Order.* New York: Schocken.
DE GRAZIA, SEBASTIAN
    1962   *Of Time, Work and Leisure.* New York: Twentieth Century Fund.
FRANKL, VIKTOR
    1963   *Man's Search for Meaning.* New York: Washington Square Press.
FREUD, SIGMUND
    1963   "Obsessive acts and religious practices." In PHILIP RIEFF, ed., *Character and Culture.* New York: Collier Books, pp. 17–26.
    1950   *The Interpretation of Dreams.* New York: Modern Library.
GARFINKEL, H.
    1956   "Conditions of successful degradation ceremonies." *American Journal of Sociology* 61 (March):420–24.
GOFFMAN, ERVING
    1969   *Strategic Interaction.* Philadelphia: University of Pennsylvania Press.
    1966   *Encounters.* Indianapolis: Bobbs-Merrill.
    1963a *Behavior in Public Places.* New York: Free Press.
    1963b *Stigma.* Englewood Cliffs: Prentice-Hall.
    1961   *Asylums.* Garden City: Doubleday.
    1959   *The Presentation of Self in Everyday Life.* Garden City: Doubleday.
HASSLER, ALFRED
    1954   *Diary of a Self-Made Convict.* Chicago: Regnery.
Iowa State Penitentiary
    1962   "Rules for inmates." In NORMAN JOHNSTON, LEONARD SAVITZ, and MARVIN E. WOLFGANG, eds., *The Sociology of Punishment and Correction.* New York: John Wiley & Sons, pp. 87–91.
KLUCKHOHN, CLYDE
    1946   *The Navaho.* Cambridge: Harvard University Press.
LOVE, EDMUND G.
    1957   *Subways Are for Sleeping.* New York: Harcourt, Brace & World.
MANN, THOMAS
    1933   *Past Masters.* London: Martin Secker.
MERTON, ROBERT
    1957   *Social Theory and Social Structure.* New York: Free Press.
MOORE, WILBERT E.
    1963   "The temporal structure of organizations." In EDWARD A. TIRYAKIAN, ed., *Sociological Theory, Values, and Sociocultural Change.* Glencoe: Free Press, pp. 161–69.
MOTT, PAUL
    1965   *Shift Work.* Ann Arbor: University of Michigan Press.
PARSONS, TALCOTT
    1951   *The Social System.* New York: Free Press.
PAVLOV, IVAN
    1960   *Conditioned Reflexes.* New York: Dover.
RIEFF, PHILIP
    1966   *The Triumph of the Therapeutic.* New York: Harper & Row.
SCHWARTZ, BARRY
    1968   "The social psychology of privacy." *American Journal of Sociology* 78 (May):741–52.
SENN, MILTON J., AND CLAIRE HARTFORD
    1968   *The Firstborn.* Cambridge: Harvard University Press.

SIMMEL, GEORG
    1959   "How is society possible?" In KURT H. WOLFF, ed., *Essays on Sociology, Philosophy and Aesthetics* by GEORG SIMMEL *et al.* New York: Harper & Row, pp. 337–56.
    1950   "The metropolis and mental life." In KURT H. WOLFF, ed., *The Sociology of Georg Simmel*. New York: Free Press, pp. 409–24.

2. Notes on the Behavior
of Pedestrians *

MICHAEL WOLFF [1]

One of the most striking and yet routine aspects of city life is the movement of large numbers of people into, around, and out of the midtown business district each day. For the New Yorker as well as the small-town visitor, walking the crowded streets of mid-Manhattan is frequently an exhausting, unpleasant experience punctuated by minor collisions, shoves, reflexive complaints, and murmured apologies. Davis and Levine (1967) have suggested that the "public in transit" constitutes a *co-acting group:* "persons who are seeking simultaneously approximately the same goal without competing or cooperating but who have an awareness of each other. . . . Incidental contacts are culturally prescribed, but little or no coordination exists. . . . Each person is concerned with himself and not with his relations to the group."

The experiment described below was designed to provide a preliminary test of the applicability of the term "co-acting group" to the behavior of pedestrians as part of a program to study the phenomena that comprise and affect the experience of living in cities. How is pedestrian behavior "coordinated"? In what sense might it be considered "culturally prescribed"? One kind of cultural prescription requires that a male yield or step aside to give a female right-of-way on a path. It was therefore hypothesized that males would step aside to let females pass on the street more often than they would yield to other males and that, conversely, females would yield less frequently to oncoming males. In addition, observations were made of the distances at which yielding occurred for the male and female

* This article, previously unpublished, appears here by permission of the author.
[1] I wish to thank Dr. Erving Goffman and Dr. Albert Scheflen for their encouragement and support. This study was originally conducted under the auspices of Dr. Stanley Milgram in partial fulfillment of course requirements and was submitted under the title "The Behavior of Pedestrians on 42nd Street, New York City" (1969). Mrs. Verena Hirsch was a co-worker in the original study, participating in the filming and in the data reduction. Her analysis of the data was submitted to Dr. Milgram in a separate and independent report.

experimenter as a function of the number of people in the immediate area of the interaction.

The Arena: Forty-Second Street

The area selected as the site for the study was Forty-Second Street between Fifth and Sixth avenues, one block from Times Square, "crossroads of the world." Running east-west through the heart of midtown Manhattan, it is a typical city block—long, wide, and straight— that is a busy thoroughfare during the day and is especially congested during the morning and evening rush hours and the noon lunch break. It is several blocks from the theater district and from the garish and seamy Eighth Avenue peep-show and pornography mecca, inhabited by hustlers, pimps, prostitutes, and other assorted "street people."

On the north side of this block are a major department store,[2] a variety of small shops, several large office buildings, and the Graduate Center of the City University of New York. The south side of the block contains the small but active Bryant Park and the monumental New York Public Library building. Although shoppers, office workers, students, executives, messengers, deliverymen, and tourists abound in this section of the city, the full range of individuals to be found in a large metropolis can be seen passing on the sidewalks of this block on any weekday in less than an hour.

Method and Procedure

One male and one female experimenter, operating independently of each other, conducted all the trial runs in the experiment. Each experimenter selected a white, adult, unaccompanied pedestrian (the subject) at random from among the pedestrians moving in the direction opposite that of the experimenter. The experimenter approached the subject from a distance of between 50 and 25 feet on a straight-line "collision course," [3] attempting to approximate the pace, gait, and posture of the majority of the pedestrians on the street at the time. The experimenter did not veer from the collision course except (1) when the subject had not yielded at all and a collision would occur on the next stride of either the experimenter or the subject or (2) when the subject moved slightly out of the path of the experimenter and indicated by a change of pace or a slight turning of the body that the experimenter was expected to follow suit. The experimenters had originally determined not to give way in any circumstance, because their intentions to swerve at some point might be communicated to oncoming pedestrians, slightly biasing the results.

[2] Was. The Stern Brothers store has since been razed and replaced by an office tower.

[3] A term independently developed and discussed by Lynette H. Lofland in an unpublished treatment entitled "In the Presence of Strangers: A Study of Behavior in Public Settings" and cited in Goffman (1971).

However, a number of "unforgivable" collisions occurred on trial runs, and the experimenters, discomfited by the victims' expressions of displeasure, changed the procedure.[4]

Both experimenters wore dark glasses to eliminate eye contact with subjects. The use of sunglasses was adopted as a control device when the experimenters found it impossible to avoid actual or apparent eye contact with the subject—especially when the subject and experimenter were separated by fewer than 15 feet. It was felt that the meaning that could be attributed to the eye contact could serve as a confounding variable (i.e., intimacy, challenge, and so forth). Although this problem might have been solved by freezing the direction of the experimenter's head and eyes or allowing the experimenter to look anywhere but straight ahead, these expedients would have changed the nature of the experiment. They would have presented the oncoming subject with a display of deliberate avoidance of monitoring responsibilities or "unnaturalness" (in the case of the frozen head and eye positions) in a situation where he might expect at least one forward-looking glance from another pedestrian over a period of time.

In all cases the experimenters located a person walking on the midline (interface) between lanes of traffic moving in the opposite direction, because it had been determined on pilot runs that a pedestrian walking in the middle of a lane but in the direction opposite to that of most other pedestrians in the lane is continually buffeted and forced to accommodate and yield to people in the majority flow (one basic cultural prescription). In the midline between two flows, the right-of-way is open to individual interpretation (in other words, "Every man for himself" or "Ladies first"?).

All interactions were filmed with a standard 8mm movie camera from the twelfth-floor window of the Graduate Center. The area of the street photographed was 50 feet long by 25 feet wide.

Results and Discussion

Because of uncontrollable differences (particularly size, posture, and pace) in the behavior of the male and female experimenters observed in the analysis of the film, the very low number of analyzable cases in some conditions, and the difficulty of making precise distance measurements, only general trends and gross differences in behavior will be discussed. It should also be noted here that the "density" measure was based on an arbitrary decision to count all the people in the photographed area of the street. In the absence of previous experimentation, a commonsense decision was made as to what constituted the effective environment. While reference is made to high

[4] For a discussion of the problems involved in attempting to disrupt routine behaviors based on "background understandings," see Garfinkel (1967).

and low densities, these densities are relative, and the high-density conditions are not quite equivalent to those of a rush hour.

Over-all, both male and female pedestrians yielded to the male and female experimenter at approximately the same distance in the low-density condition (between five and fifteen people in the area of the encounter). The median yielding distance of males and females to the female experimenter and of males and females to the male experimenter was approximately 7 feet. At higher densities (between sixteen and thirty people in the area of the encounter), oncoming pedestrians yielded at relatively shorter distances—5 feet or fewer from the male and female experimenter.

However, the experimenters may have artificially reduced the yielding distance in the low-density condition while solving a practical problem. In conditions of low density, subjects would yield and detour even at great distances (50 to 100 feet or more) when they saw another pedestrian on their line-of-walk. Because this was well beyond camera range, the experimenters waited until the subject reached the periphery of the camera range and moved into a collision course with him. This behavior may have actually induced the pedestrian to stay in the line-of-walk and not yield until much later, because the individuals who were "first" on the path (and who may have been walking on it for some time without obstruction) may have expected that the latecomer would have recognized their priority rights to the path by moving onto another line-of-walk.

In high density, numerous trials were aborted when subjects were "lost": A subject may have momentarily been on a collision course as the experimenter began walking but veered off in what appeared to be normal accommodation to changes in his immediate surroundings rather than as a response to the experimenter. In addition, the very short yielding distances that occurred in high-density conditions may be accounted for in part by (1) the possibility that the subject did not see a "collision course" until near collision, because of intervening pedestrians; (2) the subject's uncertainty as to whether the experimenter would actually continue on the straight-line course, because position on the sidewalk is subject to numerous minor changes in high-density traffic; (3) the difficulty of changing direction in high-density traffic, due to restrictions on mobility caused by close spacing with other pedestrians; and (4) the possibility that pedestrians attend to oncoming pedestrians at shorter range than in low-density traffic (the more immediate environment).

As noted earlier, there were no significant differences in pedestrians yielding to either the male or female experimenter under low-density conditions. However, despite the low number of analyzable cases in the high-density condition, certain trends are suggested. It appears that same-sex yielding occurred at shorter distances than opposite-sex yielding under high-density conditions. That is, female subjects yielded to the female experimenter at shorter distances than males yielded to the female experimenter, and male subjects yielded at shorter distances to the male experimenter than did the female subjects. This suggests that females and males, when encountering others of the same sex on the street, do not have a clearly structured sense of priority (all other things being equal), and that they may not be overly concerned with the possibility of momentary same-sex contact with strangers (as in the "step-and-slide" below). In addition, the male subjects yielded to the female experimenter at greater distances than the female subjects yielded to the male experimenter, indicating that the female subjects may have expected the male experimenter to yield—which the male subjects did for the female experimenter.

To get some measure of the distance at which people change direction and detour around a stationary obstruction to compare with the "moving" encounters, two females stood in the middle of the sidewalk fiddling around with a camera on a tripod.[5] Pedestrians generally veered off their line-of-walk at a distance of about 16½ feet. Although this distance could vary widely as a function of changes in several factors (for example, density and pace), this result is considerably different from the encounter data, where the detour distance for low-density conditions was considerably longer and that for high-density conditions was considerably shorter. Somewhat surprisingly, no one asked the two women if they had permission to obstruct traffic or to use the sidewalk, or exactly what they were doing there. In fact, no one stopped to say a word to them.

Step-and-Slide

The accommodation behaviors used by pedestrians to yield in high-density traffic are interesting in themselves. In low-density traffic, pedestrians who yielded actually changed their paths (detoured) to avoid the oncoming experimenter, while at higher densities a common behavior, especially between members of the same sex, was not total detour and avoidance of contact but a slight angling of the body, a turning of the shoulder and an almost imperceptible side step—a sort of *step-and-slide*. When a pedestrian executed a step-and-slide, he did not move enough out of the path of the oncoming pedestrian to totally avoid contact or bumping; *for a clean "pass"* [6] *to occur, the cooperation of the other pedestrian was required and given.* However, even when the step-and-slide was properly executed, some body contact, such as brushing the shoulders, chest, arms, or hip area, almost always occurred, while the hands were pulled inward or away to avoid hand-to-hand contact. In addition, bodies were twisted backward to some degree to maximize face-to-face distance during the pass. When the distance between the subject and the experimenter was approximately

[5] A full-scale study of the effects of static pedestrians on the flow of pedestrian traffic can be found in Stilitz (1969).

[6] A term suggested by Albert Scheflen.

five feet, both the pedestrian and the experimenter had to step-and-slide, because at this distance, if either of the two had walked directly ahead, there would have been a collision at the next step. Over 50 per cent of the male and female experimenters' encounters in high-density traffic were of this sort.

When the experimenters did not cooperate in the step-and-slide and bumping ensued, in addition to the pedestrians' turning around and staring, remarks were sometimes made: "Whatsa madda?" "Ya blind?" "Whyn't ya look whea ya goin'?" "Ya crazy?" These remarks are quite revealing. They suggest that the normative expectation of pedestrians is that other pedestrians will see who is before them and will cooperate in avoiding contact and inconvenience to the other: Each pedestrian is responsible for recognizing cues or displays of other pedestrians that are signals for cooperation and special consideration (for example, old age, task, disabilities, and so forth) and behaving accordingly.

This explains to some extent why people with bags and packages yielded less and made less effort to coordinate. For the same reason, people walking in couples or trios (called "withs" by Goffman, 1971) were not selected as subjects for this experiment. People walking in couples, especially when engaged in conversation, will rarely separate or yield to an oncoming single pedestrian; they make a longer-than-average eye contact—possibly indicating that they see you seeing them—and expect that the oncoming pedestrian will cooperate by detouring around them, allowing them to continue without interruption. The behavior of people with bags and packages (and in couples) explains to some extent why walking in a shopping district (for example, Herald Square) is so unpleasant and tiring, even though the pace of pedestrians there is noticeably slower than of pedestrians in other, more crowded areas of the city.

It is worth noting here that only white adults had been selected as subjects for this experiment, because it had been found on pilot runs that, if either the male or the female experimenter (both white) did not yield in low-density conditions or cooperate in high-density conditions with blacks, heated verbal abuse frequently ensued. This occurred only very rarely with white pedestrians. Because we could not have avoided altercations on the street, blacks were eliminated as subject candidates for the experiment. Perhaps, in this period of racial tensions, blacks may have been more prone to construe the failure of white persons to adhere to normative prescriptions regarding deference behaviors in public places as a direct challenge or a personal insult.

Observations

Observing pedestrians from the sidewalk, the impression formed is that the pedestrians position themselves randomly or haphazardly, and that changes in pace and direction occur in an irregular fashion

The distribution of pedestrians on the sidewalk is highly fluid—there are constant changes in position on the street—and is never homogeneous: large and small, loosely and densely packed clusters alternate with sparsely populated or open spaces. However, a number of regularities in pedestrian behavior appeared as the films (shot from the twelfth floor) were run over and over.

HEAD-OVER-THE-SHOULDER

When walking behind a person fewer than five feet away, a pedestrian strives to maintain a *head-over-the-shoulder* relationship with the person or persons in front: He positions himself so that his body is behind the shoulder (rather than the head) of a person in front. In high-density traffic, where there is less freedom to obtain a position of choice, people angle their heads so that they are peering over the shoulders of the people directly in front, even though the trunks (and heads) of their bodies may be in near parallel. Only at a distance of some fifteen feet or more will a person walk directly behind another person for any length of time. The only exceptions to this rule occur when people circumnavigate an obstruction or pass through a cluster. In these circumstances, people follow closely behind the lead person (in his "wake") until the obstruction is passed and then, almost immediately, resume the over-the-shoulder pattern.

There are two obvious explanations for the ubiquity of this phenomenon. First, it facilitates viewing what lies ahead and, second, it secures against stumbling into the feet of the person walking ahead. In fact, one normative rule of pedestrian behavior is that the person who bumps the back parts of another, for whatever reason, must initiate the apology sequence. As with automobiles, each person is responsible for seeing what is ahead, correctly evaluating the contingencies, and controlling his behavior to avoid intruding upon the unoffending back of another. It is also interesting to note that this pattern, when compressed (as in rush-hour crushes), allows for the maximum number of people to *pass through* (as opposed to *stand in*) a given area.

Consequently, as a cluster of individuals proceeds down the street, any person who changes his position within the cluster forces others to accommodate to maintain their head-over-the-shoulder relationship. This is in addition to the continual accommodations that must be made in a densely packed cluster because of individual differences in personal size, length of stride, and rhythm style of neighbors.

SPREAD EFFECT

A behavior pattern that serves to maximize the efficiency of traffic flow is the *spread effect*: People walking in one direction on a sidewalk distribute themselves to the fullest width that the natural boundaries (the curb on one side and buildings or walls on the other) will allow, if there is no appreciable flow of traffic in the opposite direction. The widths of two lanes of pedestrians moving in opposite directions on the same sidewalk are approximately equal when the *numbers* of people in these lanes are approximately equal. However, as the number of people in one of the opposing lanes increases, that lane will occupy a greater width of the sidewalk than its numerical proportionality to the sparsely populated lane would predict. For example, if the flow in one direction is three times as large as the flow in the opposing lane, the width of the lane with greater numbers of pedestrians may be three *or more* times as great as that of the other lane *despite* the fact that the people in the sparsely populated lane are much more closely spaced than the people in the well-populated lane. There is frequently unequal spacing (more room) between people in a well-populated (but not "over-populated") lane than those in an opposing sparsely populated lane.

One possible explanation for this distribution is that the *density* of the oncoming flow may *appear* to be greater than it is in fact, because the vantage point of the pedestrian might cause him to "perceptually collapse" the spaces among oncoming pedestrians. Thus, the person in the sparsely populated lane would adjust his position on the street according to what might appear to him to be a more dense and closely packed flow. This discrepancy might increase as the number of pedestrians in the opposing direction increases.

CLUSTERS

The patterned distribution of pedestrians allows them the maximum freedom of movement for accommodation and for pursuing their individual goals. By utilizing this freedom of movement, the pedestrian walking faster than a particular cluster can "thread" his way through the cluster, maintain his own pace, but not force others to accommodate to him. However, in high-density traffic, clusters are generally more tightly packed, and the fast walker will either intrude upon the members of the cluster, forcing everyone in it to accommodate, or will intrude into the oncoming pedestrians in the opposing lane while passing the cluster.

Clusters are not groups of related members but are creations of various environmental contingencies. Clusters may be created in large part by traffic signals at intersections; pedestrians bunch at corners awaiting the change of signals to cross. As the pedestrians proceed across the intersection, the large cluster breaks into smaller clusters proceeding down the block at different speeds. As noted above, it is difficult to thread through densely packed clusters. Therefore, clusters tend to grow by aggregation in the rear. In periods of low density, there are fewer clusters than in periods of high density, and these clusters are composed of fewer individuals.

DETOURING

Another behavior pattern, more difficult to account for but observed for the majority of subjects in the experiment, was attempts to revert to the "original" path or line-of-walk that the person had been maintaining before detouring around the experimenter. Although all "paths" in a lane on a sidewalk are of equal utility for the purposes of reaching the corner, it is possible that "adjustment" to temporary physical obstructions is psychologically a different situation than adjustment to longer-lasting and consequential obstructions such as those presented by personality differences, organizational structure, and so forth. In the first case, a person's goals or criteria for successful adjustment might include some notion of "return" to "original" behavior ("overcoming"), whereas in the second case there is a recognition of the need to produce "adaptations" that will result in new behaviors in new directions.[7] An alternative explanation might be that people have "position preferences" with regard to environmental boundaries and contingencies (for example, "balanced" within the "environmental order"). This hypothesis raises another question: What environmental stimuli do people take into account in choosing positions in various environments? [8]

One exception to the detouring phenomenon occurs when pedestrians have an interest or business in some area off the sidewalk lane (e.g., entering a store, window-shopping, waiting at a bus stop, and so forth). Rather than proceeding several yards farther in the same direction after detouring back onto the original line-of-walk and then making a break for the area of interest, pedestrians turned off their line-of-walk to avoid colliding with the experimenter and proceeded to make a beeline for the area of interest. This observation is particularly interesting in that it is so graphic an illustration of how individuals can be prompted to act prematurely when they are reasonably close to taking action.

PERCEPTUAL OBJECTS

People tend to treat perceptually distinct parts of the pavement, such as gratings, as obstructions to be avoided or circumnavigated when possible (reminiscent of the children's game of "don't-step-on-the crack"). Although gratings have historically been avoided by women (in high heels), it is difficult to explain why men appear to avoid them as well. This observation suggests that, if a few pavement blocks in front of large display windows were distinctly colored,

[7] Suggesting another dimension for the psychological analysis of pedestrian (and other urban) interactions: the degree to which other interactants are treated as objects and automatons.

[8] Pioneering work in this area has been produced by Robert Sommer (1969).

marked, or patterned, people standing in these areas might generally be protected from intrusions by passing pedestrians as they viewed the displays.

MONITORING

Any study of how people relate to each other on the sidewalk requires that some consideration be given to their performance of the taken-for-granted task of "monitoring" the environment. Pedestrians monitor the environment not only for the purpose of avoiding culturally proscribed intrusions but also to evaluate the potential behavior of others. As noted earlier, pedestrians normally adhere to certain position patterns; people who deviate from these patterns in various ways may be reported, avoided, or held suspect. For example, a person who walks directly behind another pedestrian at a close distance for more than a short period when the head-over-the-shoulder pattern could be sustained or a person who walks in parallel (side-by-side) at a close distance for more than a short period without making an effort to move out of this pattern is just as suspect as the person who enters an empty bus, subway car, or luncheonette and sits down beside you. Because he could have done otherwise, and because people normally do, he is suspect.

In addition to scanning frontward and to the sides, pedestrians engage in several other monitoring behaviors. First, although window-shopping, "appreciation," and curiosity viewing are common pedestrian behaviors, individuals regularly [9] turn their heads at least one quarter-turn off the perpendicular (straight ahead). This movement allows them to glance quickly and inconspicuously out of the corner of their eyes and monitor whatever is behind them without appearing to be concerned, irritated, interested, or the like. Second, pedestrians scan the faces of pedestrians coming toward them. If the oncoming pedestrians appear to be fixating in the same direction and, more importantly, are expressing surprise, fear, or general excitement, this is taken to be a cue to make a full head-turn, stop for a full check-out, or both. In this sense, pedestrians use other pedestrians as a "rear-view mirror" much as animals in herds are warned of danger by the movements of other herd members. In spite of the cultural proscriptions against ambush, attack from behind, and so forth, apparently we have developed the habit of performing several operations that enable us to "watch our back" while moving through open spaces.

These operations are more difficult to perform at night on dark streets with few other pedestrians nearby. This may explain in part why surprise attacks are historically more common at night despite increased vigilance.

[9] *How* regularly is an interesting empirical question.

CHILDREN

Children approximately seven years of age or younger appear to be treated generally as "baggage" by adult pedestrians. First, many of the people who were holding the hands of children appeared to be dragging them through traffic: The child trailed somewhat behind and was continually buffeted by oncoming pedestrians with no major objections, verbal or otherwise, issuing from the child or the accompanying adult. Second, it appeared that the oncoming pedestrians would "sight" the adult and negotiate the right-of-way with him; the child would be led, ignorant of where his next step should be and sometimes stumbling over himself and others. Third, it appeared that, for the most part, the child did not "attend to" the oncoming pedestrians. When adult couples negotiate the right-of-way with the oncoming pedestrians, they both take cognizance of the cues of oncoming pedestrians. Even though only one of the couple may do the negotiating, the other of the pair is usually aware of the arrangements that are being made.

The child suffers from several drawbacks in this situation. First, he may not have learned the cues used in negotiating behavior in public places or he may not be able to use them properly. Second, adults may not "recognize" his attempts to negotiate, on the grounds that he is not of "peer" status and thus is not entitled to deference but must always defer. Third, the child may have unwittingly abdicated his rights to negotiate as an individual by hand-holding—the "I rely on him" display—or may have had his rights usurped by an adult who insists on holding hands.

Several empirical questions can be generated from these observations. At what age or stage of development have children learned to negotiate right-of-way, territorial possession, and so forth, in public places? At what age or under what conditions is their attempted use of such knowledge "respected"?

VEHICULAR TRAFFIC

Because so much information remains to be gathered concerning the nature of pedestrian traffic, it may seem premature to compare it to vehicular traffic. On the other hand, significant insights may be obtained if they are studied analogously.

For instance, as the Sunday driver and out-of-town visitor can testify, driving in midtown Manhattan normatively requires both competitive and assertive tactics (Schor, 1964). However, pedestrian behavior, as discussed above, is coordinated to the point of being cooperative and cannot be correctly characterized as competitive or assertive. What major differences between these two types of traffic underlie this difference?

Perhaps one major difference is the large number of midtown drivers who are professional drivers, to whom the first consideration is to "make time." Would pedestrian behavior change in character if "professional pedestrians" (for example, messengers) abounded on the sidewalks? Would pace quicken? Would behavior come to be regulated by law?

Other important differences between driving and walking are the ease and speed with which a pedestrian can allow other pedestrians to maneuver around him, compared to the relative cumbersomeness of the automobile. How does behavior change as a function of the semi-vehicular traffic of the midtown "garment district," where men push carts, cartons, and racks on the sidewalk and the street? How is it possible for so many to escape injury from the spokes of umbrellas on windy and rainy days?

Vehicles are so closely packed on Manhattan streets that even those few degrees of freedom of movement available to the clumsy automobile are effectively eliminated. However, no matter how densely packed a sidewalk may be, a determined pedestrian can move through or around traffic.

How much do kinesic feedback and "action signals" play a part in facilitating pedestrian mobility? Not only are vehicles poorly equipped to communicate with each other except in the grossest and most ambiguous manner, but there is little opportunity for the driver to obtain feedback from other drivers as to whether his signals have been seen and as to the intentions of other drivers vis-à-vis those signals. This is an especially significant problem at intersections and when attempting to pass the vehicle ahead.

How much does New York's unique grid-pattern layout contribute to pedestrian and vehicular behavior? Many New York drivers habitually dash through intersections on the yellow warning light to maintain momentum and catch the "wave" of green lights on the long uptown and downtown avenues. Drivers are frustrated by the long trek across town and are harried by jaywalking pedestrians. Do similar differences between pedestrian traffic and vehicular traffic appear in other American cities? Cross-culturally?

Conclusions

While the possibility of considering the behavior of pedestrians in terms of the concept "co-acting group" had been suggested earlier, it now seems that, at best, this term might be applicable only to persons being transported on buses or subways: Pedestrians respond to one another's needs in a manner far beyond what is intended by the concept "co-acting." Indeed, a high degree of cooperation is an intrinsic part of pedestrian behavior—without it, walking would be impossible. Imagine two sets of robots marching toward each other from opposite corners.[10] If each group were to maintain its line of march, only a very few would reach the opposite corner.

Secondly, despite the existence of shared norms, it is difficult to characterize the multitude of pedestrians as a "group"; even cluster members share neither a sense of groupness nor a sense of belonging, nor do pedestrians relate directly to each other except for the briefest of moments—and then only for the purpose of avoiding mutual intrusions rather than to produce a sustained effort toward a goal. (Although it could be argued that the goal of each pedestrian is passage over a stretch of sidewalk, this is basically a solitary activity that could best be accomplished without other, uninvited, presences.) Additionally, the use of the term "group" suggests a frustrating, if not impossible, search for boundary criteria to distinguish those who are members of the group from those who are not. On the other hand, traditional labels, such as "aggregate" and "pedestrian," leave the boundary problem open without suggesting analytic advantages. Then, too, are loiterers, couples, mendicants, messengers, shoppers, and sight-seers all quite the same as "pedestrians"?

Erving Goffman has suggested (in a personal communication) that "the concept of *social order* is the key term (in the sense in which order can be distinguished from organization) in the examination of the structure of various traffic systems (each an instance of order). In that various orders incorporate individuals into 'ordered regions' that are often much larger than nation-states or language communities, traditional notions of structure do not quite apply."

Perhaps the term *coordinate* can be used to describe individuals in "public orders" such as pedestrian and vehicular traffic systems, crowds, and queues. First, as a noun, it describes individuals in such systems as occupying related points within a patterned array. The mere physical copresence of individuals establishes them as coordinates—as are trees, pillars, curbs, and walls. The relationship between (groupings or sets of) coordinates in a patterned array (in other words, opposing lanes, clusters, queues) guides the behavior of individuals in that field. In addition, because they are mobile and flexible, individuals are potentially facilitators as well as obstructors of each other's progress. The term *coordinate* as a verb describes the normative baseline requirement for encounters in the public order on the facilitate-obstruct dimension: equal responsibility and equal effort for common progress (see discussion of step-and-slide, above).

Over-all, one of the most intriguing observations of pedestrian behavior concerns the pivotal function of patterns of relationships between pedestrians and their reactions to changes in these patterns. To what extent do patterns in the environment and "reflexive" responses to these patterns play a part in our everyday activities? And

[10] Suggested by Stanley Milgram.

how do these responses develop? To what extent are they mediated by various dimensions of personality? To what extent are they shared cross-culturally? The observations above suggest that array patterns provide the structure that supports the routine and automatic coordination that occurs in periods of low and medium density. In periods of high density, the overload on individuals within arrays (in other words, reduction of degrees of freedom of movement, the necessity for simultaneously negotiating with and monitoring a dozen other pedestrians, the impelling force of the crowd at a pedestrian's back), compounded by the psychological states of people rushing to and from work places, produces the failures that are common in the city at these times. Even the most energetic and well-bred pedestrian soon tires under the strain of the efforts necessary to extend to everyone the full measure of cooperation while maintaining his own progress. Knowledge of, and competence in, monitoring and negotiating behavior, body control, and positioning patterns are the taken-for-granted parts of every pedestrian's repertoire, and failures in any of the above behaviors that result in intrusions or array disruptions may quickly be attributed to a lack of effort or concern, eliciting complaints or challenges.

In conclusion, it can be said that among the most outstanding characteristics of pedestrians that have emerged from this study are the amount and degree of cooperative behavior on the streets of the city. While at the immediate and superficial level encounters on the street are hardly noticeable and devoid of pleasantry and warmth, pedestrians do, in fact, communicate and do take into account the qualities and predicaments of others in regulating their behavior. The major hypothesis generated by the observations above is that *the most significant factor in affecting and modifying the behavior of pedestrians in a metropolis is the number of people in their immediate environment.*

References

DAVIS, M., and S. LEVINE
    1967   "Towards a Sociology of Public Transit." *Social Problems* 15:84–91.
GARFINKEL, HAROLD
    1967   *Studies in Ethnomethodology.* Englewood Cliffs: Prentice-Hall.
GOFFMAN, ERVING
    1971   *Relations in Public.* New York: Basic Books.
SCHOR, R. E.
    1964   "Shared Patterns of Nonverbal Normative Expectations in Automobile Driving." *Journal of Social Psychology* 62:153–63.
SOMMER, ROBERT
    1969   *Personal Space.* Englewood Cliffs: Prentice-Hall.
STILITZ, IVOR
    1969   "The Role of Static Pedestrian Groups in Crowded Spaces." *Ergonomics* 12:821–39.

3. Pinball Occasions *

WILLIAM B. SANDERS

Participants in social occasions are expected to involve themselves in such a manner as to preserve the sanctity of the occasion (Goffman, 1963). In most situations the proper allocation of involvement can at least be presented by participants even though they do not feel what they present. That is, they can fake engrossment, both cognitive and affective, and, as long as they appear to be appropriately involved, the integrity of the occasion has not been violated (Goffman, 1959).

Some situations, however, require a special kind of involvement that is not easily faked. A bomb defuser, for example, must display a calm, steady hand while he detaches wires and fuses from explosive packages. His actions function in two importantly different ways. On the one hand, shaky movements may set off the bomb, and, on the other hand, such nervousness reveals a weakness of character (Goffman, 1967:217). In either case, the trembling defuser blows his performance, pointing to an instrumental as well as an expressive stake in acting calmly. Moreover, the instrumental and expressive aspects of the performance are linked. The risky commitment happens simultaneously with the resolution requirements.

However, not all risks are so linked. In horse racing, for instance, the bettor places his bet in an act that is divorced from the requirement for him to win. Once he has committed himself, the racing fan can tear his hair and bite his nails, but, while these actions may show weakness of character, they in no way jeopardize or enhance his chances of winning (Scott, 1968). His commitment move, then, is separated from the resolution requirement. However, in the case of the bomb defuser, as well as in cases of poker playing, skiing, surfing, and similar activities where composure is a technical requirement, the actor's performance after the commitment move is fatefully linked to the outcome.

The interest in such activities concerns the two issues of social control and social evaluation. Social control can best be seen in those situations where an individual's inner state contradicts his outward

* This article, previously unpublished, appears here by permission of the author.

appearance. Just as a bomb defuser would be blown to bits if he followed an inner urge to rip apart a bomb package, so too would social occasions be wrecked if the participants followed inner urges to do what they felt (Goffman, 1961:51).

A final interest centers around how and why social members spend their time as they do. Involvements of various sorts are found on various occasions, and one interesting occasion where people spend time is pinball. What happens in these occasions in terms of the actors' involvements will be the focus of the following discussion.

Methodology

In order to come to terms with the world of pinball, I spent three months observing players in a West Coast poolhall where several pinball machines were located. The poolhall was in a student community located adjacent to a public university. Separated from a nearby city, the community is unique in that it is composed almost wholly of college-age youth, most of whom are students, but it also includes many nonstudents in its population of 13,000.

The observation period spanned a time from early March to the beginning of June; thus, the study took place while school was in session and the students, most of whom moved away during the summer, were in residence. Even though the average income of the students' families is in excess of $20,000, the character of the community lacks the flavor of most middle- and upper-middle-class communities. Composed of inexpensively built apartments, residence halls, and a few houses, the community is transient and youth-oriented. From early 1970 to the present, there have been annual riots, and the students have what would be considered a radical life-style, which includes, for example, drug use, left-wing politics (in the 1970 state-wide election, the Peace and Freedom Party candidates received more votes than the Republicans), and heterosexual unmarried cohabitation.

Observational procedures and recording had to be tailored to the setting. It was decided that all data would be collected unobtrusively to control for researcher contamination (Webb et al., 1966:138), and interviewing was done in such a manner that it was not seen to be "interviewing" by the subjects, in other words, questions concerning features and practices were asked in normal conversations. The observations were conducted from the stations of a "loiterer" and a "game watcher," two normal roles in the setting (Gold, in Denzin, 1970:373).

Because it was an unobtrusive study and I could find no way to take notes in the setting without drawing attention to myself, I waited until I returned home to write up the findings. It was a five-minute walk from where I lived to the poolhall; thus, there was a minimum amount that was forgotten or left out. Observation time lasted from fifteen minutes to an hour and a half, covering all days of the week and all hours that the establishment was open for business.

Characteristics

THE SETTING

The setting where the pinball machines are located is a poolhall, but the area reserved for pool tables is clearly set off from the pinball area. In addition to pinball and pool, there are two "Foosball" [1] tables located in the area formed by the two legs of the "L" formed by the pinball machines, giving the pinball and pool areas an even more distinct border. Business hours are not regular or at least not strictly so, but the establishment usually does not close until two in the morning and opens around ten or eleven in the morning. If business is good, however, the place sometimes stays open longer, as the following observation illustrates:

4/22: When I walked in I asked the guy at the counter how late they stayed open. He asked how late I wanted it to, and I told him I just wanted to know if they had a particular hour they closed. He said that as long as there was enough business, he would stay open.

The setting was used for other than "business" purposes, however. Activities such as looking for people, looking for money (either by panhandling or by checking the coin return slots), talking to the cashier, talking to one another, watching the pinball players, smoking marijuana (generally outside of the building, in front of the door), waiting for friends or drug contacts, and simply loitering took place in and around the setting. The following are some instances:

3/6: Two girls about high school age came in and began panhandling without much success. One came up to me and asked for a penny, which I gave her. She put it in one of the candy machines.
4/14: A girl walked in, looked around, then left.
4/15: A guy asked me for spare change. I told him that my last dime was in the machine and he walked away. Later, I saw him standing by the window looking out.
4/22: A couple of girls with a baby were talking with Rick at the counter.
4/28: A guy walked in and gave Roberta the peace sign, and she said hello. He walked by the two guys at the juke box and one of them said something to him, and he went over and talked to them. After the music stopped, they left together.

There are, however, limitations as to activities on the scene. The cashier and owner admonish children when they pound on the pinball machines, even if they are spending money. Also, a bystander is obliged to move away from a pinball machine if someone wishes to

[1] "Foosball" is a machine game similar to hockey but using a table-tennis ball as a puck. It is not a pinball game, although it is often found in the same locales as pinball machines.

play. Furthermore, if all of the machines are being used, there is nothing other than the juke box and the "Foosball" machines to lean on while watching a game of pinball, and, because neither of these provide a good vantage point, people may be forced to leave. That is, even if one wishes to loiter, the spatial arrangements make it extremely difficult to loiter if certain strategic niches in the setting are taken.

PATRONS

People who enter the pinball scene can be divided into "regulars" and "occasionals" (Cavan, 1966:65; Scott, 1968:81–112; 113–16). Regulars are those who normally include the setting in their daily round of activities. Some of the regulars are pool players, some are street people who come to see if anything interesting is happening (for example, friends are present), some are friends of the cashier's who come to visit him, and some are pinball players. I will focus on the pinball regulars.

The regulars who come primarily to play pinball can be divided into three age groups. First, there are the "little kids," aged between nine and junior high or early high school age. This group is there mostly in the afternoon and early evening, and, although it includes some very good pinball players, they are treated as nonserious players, merely coming in to "play" the way kids "play." Second, there is a group aged from late high school to late college age whom I will refer to as the "regulars." (Almost all of the "kids" are regulars, but, for simplicity, I will use the terms "kids" and "regulars" to differentiate between the two groups.) A third set is the "teeny boppers," or the young adolescents; however, the members of this group are more likely to be treated as "kids" if they are younger and as "regulars" if they are more mature.

Most of the pinball regulars are young men, and the only girls who can be considered pinball regulars are those who come in with their boyfriends; however, there are only a few pinball players who bring their girlfriends. On any given day, while it would not be unusual to see girls on the scene, it is not very common to see them playing pinball. No girls come in who are not accompanied by boys who are pinball regulars.

The pinball occasionals consist of pool players who shoot a game of pinball every now and then, street people who are passing through, students who wander in, and others who drop in on an irregular basis. Other than the pool players, the occasionals do not generally know one another or the people who work in the establishment. In general, their presence is "in" the setting but not "of" the setting.

A final note of interest concerning both regulars and occasionals involves their dress and general appearance. On a continuum from "straight" to "hippie," every gradation of appearance could be observed in the setting. For reasons that will become apparent later, an individual's appearance is simply not relevant to playing pinball or to the other activities in the setting.

Pinball Encounters

GETTING STARTED

I will assume that a person who wants to play pinball knows enough to activate a pinball machine by putting a coin in the coin slot, but I would like to discuss the various means of getting started in a game of pinball. Machines have signs indicating that one game can be played for a dime and three for a quarter. Thus, for ten cents, the player can shoot five balls, the game beginning with the first ball and ending when the last ball rolls out of play.

However, there are other ways to get started. First, people sometimes leave free games on the machine, and all the next person has to do to play is press the replay button. Another way of getting free games is to be invited to play by the person who is playing. The following happened in the course of my observations:

4/19: When I first came in, three guys were playing the "Baseball" machine. As I began watching, two of the players left the player who appeared to be winning most of the games. He asked me if I wanted to play. I shot two games, lost both of them, and he shot some more. Finally, he said, "I'm tired of playing. You can have them." He left me four games, which I played out.

On other occasions, I have been invited to play or been given free games. "Giving away games," however, is apparently somewhat peculiar to this setting, as I learned from one informant.

5/5: A young player who is around a lot was given three games by a couple of players. He thanked them and started to play. I commented on their giving the games to him, and he said this was the only place he knew of where that happened and indicated that he appreciated it a great deal.

Free games are also "hustled" by the kids. The above-mentioned player who was given free games was observed flattering players, including myself, in the hope that he would be given some games.

4/21: As I began playing, the observer commented on what a good player I was after the first ball. I had only scored 3,000 points out of 30,000 needed for a free game and I commented that I hadn't done too well. He looked up and said, "I thought you had done better with all the bells ringing," and agreed that I was not doing too well.

This form of hustling does not include the type practiced by pool

players, whereby they attempt to win money (Polsky, 1967:41–44).
Moreover, it is usually done only by the kids, and, unlike pool hustling,
where the player's hustling activity increases with age and skill, the pinball player's decreases as he grows up and gets better.

A final way of getting started in a pinball game is to "buy" games
from players. This happens when a player has won a number of games
and would rather sell them to someone than play them himself. For
instance:

> 4/19: I was watching a player winning several games on a machine.
> When he had four games left, he asked me if I wanted to buy them
> for "two dimes." I told him I did not, and he went on playing. When
> he was down to two games, I offered to buy them for a dime and he
> agreed. As he backed away from the machine he let out a sigh of relief
> and said he had been at the machine for an hour and a half. When
> I started to play, I noticed it was extremely warm around the flipper
> buttons.
>
> 5/23: A kid came over and asked if I wanted to buy four games for
> a dime, and I told him I did. When I finished shooting my game,
> I went over and asked if they had change for a quarter. They did not
> and suggested asking the cashier. When I came back I asked them
> if they'd take a nickel so that I could use my two dimes on other
> games. They agreed, and so I got four games for a nickel.

As can be seen from the above examples, there are no set prices in
buying and selling games. However, it should be pointed out that a
player always pays less for games he buys from other players than he
would pay a machine.

Before going on to playing pinball, I would like to briefly mention
money and pinball players. Early in my observations, I began evaluating
my change in terms of the number of pinball games I could buy at
machine prices. Later, I found this to be true of many regular pinball
players. In a previous example, a player offered to sell games for "two
dimes." He could have said "twenty cents," but in the reality of the
pinball occasion, "twenty cents" means less than "two dimes," because
the latter represents what can be put in the machine. The following
also illustrates counting money in terms of the tokens the machine will
accept.

> 5/9: I had been watching a player who had been losing several games.
> When he finally began winning, I commented on the wins, and he
> said, "Yeah, but it cost me two quarters and two dimes."

Thus, he told me that he had spent money on eight games—three
apiece for the two quarters and one apiece for the two dimes. If he had
said "seventy cents," he would not have given the same information,
and if he had spent any other combination that would have added up
to seventy cents, he would have reported it in terms of the number of

tokens dropped in the machine. Similarly, the cashiers always give pinball players tokens that can be used in the machine without asking the
players to specify what they need. They know what it takes to play and
need not be told.

PLAYING

In pinball, as in other games, the players attempt to win, but "winning" in pinball, unlike other games, does not involve beating an
opponent. To get more points than another player may constitute
winning for some occasional players, but, for the regulars, winning is
to receive the number of points or other play conditions needed for a
free game. This is crucial for understanding pinball and pinball players;
for, unlike many games where winning routinely entails beating a
human opponent, winning at pinball constitutes beating the machine.
Linked with the lack of competition in the setting studied was also
a lack of gambling among pinball players. However, this cannot be
accounted for by any lack of gambling ethic either in the establishment
or among its patrons. The following observations point to this:

4/29: I was trying to get the cashier to talk about payoffs or gambling
by saying that I had heard of certain bars paying off pinball players
for winning a certain number of games. In response, he told me that
there was a "Bowl-O" game in the Las Vegas bus station that paid
off in cash for wins and that he had a friend who won a good deal
of money playing it.

4/30: Rick said that he had lost $3.00 playing pool. I asked if he
ever saw pinball players gambling, and he said he had. When I told him
I had never seen it, he said it was extremely rare.

4/20: Two boys about sixteen or seventeen were playing "Paul
Bunyan," taking turns on a one-player game. One had just won a game
on the fourth ball and the other shot the fifth. "You blew it," the one
said to the second when he failed to score enough points to win a
second game.

The conversation with the cashier (Rick) indicates that, while gambling
is common in the building, pinball players are not generally gamblers,
at least in the setting studied. The two boys who were taking turns
shooting were not trying to get more points than one another, but they
were trying to beat the machine, that is, win a free game. A player who
was trying to sell his games further illustrates that competition is against
the machine and not against human opponents.

5/9: A guy told me that he believed that people would not buy the
seventeen games he was trying to sell because the machine had already
been beaten and there was no challenge left.

The pinball player who is serious about playing will attempt to win a
game with some belief that, if he concentrates, he can do so. The most

common type of win entails getting a certain number of points that are electronically recorded and displayed when the ball hits or rolls over various devices on the sloped surface of the machine.

Besides winning by getting the needed number of points, some games have "specials" that also give the player a free game for meeting specified requirements. For example, one game has a special win if numbers in a series from one to twelve are hit. When all twelve numbers are hit, one of the numbers lights up, and, if the player hits that number again, he wins a game.

A final way of receiving a free game is by a "match." This is not considered "winning," nor is the player considered to have beaten the machine. A match occurs at the end of the game. If a player's last number or last two numbers match the number or numbers that light up on the upright board of the machine, he gets a free game. Matches are considered matters of luck and are not believed to reflect the player's ability to play.

To begin playing, the player shoots the ball up a corridor by means of a spring-loaded plunger. Some players consider shooting important, especially if a special is pending on one of the scoring devices at the top of the machine; however, it is generally considered the least important of the skills involved in playing pinball. Sometimes the kids will go around and ask to "hit the ball up" for a player, and, because this aspect is relatively unimportant, the players usually let the kids do it.

Once the ball is in play, the pinball player's skill in using the flippers and shaking the machine comes to the fore. The flippers are two arms at the bottom of the machine that pivot on pins and flip upward when the flipper buttons are pressed. Depending upon when the player presses the flipper buttons in relation to the position of the ball, the ball will be hit, missed, go where he wants it to go, or go where he does not want it to go. Hence, the player's skill rests on his ability to press the buttons at the most opportune moment. The inexperienced player will frantically start flapping the flipper buttons, and hits and misses become random. The better player will catch the ball on the rail with the flipper button, letting the ball roll down the flipper to the point he wants, and then press the button, sending the ball where he wants it to go. Or else he will simply hit it at the right moment to keep it in play if it is moving too fast to catch or slow enough for him to hit it correctly without stopping it.

Likewise, shaking the machine requires an artful touch. If the machine is shaken too hard or incorrectly, it will indicate "tilt," and the player will receive no more points for the ball in play or, on some machines, for the entire game. One very good player explained it to me:

4/19: "You don't push it or it'll tilt. You shake it hard, quick."

Another player who did not shake it explained:

4/22: "I put the machine right up against the wall and don't jiggle it. I don't have the touch."

The object, of course, in working the flippers and shaking the machine, is to get points to win the game, or to get the special. To do this while the ball keeps rolling downward to a hole near the front of the machine requires some self-control. Goffman (1967:225) refers to the ability to think clearly under circumstances that may muddle the brain as "presence of mind," and Lyman and Scott (1970:145) define "coolness" as the ability to keep calm under pressure. These attributes are essential for good pinball playing; for, as was pointed out at the beginning of this discussion, the resolution requirement, that is, hitting the ball so that it will score points, occurs after the commitment and before the outcome. Thus, the sign of good pinball playing, namely, winning free games, is also a sign of strong character; for, in order to meet the resolution requirements, the player has to maintain a clear head as well as his "cool."

The pressure and actions under pressure are in the structure of the pinball situation. In every game there are five balls, and, in every series of games, there is a first and a last game. When the player puts money in the machine and begins to play, it is his "first game." On any given occasion, he may have several "first games," depending on how often he has to put money in the machine. If the player has only put a dime in the machine, he will either have to win a game, get a match, or put more money in the machine; hence, there is added pressure to win. One player who always put a quarter in the machine explained that he always got nervous on the first game and could never win. If he lost, he knew he had two more games, and, because of this knowledge, he relaxed more and consequently did better.

The "last game," on the other hand, is the last of whatever series of games is played before more money has to be spent, and as in the first game of a dime's play, there is added pressure. One player told me he always "blew it" on the last game because of this. There can be several last games in a series, because whenever the game counter reaches "zero" the game being played is the "last game." If the player wins games, the game counter will register the number of games won, and the game no longer is the last one.

As with games, there are "balls to be played," but it is only the last, the fifth, ball, under certain conditions, that creates added pressure. As soon as the player has the number of points needed for at least one free game, he can relax to some extent because, no matter what happens, he will have another game. However, it is not uncommon for the player to find himself in a situation where he has shot four balls and is short of the needed number of points for a free game. If it happens to be the last ball of his last game and he is "within range" of a free game, the pressure is multiplied. (By "within range" I mean that the player can expect to get the needed number of points with close attention to the game.) The player who calmly shakes the machine without tilting it and catches the ball, and then shoots it off the tip of the flipper on the last ball of his last game, when he still needs points to win, is considered cool indeed.

PINBALL RELATIONSHIPS

Most players have a single machine or a limited number of machines that they play. The choice of a machine by a player is not determined so much by its being fun to play as by the player's ability to beat the game. For example, I found "Jive Time" more fun than "On Beam," simply because I liked the spinner on "Jive Time," but I rarely won playing "Jive Time," so I usually played "On Beam." Other players have similar sentiments and know a good deal about the machine they usually play.

> 4/28: After a while a guy came over and started watching and said, "This is the only machine I can win on." I told him there was a whirling sound every now and then, and I had to wait a long time for the ball to come out. He told me that the last time it happened there was an "Out of Order" sign on it the next time he came in after hearing the same sound.

"Getting to know" the machine means becoming accustomed to the various specials, point-scoring systems, and other quirks of the machine. For example, one machine has a left flipper button that sticks slightly, and it is necessary to hit the button before one normally would to strike the ball properly. The list of idiosyncrasies for almost any machine is quite long and deals with so many variables that even a player who is well acquainted with a machine may not understand all of the machine's characteristics. Concerning one machine, even the proprietor had problems figuring out how the points were scored.

> 5/11: I was talking with Roberta about the broken glass on the "Student Prince" machine and we got to talking about playing the various machines. Discussed "On Beam." Roberta said that she thought that if the space ship and the space station came together on the same beam, the special would be activated, but she said she had to watch the place and was unable to concentrate on the game enough to figure it out.

Nevertheless, a player who has his "own" machine has considerably more knowledge about that machine than one who only occasionally uses the same machine.

Sustained playing of the same machine or same group of machines usually leads to a form of acquaintanceship with other players who use the same machine. In getting to know a machine, the player also gets to know those who regularly play it. Regular players will inform other players as to the machine's characteristics and how best to play the machine in order to get a replay. One of the kids, for example, told me to hit the shooter as hard as I could on the "Paul Bunyan" machine so the ball would go through a 500-point gate at the top of the machine. Players are advised by regulars of another machine to shake the table when the ball comes back out between the flippers on the special. Thus, in discussing the machine, "pinball relationships" develop.

The relationships between pinball players appear to be strictly situational and formal. Players who strike up these situational acquaintance-ships do not seem to maintain them beyond the boundaries of the setting; nor does it appear that even knowing the other's name is important. Each will acknowledge the other's presence when he comes over to watch or play a game, but the talk does not go beyond discussion about playing pinball and how the particular machine has been behaving.

5/9: When I came in, the guy who had been playing "On Beam" earlier was still there. He had been having difficulty when I left, but now he had twenty games on the counter. He said that the most he had ever seen on the counter was twenty-three and he was trying for twenty-four. We discussed the machine and how it was not responding well earlier. He said that the "D" slot was a bad one to get, because the ball would go through it and head straight for the flippers without getting any points on the way. He let me shoot three games, and I won only one. Also, he mentioned that he had once gotten 94,000 and was trying to get the point counter back to zero so that he could get more free games by working it back up to 30,000 or more.

The difference between a "pinball acquaintanceship" and two players who come in together can be seen in the way the people treat each other. The pinball acquaintances will be very circumspect and never deride the player for losing or handling the ball poorly. Friends, on the other hand, will tease one another about their play, take turns shooting the same game, and stand closer to the machine and player. Friends may even jostle one another in a playful attempt to make the other lose. Pinball acquaintances, while they may let one another take turns on games or give a series of games to one another, will rarely take turns shooting the same game. In general, pinball acquaintances watch one another shoot, make comments about the machine or about techniques for beating the machine, and formally console the player if he muffs a ball or loses a game.

In getting to know a pinball acquaintance, the "knowing" has to do with his style of play, his ability to win the game, and his general knowledge of pinball. For example, some pinball players sit when they play and some stand, some are tense and some are loose, some can beat only one game and some can beat several. The players also have a variety of personal habits. However, the acquaintanceship is thoroughly occasioned in terms of the pinball situation, and the knowing does not extend beyond that occasion.

Even though pinball acquaintances may talk with one another readily, a player does not have to have sustained copresence with other players to initiate conversation. Because most of the talk is about pinball, it takes a minimum of contact to engage in discussions. One player I had met for the first time was asking me about the game he was playing and the characteristics of various other games. When he had finished playing, I asked him to hold the machine for me while I went to get change, and he obliged. On other occasions I have been invited to play some games, been engaged in conversations, and been asked advice by players I had never seen before. Like the relationships between horse players, pinball relationships are temporary and diffuse, being an emergent property of the pinball setting and not necessarily the primary reason for players' coming there (Scott, 1968:115).

To some extent, then, the pinball setting is an "open region" in that "any two persons, acquainted or not, have a right to initiate face engagement" (Goffman, 1963:132). However, it is not the case, as it is in bars, for example, that face engagements have priority over other forms of involvement (Cavan, 1966:156). For instance, if an observer came up to watch a game being played and began commenting on the play, the machine, or anything else to a player he did not know, his right to engage in such talk would not be questioned, but the player would not be expected to take his attention away from the game to make small talk with the observer. Between balls, the player might say something or look over at the observer, but even this much attention is not demanded or expected from someone who is playing. If the player is very close to winning a game and is on his last ball, or even appears to be concentrating very hard, little talk is offered by the observer or the player, and talking observers have been heard to stop in midsentence on seeing that a tense situation is developing. Exceptions to this rule occur among occasionals and kids, but regulars adhere to it, and in all my observations I never saw regulars break it.

Conclusion

A player's style of play is linked very closely to the features of involvement of the pinball occasion. Unlike the case in settings where pinball is a subordinate involvement, pinball is the dominant involvement, for the most part, for those who come to the pinball area. By certain players, such as pool players who shoot a game of pinball between games of pool, pinball is treated as a subordinate involvement, but, on the whole, it is the dominant one for the people in that part of the building.

The extent to which a player treats the play as serious determines the amount of concentration he will give the task of winning and the amount he is expected to give it by others (Goffman, 1961:17). The less serious the endeavor, the less the concentration and the less the player is expected to win. Thus, a player whose body idiom is loose and casual, who looks around while the ball is in play and pays a considerable amount of attention to an observer or friend, can claim he is playing for "fun." Of course, if a player is losing more or less consistently, he may claim *post facto* that all along he was playing for fun. Such a claim by an occasional is believable because he is not expected to win except by luck, anyway, but for a regular to make such a claim requires a special set of circumstances. If, for example, a regular finds that his machine is occupied, he may play another, which he does not expect to beat, until his machine is free. Under such circumstances, he may claim that he was playing the machine for fun; however, even under these conditions, a regular will give the play more concentration and effort than would an occasional who plays for fun.

The move from casual to serious play usually takes place when the player realizes that he has a good chance of winning. As this happens, the tension increases, along with the attention given by the player. In this way, playing pinball is transformed from an idle pastime to serious business.

As the serious concern with winning increases, engrossment to the point of shakiness or "overinvolvement" (Goffman, 1963:62) occurs. With this overinvolvement, the player's self-control decreases, and he increases the chances of tilting the machine and misjudging flipper shots. (Players have been observed to hit and break the glass on a machine as a result of such overinvolvement.) It is one thing for the kids who play to jump up and down and shout while they play, because they are not expected to demonstrate control over the situation, but, for a person who wishes to communicate dignity, composure, and presence of mind in a tense situation, it is altogether another matter. Likewise, for a player who sees that he is going to lose the game, barring a small miracle, it is not too difficult to maintain calmness and poise. The true test of pinball character comes when the player tacitly indicates that he is a serious player but can remain unruffled and clearheaded when the last ball of the last game rolls dizzily toward the flippers.

These attributes are recognized by players, and a good player who maintains his dignity while shooting a tight game is well thought of. Some players believe that they can play better when they smoke marijuana, and, if marijuana has a calming effect, it probably does help. Thus, the presentation of a calm, cool, dignified front, while problematic in a tense situation in pinball, can be maintained, if not through strength of character, by other means.

Finally, it should be noted that the maintenance of character and preservation of grace and face among pinball players are joint efforts (Goffman, 1967:27–31). As mentioned earlier, pinball acquaintanceships are formal and circumspect, and pinball acquaintances never make derogatory remarks about a player they are watching and will often attempt face-saving remarks by blaming the loss on ill fortune and not on the player. Observers will give the player all the room he needs by not leaning on the machine and by not creating other distractions. For, while a player is operating a machine, his play is the center of attention, and the player on.stage is trying to win against an impersonal force. If he wins, the observers will help him celebrate his victory, and, if he loses, they will help him lessen his defeat (Goffman, 1952).

References

CAVAN, S.
    1966   *Liquor License: An Ethnography of Bar Behavior*. Chicago: Aldine.

GOFFMAN, E.
    1967   *Interaction Ritual: Essays on Face-to-Face Behavior*. Garden City: Doubleday.
    1963   *Behavior in Public Places: Notes on the Social Organization of Gatherings*. New York: Free Press.
    1961   *Encounters: Two Studies in the Sociology of Interaction*. Indianapolis: Bobbs-Merrill.
    1959   *The Presentation of Self in Everyday Life*. Garden City: Doubleday.
    1952   "On Cooling the Mark Out: Some Aspects of Adaptation to Failure." *Psychiatry* 15 (November):451–63.

GOLD, R. L.
    1970   "Roles in Sociological Field Observations." In NORMAN K. DENZIN, ed., *Sociological Methods: A Sourcebook*. Chicago: Aldine, pp. 370–80.

LYMAN, S. M., and M. B. SCOTT
    1970   *A Sociology of the Absurd*. New York: Appleton-Century-Crofts.

POLSKY, N.
    1967   *Hustlers, Beats and Others*. Garden City: Doubleday.

SCOTT, M. B.
    1968   *The Racing Game*. Chicago: Aldine.

WEBB, E. J., D. T. CAMPBELL, R. SCHWARTZ, and L. SECHREST
    1966   *Unobtrusive Measures: Nonreactive Research in the Social Sciences*. Chicago: Rand McNally.

II. In Place and Out of Place: Conformity and Deviance

II. In Place and Out of Place: Conformity and Deviance

It may not be true, as the old saw has it, that "there is a time and a place for everything"; certainly not, if what is meant is that there is a time and place when anything at all is acceptable. But, taking the statement one step farther and reading into it as most of us do, there are activities that are considered proper and appropriate at a given or expected time and in a given setting and surrounding that become absurd, open to ridicule and even stronger sanctions, if performed at other times and in other settings. Whereas some acts are deviant no matter who does them or when they are done, others are approved if only we wait until the hour is struck, or if only we take note of who is present and what is the occasion.

"Deviance" is a term denoting a broad spectrum of acts that incite ridicule, anger, indignation, sarcasm, official condemnation, mild punishments, or sanctions as severe as long-time denial of liberty. We think of deviance in terms of crime or in terms of such widely condemned performances—even when they are not criminal—as public intoxication, drug addiction, prostitution, homosexuality, and transvestism. Deviance thus ranges from the outlandish to the intolerable, and a society displays its major values by indicating what behavior its dominant forces consider to be deviant, and how deviant they consider it.

Deviance, usually in rather mild forms, nevertheless exists in everybody's everyday life. There is a slip of the tongue, and we have called a current girlfriend by the name of an ex-wife; or a little forgetful gaucherie, as when the professor in Bernard Malamud's A New Life stands before his students on the first day of class, pleased that he has the rapt attention of the young men and women, only to discover at the end of the hour that his fly has been wide open throughout the lecture. In such instances, it can be said that we perform a deviant act, but that we have not assumed (or been assigned) a deviant identity.

To avoid reproach, we must not only do the right thing, and at the right time and place; it is inherent in this notion that we must also establish our credentials as the one deemed competent to do that thing, and hence permitted and expected to do it. If a person finds, for whatever reason, that he is doing something that will meet scorn, no matter how mild, he is faced with two tasks: to restore his own face as a

65

competent and decent member of society and to keep an ongoing social interaction from being disrupted by actions on his part that have been deemed improper. That these occasions take place frequently—in family life, in classrooms, among friends and strangers—is apparent. It may be a small matter, sometimes involuntary, as when one sneezes at a concert or breaks wind at a meeting with one's employer. Or it may be something over which one has more control, such as not wishing to take a drink when everyone else is drinking.

In a contribution by the editors of this volume, the problem of the nondrinker is examined. What is involved here, Birenbaum and Sagarin maintain, is the need to handle the deviance in such a way that the nondrinker establishes the legitimacy of his presence and does not disrupt an ongoing occasion. In this instance, they contend, the deviant becomes the stage manager, the medium through whom the interaction is maintained. They suggest that his behavior can be called "cohesive deviance."

The nondrinker at a cocktail party is both in place and out of place, but the person performing his everyday errands in the most humdrum manner is very much in place—or is he? Doing errands may be a way of meeting one's obligations, but it is not a crystallized role; therefore, it is an ambiguous experience for the doer. Moreover, a person can get too far into his errands or become too involved in doing them, and then be out of place because he has strayed from the expectations associated with a specific role. Martin Wenglinsky, in his essay, clearly reveals the personal and hence sociological significance of trivia, the petty things that make up the day, in which we all become so enmeshed. Our errands are side-involvements, peripheral to our major activities and to most of our role-related tasks, that constitute a central problem in just getting through a day.

In their essay on embarrassment, Gross and Stone deal with role requirements that demand a structured display of emotion. They demonstrate the rich potential of everyday acts for sociological analysis. This dovetails with the psychoanalytic approach, as one can see by comparing their essay with the Freudian literature on slips, forgetfulness, misnaming, and other such acts. In psychoanalysis, there is a concern with what both mistake and embarrassment reveal about the performer; Gross and Stone are concerned, rather, with what they reveal about the nature of roles and expectations. Psychoanalysis seeks to understand the genesis of the error; Gross and Stone, the nature of the transaction that made the error possible and in which it became defined as embarrassment and hence labeled and handled as such.

Embarrassment and role relationships are also explored in the excerpt from Erving Goffman's book *Encounters*. Goffman is here concerned with people who fear that they may be regarded as out of place. He therefore clarifies the nature of deviants and deviance, particularly how people use impression management to disarm those who might see them as deviant. As Freud studied the abnormal to understand the normal (and to a lesser extent the reverse), so Goffman illuminates the actions of deviants in order to understand the actions of essentially conforming individuals in ordinary settings. This is not to suggest, as some might, that we are all deviants; certainly we are, at one time or another, and in some situations that we face from time to time. But, rather, the point here is that deviance and conformity are in dynamic interplay. In Goffman's world, this interplay is seen when people handle what might otherwise be deviant acts in such a manner that the acts are redefined as acceptable. The adolescent merry-go-round rider, older than those who are expected to be seen on a carousel, may be thought of as out of place. He manipulates the situation, however, so as to save face—and saving face is supremely important to the people inhabiting Goffman's world. That is what makes it our world, the world of all of us.

1. The Deviant Actor Maintains His Right to Be Present: The Case of the Nondrinker *

ARNOLD BIRENBAUM AND
EDWARD SAGARIN

Every social occasion brings together people who have some claim to be in that situation and some knowledge about what to do and say to others who are present (Goffman, 1963:2). This claim by the participants, and the knowledge that each has and that they share, is generally approved by all in the situation, forming a kind of collective (albeit often unstated) set of rules to which individuals comply. The rules make possible the development of a network of interconnections between persons transacting business, the creation of a common vocabulary for discourse between negotiators in disputes, and agreement on what to disagree on between opposing sides in debates. In short, these aspects of organized social life are aptly called the "noncontractual elements of contract" (Durkheim, 1960:211).

These rules are generally maintained through a network of relationships, temporary or permanent, in which is created some consensus within groups as to the values and models of behavior that are proper in the particular setting. Thus, human behavior is patterned so that people can have expectations of what others will do, and a reservoir of responses to such expected behavior from which they can draw. By and large, people do what they are expected to do, and these actions are within socially approved boundaries. We follow scripts and scenarios written for us by eons of humanity we never knew and from whom we have obtained a great social legacy, and human freedom often consists of making choices within the parameters laid down for us. No wonder, then, that the sociologist refers to the individual in these circumstances as an actor: in the sense not merely of one who performs an act, but of one who follows the script.

* This article has not been published previously.

68

As competent actors, we often attribute to others a variety of traits that promote the condition of certainty necessary to maintain these networks of relationships. Most often these attributions begin in anticipation of an encounter, being based on prior experience with the same people or with those whom we recognize as being similarly situated. We know that if we have to cash a check we do not have to look for the very same bank teller every time, for any bank teller will do. Furthermore, these attributions extend beyond actual performance to other characteristics that we impute to the person who, according to our expectation, will perform a given task. We create a model of responses of others to ourselves, and this model goes beyond specific acts to other aspects of the person (Schutz, 1962:19). These characteristics form a set of background expectations that are as important as the acts we anticipate others will perform. When these background expectations are fulfilled, social life flows smoothly, for each actor shows that he has a right to be present on a particular occasion, that he commands a knowledge of what to do and say to others. In other words, he knows the rules about how to be sociable.

Yet social life is filled with its surprising moments. These moments are dangerous, not in the sense of constituting a threat to our physical well-being but, rather, in that they may disrupt the ongoing and desirable social interaction or cause one or several of the actors to feel ill at ease. People are occasionally shocked or taken aback when they find that some cab drivers are women, or that mechanics in some garages are amputees. Similarly, Miles Davis, the great black jazz composer-musician, owned a building where people seeking apartments invariably mistook him for the superintendent because a black landlord seemed an unlikely phenomenon to them. Such unexpected combinations of traits are likely to appear in a society in which acquired and ascribed social characteristics meld in uneasy coexistence.

These anomalous situations are often full of embarrassment, awkwardness, and confusion. They are sometimes humorous, sometimes disruptive. But the purposes for which the occasion was brought into existence can generally go forward, even if lacking in smoothness or with hesitation and improvisations. Once the right of participation is reconfirmed, usually by a demonstration of competence in the performance by those present of the primary roles for which their presence is requested, desired, or tolerated, the interaction is resumed. In short, the actors who are suspect can show that they know what to do and say, and so be redefined by others; they can offer positive cues to their claim to a right to be in the situation.

To add a further refinement, there are anomalous situations in which actors create uncertainty by not providing support for their presence through expected or positive means. Such people cannot emit effective cues, because their incongruous images result not from actions that deflect from the stated purposes of the occasion but from things they cannot or will not do. Their right to be present is not called into question, but their demeanor, which is unsupportive of the occasion, makes their commitment to the encounter suspect. Others in this situation are uneasy about what additional actions might not be forthcoming. The smooth flow of interaction is disrupted by the failure to offer a cue at the right time. The awkwardness and embarrassment that ensue cannot be removed by a show of activity that reaffirms one's claim to be present, because this is not what is in question. Suspicion is cast upon the actor's sociability skills, and the conventionally behaving actor may lose the certainty that he is dealing with a fully competent person who knows what to say and do. For a moment, easeful interaction is threatened.

An actor who fails to perform an important sociability rite is usually the one who must do something to restore an easy flow of interaction; however, this task can be performed by another who saves a situation although he had not been the one to threaten it. In either case, someone must attempt to give off impressions that support the goals of the situation and, more importantly, support its underlying collective character.

The person who threatens the unstated norms of the group by refusing to do what is expected of him must show signs of recognition that others have the right to do what he does not choose to do. Then, he can save the situation by showing his encouragement for conventional behavior. In some ways he becomes a kind of "floor manager" of the collective life of the occasion, at least until smooth-flowing sociability is restored. This permits the participants to get on with achieving their purposes, because further direct attention does not have to be paid to the collective character or ambience of the occasion. The social occasion goes on despite the presence of a person who is a "wet blanket," who fails to support the concrete activities that usually create the collective character, but who supports the collectiveness itself. In this essay, we will follow one such floor manager, who differs from those around him in that he is a nondrinker. In his effort to restore the purpose and ambience of the encounter, he restores his image as a competent actor, as one who can correctly assess the meaning and value of his failure to do the expected.

There are many people who are distinguished from all others—distinguished, one might say, from the majority—by their *failure* to do something, or by their unwillingness or inability to do it. Usually, as restorers of the moral order, we focus attention on those who perform an offensive act, rather than on those who fail to do a trivial but expected one. If human actions are seen as voluntary and essentially rational (although one would not dispute that there are degrees of voluntarism, going into the Army presumably being less voluntary for a draftee than going to college, and degrees of rationality, the kleptomaniac presumably being less rational than the bank thief), then failure to act can often be omitted from consideration, if only because it may not involve a decision. That is to say, millions of people do not drink coffee, do not read a morning newspaper, or do not make transatlantic telephone calls. In these instances, they are not specifically making decisions to fail to commit these acts but are allocating their time, energy, and money elsewhere.

Yet sometimes society, or groups within it, evokes punitive sanctions against those who fail to act. People are punished, or at least they would be if the failure were known, for deliberately refusing to file an income tax return; others, for unwillingness to provide for the family if one is head of a household. These people may be said to be occupying socially defined statuses, and then failing to live up to the norms incumbent upon them. It is the role of the person who has an income to file a tax return, and it is the role of the husband who is physically and mentally capable to support his family. But why should a person *have* to drink, or why should he *feel* that he has to do so, and how does he manage to maintain a pattern of interaction in a small group if he is unwilling or unable to perform?

Although alcoholic beverages have ubiquitous purposes in our society, their use to convey a special meaning to an occasion remains most important, at least in middle-class and middle-aged settings. Culturally, "having a drink" still connotes a set-apart occasion, one in which the routines of the workaday world are either halted or enhanced by the presence of whisky or some other distilled or fermented beverage. We no longer pour an elaborate drink for the gods, as the Greeks of Homer's time did when they made their libations, but the term "libation" is sometimes used to suggest that it is now the right time and the right place to recognize or cement the bonds between us that transcend our individual interests or projects.

Alcohol still has a sacred meaning, even though the meaning of the sacred has lost much of its divine character. Consequently, encounters that call for the use of spirits retain their ritual character. In turn, the nondrinker is not merely proffered an opportunity to drink but commanded or summoned to recognize the sacredness of an occasion. The innocent question "Would you like a drink?" is never formulated randomly or limited to its literal meaning: It is a symbolic beginning of one focus for activity, an opener for recognizing an alteration of the definition of the situation. When the nondrinker answers this summons with a refusal, he is rejecting, in essence, the new direction of meaning that others seek to bestow upon the situation. The nondrinker, if he is willing to support the occasion, must convey in some way that he does not reject the symbolic character of the question and the hidden sacred meaning that the words imply.

At times, when he is a guest at a party or a reception, an already established occasion in which the sacred and sociable meaning requires no initiation, the nondrinker may sustain the definition of the situation more easily and yet not completely effortlessly. When the host or hostess offers him a drink and he refuses this hospitality, he may still be able to receive some other token as a sign of being supportive of the occasion, as when he is proffered a nonalcoholic beverage or food. Thus, the host can still provide hospitality, and the nondrinker can still accept an alternative offering, although this may produce some minor inconvenience for the busy party-giver.

Despite the acceptance of the substitute gift of food or drink, the nondrinking guest remains somewhat of an enigma to the host and other guests. It is taken for granted that alcohol opens one up for sociability, and, whatever its physiological effects, the person at a party who consumes no spirits may be regarded as less spirited—less caught up in the festivity of the occasion. Some suspicion may still remain among those who monitor the nondrinker's careful avoidance of whisky or wine: that he is not showing the appropriate deference to the occasion, that his refusal reveals a lesser commitment to the party than is required by those who are present and who sustain the ambience of the occasion. Consequently, the nondrinker may have to double his effort at celebrating the occasion, by becoming an overly energetic participant in order to disidentify with his temporarily assigned position as a deviant.

Moreover, in some instances, a person's character may become open to question if he cannot or will not make this effort to live up to the rules of sociability. A woman's refusal to drink is understandable to all who are present: Of course, we all "know" in a commonsense way that women are the weaker sex, and their not taking a drink, or drinking a "lady's drink," is perfectly permissible. To some extent it is even secretly encouraged because of the general revulsion on seeing women drunk, particularly in public places. The drunkenness of a man is never treated with as much disgust or public comment. Similarly, the displays of coquettishness that middle-class males expect and demand of women at parties require that the women keep their heads, lest they turn a harmless flirtation into something more serious, such as an exhibition of passion, perhaps with someone else's husband, or a nasty scene in which some male mistakes excessive responsiveness as an invitation to a more serious encounter, ending in verbal rejection of his advances. Therefore, attitudes toward unwillingness to be a participant in the drinking party differ according to the sex of the reluctant person, with the differing attitudes validating our view of sex roles and expectations.

Interestingly, in contrast, men are encouraged to imbibe, and one who does not drink is suspect to those present; for, if one of the expected components of his identity is absent, perhaps there are other things about him that might be revealed under different circumstances. This suspicion is known all too well to the suspect—the nondrinker—and to those who might find the absence of drinking in a man somewhat peculiar. Therefore, the man who does not drink will quickly offer some justification for this lack of social grace. As the Irish say, drinking is a "good man's failing." The justification may be in the form of a joke that follows the statement "No thanks, I don't drink," for example, "But I do smoke, curse, and like sex." Alternatively, one might explicitly recognize the social import of the occasion by making a verbal statement that he is certainly open for sociability, by claiming that he does not need alcohol to become loose and open with others.

Sometimes these efforts to reaffirm the meaning of the occasion, and one's recognition of his duty to participate and show commitment to it, become the focus of interaction, as when conversations turn to the subject of drinking and related topics. To some extent, the differentness that the nondrinker exhibits in his polite refusal of alcohol can become a basis for sociability or for its initiation. At a party, or any other social occasion, as Georg Simmel has noted (1950), external statuses and interests cannot be invoked, lest they ruin the spontaneity and equalitarian nature of the gathering. Yet one can and is expected to make the effort to be interesting and distinctive, and one usually finds that effort rewarding, so long as the concerns of the serious and workaday world remain outside of the occasion. Parties may have no central task or focus of concern in the form of realizing a goal beyond the maintenance of easeful interaction, which playful concern with personality may help to sustain.

For the person who has nothing to hide, save his slightly peculiar characteristic of not drinking, the offer to disidentify with the socially assigned role of the "wet blanket" may be of small moment. But, for the person who has some other characteristic that he wishes to keep secret, the disclosure of this harmless little peculiarity may be more dramatic. Suspicion and doubt about that person's right to be present, his qualifications to participate as a peer, may breed as a result of his generally harmless disclosure. Most important for such a nondrinking person, if doubt is not dispelled, the potentially discreditable person (Goffman, 1963:30) may not be able to sustain the conventional-appearing image he wishes others to accept. Therefore, the person who has something else to conceal may readily admit to being a nondrinker, not only to quickly recover his right to be present but also to prevent himself from conveying the image of being a person with a more stigmatizing characteristic. To the extent that the stigma he wishes to keep secret has been acquired involuntarily, this strategy might be followed with great consistency in his presence at all occasions when one is summoned to drink. On the other hand, when this deviant identity involves more active and voluntary participation, there is some likelihood that more ambiguous efforts at self-concealment will occur. Voluntary deviance, even in hostile settings, is an aspect of the self that might find a sympathetic ear, or one might even encounter another person with the same characteristics or interests. Thus, through hints and cues, the nondrinking voluntary deviant may get others to respond to this aspect of his life-style by interesting them in himself through the disclosure of what appears in a given setting as a flaw, however minor it may be.

The element of nondrinking in a person's identity does not always require the elaborate explanation that it would demand in a character on the stage, where such a strange or peculiar trait must be accounted for in the script. Yet, on the part of conventional and deviant actors alike, there is some general sensitivity to differentness in everyday life. Moreover, voluntary and involuntary deviants are extraordinarily sensitive to the dramaturgical quality of everyday life and may be particularly suspicious of unusual traits that others display. This is (1) a way of protecting themselves against being exposed and discredited and (2) a way, particularly for those who are voluntary deviants, of locating others who share their fate and interests. The pot-smoking business executive, for example, may ask another guest at a party, in a circumspect way, if he also indulges in the use of marijuana, by inquiring if he smokes, hoping that the answer will be something like "Yes, but only when I can pass it" or "Not tobacco." If the answer is of a more conventional variety, nothing has been revealed in asking the question, and the questioner can retrace the tentative steps forward without having jeopardized his status with an unfortunate revelation. Similarly, nondrinking may be used as an index of the use of other stimulants. Among those who share such nonconforming proclivities, confession of such a minor flaw may lead to conversations that produce more interesting revelations.

That there are a few "oddballs" who don't drink is taken for granted (Schutz, 1962:74), but we seldom stop to consider that such people stand in danger of being catapulted into the socially undesirable position of "wet blanket" (ironical language, indeed, when we invoke the terminology of the Prohibition era). What places the nondrinker in this precarious position, where he becomes subject to strong but unofficial sanctions, is that he, like any other person present, fills a status in which drinking is part of the expected normative procedure, namely, the social mingler. He socializes for reasons that have nothing to do with drinking, and his failure to participate in this aspect of other people's activity becomes prominent, visible, and disruptive of group solidarity. We can contrast his position with that of others who do not participate, and we will see that each in a unique way must come to grips with the onus of being an outsider, and each develops mechanisms that can be called safety valves and escape hatches.

These devices are of two kinds: The first prevents the situation in which the nondrinker will experience embarrassment and awkwardness from arising, and the second deals with the confusion that is promoted by the nondrinker's failure to follow expected normative procedures. Even in the latter case, the nondrinker may attempt to escape notice rather than state plainly that he does not drink. Moreover, in such situations, attention can be reduced by introducing a socially acceptable excuse. Let us examine the ways in which such situations are skirted by the inveterate nondrinker or the person who seeks even to stay away from alcohol in situations in which he must be present.

Start, for example, with the person who does not play bridge or golf. The escape hatch here is the ability not to attend gatherings brought together primarily for such purposes. One can easily avoid the bridge party or the golf course. On some occasions a person might be present when a bridge foursome is desperately needed, but ordinary, everyday activities are unlikely to lead a person into such a situation with any frequency. As a matter of fact, bridge players and golfers are usually not desirous of having the nonparticipant present, unless it be as caddy or bartender; so, mingling in a milieu in which "everybody" plays bridge or "everyone" spends time on the golf course, the nonperformer or the person who is deviant by virtue of being the nonactor maintains relationships by the technique of selective avoidance: He deliberately avoids situations in which the particular act is to be performed. The avoidance is reciprocated, and the prominence of the deviance is not so much diminished as it is devoided of its annoyance qualities.

In a somewhat different position is the nonsmoker. At the moment, he is prominent and something of a hero, particularly if he is an ex-smoker, owing to the current health campaign against smoking. People carry their own cigarettes if they are smokers, and, although they often offer their open package to others, they are not inhibited in their activity if these others refuse. A nonsmoker can refuse almost unnoticed, and there is little interest in whether he does so because he never smokes, has another brand, has his own in a pocket or purse, or just is not in the mood at the particular moment. Smoking is an individual act, contributing little to social interaction or group cohesion (except in adolescent circles or in youthful marijuana-using groups). Under ordinary conditions, the interactive element may have begun and ended simply with the offer of one cigarette and its acceptance or refusal.

In contrast to smoking, drinking is often part of a ceremony. Sometimes the ceremony is integrated into the legitimate activities of an institutionalized religion, as at the Catholic Mass or the Jewish Passover service. At other times, it is a mechanism for the expression of the common aims and wishes of a small collectivity, and in such a case the failure to participate can be interpreted as a failure to support the goals that are being articulated. Let's have a drink for peace, or for the bride, or for the trip to Europe, or for the new Ph.D. program. One does not strike a match, light up a cigarette, take a deep breath of smoke within the body and exhale a well-formed ring while one of the party is saying, "Here's a smoke to Mary and Joe." Thus, the pressure to smoke is slight, even when one is within a group, and the failure to join in the activity does not disturb group cohesion and label one an outsider.

Somewhat closer to the nondrinker is the nondancer, who may likewise find himself in groups that have come together for purposes other than dancing. At a wedding, many people dance, but, because all do not dance simultaneously, the visibility of a nonparticipant is reduced. Moreover, the nondancers constitute an audience for the dancers, a socially acceptable form of nonparticipation. Except for the adolescent and young adult, the nondancer finds himself in a milieu in which everybody is dancing only infrequently. It is far easier to avoid such a situation than it is for the nondrinker to avoid an analogous one.

Somewhat similar to the nondrinker, but perhaps with more social repercussions, is the nonparticipant in religious affairs in a small and isolated community. The members of a specific religious group become sufficiently acquainted with one another to form almost a primary group of their own, and one of the social expectations for someone belonging to the ethnic community is that he participate in its religious activity. Not to participate, at least in a somewhat perfunctory manner, is deviance by virtue of the nonact. Here, group belonging is ascribed by ethnicity and achieved by residence, the norm of participation derives from the status, and the deviation from the norm becomes visible because of the small size of the group.

People who drink alcoholic beverages are generally divided into two main categories, but there is a continuum between the extremes. Generally, it can be said that some people are social drinkers while others are alcoholics. The former are those who have no compulsion to drink, do not suffer when deprived, and are capable of enjoying a drink frequently or infrequently, regularly or irregularly, without their functioning being impaired by the use of alcohol. On the other hand, alcoholics, who have been studied at length and in depth, are people who have a personal problem and who constitute a social problem. They are more or less unable to control their drinking, and they allow it to interfere with normal functioning in their economic, familial, and general social roles. They spend more money and time than they can afford on liquor, and they usually drink more than they can handle.

Nondrinkers are also divisible into categories. There are total abstainers and more flexible and partial ones; there are former drinkers and those who never drank; and there are former excessive drinkers who have become total abstainers. Some abstain because of principle, some because of ill health, and some because they "just don't like the stuff."

Former alcoholics are sometimes known as ex-alcoholics (a term that meets strong disapproval from Alcoholics Anonymous), dry alcoholics, sober alcoholics (in the sense that they are permanently sober), or, in the ordinary vernacular, people who are on the wagon. To be on the wagon means to have been a drinker and to be permanently abstaining; in other words, one is an ex-drinker, although not necessarily, albeit often, an ex-alcoholic. Thus, an ordinary nondrinker who has never been a drinker cannot be on the wagon.

Linguistically, the key to this is that one *climbs* on the wagon and does not merely find oneself there. Nor can an ordinary drinker be off the wagon. In fact, one is not said to *be* off the wagon, but rather to *fall* off it, and the word "fall" here is both symbolic (there is downfall) and at the same time an expression of one's helplessness. Climbing is voluntary; falling is something that happens to a person and is beyond his control.

Thus, to be off the wagon, one must formerly have been on it. A person off the wagon, therefore, is one who was a drinker, then renounced intoxicating beverages, and then (in the words of Oscar Wilde) "sinned a second time." To be off the wagon, in sum, is to be an ex-ex-drinker. One is hard pressed to find another expression in the English language describing an ex-ex-anything, and this fact may be an indication of the American obsession with the renunciation of alcohol.

The term "abstainer," often used of the nondrinker, carries no connotation that one was or was not a drinker in the past. Like the word "drinker," "abstainer" (and the verb "to abstain") carries an implication that the matter under discussion involves alcoholic beverages, but, just as one can drink milk or tea, when this is spelled out or clearly implied, so one can abstain from ice cream, cigarettes, or sexual activity, without doing injustice to the word.

What makes the nondrinker's position peculiar is that he frequently finds himself in the presence of drinkers and in a situation where he becomes an outsider if he does not participate. The cocktail party has become a part of a large segment of American society, probably at all but the lowest socioeconomic levels. In business and professional groups, one goes to lunch or to dinner with colleagues, and a round or two of drinks is expected to precede any solid food.

The important factor here is that such gatherings, even those specifically called cocktail parties, are not arranged for the purpose of drinking, in the sense that the bridge party is to play bridge and the day on the golf course is to play golf. One goes to the cocktail party to socialize—to talk, meet people, conduct business—and, during the pursuit of such activities, one drinks. The purpose of the gathering is fulfilled by attending, but to attend without drinking is to be disruptive by failing to fulfill one of the social expectations incumbent upon all those present.

Now, how does the nondrinker handle his problem so that he is least disruptive of group cohesion and obtains the slightest possible social sanctions for his behavior?

First, he sizes up a situation to determine the visibility of his non-participation. His failure to drink may be prominent, or it may go hardly noticed. Prominence is illustrated by the waiter at the table, going from one person to the next, taking orders for cocktails and highballs, perhaps starting with the nondrinker. The situation of the nondrinker becomes particularly acute when he is at a table and, upon declining to order a drink, finds that the others follow suit, sometimes even articulating, "Well, I don't drink alone" or "If you won't have one, I won't either." Here the drinker is the potential redefiner of the occasion, and the abstainer must show clearly that he does not object to others drinking.

A method for coping with the prominence of failure to join in group activity is to shake one's head unobtrusively or to decline the invitation *sotto voce*. This is often done at a table after two or three other drinks have been ordered, and it is sometimes accomplished by hiding one's head in the menu (particularly easy if the menu is large) and pretending to read and study the offerings while orders are being taken. By the time the nondrinker has been reached with the query as to what he will have and he has declined, it is too late for the others to retract their own orders.

A common device is to order a ginger ale or Coca-Cola. If this is done at a party, one can pretend to be drinking an alcohol-containing liquid. At the table, where this pretense is not possible, one can at least have a glass filled with something to lift to the lips when a toast is given (the ceremony thus becoming a ritual). True, one can lift a glass of water while the others have champagne or Scotch, but its being water is too prominent as a norm violation and makes nonparticipation sufficiently obvious to be embarrassing. At a cocktail party, where the liquid mixture is not identifiable to the eye and has been obtained while one's companions were not present, the nondrinker-drinker permits the assumption to be made that his beverage is alcoholic, although this is not the case, and he is never challenged. Nondrinking, in such an instance, can be explained in the words of Goffman (1963:30) as being a discreditable rather than a discredited stigma.

The alcoholic who is on the wagon is usually less embarrassed by being a nondrinker than the permanent abstainer. He wears his badge more proudly, the prominence being perhaps a reinforcement of his will to refrain. He will say "no" loudly and will often add, with a gleam in his eye, "I'm on the wagon." He feels no stigma, and, if his failure to drink provides an atmosphere in which the other participants have difficulty falling into their social roles, that is their problem. He may be pre-empting others from their negative labeling by forcing on them positive labeling of himself as a reformed and redeemed soul. To be an Alcoholics Anonymous member is a source of pride, not shame. To have fallen into the gutter (perhaps literally as well as figuratively) and have risen out of it deserves a tribute because one has risen—which is the American dream of self-help and upward mobility, of every man the master of his own fate.

Because the wagon can also be boarded by one who is on medical orders not to drink and abstention is a mechanism that enables such a person to continue to function, rather than fall victim to the nonfunctioning that is inherent in the sick role, the ulcer sufferer can also refuse a drink without the embarrassment and stigma of being an outsider. If it is proper to go to an analyst, it is respectable to have ulcers. One need not conceal being a victim of such a physiological disorder, as he would if it were a case of hemorrhoids or a colostomy operation.

It is interesting to note that nondrinkers know that there is a priority of "accounts" (Lyman and Scott, 1970:112) that one can introduce here to explain why one is not drinking at a party or at a luncheon. This is illustrated by the way in which the person who simply does not like the taste of alcoholic beverages will sometimes claim that his lapse from the expected behavior in the situation is justified by having an alcohol problem or a physical ailment that makes drinking detrimental to his health. In using expressions like "I'm on the wagon" or "I'm a teetotaler," the nondrinker masks his dislike with socially acceptable excuses, thereby saying to all who are present that he is not to be judged as deficient in social graces; nor do they have to judge him as harshly as he judges himself. Saying flatly "I don't drink at all" or "I don't like the stuff" makes the person more suspect and less of a "regular fellow" either by virtue of the moral superiority invoked in the former statement or the image of the "pantywaist" or "sissy" invoked by the latter. In avoiding these labels, the nondrinker proffers an image accompanied by an excuse, making it easier to restore easeful interaction.

Recognition of the difficulty of the nondrinker was made official when a new drink made its appearance in some sophisticated bars; called a Virgin Mary, it consists of tomato juice (without vodka). The name may be considered an index of the degree to which ours is a secular (if not outrightly blasphemous) society. The product itself may be considered as an indication of the society's desire neither to punish the deviant nor to suppress the deviant behavior but merely to make such deviance less visible and less disruptive of social relations.

Occasionally nondrinkers handle their role aggressively. One method, usable only in the presence of a child, is practiced after the child has ordered what is called a kiddie cocktail (or such synonyms as a Shirley Temple or a Buck Rogers, for female and male children, respectively). The drink consists of ginger ale, with a Maraschino cherry and a little Maraschino juice. After the abstaining adult has heard the child give this order, he may remark, "Make that two." The self-mockery is too mild to be disturbing, but sufficient to permit reduction of tension and to create an atmosphere of joviality in which the nondrinker can rightfully join. The humor may be seen as a mechanism to establish distance from the role in which the abstainer has placed himself, that of a child who does not have the right to perform adult activities (Goffman, 1961:85–152).

If the nondrinker is not an alcoholic or total abstainer but merely dislikes the taste or effect of liquor, he may take a single alcoholic drink, preferably in a weak mixture if this can be obtained, and sip it slowly. To use a colloquialism, he "nurses" his drink. The expression may be derived from a description of a child at his mother's breast, prolonging the drinking of the milk over a long period of time. However, the marked difference between the two situations should be apparent. The child often starts sucking avidly and enthusiastically and slows down later; furthermore, the child nurses the drink in order to prolong gratification, rather than to avoid distaste.

A man may refuse a drink, and certainly may refuse a refill when he is nursing one, and at the same time avoid the stigma of being an outsider, by invoking the socially accepted role of the sober driver. Particularly at such ceremonies as weddings, where the drinks may flow freely and the pressure to participate may be strong, the statement "I have to drive home" provides the abstainer with a mechanism for arriving at his desired goal (nonparticipation) without disrupting the camaraderie.

Finally, the nondrinker can handle his problem by avoiding social activities that bring him into contact with drinks and drinkers. Whatever possibilities this may still have in small towns and in what was known at one time as dry territory and the Bible belt, it is increasingly difficult to use as a mechanism for avoiding moments of embarrassment and awkwardness, particularly in large cities, in industry, and in the academic community.

Conclusion

The pressures in the society toward conformity are many, and the strongest may be coming from primary group, peer group, and other face-to-face associations. The nondrinker is tolerated. He is not condemned or disapproved, and hence it is difficult to label his behavior deviant. Neither, however, is he approved. His nonconformity is troubling to others; it is upsetting but only mildly so and is easily overlooked if he does not insist on imposing his mode of behavior on others.

Thus, to conceptualize the nondrinker as deviant is inaccurate, if only because of the high degree of disapproval inherent in labeling a person with that term, either by his peers or by the sociologist analyzing the attitudes of these peers. Perhaps Howard Becker's term "outsider" (1963) is more properly descriptive, but the nondrinker differs from Becker's outsiders (particularly the jazz musicians and the marijuana-users) in that those Becker describes usually mingle in a primary group of similarly oriented outsiders and a person specifically emerges as a nondrinker only when mingling with a small group in face-to-face interaction in which he is the outsider. The marginality of the jazz musician is in relationship to the American society; the marginality of the nondrinker is in his relationship to a group around a table or at the party. If, then, the label of "deviant" is less properly applicable to the nondrinker than to the marijuana-user, the label of "outsider" may be more properly applicable to the nondrinker.

In the management of his problem, the nondrinker often seeks what Davis (1964:119–37) calls "deviance disavowal." This can take the form of concealment of his nonconformity (drinking ginger ale and pretending that it is a highball) or a plea that the nonconformity not be disruptive ("No, I don't drink, but you go right ahead if you want to"). When his deviance becomes visible, he becomes uncomfortably conscious of the supposed link between abstention and a puritanical and ascetic goodness. Thus, overconformity, as Merton (1957) has noted, is a form of deviance too, a saintliness regarded with skeptical derision in contemporary society.

The conflict of the nondrinker, produced by this discrepancy between self and social expectations, is derived from the social nature of drinking, whereby the failure to participate leaves one outside the group, weakens its solidarity, and disrupts the group spirit. He improvises because there are no institutionalized norms for him to follow. It is indicative of the long road America has traveled since Prohibition that he does not clothe himself in virtue and openly proclaim his status but either slinks into a corner and hides his nonconformity or works carefully at maintaining interaction.

In a sort of tacit manner, the role is called into being on every social occasion. Those absent who should be present are noted; those present who cannot validate their right to be present usually are more clearly noticed. One must show that he not only is but is supposed to be a member of the wedding, a member of the party, a member of the dinner-table gathering. This means performance, among other things, but the nondrinker is the nonperforming—and hence nonconforming—member.

Through many adaptations, he promotes the maintenance of both the purpose and the atmosphere of the occasion. He recognizes his own deviance and does not permit it to become obtrusive. In so doing, he never calls the behavior of the drinkers into question, and they may unhesitatingly take up their drinking. More important, they may give up their suspicion that the nondrinker will do other unexpected things, or will fail to do expected things. The occasion and all of its members are reunited to their full collectiveness despite the presence of a nonconforming member.

References

BECKER, HOWARD
   1963   *Outsiders*. New York: Free Press.
DAVIS, F.
   1964   "Deviance disavowal: the management of strained interaction by the visibly handicapped." In HOWARD BECKER, ed., *The Other Side*. New York: Free Press, pp. 119–37.

DURKHEIM, EMILE
  1960   *Division of Labor in Society*. Trans. by GEORGE SIMPSON. Glencoe:
         Free Press.
GOFFMAN, ERVING
  1963   *Stigma: Notes on the Management of Spoiled Identity*. Englewood
         Cliffs: Prentice-Hall.
  1961   *Encounters*. Indianapolis: Bobbs-Merrill.
LYMAN, STANFORD M., and MARVIN B. SCOTT
  1970   *The Sociology of the Absurd*. New York: Appleton-Century-Crofts.
MERTON, ROBERT K.
  1949   *Social Theory and Social Structure*. Glencoe: Free Press.
SCHUTZ, ALFRED
  1962   *Collected Papers*. Vol. I: *The Problem of Social Reality*. The Hague:
         Martinus Nijhoff.
SIMMEL, GEORG
  1950   *The Sociology of Georg Simmel*. Trans. and ed. by KURT H. WOLFF.
         New York: Free Press.

2. Errands *

MARTIN WENGLINSKY

I

Some of the alienation, frustration, anxiety, and other afflictions that exist in society may not be due to overt repressions or exploitation. Rather, they may be due to aspects of the social structure that are so pervasive and mundane as to elude specification and analysis while yet creating social imbalances and strains, contradictory or overburdening demands on individuals, and generally ineffective techniques for the carrying on of social life. Moreover, the problems that these features of the social structure present may be exacerbated by the forms they take on in the context of modern society, and these forms may be the vehicles through which repression and exploitation find or sustain their expression.

In engaging in day-to-day life, people perform their jobs, deal with their spouses, argue with their children's teachers, and exchange intimacies with their friends, besides paying taxes, marketing, and carrying out the garbage. Many of these activities are among those publicly acknowledged rights and responsibilities that are part of one or another status. One can expect a butcher to have meat for sale, or that it is deemed appropriate to ask a teacher why a student of his is doing badly. There are other activities, such as exchanging pleasantries with a stranger on a train, or running with a crowd that is attacking a police station, or arguing with a neighbor, that are governed more by the general usages of a society or the dramaturgical structure of a situation.

There is another category of activities (undoubtedly one of many other categories) worth calling to some attention. These activities include filing a tax return, getting a driver's license, finding an apartment, buying enough subway tokens for the week, visiting the dentist, locking the doors before going to sleep, buying groceries, calling the plumber, and sending transcripts to colleges. These activities are errands. They have the flavor of tasks that need accomplishing,

* This article, previously unpublished, appears here by permission of the author.

the busywork of day-to-day existence, the time-consuming, ever present, usually dull necessities of social life that for the most part are hardly memorable in themselves but are, however, impressive in a sociological sense.

Three types of errands can be readily distinguished. There are those that provide the material wherewithal of life and alter the material circumstances in which people live. These include cleaning out the garage or the file cabinets, going to the grocery or department store to shop, finding a place to live, preparing and cleaning up after meals. Another kind of errand involves legal or pseudolegal requirements placed upon individuals, like getting licenses, filing tax returns, going to court to pay fines, or getting a letter of reference for a job. A third kind of errand involves smoothing the course of interpersonal relations by attending dinner parties, buying flowers for a wife or girl friend, paying compliments to a friend.

Errands are not only part of many situations in life but are a prevalent kind of situation themselves. This is readily seen in the problems that arise in going to a supermarket for the week's groceries: a clear-cut errand involving a number of subsidiary errands and exhibiting many of the characteristics that arise in going about other errands. The shopper must keep a running inventory of his larder in mind between shopping trips in order to know what needs replacing or adding. This requires a discipline that, though sometimes mildly annoying, is much less annoying than the extra errands involved in running out of milk or gin at inappropriate moments, and may even give a slight sense of mastery over a household if done successfully. But added to this are the running inventories that must also be held for paying bills, checking on the work of subordinates in an office, and keeping professional and personal licenses up to date.

A great deal of repetitive work is involved in shopping. Except when it is used by the very efficient, a cart is run up and down the same aisles in order to find the jar of pimentoes, just as applications for bank accounts or school registration require filling in the same information over and over again. But disappointments are frequent, and are disproportionately severe considering the triviality of the task. Some energy had to be focused in order to pursue the pimentoes, only to find out the store has run out of them. The shopper is co-opted into unloading his cart while the checker rings up the items; the shopper also helps the packer bag his groceries so he can get out of the store more quickly (and doesn't the supermarket count on that assistance?), which keeps the shopper from checking whether the prices and number of items charged for are accurate (and doesn't the supermarket count on that, too?). It would take an extra and quite tedious errand to check whether the register slip, so thoughtfully provided, matches the purchases.

When arranging a daily schedule of errands, a person must consult the needs of the institution he is dealing with rather than his own.

It is more difficult to shop on Saturdays, because everyone wants to shop then; so one tries to find another time, which is inconvenient for the shopper but distributes the work for the supermarket better. Similarly, bank procedures penalize unusual transactions that will inconvenience the computer or accounting procedures—like a check without computerized account numerals or a withdrawal a few days before an automatic deposit will be made—but do not penalize themselves for inconveniences caused to customers. It falls upon the customer, should he find a mistake, to call it to the institution's attention, and it is the customer who retraces the steps the institution should have taken, as when a supermarket has failed to deliver an order or a bank has not processed a loan because a clerk had not seen that all the criteria for the loan had been met.

These problems and their attendant frustrations adhere not only to dealings with bureaucracies but also to dealings with friends and to other errand-filled situations. If the phone does not work, a friend must find a way of indicating he really did try to call, or in some way make up for the lapse. If the barber cuts your hair badly, you have to walk around that way. If your wife burned dinner, you go out for pizza.

Errands are a kind of task and so must be performed according to criteria of success. What they purport to provide or cause must indeed be provided or caused. They are, however, unlike ordinary work tasks in that their failures are more notable than their successes. One is less pleased by an errand accomplished than annoyed by an errand protracted, delayed, or not completed. In this sense, errands are part of ordinary activity and so are not dignified, as work is, by usually being selected for attention.

Specifically, errands cannot be examined fruitfully by noting the alienation they cause. Certainly an analogy can be drawn between work situations and going to the supermarket: The shopper engages in repetitions, acts in a situation over which he has little power, gathers little meaning, and exercises little skill. But the significance of errands lies elsewhere. Work is a part of your life, a consciously delineated part. Errands are aspects of all of your life, a characteristic of getting along itself. Work is thought of as time assigned to specific tasks or problems, even—in its alienated, ritualized form—as time of availability assigned in return for monetary reward. Errands, on the other hand, are assignments that are made in the course of one's own time, for one's own purposes, in the pursuit of that part of life not assigned as a legitimate, overt form of recompense. Work time is exchanged. Time with a friend is recognized as exchanged for love only cynically, pathetically, or as part of psychological analysis. A psychiatrist is untrue to a situation if he suggests that friends are "useful" to one another, and a patient has become callous if he accepts that as an accurate description of the import or process of a friendship. Friendship, like the rest of ordinary life, is behavior taken seriously for its own sake. Customs and most social usages are of this character, whereas work, however serious, has a built-in hypocrisy that comes from a job's being assumed as a set of duties that the job-holder would feel no such strong obligation to carry out were it not his job. Of a job, it can be said, "I am doing this for a living." To admit the same of a friendship would be considered not merely hypocritical but also dishonorable.

Similarly, on-the-job errands are assignments in the pursuit of the job, rather than extra or intense forms of work alienation. For example, a secretary goes out for coffee as part of her job. To ask her to procure for her boss would be an insult, not part of her job, even if she would willingly do it outside of office hours. The boundaries of the job allow errands in its terms, but not errands outside its compass, even if they are perfectly acceptable errands in other circumstances. Within the fiction of the job, as an "ordinary" situation, errands of the job will be done, but a job is ordinary life only as a fiction. When a secretary says she will do anything, she doesn't usually mean it.

Moreover, though errands are voluntary in the sense that one decides to have a telephone installed or cook a steak they are not "free." They cannot be done without, even if any particular one of them can be done without. They are requirements of a social structure. Careful budgeting of time can achieve efficient errand performance, and self-discipline and privation can allow errand frugality. Some people can shop a long list in their supermarkets in half the time others take, and some people can live off frozen dinners, but, clearly, there is a price paid; energy and attention expended or pleasures precluded. It is very difficult to alter seriously an errand-time budget without altering seriously a style of life. Furthermore, though it is possible to use errand-running as an occasion for pleasure, this can be considered a rationalization in the sense that one has altered one's evaluation of the situation rather than the situation itself. One can enjoy going to the supermarket hand-in-hand with a loved one, and this may bring personal psychological gains, but the supermarket would have to change its format significantly for this to alter the errand-running or make it something else. Supermarkets would need to do more than instruct their employees to compliment young lovers, or run displays and advertisements designed to draw young lovers to supermarkets as the place to be. In other words, it is difficult to see how most errands can become authentically pleasurable.[1]

In sum, errands need to be seen as a social phenomenon *sui generis*. They are not a degree of something else—alienation, slavery, achievement-orientation, or whatever—however much they may be similar in consequences or causally related.

Moreover, and most significantly, the distinctive character of a set

[1] The concept "authenticity" is meant in the sense used by Amitai Etzioni to point out fundamental rather than manufactured or inculcated human needs (Etzioni, 1968: Ch. 21).

of errands gives rise to a sense of ordinary life, even though errands are not the whole of it. This sense, when itself characterized, constitutes what is ordinarily meant by a style of life. Clearly, the distinction between urban and suburban living is not a geographical or class distinction (except in so far as different classes perform different errands). Living in a suburb means shopping at a shopping center, using a car on all occasions from shopping to taking the kids to school, meeting neighbors for the organization of required services, like schools and churches, more often having guests stay the weekend when they visit, rather than just for dinner, worrying about the weather and the commuter line, and having major and specialized medical or entertainment services at a distance, whereas urban living tends toward the opposite of all of these. And a high-rise apartment in the middle of a city can be suburban while relatively open areas outside a city or on its borders can seem very urban. Thus, while trivial as individual experiences, a person's round of errands is a very important part of his life.

II

More formally, errands can be defined as that set of activities required to sustain a status or an ordinary activity. This is so whether or not particular errands are themselves defined as part of a status. Standing on line for a bus is an errand whether the bus trip is a joyride, a way to get to work, or part of one's duties as a messenger. It is not an errand if it is done for its own sake, independently of what it allows to be done. This definition includes activities that initiate statuses or activities and those that maintain them.

In particular cases, it may seem difficult to separate activities of a status from errands of a status. This problem reflects some of the theoretical peculiarities of the concept of an errand. A father, for example, scolds his child. In doing so he maintains his authority (an errand), besides achieving immediate obedience (an act within his authoritative status). Indeed, one could argue, as is commonly done, that much authority is exercised to sustain the principle of authority rather than to exercise immediate control. If the authority were well established, obedience would not be problematic. Similarly, a grocer selling canned goods to a customer is not simply engaged in a transaction that is usual to his position; he could not continue to be a grocer unless he succeeded in maintaining a certain volume of sales.

However, while it may be true that engaging in the behavior of a status is necessary to sustain some statuses (although there are writers who do not write and husbands who do not see their wives), it is also true that there are other activities, minimal for trying to make a go of the status at all, that are requisite whether the status is well or badly performed. A bartender may run out of beer, but he needs a license to sell beer at all. The conditions that allow the completion of an errand for a status may affect the carrying out of the status and, indeed, provide its major drama, but they can still be distinguished from other status behavior. The rest of the status behavior surrounds the idea of the status, what it is for, while the errands are means to the end of engaging in the means whereby the end of the status is achieved. The errands are those second-order means, whereas the ordinary status behaviors are first-order means. This distinction holds whether the ends of the status are task performances, as in work, or simply the presentation of a self or a stereotype, as in statuses that are used in ordinary life.

Accepting an award is an errand for a writer, though a pleasant one, but dickering with a publisher is not an errand, even if it is unpleasant. A writer may never win an award, yet continue to write. He may not dicker at great length with a publisher, but some negotiation is necessary to present his work to the public—and such presentation to a publisher and thence to the public, or at least the attempt, is usually thought to be in keeping with a writer's status. Writing for his own drawer, as in diaries, may be an important part of a person's identity but hardly constitutes one of his statuses, unless it becomes known that, for example, he is not to be disturbed from three to five o'clock in the afternoon because he is working on his diary. A status involves responsibilities to, and expectations of, others, inevitably multiple and not all equally pleasant or even uniformly regarded as status requirements by all status-holders.

A writer is sufficiently in control of his own status definition to let it be known that he writes for posterity and not immediate publication. He can do the work required to alter his status as a writer so that people will stop asking him when his books came out or will come out when he tells them that he spends his time writing. Not all professionals can do that. A doctor is, for the most part, not free to decide that he will only examine his patients and not talk to them. Talking to them is part of his status. Making appointments and leaving time to talk to them constitute an errand, though it is part of his status that he will be available for appointments. Many doctors in private practice collect their fees from patients in person and in cash. Under the pressure of tax regulations and health insurance, many who used to collect cash are now compelled to keep records of receipts. Resistance to this new practice not only was based on the financial accountability it made possible, but also included resistance to using a nurse as a part-time bookkeeper. It seemed more "free" to keep in mind that a patient had not paid in a while, or to find some extra cash in hand at the end of the day. Part of the difficulty of unambiguously distinguishing errands comes from the fact that statuses themselves are subject to change and ambiguous definition, and people who determine an occupational ideology may have difficulty accepting certain errands explicitly as such, even if to do so would decrease work.

Another difficulty of determining the errands of a status is exhibited most clearly with reference to statuses that are business ventures. The storekeeper sells his wares, pays his mortgage or rent, and gives money to the local policeman and the neighborhood charities. Charitable payments may be out of the goodness of the storekeeper's heart, but clearly one of their not too latent functions is to allow the storekeeper to remain in business. How, then, is it possible to separate the operation of the business from what is required to keep the business in operation? One solution would be to regard almost all of the activities of such an enterprise as errands. That is, after all, the service that the storekeeper provides: assembling at a convenient outlet the products of a number of manufacturers. Such an approach would be tendentious, because the definition of the status, by both the storekeeper and the customer, accepts a distinction between the business and the requirements of staying in business. Selling a pound of butter is not a problem for the storekeeper, in the sense of whether or not he is expected to do it, but giving a bribe to a deliveryman may be. A bribe may be seen as a necessary evil or merely part of normal business operations.

The difficulty here comes from the congruence of the status with its bookkeeping as an economic enterprise. All behavior in the status becomes collapsed into profit and loss, into the over-all question of the economic well-being of the status. A distinction could be made only between profit levels and expenses necessary for short-term survival and those required for long-term survival or prosperity. Indeed, one of the psychological problems that derive from such a status comes from the seriousness with which each behavioral transaction is looked to for its direct or indirect economic benefit: A compliment to a customer may mean retaining that customer's trade. Some may find sufficient compensation for the constant ulterior motivation in the ideology of "being in business for yourself." Such a view is hardly preponderant among small retailers. Many would prefer a job whose status is secure, even if the job itself is not, where the two do not hinge upon one another.

The difficulty just discussed is less troublesome in large retail establishments—chain stores—where the division of labor and large volume make the statuses of clerks and managers subject to organizational guidance and only indirectly subject to profit and loss. In other words, the clerk may be hired and fired, may have to fill in W-2 forms and occasionally buy the manager coffee to maintain good relations, but such errands are distinct from serving customers or handling stock or taking orders from the manager. Employees know when they "have to" do the boss a favor beyond the usual demands of the job. They know they are contributing to his sense of solidarity with them so that they will be retained in, or promoted from, their position, rather than contributing to the solidarity of the position itself in the organization, although on occasion a position may be retained or dissolved in order to deal with the person who holds it.

Indeed, gestures of office solidarity may be so routinized as to become overt errands—as when a collection to buy a present for a secretary's new baby is done without sentiment or even, in some cases, through a weekly deduction taken from everyone's paycheck like Social Security. This does not mean that the distinction between errands and status is a matter of self-definition. What it does mean is that the status-holder's perceptions are reliable though possibly mistaken indicators of errands. Moreover, errands may not be distasteful. Sleeping with a producer may be an errand for an actress, but she may find it both fun and profitable, and deny the connection between the two.

Errands, then, are a set of role relations that overlap somewhat with the set of role expectations that make up a status. They are those roles that contribute to sustaining the entire status or the relations between the roles of the status. They are actions distinct from the performance of the status itself. Errands provide the status with the adaptive, allocative, pattern-maintenance and value support that allow the status to keep going. Listening to a speech to buck up morale is an errand as much as checking the tires before flying a plane. A status differs from a social system in that it is expected to do something more than hold itself together, a demand only sometimes made of societies. It is also possible, however, that the successful performance of the status may itself be required for the status to be sustained, and that, in a given case, whether a behavior is an errand or part of the status performance may be both ambiguous and indeterminate. For example, a clerk may not know whether he has to be pleasant to his immediate supervisor or invite the boss home to dinner, and the boss may feel that the invitation to dinner by his employee was not required but only a part of the extension of their growing friendship beyond the office. But, should no invitation be proffered, the boss may feel that his status as boss has been slighted. Thus, a dinner invitation may be an errand of a job, even if neither party defines it as such but both see the pleasant relations either as not job-related or as part of the job itself: One must get along with colleagues. The formulation is usually after the fact. It gives definition to a violation that comes to be perceived for a variety of possibly circumstantial reasons: The clerk has not been performing the job well; the boss is having personal difficulties; the office's over-all performance has diminished. Errands, then, have exteriority and constraint and are thus not simply a matter of personal definition.

One other problem of the concept of errands is purely verbal. A copy boy has a status in which status behavior is also errand behavior. His job is to get files for other people, but what are errands for others are not errands for him. His status is discussed in terms of tasks that are a collection of other people's errands, which he assumes so that their work can proceed more easily. These errands may be work-related (picking up copy) or personal (ordering flowers for someone's wife). These are clearly distinct from the boy's own errands, such as collecting his paycheck. Jobs with any dignity allow even errand boys their own errands. They get to eat lunch and go to the bathroom. This is not true of all jobs.

One kind of errand is easily recognized. This is the personal errand necessary for presenting oneself in social life. It includes such behavior as bathing, shaving, dressing, and eating. As with more public errands, personal errands seem to consist largely of establishing material conditions for engaging in a status. The storekeeper needs a place of business and stock; the individual needs his body. But, as in the case of the storekeeper, these conditions are not simply physical. A person must put on his face (which is not the same as his mask) in order to go about the day's activities. He must form his face into its characteristic pose. This takes effort, though in ordinary life it is habitual. Without the effort, a face would seem less animated and would be likely to prompt some comment. When they sleep or are in repose, people look different—and not necessarily better or more communicative of their emotions, unless one makes an ideological assumption that emotions communicated effortlessly are more significant than emotions for which an effort has been made. Children, for example, tend to show less difference in their facial composition between sleeping and being awake then adults do, which may mean that they do not yet have a character to sustain, although they may have traits of character to exhibit.

In fact, the efforts required to perform personal errands are regarded as so ordinary that failure to sustain them is interpreted as a sign of severe mental distress. "Habit deterioration," as it is called, may be taken, at the least, as severe depression and may be a concomitant of psychological crises. Everyone lapses in personal errands for a variety of reasons. A man who does not shave on a day he need not go to the office is giving himself something of a vacation. A person who does not bathe may be exercising a protest against the errand requirements of certain social usages—though he may exercise considerable effort in performing the errands surrounding, for example, personal friendship. A student who temporarily neglects certain errands (like doing the laundry or sleeping) may do so in order to concentrate on the tasks of a status (like writing papers or cramming for examinations). Indeed, one sign of the significance of a status, of its dominance, is regarding personal errands, which are necessary for all statuses, or physical behavior, which is not usually regarded or noticed as an errand—like eating—as an imposition in the performance of the status. Another sign is neglecting other statuses entirely.

Though with somewhat less clarity, failures to perform social errands —that is, those errands necessary to sustain public statuses—are noticed. Perhaps at first seen as lapses or willfulness, they too, if sufficiently egregious or repeated, are taken as indications of mental distress. Indeed, insufficient zeal in school work is a primary cause of referrals of children for therapy. The consequences of such failure loom large to parents, and, because no other institution is available in which a child can display interest in, or energy for, attaining some significant life goal, insufficient zeal is taken as an indication of problems of psychological organization rather than of the school, a social organization so universal that it is taken to be natural (Sullivan, 1953).

In schools, one finds an organizational bookkeeping similar to that of the small commercial enterprise: All activity becomes debit or credit, so that performing the errands of the status is difficult to distinguish from the tasks of the status itself. As with the storekeeper, failure in errand performance by a student—not making efforts to be called on or noticed by the teacher, not displaying skill in taking examinations—is closely associated with over-all lack of ability. In the case of the student, unlike that of the storekeeper, such deficiencies are generalized far beyond the status in which they apply. A storekeeper may be poor at keeping any store, but not necessarily any kind of work. For the student the situation is different; the judgment, over-all.

Among adults, there are many varieties of failure to perform errands. Failure to keep "in touch" with friends through letters, phone calls, or continual contact is sometimes taken as a reproof or a slight. Failure to report to work on time (an errand in the sense of the preparatory efforts required to meet the status obligation of being at a certain place at a certain time) is taken as lack of interest or inattentiveness to duties when it may sometimes mean difficulty in organizing to do a job rather than difficulty in doing the job itself. Getting promoted may testify more to the ability to master promotion procedures than ability to do the job itself. Indeed, some bureaucratic jobs place more emphasis on the errands than on the job itself. High school diplomas are required for stock clerks, to ensure attendance as well as performance. It is possible that a separation can be made between the errands and performance of many jobs so that people unskilled in errands can sustain employment.

Failure at social errands is less acceptable or excusable than failure at personal errands. In general, this may be because social errands affect more people. Those who are failed in social errands have less personal interest in the failing individual and so have less reason to forgive. Social failures are also apt to be less dramatic and not have a developed set of explanations available, as psychotic or neurotic behavior has. On the whole, we can notice and take into account personal habit deterioration, but we find this more difficult with social habit deterioration.

A striking example of this fact is that applicants at therapeutic clinics are expected to go through the routines of processing and accept placement on a long waiting list when seeking assistance for, among other things, personal errand failure. While social usages concerning taboo topics, politeness, and other incidentals of self-presentation are allowed to lapse for therapy, social errands cannot lapse. Freud explains this as necessary in order that a private practitioner does not jeopardize his livelihood. Similarly, a bureaucracy does not wish to jeopardize the rationality of its procedures. Nonetheless, however practical the reasons, social errand lapses are not permitted or, at least, are less tolerated. To be tolerant of failures is not just to violate a kind of mechanical solidarity but also to cause immediate inconvenience because of the lapse in the cooperation between statuses—the client and the practitioner, the courtier and the courted—that is necessary for social life (organic solidarity) to continue. It is possible to forgive a friend who falls into abuse when he might be expected to work at sustaining a friendship by being polite even without sincerity; it is also possible to forgive or accept a friend who is regularly late for appointments. The former failure, however, is better tolerated than the latter, partly because the latter seems merely trivial and instrumental, connected to the circumstances rather than the character of the friendship.

III

Errands are universal phenomena in the sense that they arise out of the most generalizable features of social life and, therefore, are present for all men at all times. Cave men ran errands. Religious virtuosi run errands, though we may find it shocking to remember that they go to the bathroom and argue with landlords. But certain kinds and degrees of errand-running follow from two features that are identified with modern society: It is voluntary, and it is bureaucratic. Modern society is voluntary in that modern men have to decide to engage in certain statuses, and do something about it, which usually means running a number of errands. If a person wants to drive a car, he needs to get a license. In part, as this example indicates, statuses are voluntary because society is achievement-oriented, which, in turn, is the result of its technical orientation. There are specific skills required for statuses, for which a potential status-holder must show himself qualified.

In part, modern society is voluntary because it is universalistic, which means that, because everyone is judged by similar criteria, and, indeed, in some cases anyone can meet those criteria, holding a status may simply depend on going through the sometimes protracted routines of declaring an interest in holding the status. Sometimes, of course, the routines are arranged to be so time-consuming that, while few would not be able to do them, few would wish to do them. In both fraternities and political clubs, such work is used as a self-selection procedure to indicate and inculcate dedication to the status. Making it through the procedures is itself an achievement.

But, more generally, procedures of self-declaration are required simply for identification of the applicant by those who confer the status, because there is no other way to do it in a universalistic situation where other criteria cannot be used to qualify for a status. In other words, in a universalistic society, statuses must be applied for because that is the only way to make visible the desire to hold the status. A prince need not apply for his princedom, or an Irishman for certain jobs in nineteenth-century Boston; a woman, until recently, did not need to declare her interest in consideration as a sexual object. Similarly, it is necessary to give voluntary clues to have a status maintained. One may need to keep wearing a button or attending meetings to uphold a political affiliation. Transactions must take place in bank accounts to keep them from lapsing. Friends, unlike relatives, need interaction to maintain the relation, though with a little extra work it is possible to renew or reinvigorate friendships that have not lapsed but in which there has been little contact for some time. All this requires work, though some of it, like reinvigorating a friendship, may seem less routine, distasteful, or alienating than the work required in other cases.

The bureaucracy of modern society is partly founded in the fact that there is a proliferation of rather precisely defined statuses for whose qualification and maintenance it is necessary to file pieces of paper as records of activities undertaken preparatory to, and as part of, a status. These records are often largely composed of notations of errands, and the filing or creation of such records is a major aspect of errand-running in modern society. It is necessary to keep track of consumer, banking, work, and citizenship transactions by seeing that accurate records have been made and tallied. This record-keeping is quite important, because it takes on a life of its own. Significant consequences arise from what has been recorded rather than from what may have actually happened. A record is neither an indicator, nor only a trace of activity; it is itself a fact of reality, constituting a social circumstance of the individual. In this respect, every individual has, in effect, a permanent record card that includes entries somehow related to life activities. The entries, among their other uses, act as tools for advancement in bureaucracies and careers. As in the case of the elementary school student who wonders if the teacher is entering a gold star or a demerit for him in his grade book, it is well to consider what sorts of relations exist between what is done and what is recorded.

A great many errands, for example, may be required to rectify a faulty, erroneous, or disadvantageous errand: locating old birth certificates or insurance policies, tracing down old employers to provide different forms, negotiating with landlords or employers on alternative credentials. Not only do liars need to have good memories. Everyone does, in order to make sure the records have indeed recorded what should have been or now needs to have been recorded. A good deal of errand running consists of just such activity: checking and updating insurance coverage, reconciling bank statements, seeing that one's name is in the proper place on the vacation list, calling the comptroller to check on a lost expense voucher, calling the storekeeper because he has lost or misplaced a delivery that was supposed to be sent in time to cook for the dinner party, not in time for the delivery boy to greet the guests. Thus, errand running takes on not only a special significance but also a special character in a voluntary, bureaucratic society.

The sort of errand running required in the modern world has a number of uses and disadvantages for the pursuit of a happy life. One use is that it may prompt involvement in new situations and so provide an occasion for broadening horizons or commitments. For example, payroll checkoff allows for a more secure financial base for the union but does not promote the contact with the union and its services that would result if members had to attend union functions or come to a union office to pay their dues. Similarly, the errand of jury duty or dealing with an insurance company over a claim may provide insight—and possibly animus—not otherwise granted. We usually expect such rewards only from voluntary associations like VISTA or the Cerebral Palsy drive. They come to us also from errands, even if the rewards do not seem worth the bother.

Moreover, there is a danger that the errands will seem a more significant contribution than they are and the only way in which the work can be handled. In suburban communities, citizens engage in the formal creation and definition of institutions such as schools and churches, which can be taken for granted in cities because there will be a sufficient number of people of diverse interests so that one can expect someone to take on the citizen's public responsibility. In suburban communities, participation becomes more burden than opportunity for the display of talents and the taking of responsibility, because lack of citizen participation may mean that essential services will not be instituted or maintained.[2] It does not matter that a parent is not particularly interested in education or sewage systems. He may need to participate to see that the services are provided.

In such circumstances, social life may become intimately tied to political life. First, political life is a significant occasion for social life, and, second, social life becomes the vehicle for politics. This relationship makes politics less rational (though more supported) in that, first, the rewards of politics include not only effectiveness but also participation itself and, second, participation rests on personal loyalty and the most immediate self-interest.

In some cases, an errand is clearly worth the trouble, even if it is itself unwelcome, because of the satisfaction it brings in having dealt with record keepers and their attendants. Managing to get your money back for the faulty appliance or arguing the income tax people to a standstill gives a sense of accomplishment far greater than the actual financial gain merits. It means one has beaten the errand system, has exhibited competence in dealing with the world, has, in fact, established oneself as a responsible individual.

A cultural anachronism of modern society allows us to give credit and prestige to adroit errand running only when it is done by already powerful people. If a corporation invokes the proper bureaucratic procedures to get its way, that is considered business acumen, a reflection of free enterprise, and initiative, even if, in fact, it means becoming more tied to government financing. Business, of course, is able to finance displaying such errand acumen as a kind of rugged individualism: the business outguessing the system. Others, however, who are more dependent on errand running and less well trained for it, find themselves castigated

[2] For a discussion of such a political situation, see Gans (1967).

for their successes and penalized severely for their failures at maneuvering within the system. The welfare mother is not given credit for having run the gauntlet of errands to keep on welfare and to live off a welfare check; much less is she praised for having worked the system well enough to get more out of it than it cares to offer. A person on small charity is not expected to master the rule book in order to persist in making claims and is not honored for doing so, whereas a corporation petitioning the government for its largesse is highly rewarded and respected.

The small-scale errand runner is, moreover, at a great disadvantage in the competition to achieve rewards from the social structure. Every society has a minimum level of competence expected of each of its citizens, for the absence of which ignorance or inadequacy is no excuse. One is expected to know that stealing is against the law and that income tax forms are to be filed annually. Indeed, failure to respond on the society's level of adequacy is taken as a sign of biological or psychological inadequacy. A person is "retarded" because he cannot get through school well, even if he can function adequately in a family environment or in a low-skilled occupation (Tobias *et al.*, 1969, Ch. 10).

One feature of modern society is that this minimum level of intellectual competence for ordinary life seems to be significantly higher than in early industrial society. Not only are all people expected to perform satisfactorily in the formal learning of the school system, but they are also expected to be able to manage a wide and complicated set of errands. Functional illiteracy may be a mitigating circumstance but does not constitute an excuse. The illiterate is expected to find someone who will explain the situation or represent him in negotiations. Bluster and refusal to be cowed by one's own ignorance must often serve in the stead of knowledge in trying to protect one's rights and resources in the labyrinth of errands.

Yet, most people are functional illiterates in their errands, however much knowledge or skill they think they have or are encouraged to think they have. Whether negotiating bank loans, finding a doctor, demanding that the landlord paint their apartment, choosing alternative insurance policies, or deciding whether the boss really has been holding out on the raise to which they think themselves entitled, middle-class people are readily fooled and often are not sufficiently cynical to know it or use brass to press claims. In all these cases, the ordinary citizen is expected to have sufficient judgment not simply to read the forms placed before him but also to evaluate whether the social usages of the transaction should be identified as sharp practices. When an administrator or salesman suggests you should sign before you really have had time to consider all the fine print, is this an indication he is trying to fool you? It seems unlikely because it would be impossible for you to sift through all that material even at your leisure. Therefore, you accept the assumption that the technicalities are only the usual ones that you would not be in a position to negotiate anyway. Few consult the civil-service regulations to find out if the practices in their offices are the official ones.

For the most part, middle-class people depend on their display of their social category to safeguard them when accepting the authority of their errand antagonist. Lower-class people, not college people, get fooled, many believe. And it would be a waste of time for an educated person to try to check on whether he is being fooled in any usual situation. The time, energy, and legal skills required for adequate comparison shopping for insurance policies or administrators who would be more congenial to one's claims or stated needs would be prohibitive if it were done more than occasionally for symbolic effect. Who, after all, can be expected to find out that the organization has an officer somewhere in its system who is charged with doing what one wants, or that a fourth assistant to the vice-president one consults will turn out to be willing to interpret the regulation more liberally than anyone said was possible?

We are, of course, all expected to know the relevant facts and understand the alternatives. Just as *caveat emptor* was a doctrine that placed on the consumer a burden that exceeds his ability to challenge the offers of the powerful, so contemporary law and usage place on the errand runner a burden far in excess of his ability to contend with the powerful who manipulate and create the errands. Indeed, the legitimacy of unequal resources between seller and consumer is so ingrained that remedial legislation has been based on the assumption that fairness in the relationship can be achieved by giving extra errands to the consumer. In unit pricing, for example, as in many other consumer-oriented reforms, the consumer is given information that allows comparison shopping only if he adds more time, effort, and skill in computation to the performance of his supermarket errands. It is as if the resources for errands on the part of the consumer are inexhaustibly elastic and can be drawn upon without compensation. Moreover, the inconvenience of the scheduling of errands is borne by the errand runner rather than the institutions with which he deals. Appointments are largely made at their convenience rather than his. Moreover, people who handle errands as part or all of their job duties are paid to do so. For them, a day of errand servicing can be a satisfying work day. For the company, it is part of the overhead for which the consumer eventually pays. For the consumer, it is part of his own time. A consumer has not won when a dozen telephone calls finally get a building maintenance man to come to his apartment. In short, whether it is the phone company, the garage, or the school system that is dealt with, the characteristics of the relationship remain so constant as to warrant the perception that the errand runner is dealing with "them"—a coordinated monolith with its own interests. The working man in nineteenth-century England experienced the blacklist and other coordinated economic activity that gave rise to a sense of a single enemy and thus a consciousness of an identity with other members of his class (Thompson, 1963). Similarly, consumers, whatever their differences, may come to make common cause because of the systematic character of the errand running required of them.

IV

A differential description of errands can be achieved by noting the characteristics of errands and the combination of characteristics that constitute and are perceived as differing kinds of errands.

Errands can be *pivotal* in the sense that no or very few other completed activities can be satisfactorily sustained without them. Job hunting is pivotal for most of us, as is getting a driver's license for anyone living in the suburbs. Like apartment hunting, these pivotal errands are not *continual*, whereas getting dressed properly is both continual and pivotal. Noncontinual errands, like filing income tax forms, are nonetheless *permanent*, though some errands are only *one-shot*, like getting a degree, a driver's license (though not its renewal), or certain immunity injections. It seems that a sense of release is experienced at the completion of one-shot, pivotal errands. People out of school or the army can think of themselves as "free," in the sense of having that kind of errand out of the way. Indeed, adulthood is often seen as a situation where such one-shot, pivotal errands are past, and so life can begin unshadowed by such preoccupations and difficulties.

Of course, there are errands during the rest of life as well, and they have been there before, even if overshadowed. This is one reason it is romantic to have a sense that people live "happily ever after" once certain errands are accomplished. Errands that remain can prove *problematic*. There may be considerable doubt whether the efforts made will be satisfactorily processed. Meeting all the requirements for a promotion may not get the job. The existence of universalistic criteria is not sufficient; it is necessary to go through the process of appealing to those criteria. Even should those standards be met, the fact must be registered. A promotion may thus be problematic even if competence is not a problem. Other factors, like the boss's disposition to accept competence as a determining criterion, or the formal procedures of making competence legitimately registered, may intervene.

One version of registration is required when episodes of past history need to be reactivated; this could involve, for instance, records of courses taken at different universities, or birth certificates for use in citizenship applications. Such errands are *burdens* whether or not they are highly problematical when they no longer convey a sense of personal significance or accomplishment but are simply recognitions of what is or should be over and done with. They are to be distinguished from *hurdles*, where there is a congruence between the psychological change or transformation, on one hand, and the social recognition and working of such change or transformation, on the other. One of the criticisms of the errand process in higher education is the lack of such congruence so that the accomplishment of institutional certification is a burden rather than a hurdle, merely a registration of long-past learning experiences.

This, in some part, is a way of understanding a sense of alienation from an institution. Unlike dramatic, athletic, or aesthetic experiences, most dealings with bureaucracies provoke a sense of frustration and cynicism because they are only burdens. When you finally close the deal on the house, it is an anticlimax because of all that has intruded between the decision to take the house and the actual, officially acknowledged event. The same is not true of divorce, where the legal mechanisms may deepen a sense of the separation of the individuals, and so be part of the hurdle of achieving emotional independence. On the other hand, the ceremonials of marriage have become for many so clearly a burden, so attenuated from the experience of a commitment to emotional intimacy, that they are more and more likely to be perfunctory or unused.

Minor or major disasters, such as an auto accident, a city or household electrical failure, or an arrest, increase the number of errands that are required and that are likely to need performing in a short, immediately subsequent span of time. These errands are *bothers* —annoying, rather troublesome, depending upon how minor the disaster. We may hypothesize that a high number of bothers associated with a status indicates the status is badly constructed. It probably needs differentiation or a realignment of its relations with other statuses. Like boilers that regularly need repair, a status that requires a great deal of servicing probably needs rebuilding and not just repatching. Such a status is inefficient and probably ineffective. Whether this is because of insufficient legitimation, inordinate demands, or whatever, the idea that a status can be too much of a bother allows a more precise and objective notion of the requirements of a status and its relation to other social behavior.

Using such criteria, it is possible to recognize what kinds of structural innovation are called for if statuses are to be at least viable, much less occasions for happiness. Providing assistance for, or lowering expectations of, errand-running competence would, in general, allow statuses to be more satisfactorily filled. Specifically, this would mean legislation making producers shift fewer of their errands to the consumer, whereas at present more errands are created for the consumer in his or the company's attempt to bring about better service. It would also mean legislation providing errand-running services for the poor that are now partly provided by welfare and legal-assistance agencies. It would mean designing institutional procedures that reflect rather than postdate psychological processes. Student participation in university government is just an additional set of uncompensated errands if it does not effect such a reform and, if such a reform is achieved, would probably bring little motivation outside the ideologically relevant issue of the right of participation. If the university does its job, the students will not need to do the university's work.

In conclusion, errands represent demands that are sometimes trivial and sometimes significant, but they require action lest a status of the individual—his liberties as a citizen, his membership in the local library—be terminated or interrupted. These tasks surround and punctuate the course of his continued activities. In an important sense, errands frustrate a person's desire to be left alone, to be immersed in his own individuality, whether in private or in the company of others.

References

Etzioni, Amitai
    1968   The Active Society. New York: Free Press.
Gans, Herbert
    1967   The Levittowners: Ways of Life and Politics in a New Suburban Community. New York: Pantheon Books.
Sullivan, Harry Stack
    1953   The Interpersonal Theory of Psychiatry. New York: Norton.
Thompson, E. P.
    1963   The Making of the English Working Class. New York: Vintage.
Tobias, Jack, Ida Alpert, and Arnold Birenbaum
    1969   A Survey of the Employment Status of Mentally Retarded Adults in New York. Report to the Office of Manpower Research, Manpower Administration, U.S. Department of Labor.

3. Embarrassment and the Analysis of Role Requirements *

EDWARD GROSS AND GREGORY P. STONE

Attitudes, in the view of George Herbert Mead, are incipient acts. Meaningful discourse requires that discussants take one another's attitudes—incorporate one another's incipient activities—in their conversation. Since all social transactions are marked by meaningful communication, discursive or not, whenever people come together, they bring futures into one another's presence. They are ready, balanced, *poised* for the upcoming discussion. The discussion, of course, remands futures to a momentary present, where they are always somewhat inexactly realized, and relegates them in their altered form to the collective past we call memory. New futures are constantly built up in discussions. Indeed, they must be, else the discussion is over and the transaction is ended. Without a future, there is nothing else to be done, nothing left to say. Every social transaction, therefore, requires that the participants be poised at the outset and that poise be maintained as the transaction unfolds, until there is an accord that each can turn to other things and carry other futures away to other circles.

Poise is not enough. The futures that are presented, imperfectly realized, and re-established must be relevant. Relevance is achieved by establishing the *identities* of those who are caught up in the transaction. Futures or attitudes are anchored in identities. We speak of *role* as consensual attitudes mobilized by an announced and ratified identity. In social transactions, then, persons must announce who they are to enable each one to ready himself with reference to appropriate futures, providing attitudes which others may take or assume. Often announced identities are complementary, establishing the transaction as a social relationship, for many identities presuppose counteridentities. Whether

* Reprinted from *American Journal of Sociology*, Vol. 70 (1964), pp. 1–15.

or not this is the case, the maintenance of one's identity assists the maintenance of the other.[1]

Furthermore, all transactions are transactions through time. It is not enough that identity and poise be established. They must be continuously reaffirmed, maintained, and provisions made for their repair in case of breakdown. Role performers count on this. We attempt here to limn the structure of transactions by examining instances where identities have been misplaced or forgotten, where poise has been lost or destroyed, or where, for any reason, confidence that identities and poise will be maintained has been undermined. We have in mind instances of embarrassment, whether or not deliberately perpetrated.

Embarrassment and the Analysis of Role Requirements

Embarrassment exaggerates the core dimensions of social transactions, bringing them to the eye of the observer in an almost naked state. Embarrassment occurs whenever some *central* assumption in a transaction has been *unexpectedly* and unqualifiedly discredited for at least one participant. The result is that he is incapacitated for continued role performance.[2] Moreover, embarrassment is infectious. It may spread out, incapacitating others not previously incapacitated. It is destructive dis-ease. In the wreckage left by embarrassment lie the broken foundations of social transactions. By examining such ruins, the investigator can reconstruct the architecture they represent.

To explore this idea, recollections of embarrassment were expressly solicited from two groups of subjects: (1) approximately 800 students enrolled in introductory sociology courses; and (2) about 80 students enrolled in an evening extension class. Not solicited, but gratefully received, were many examples volunteered by colleagues and friends who had heard of our interest in the subject. Finally we drew up many recollections of embarrassment we had experienced ourselves. Through these means at least one thousand specimens of embarrassment were secured.

We found that embarrassments frequently occurred in situations requiring continuous and co-ordinated role performance—speeches, ceremonies, processions, or working concerts. In such situations embarrass-

---

[1] Alfred R. Lindesmith and Anselm L. Strauss assert that *every* role presupposes a counter-role. There is a sense in which the assertion is correct, as in Kenneth Burke's "paradox of substance," but it may also be somewhat misleading in sociological analysis. Specifically, there is a role of cigarette smoker, but the role is not really dependent for its establishment on the counter-role of non-smoker in the sense that the parental role is dependent upon child roles and vice versa. Thus, in some social transactions the establishment and maintenance of one identity may be very helpful for the establishment and maintenance of a counter-identity; in other transactions, this may not be the case at all (see Lindesmith and Strauss, 1956:379–80; and Kenneth Burke, 1945:21–58).

[2] Not all incapacitated persons are always embarrassed or embarrassing, because others have come to expect their *incapacities* and are consequently prepared for them.

ment is particularly noticeable because it is so devastating. Forgetting one's lines, forgetting the wedding ring, stumbling in a cafeteria line, or handing a colleague the wrong tool, when these things occur without qualification, bring the performance to an obviously premature and unexpected halt. At the same time, manifestations of the embarrassment—blushing, fumbling, stuttering, sweating [3]—coerce awareness of the social damage and the need for immediate repair. In some instances, the damage may be potentially so great that embarrassment cannot be allowed to spread among the role performers. The incapacity may be qualified, totally ignored, or pretended out of existence.[4] For example, a minister, noting the best man's frantic search for an absent wedding ring, whispers to him to ignore it, and all conspire to continue the drama with an imaginary ring. Such rescues are not always possible. Hence we suggest that every enduring social relation will provide means of preventing embarrassment, so that the entire transaction will not collapse when embarrassment occurs. A second general observation would take into account that some stages in the life cycle, for example, adolescence in our society, generate more frequent embarrassments than others. These are points to which we shall return.

To get at the content of embarrassment, we classified the instances in categories that remained as close to the specimens as possible. A total of seventy-four such categories were developed, some of which were forced choices between friends, public mistakes, exposure of false front, being caught in a cover story, misnaming, forgetting names, slips of the tongue, body exposure, invasions of others' back regions, uncontrollable laughter, drunkenness in the presence of sobriety (or vice versa), loss of visceral control, and the sudden recognition of wounds or other stigmata. Further inspection of these categories disclosed that most could be included in three general areas: (1) inappropriate identity; (2) loss of poise; (3) disturbance of the assumptions persons make about one another in social transactions.

Since embarrassment always incapacitates persons for role performance (to embarrass is, literally, to bar or stop), a close analysis of the conditions under which it occurs is especially fruitful in the revelation of the requirements *necessary* for role-playing, role-taking, role-making, and role performance in general. These role requirements are thus seen to include the establishment of identity, poise, and valid assumptions about one another among all the parties of a social transaction. We turn now to analysis of those role requirements.

Identity and Poise

In every social transaction, selves must be established, defined, and accepted by the parties. Every person in the company of others is, in

---

[3] Erving Goffman (1956) describes these manifestations vividly.

[4] A more general discussion of this phenomenon, under the rubric civil inattention, is provided in Goffman, 1963a:83–88; *passim*.

a sense, obligated to bring his best self forward to meet the selves of others also presumably best fitted to the occasion. When one is "not himself" in the presence of others who expect him to be just that, as in cases where his mood carries him away either by spontaneous seizure (uncontrollable laughter or tears) or by induced seizure (drunkenness), embarrassment ensues. Similarly, when one is "shown up" to other parties to the transaction by the exposure of unacceptable moral qualifications or inappropriate motives, embarrassment sets in all around. However, the concept, self, is a rather gross concept, and we wish to single out two phases that frequently provided focal points for embarrassment—identity and poise.

Identity.—Identity is the substantive dimension of the self (Gregory P. Stone, 1962:93).

> Almost all writers using the term imply that identity establishes what and where the person is in social terms. It is not a substitute word for "self." Instead, when one has identity, he is *situated*—that is, cast in the shape of a social object by the acknowledgement of his participation or membership in social relations. One's identity is established when others *place* him as a social object by assigning the same words of identity that he appropriates for himself or *announces*. It is in the coincidence of placements and announcements that identity becomes a meaning of the self.

Moreover, as we have already pointed out, identity stands at the base of role. When inappropriate identities are established or appropriate identities are lost, role performance is impossible.

If identity *locates* the person in social terms, it follows that locations or spaces emerge as symbols of identity, since social relations are spatially distributed. Moreover, as Goffman has remarked (1959a:25), there must be a certain coherence between one's personal appearance and the setting in which he appears. Otherwise embarrassment may ensue with the resulting incapacitation for role performance. Sexual identity is pervasively established by personal appearance, and a frequent source of embarrassment among our subjects was the presence of one sex in a setting reserved for the other. Both men and women reported inadvertent invasions of space set aside for the other sex with consequent embarrassment and humiliation. The implication of such inadvertent invasions is, of course, that one literally does not know where one is, that one literally has no identity in the situation, or that the identity one is putting forward is so absurd as to render the proposed role performance totally irrelevant. Everyone is embarrassed, and such manifestations as, for example, cries and screams heighten the dis-ease. In such situations, laughter cannot be enjoined to reduce the seriousness of the unexpected collapse of the encounter, and only flight can insure that one will not be buried in the wreckage.

To establish *what* he is in social terms, each person assembles a set of apparent [5] symbols which he carries about as he moves from transaction to transaction. Such symbols include the shaping of the hair, painting of the face, clothing, cards of identity, other contents of wallets and purses, and sundry additional marks and ornaments. The items in the set must cohere, and the set must be complete. Taken together, these apparent symbols have been called *identity documents*,[6] in that they enable others to validate announced identities. Embarrassment often resulted when our subjects made personal appearances with either invalid or incomplete identity documents. It was embarrassing for many, for example, to announce their identities as customers at restaurants or stores, perform the customer role and then, when the crucial validation of this identity was requested—the payoff—to discover that the wallet had been left at home.

Because the social participation of men in American society is relatively more frequently caught up in the central structures, for example, the structure of work, than is the social participation of women who are relatively more immersed in interpersonal relations, the identities put forward by men are often *titles*; by women, often *names*. Except for very unusual titles,[7] such identities are shared, and their presentation has the consequence of bringing people together. Names, on the other hand, mark people off from one another. So it is that a frequent source of embarrassment for women in our society occurs when they appear together in precisely the same dress. Their identity documents are invalidated. The embarrassment may be minimized, however, if the space in which they make their personal appearance is large enough. In one instance, both women met the situation by spending an entire evening on different sides of the ballroom in which their embarrassing confrontation occurred, attempting to secure validation from social circles with minimal intersection, or, at least, where intersection was temporally attenuated. Men, on the other hand, will be embarrassed if their clothing does not resemble the dress of the other men present in public and official encounters. Except for "the old school tie" their neckties seem to serve as numbers on a uniform, marking each man off from every other. Out of uniform, their structural membership

[5] We use the term "appearance" to designate that dimension of a social transaction given over to identifications of the participants. Apparent symbols are those symbols used to communicate such identifications. They are often non-verbal. Appearance seems, to us, a more useful term than Goffman's "front" (1959a), which in everyday speech connotes misrepresentation.

[6] Erving Goffman (1963b:59–62) confines the concept to personal identity, but his own discussion extends it to include matters of social identity.

[7] For example, the title "honorary citizen of the United States," which was conferred on Winston Churchill, served the function of a name, since Churchill was the only living recipient of the title. Compare the titles, "professor," "manager," "punch-press operator," and the like.

cannot be visibly established, and role performance is rendered extremely difficult, if not impossible.[8]

Not only are identities undocumented, they are also misplaced, as in misnaming or forgetting, or other incomplete placements. One relatively frequent source of embarrassment we categorized as "damaging someone's personal representation." This included cases of ethnically colored sneers in the presence of one who, in fact, belonged to the deprecated ethnic group but did not put that identity forward, or behind-the-back slurs about a woman who turned out to be the listener's wife. The victim of such misplacement, however inadvertent, will find it difficult to continue the transaction or to present the relevant identity to the perpetrators of the embarrassment in the future. The awkwardness is reflexive. Those who are responsible for the misplacement will experience the same difficulties and dis-ease.

Other sources of embarrassment anchored in identity suggest a basic characteristic of all human transactions, which, as Strauss puts it, are "carried on in thickly peopled and complexly imaged contexts" (Anselm L. Strauss, 1959:57). One always brings to transactions more identities than are necessary for his role performance. As a consequence, two or more roles are usually performed at once by each participant.[9]

If we designate the relevant roles in transactions as *dominant roles* [10] then we may note that *adjunct roles*—a type of side involvement, as Goffman would have it,[11] or better, a type of side *activity*—are usually

[8] The implication of the discussion is that structured activities are uniformed, while interpersonal activities emphasize individuation in dress. Erving Goffman suggests, in correspondence, that what may be reflected here is the company people keep in their transactions. The work of men in our society is ordinarily teamwork, and teams are uniformed, but housework performed by a wife is solitary work and does not require a uniformed appearance, though the "housedress" might be so regarded.

[9] This observation and the ensuing discussion constitute a contribution to and extension of present perspectives on role conflict. Most discussions conceive of such conflict as internalized contradictory obligations. They do not consider simultaneous multiple-role performances. An exception is Everett C. Hughes' discussion of the Negro physician innocently summoned to attend a prejudiced emergency case (1945).

[10] We have rewritten this discussion to relate to Goffman's classification which came to our attention after we had prepared an earlier version of this article. Goffman distinguishes between what people do in transactions and what the situation calls for. He recognizes that people do many things at once in their encounters and distinguishes those activities that command most of their attention and energies from those which are less demanding of energy and time. Here, the distinction is made between *main* and *side involvements*. On the other hand, situations often call for multiple activities. Those which are central to the situation, Goffman speaks of as *dominant involvements*; others are called *subordinate involvements*. Dominant roles, therefore, are those that are central to the transactional situation—what the participants have come together to do (see Goffman, 1963a:43–59).

[11] Adjunct roles are one type of side involvement or activity. We focus on them because we are concerned here with identity difficulties. There are other side *activities* which are *not* necessarily adjunct *roles*, namely, sporadic nosepicking,

performed in parallel with dominant role performance. Specifically, a lecturer may smoke cigarettes or a pipe while carrying out the dominant performance, or one may carry on a heated conversation with a passenger while operating a motor vehicle. Moreover, symbols of *reserve identities* are often carried into social transactions. Ordinarily, they are concealed, as when a court judge wears his golfing clothes beneath his robes. Finally, symbols of abandoned or *relict identities* may persist in settings where they have no relevance for dominant role performances.[12] For example, photographs of the performer as an infant may be thrust into a transaction by a doting mother or wife, or one's newly constituted household may still contain the symbols of a previous marriage.

In these respects, the probability of avoiding embarrassment is a function of at least two factors: (1) the extent to which adjunct roles, reserve identities and relict identities are not incongruent with the dominant role performance;[13] and (2) the allocation of prime attention to the dominant role performance so that less attention is directed toward adjunct role performance, reserve identities, and relict identities. Thus the professor risks embarrassment should the performance of his sex role appear to be the main activity in transactions with female students where the professorial role is dominant—for example, if the student pulls her skirt over her knees with clearly more force than necessary. The judge may not enter the courtroom in a golf cap, nor may the husband dwell on the symbols of a past marriage in the presence of a new wife while entertaining guests in his home. Similarly, should adjunct role performance prove inept, as when the smoking lecturer ignites the contents of a wastebasket or the argumentative driver fails to observe the car in front in time to avert a collision, attention is diverted from the dominant role performance. Even without the golf cap, should the judge's robe be caught so that his golfing attire is suddenly revealed in the courtroom, the transactions of the court will be disturbed. Fetishistic devotion to the symbols of relict identities by bereaved persons is embarrassing even to well-meaning visitors.

However, the matter of avoiding incongruence and allocating attention appropriately among the several identities a performer brings to a transaction verges very closely on matters of poise, as we shall see. Matters of poise converge on the necessity of controlling representations of the self, and identity-symbols are important self-representations.

Personal poise.—Presentation of the self in social transactions extends

---

scratching, coughing, sneezing, or stomach growling, which are relevant to matters of embarrassment, but not to the conceptualization of the problem in these terms. Of course, such activities, insofar as they are consistently proposed and anticipated, may become incorporated in the *personal role* (always an adjunct in official transactions), as in the case of Billy Gilbert, the fabulous sneezer.

[12] This phenomenon provides the main theme and source of horror and mystery in Daphne du Maurier's now classic *Rebecca*.

[13] Adjunct roles, reserve identities, and relict identities need not cohere with the dominant role; they simply must not clash so that the attention of participants in a transaction is not completely diverted from the dominant role performance.

considerably beyond making the appropriate personal appearance. It includes the presentation of an entire situation. Components of situations, however, are often representations of self, and in this sense self and situation are two sides of the same coin. Personal poise refers to the performer's control over self and situation, and whatever disturbs that control, depriving the transactions, as we have said before, of any relevant future, is incapacitating and consequently embarrassing.

Loss of poise was a major dimension in our scrutiny of embarrassment, and its analysis can do much to shed light on the components of social situations—a necessary task, because the concept, "situation," is quite difficult to specify and operationalize. Working from the outside in, so to speak, we wish to single out five [14] elements of self and situation with reference to which loss of control gave rise to considerable embarrassment.

First, *spaces* must be so arranged and maintained that they are role-enabling. This is sometimes difficult to control, since people appear in spaces that belong to others, over which they exercise no authority and for which they are not responsible. Students, invited to faculty parties where faculty members behave like faculty members, will "tighten up" to the extent that the students' role performance is seriously impeded. To avoid embarrassment, people will go to great lengths to insure their appearance in appropriate places, and to some to be deprived of access to a particular setting is to limit performance drastically.

Spaces are often fixed in location and have boundaries. As such they may partake of the character of territories or domains: a particular person (or persons) is "in command" (it is "his" domain) and most familiar with it, and the territory is in continual danger of being invaded (deliberately or inadvertently). Embarrassments were reported for both of these features of space. Being "in command" and familiar with an area means knowing where the back regions are and having the right of access to them. The host at a party in his own home, however much he may be vanishing (Riesman *et al.*, 1960), is at least the person in whose territory the gathering takes place. Should a guest spill food on his clothes, he has no choice but to suffer embarrassment for the remainder of the party. The host, by contrast, can retire to his bedroom and change his clothes quickly, often before the momentary loss of poise becomes known. A striking case of the man "in command" of a territory is the person delivering a speech to a fixed audience in a closed room. In being presented to the audience, he may even be told, "The floor is yours." To underline his exclusive domain, the speaker may wait until waiters clear the last table of cups and saucers and the doors are closed. In such a setting, where the audience is not free to leave, the speaker is now in great danger of embarrassing

[14] The five components to be discussed—spaces, props, equipment, clothing, and the body—are not offered as an exhaustive list. We have been able to distinguish close to forty such elements.

his audience unless his speech is such that the audience is not let down. Should he show lack of poise, the audience will feel embarrassed for him, yet be unable to escape, for that would further embarrass him. Hence they will suffer silently, hoping for a short speech.

In a situation reported to us, the discussant at a professional meeting was able to save the situation. The speaker was a man of national reputation—one of the pillars of his discipline. To everyone's dismay and embarrassment, he proceeded to give a pedestrian address of the caliber of an undergraduate term essay. Everyone hoped the discussant would save them, and he did. His tactic was to make clear to the audience that the identity presented by the speaker was not his real identity. This result he accomplished by reminding the audience of the major contributions of the speaker, by claiming the paper presented must be interpreted as evidence that the speaker was still productive, and that all could expect even more important contributions in the future. When the audience thundered applause, they were not simply expressing their agreement with the discussant's appraisal of the speaker: they were also thanking him for saving them all from embarrassment by putting the speaker back in command of the territory.

We have already touched upon problems presented by invasions of spaces, and little more need be said. Persons lose poise when they discover they are in places forbidden to them, for the proscription itself means they have no identity there and hence cannot act. They can do little except withdraw quickly. It is interesting that children are continually invading the territories of others—who can control the course of a sharply hit baseball?—and part of the process of socialization consists of indications of the importance of boundaries. Whether territories are crescive or contrived affects the possibility of invasion. When they are contrived and boundaries are marked, the invader knows he has crossed the boundary and is embarrassed if caught. With crescive territories inadvertent invasions occur, as when a tourist reports discovery of a "quaint" area of the city only to be met with the sly smiles of those who know that the area is the local prostitution region.

Such considerations raise questions concerning both how boundaries are defined and how boundary violations may be prevented. Walls provide physical limits, but do not necessarily prevent communications from passing through (Goffman, 1963a: 151–52). Hence walls work best when there is also tacit agreement to ignore audible communication on the other side of the wall. Embarrassment frequently occurs when persons on one side of the wall learn that intimate matters have been communicated to persons on the other side. A common protective device is for the captive listeners to become very quiet so that their receipt of the communication will not be discovered by the unsuspecting intimates. When no physical boundaries are present, a group gathered in one section of a room may have developed a common mood which is bounded by a certain space that defines the limits of their engagement to one another. The entry of someone new may be followed by an embarrassed hush. It is not necessary that the group should have been talking about that person. Rather, since moods take time to build up, it will take time for the newcomer to "get with it" and it may not be worth the group's trouble to "fill him in." However unintentionally, he has destroyed a mood that took some effort to build up and he will suffer for it, if only by being stared at or by an obvious change of subject. In some cases, when the mood is partially sustained by alcohol, one can prepare the newcomer immediately for the mood by loud shouts that the group is "three drinks ahead" of him and by thrusting a drink into his hand without delay. So, too, a function of foyers, halls, anterooms, and other buffer zones or decompression chambers around settings is to prepare such newcomers and hence reduce the likelihood of their embarrassing both themselves and those inside.

Spaces, then, include bounded areas within which transactions go on. The boundaries may be more or less sharply defined, that is, walled in or marked off by the distances that separate one encounter from another. Overstepping the bounds is a source of embarrassment, signaling a loss of poise. Consequently, the boundaries are usually controlled and patrolled and come to present the selves of those who are authorized to cross them.

A second component of self and situation that must be controlled to maintain poise is here designated *props*. Props are arranged around settings in an orderly manner commonly called décor. Ordinarily they are not moved about during a transaction, except as emergencies arise, to facilitate the movement of people about the setting and to protect the props from damage. In some cases, their adherence to settings is guaranteed by law. Wall-to-wall carpeting, mirrors attached to walls, and curtain fixtures, for example, may not be removed from houses, even though ownership of such domestic settings may change hands. The arrangement of less adhesive props within a setting may mark off or suggest (as in the case of "room dividers") smaller subsettings facilitating the division of large assemblies into more intimate circles. Moreover, although props are ordinarily not moved about *during* transactions, they are typically rearranged or replaced between major changes of scene, marking off changes in life situations.[15]

Perhaps just because of their intimate connection with the life

[15] David Riesman and Howard Rosenborough, in a discussion of family careers, indicate the linkage between the rearrangement of props and the rearrangement of life situations: "One of our Kansas City respondents, whose existence had been wrapped up in her daughters' social life, when asked what she did when the daughters married and moved away, said that she slept more—and redecorated the living room. Still another became more active in church work—and redecorated the vestry" (1955:14).

situations of those who control them,[16] loss of control over props is a more frequent (though usually milder) source of embarrassment than the violation of boundaries. When one stumbles over his own furniture or slips on his own throw rug, doubt may be cast on the extent to which such props represent, in fact, the self and situation of the person or team members who have arranged them. Gifts of props are frequently embarrassing to the recipients. Thus an artist (or would-be artist) may foist a painting on a friend without recognizing that the painting is contrary to the recipient's aesthetic taste. Moreover, the artist may expect that his work will be given a prominent display commensurate with his investment. A conflict is immediately established between loyalty to the artist-friend and loyalty to the recipient's self. A way out is to include the prop in question only in those situations where the donor is present, but this may become tedious, depending on the frequency and scheduling of visiting. A classic case is the wealthy relative's gift of a self-photograph, which must be dragged out of the closet for display when the relative visits.

Clashing differences in domestic décor will usually terminate or restrict house-to-house visiting. Because of this, many wartime friendships have been abruptly ended shortly after the cessation of hostilities and demobilization. In a common military setting, servicemen would meet and become close friends, sometimes building up life-and-death obligations to one another. They would eagerly anticipate extending their hard-won intimacy into the workaday world of peacetime. Then, when they met in one or the other's home, the glaring incompatibility in décor would silently signal an incompatibility in life situation. Such embarrassing confrontations would be covered over with empty promises and futile vows to meet again, and the former friends would part as embarrassed strangers. If incompatibilities in décor can bring about the estrangement of friends who owe their lives to one another, we can see how props and their arrangement become powerful guaranties of the exclusiveness of social circles and status strata.

Much of our earlier discussion of adjunct roles, reserve identities, and relict identities applies to props. The porcelain dinnerware may always be kept visibly in reserve for special guests, and this very fact may be embarrassing to some dinner guests who are reminded that they are not so special after all, while, for other guests, anything but the everyday props would be embarrassing. Relict props also present a potential for embarrassment, persisting as they do when one's new life-situation has made them obsolete. The table at which a woman used to sit while dining with a former husband is obviously still quite serviceable, but it is probably best to buy another.

Third, every social transaction requires the manipulation of *equip-*

---

[16] Striking examples are provided by Harvey W. Zorbaugh (1926:103-4); and in Anonymous (1962:46-48).

ment. If props are ordinarily stationary during encounters, equipment is typically moved about, handled, or touched.[17] Equipment can range from words to physical objects, and a loss of control over such equipment is a frequent source of embarrassment. Here are included slips of the tongue, sudden dumbness when speech is called for, stalling cars in traffic, dropping bowling balls, spilling food, and tool failures. Equipment appearances that cast doubt on the adequacy of control are illustrated by the clanking motor, the match burning down to the fingers, tarnished silverware, or rusty work tools. Equipment sometimes extends beyond what is actually handled in the transaction to include the stage props. Indeed, items of equipment in disuse, reserve equipment, often become props—the Cadillac in the driveway or the silver service on the shelf—and there is a point at which the objects used or scheduled for use in a situation are both equipment and props. At one instant, the items of a table setting lie immobile as props; at the next, they are taken up and transformed into equipment. The close linkage of equipment and props may be responsible for the fact that *embarrassment* at times not only *infects* the participants in the transaction but the *objects* as well. For example, at a formal dinner, a speaker was discovered with his fly zipper undone. On being informed of this embarrassing oversight after he was reseated, he proceeded to make the requisite adjustment, unknowingly catching the table cloth in his trousers. When obliged to rise again at the close of the proceedings, he took the stage props with him and of course scattered the dinner tools about the setting in such a way that others were forced to doubt his control. His poise was lost in the situation.

Just as props may be adjunct to the dominant role performance, held in reserve, or relict, so may equipment. Indeed, as we have said, reserve equipment is often an important part of décor.

Fourth, *clothing* must be maintained, controlled, and coherently arranged. Its very appearance must communicate this. Torn clothing, frayed cuffs, stained neckties, and unpolished shoes are felt as embarrassing in situations where they are expected to be untorn, neat, clean, and polished. Clothing is of special importance since, as William James observed (1892:177–78), it is as much a part of the self as the

---

[17] Whether objects in a situation are meant to be moved, manipulated, or taken up provides an important differentiating dimension between equipment on the one hand and props (as well as clothing, to be discussed shortly) on the other. Equipment is meant to be moved, manipulated, or taken up *during* a social transaction whereas clothing and props are expected to remain unchanged during a social transaction but will be moved, manipulated, or taken up *between* social transactions. To change props, as in burning the portrait of an old girl friend (or to change clothes, as in taking off a necktie), signals a change in the situation. The special case of the strip-tease dancer is no exception, for her act transforms clothes into equipment. The reference above to the "stickiness" of props may now be seen as another way of describing the fact that they are not moved, manipulated, or taken up during transactions, but remain unchanged for the course of the transaction. Clothing is equally sticky but the object to which it sticks differs. Clothing sticks to the body; props stick to the settings.

body—a part of what he called the "material me." Moreover, since it is so close to the body, it conveys the impression of body maintenance, paradoxically, by concealing body-maintenance activities.[18] Hence, the double wrap—outer clothes and underclothes. Underclothes bear the marks of body maintenance and tonic state, and their unexpected exposure is a frequent source of embarrassment. The broken brassière strap sometimes produces a shift in appearance that few women (or men, for that matter) will fail to perceive as embarrassing.

Fifth, the *body* must always be in a state of readiness to act, and its appearance must make this clear. Hence any evidence of unreadiness or clumsiness is embarrassing. Examples include loss of whole body control (stumbling, trembling, or fainting), loss of visceral control (flatulence, involuntary urination, or drooling), and the communication of other "signs of the animal." The actress who is photographed from her "bad side" loses poise, for it shakes the foundation on which her fame rests. So does the person who is embarrassed about pimples, warts, or missing limbs, as well as those embarrassed in his presence.

Ordinarily, persons will avoid recognizing such stigmata, turn their eyes away, and pretend them out of existence, but on occasion stigmata will obtrude upon the situation causing embarrassment all around. A case in point was a minor flirtation reported by one of our students. Seated in a library a short distance from a beautiful girl, the student began the requisite gestural invitation to a more intimate conversation. The girl turned, smiling, to acknowledge the bid, revealing an amputated left arm. Our student's gestural line was brought to a crashing halt. Embarrassed, he abandoned the role he was building even before the foundation was laid, pretending that his inviting gestures were directed toward some imaginary audience suggested by his reading. Such stigmata publicize body-maintenance activities, and, when they are established in social transactions, interfere with role performances. The pimples on the face of the job applicant cast doubt on his maturity, and, consequently, on his qualifications for any job requiring such maturity.

All this is to say that self and situation must be in a perpetual condition of poise or readiness, adequately maintained, and in good repair. Such maintenance and the keeping of self in a state of good repair obviously require energy and time. While engaged in maintenance or repair, the person is, for that time, unable to play the role. Hence we may expect that persons will, in order to avoid casting doubt on their ability to play a role, deliberately play down or conceal maintenance and repair activity. Speakers know that spontaneity cannot be left to chance but must be prepared for, even rehearsed. Yet obviously information on the amount of preparation it took to be spontaneous would destroy the audience's belief in the spontaneity. Outer clothes

[18] A complete exposition of the body-maintenance function of clothing is set forth in an advertisement for Jockey briefs (*Good Housekeeping*, 1963).

require underclothes, as social life requires an underlife (which is, of course, also social).[19]

Maintenance of Confidence

When identities have been validated and persons poised, interaction may begin. Its continuation, however, requires that a scaffolding be erected and that attention be given to preventing this scaffolding from collapsing. The scaffold develops as the relationship becomes stabilized. In time persons come to expect that the way they place the other is the way the other announces himself, and that poise will continue to be maintained. Persons now begin to count on these expectations and to have confidence in them. But at any time they may be violated. It was such violations of confidence that made up the greatest single source of embarrassment in our examples. Perhaps this is only an acknowledgment that the parties to every transaction must always maintain themselves *in role* to permit the requisite role-taking, or that identity-switching ought not be accomplished so abruptly that others are left floundering in the encounter as they grope for the new futures that the new identity implies.

This is all the more important in situations where roles are tightly linked together as in situations involving a division of labor. In one instance, a group of social scientists was presenting a progress report of research to a representative of the client subsidizing the research. The principal investigator's presentation was filled out by comments from the other researchers, his professional peers. Negatively critical comments were held to a bare minimum. Suddenly the principal investigator overstepped the bounds. He made a claim that they were well on the road to confirming a hypothesis which, if confirmed, would represent a major contribution. Actually, his colleagues (our informant was one of them) knew that they were very far indeed from confirming the hypothesis. They first sought to catch the leader's eye to look for a hidden message. Receiving none, they lowered their eyes to the table, bit their lips, and fell silent. In the presence of the client's representative, they felt they could not "call" their leader for that would be embarrassing, but they did seek him out immediately afterward for an explanation. The leader agreed that they were right, but said his claim was polite, that new data might well turn up, and that it was clearly too late to remedy the situation.

[19] Consider the fact that the physician often needs time and opportunity to consult medical books and colleagues before he can render an authoritative medical diagnosis. A structural assurance is provided by his having been taught to make diagnoses slowly. Through time thus gained, he takes advantage of informal encounters with colleagues and spare moments between patients when he can consult medical books. A direct revelation of his need for such aids and his rather unsystematic way of getting them would be embarrassing. Yet it is in the patient's best interest that they be kept secret from him, otherwise the patient would be in the position of having to pass judgment on a professional practice when he is, in fact, too involved to render an objective judgment.

Careful examination of this case reveals a more basic reason for the researchers' hesitance to embarrass the leader before the client's representative. If their leader were revealed to be the kind of person who goes beyond the data (or to be a plain liar), serious question could have been raised about the kind of men who willingly work with such a person. Thus they found themselves coerced into unwilling collusion. It was not simply that their jobs depended on continued satisfaction of the client. Rather they were unwilling to say to themselves and to the client's representative that they were the kind of researchers who would be party to a fraud. To embarrass the leader, then, would have meant embarrassing themselves by casting serious question upon their identities as researchers. Indeed, it was their desire to cling to their identities that led, not long afterward (and after several other similar experiences), to the breakup of the research team.

Just as, in time, an identity may be discredited, so too may poise be upset. Should this occur, each must be able to assume that the other will render assistance if he gets into such control trouble, and each must be secure in the knowledge that the assumption is tenable. Persons will be alert for incipient signs of such trouble—irrelevant attitudes—and attempt to avert the consequences. Goffman has provided many examples in his discussion of dramaturgical loyalty, discipline, and circumspection in the presentation of the self, pointing out protective practices that are employed, such as clearing one's throat before interrupting a conversation, knocking on doors before entering an occupied room, or begging the other's pardon before an intrusion (Goffman, 1959a:212–33).

The danger that one's confidence in the other's continued identity or his ability to maintain his poise may be destroyed leads to the generation of a set of *performance norms*. These are social protections against embarrassment.[20] If persons adhere to them, the probability of embarrassment is reduced. We discovered two major performance norms.

First, *standards of role performance almost always allow for flexibility and tolerance*. One is rarely, if ever, totally in role (an exception might be highly ritualized performances, where to acknowledge breaches of expectation is devastatingly embarrassing).[21] To illustrate, we expect one another to give attention to what is going on in our transactions, but the attention we anticipate is always *optimal*, never total. To lock the other person completely in one's glance and refuse to let go is very embarrassing. A rigid attention is coerced eventuating in a loss of poise. One is rapt in the other's future and deprived of control almost like the hypnotist's subject. Similarly, never to give one's attention to the other is role-incapacitating. If one focuses his gaze not on the other's eyes, but on his forehead, let us say, the encounter is visibly

[20] Implicit in Georg Simmel, 1950:308.
[21] See the discussion of "role distance" in Erving Goffman, 1961:105–52.

disturbed.[22] Norms allowing for flexibility and tolerance permit the parties to social transactions ordinarily to assume that they will not be held to rigid standards of conduct and that temporary lapses will be overlooked. The norm is respected by drinking companions who both understand how it is to have had a drop too much and who can also be counted on not to hold another to everything he says, does, or suggests. So, too, colleagues are persons who know enough to embarrass one another but can ordinarily be trusted not to do so. The exclusiveness of colleague groups can be seen, therefore, as a collective defense against embarrassment.

The second performance norm was that of *giving the other fellow the benefit of the doubt.* For the transaction to go on at all, one has at least to give the other fellow a *chance* to play the role he seeks to play. Clearly, if everyone went around watching for chances to embarrass others, so many would be incapacitated for role performance that society would collapse. Such considerate behavior is probably characteristic of all human society, because of the dependence of social relations on role performance. A part of socialization, therefore, must deal with the prevention of embarrassment by the teaching of tact. People must learn not only not to embarrass others, but to ignore the lapses that can be embarrassing whenever they occur. In addition, people must learn to *cope* with embarrassment. Consequently, embarrassment will occasionally be deliberately perpetrated to ready people for role incapacitation when it occurs.

Deliberate Embarrassment

Although we have emphasized up to this point instances of embarrassment which arise from wholly unexpected acts and revelations, the unexpected is often deliberately perpetrated. Examples are practical jokes, teasing, initiation into secret societies, puncturing false fronts, and public degradation. Since embarrassment appears to represent social damage that is not at all easily repaired, we might well ask why the condition may be deliberately established. The embarrassed person stands exposed as incapable of continued role performance—a person who cannot be depended upon. In his presence, all must pause and review their assessments and expectations. Whatever they decide, the transaction is halted, and those dependent upon it are deprived of the realization of the futures that they have entrusted to others.

Embarrassments, therefore, always have careers. One person embarrasses others whose hurried attempts to salvage the situation merely call further attention to the embarrassment. A point may be reached where no repair is possible—the embarrassed person breaks into tears, flees, or, in the classic case, commits suicide—not to save face, but because face has been destroyed beyond repair (Goffman, 1955). Other

[22] Here we are speaking of what Edward T. Hall calls the "gaze line." He points out there are cultural variations in this phenomenon. See Hall, 1963.

terminations are possible, as we have shown. The embarrassing situation may be transformed by humor—laughed off—to define it as unserious and to invite others to symbolize their solidarity with the embarrassed person by joining in the laughter (see Rose Laub Coser, 1959). Blame may be diverted away from the transaction and placed on others on the outside. The embarrassed one may fall sick. There are numerous outcomes, and, while some are less drastic than others, none is completely devoid of risk. Why is it, then, that embarrassment may be deliberately perpetrated? There are at least three reasons or social functions that may be attributed to deliberate embarrassment.

First, since embarrassing situations are inevitable in social life, persons must be schooled to maintain poise when poise is threatened, to maintain the identities they have established in social situations in the face of discreditation, and to sustain the confidence others have built up about such matters. Deliberate embarrassment acts to socialize young people with these skills. Consequently, all young children trip one another, push, disarrange one another's clothing and other items of personal appearance. Besides being fun, such play [23] socializes the child in the maintenance of poise despite direct physical attacks on his "balance." Indeed, young children will spin about, inducing dizziness as they unknowingly test their ability to handle the imbalance in the play that Roger Caillois speaks of as *ilinx* or *vertigo* (1955). But socialization continues throughout life, and adult men, for example, test who can maintain poise in the face of the other's loss by playing at "drinking the other under the table." The roller coaster and tilt-a-whirl, and less upsetting machines like the merry-go-round and ferris wheel can be interpreted as a technology available to test poise.[24] Almost by definition, every game is a test of poise, but some sports place particular emphasis upon such tests—ski-jumping and gymnastics.[25] Announced identities are also challenged and impugned in play, as in "name-calling," and such teasing often reaches out to call into question everything one seeks to establish about himself in social encounters:

> Shame! Shame! Double shame!
> Everybody knows your name!

The child, of course, learns the institutionalized replies to such tests of identity and self-confidence which throw the challenge back:

[23] Careful attention must be given to all phases of children's play, which includes very much more than the anticipatory and fantastic dramas emphasized by George H. Mead.

[24] A definite age-grading of the technology may be noticed in our society. The mildest test of poise is provided for the very young—the merry-go-round—and the devilish devices seem to be reserved for the middle and late teen-agers.

[25] Poise is an essential part of the commercialized tumbling exhibitions we call wrestling. Interviews with professional wrestlers by one of the writers establish that the most feared "opponent" is not at all the most fierce, but the neophyte, upon whose poise the established professional cannot rely.

My name, my name is Puddin' Tame.
Ask me again and I'll tell you the same!

As others have noted, the challenges and responses inherent in such tests of poise, identity, and self-confidence often assume a pattern of interactive insult. The classic case is "playing the dozens." [26]

If one function of deliberate embarrassment is socialization, we would guess that such tests would be concentrated in the formative years and in other periods of major status passage. Our survey of adults in the evening extension class showed this to be true. When we asked them to recall the time of their lives when they were frequently embarrassed, the adolescent years were most commonly mentioned. Instances of deliberate embarrassment also included hazings and the humiliation which accompanied socialization into the armed forces. It may well be that every move into an established social world—every major *rite de passage*—is facilitated by the deliberate perpetration of embarrassing tests of poise, identity, and self-knowledge.[27]

Second, embarrassment is deliberately perpetrated as a negative sanction as in "calling" the one who is giving an undesirable performance. Since embarrassment does incapacitate the person from performing his role, it can clearly be used to stop someone from playing a role that might discredit a collectivity. Empirical categories include public reprimands, exposure of false fronts, open gossip and cattiness, or embarrassment perpetrated as a retaliation for an earlier embarrassment. In some of these cases, a person is exposed as having no right to play the role he has laid claim to, because the identity in which his role is anchored is invalid. In others, the person is punished by terminating his role performance so that he can no longer enjoy its perquisites.

A third function of deliberate embarrassment is the establishment and maintenance of power. The technique here is rather more subtle than those we have discussed. Specifically, the scene may be laid for embarrassment so that only by following the line established by one who sets the scene may embarrassment be avoided. In this case, one

[26] This game, found most commonly among American Negroes, is never carried on between two isolated antagonists, but requires the physical presence of peers who evaluate each insult and goad the players to heightened performances. The antagonists and their peers are usually members of the same in-group, again emphasizing the socializing function of the play. As the insults become more and more acrid, one antagonist may "break down" (lose poise) and suggest fighting. That person is perceived as having failed the test and the group then moves to prevent a fight from actually occurring. For Negroes, the ability to take insults without breaking down is clearly functional for survival in Negro-white interaction (see John Dollard, 1939; Ralph E. Berdie, 1947; and Cornelius L. Golightly and Israel Scheffler, 1948).

[27] An interesting comment on this point was made by Erving Goffman in a personal communication: "Since the theater is *the* place for the issue of poise, could our extensive high-school theatrical movement then be part of the socialization you speak of?"

assures himself that his decision will carry the day by guaranteeing that any alternative will result in irreparable damage to the whole collectivity. Organizational policy changes, for example, may be accomplished by cloaking them in a cover story impregnated with the organizational ideology. To resist the proposed changes, consequently, risks the discreditation of the entire organization. Another example is to be found in "kicking an official upstairs." The decision will be reached in a policy-making discussion where the official in question may be present. In the discussion, emphasis will be given to the official's qualifications for the new post so that the "stage manager" leads a new self forward to replace the old self of the official in question. Discreditation of the new self, particularly in the official's presence, would wreak such damage on the transaction that it must be foregone and the "manager's" decision conceded.[28]

Conclusion

In this paper, we have inquired into the conditions necessary for role performance. Embarrassment has been employed as a sensitive indicator of those conditions, for that which embarrasses incapacitates role performance. Our data have led us to describe the conditions for role performance in terms of identity, poise, and sustained confidence in one another. When these become disturbed and discredited, role performance cannot continue. Consequently, provisions for the avoidance or prevention of embarrassment, or quick recovery from embarrassment when it does occur, are of key importance to any society or social transaction, and devices to insure the avoidance and minimization of embarrassment will be part of every persisting social relationship. Specifically, tests of identity, poise, and self-knowledge will be institutionalized in every society. Such devices, like all mechanisms of social control, are capable of manipulation and may well be exploited to establish and maintain power in social transactions. Yet, deliberate or not, embarrassment is as general a sociological concept as is role.

References

ANONYMOUS
    1962   *Street-Walker*. New York: Gramercy.
BERDIE, RALPH E.
    1947   "Playing the Dozens." *Journal of Abnormal and Social Psychology* 42 (January):120–21.
BURKE, KENNETH
    1945   A *Grammar of Motives*. New York: Prentice-Hall.
CALLOIS, ROGER
    1955   "The Structure and Classification of Games." *Diogenes* No. 12 (Winter):61–75.

[28] Erving Goffman describes a similar process by which persons are channeled through a "betrayal funnel" into a mental hospital (see Goffman, 1959b).

COSER, ROSE LAUB
  1959 "Some Social Functions of Laughter: A Study of Humor in a Hospital Setting." *Human Relations* 12 (May):171–82.
DOLLARD, JOHN
  1939 "The Dozens: Dialectic of Insult." *The American Image* 1 (November):3–25.
GOFFMAN, ERVING
  1963a *Behavior in Public Places*. New York: Free Press.
  1963b *Stigma*. Englewood Cliffs: Prentice-Hall.
  1961 *Encounters*. Indianapolis: Bobbs-Merrill.
  1959a *The Presentation of Self in Everyday Life*. Garden City: Doubleday.
  1959b "The Moral Career of the Mental Patient." *Psychiatry* 22 (May):123–42.
  1956 "Embarrassment and Social Organization." *American Journal of Sociology* 62 (November):264–71.
  1955 "On Face-Work." *Psychiatry* 18 (August):213–31.
GOLIGHTLY, CORNELIUS, and ISRAEL SCHEFFLER
  1948 " 'Playing the Dozens': A Research Note." *Journal of Abnormal and Social Psychology* 43 (January): 104–5.
Good Housekeeping
  1963 "A Frank Discussion: What Wives Should Know About Male Support." (May):237.
HALL, EDWARD T.
  1963 "A System for the Notation of Proxemic Behavior." *American Anthropologist* 65 (October):1012–14.
HUGHES, EVERETT C.
  1945 "Dilemmas and Contradictions in Status." *American Journal of Sociology* 50 (March):353–59.
LINDESMITH, ALFRED R., and ANSELM L. STRAUSS
  1956 *Social Psychology*. New York: Dryden Press.
RIESMAN, DAVID, ROBERT J. POTTER, and JEANNE WATSON
  1960 "The Vanishing Host." *Human Organization* 19 (Spring):17–21.
RIESMAN, DAVID, and HOWARD ROSENBOROUGH
  1955 "Careers and Consumer Behavior." In LINCOLN CLARK, ed., *Consumer Behavior*. Vol. II: *The Life Cycle and Consumer Behavior*. New York: New York University Press.
SIMMEL, GEORG
  1950 *The Sociology of Georg Simmel*. Translated by KURT H. WOLFF. Glencoe: Free Press.
STONE, GREGORY P.
  1962 "Appearance and the Self." In ARNOLD ROSE, ed., *Human Behavior and Social Processes*. Boston: Houghton-Mifflin.
STRAUSS, ANSELM L.
  1959 *Mirrors and Masks*. Glencoe: Free Press.
ZORBAUGH, HARVEY W.
  1926 In ERNEST W. BURGESS, ed., *The Urban Community*. Chicago: University of Chicago Press.

4. Role Distance*

ERVING GOFFMAN

Situated Activity Systems

An object of this paper is to adapt role concepts for use in close studies of moment-to-moment behavior. At the same time, I do not want to gloss over the fact—already stressed—that the "system of reference" in role analysis is often vague and shifting. I therefore limit myself to activity that occurs entirely within the walls of single social establishments. This is already a grave limitation. The role of doctor can hardly be considered fully by noting what he does in a particular hospital that employs him; a full treatment must cover his round of work visits in the community and, what is more, the special treatment he is given when not ostensibly involved in medical matters at all—a treatment he facilitates by having a special license plate, a special door plate, a special term of address, and a special title on his official documents.

But even limiting interest to a particular establishment is not enough. We can look at the individual's regular participation in such an establishment as a regular sequence of daily activities: our doctor makes rounds, writes out clinical notes, places calls to his office, has staff conferences, spends time in surgery, has coffee and lunch breaks, and so forth. Some of these activities will bring him into face-to-face interaction with others for the performance of a single joint activity, a somewhat closed, self-compensating, self-terminating circuit of interdependent actions—what might be called a *situated activity system*. The performance of a surgical operation is an example. Illustrations from other spheres of life would be: the playing-through of a game; the execution of one run of a small-group experiment; the giving and getting of a haircut. Such systems of activity are to be distinguished from a task performed wholly by a single person, whether alone or in the presence of others, and from a joint endeavor that is "multisituated," in that it is executed by subgroups of persons operating

* From *Encounters* by Erving Goffman, copyright © 1961 by The Bobbs-Merrill Company, Inc.; reprinted by permission of the publisher.

from different rooms. I would like to add that in English it is convenient to allow the context to decide the class-member issue, that is, whether one is referring to a class of like activities and a pattern of similarities, or referring to any occasion, trial, or run during which one complete cycle of phases occurs and provides a single illustration of the class and pattern.

Given any individual's sequence of regular activities in a social establishment, *one* regular activity involving a situated system can be singled out for study, since this provides the student with a context in which he can get as close as he is able to raw conduct. We deal, then, with "small group" phenomena in a natural setting.

When the runs of a situated system are repeated with any frequency, fairly well-developed *situated roles* seem to emerge: action comes to be divided into manageable bundles, each a set of acts that can be compatibly performed by a single participant. In addition to this role formation, there is a tendency for role differentiation to occur, so that the package of activity that the members of one class of participants perform is different from, though dependent on, the set performed by members of another category. A situated role, then, is a bundle of activities visibly performed before a set of others and visibly meshed into the activity these others perform. These kinds of roles, it may be added, differ from roles in general, not only because they are realized and encompassed in a face-to-face social situation, but also because the pattern of which they are a part can be confidently identified as a concrete self-compensating system.

The part that an individual plays in a situated circuit of activity inevitably expresses something about him, something out of which he and the others fashion an image of him. Often, this will be more than what is conveyed by mere accidents and incidents, and different from what is conveyed by membership in the establishment as such and by location in its ranks and offices. A situated self, then, awaits the individual.

As an initial example of a situated system, I would like to draw on some brief observations of merry-go-rounds. There are senses in which any patronized ride on a merry-go-round provides an instance of a natural and objective social unit, an activity circuit, providing we follow the ride through its full cycle of activity involving a cohort of persons, each one getting a ticket and using it up together on the same ride. As is often the case with situated activity systems, mechanical operations and administrative purpose provide the basis of the unit. Yet persons are placed on this floor and something organic emerges. There is a mutual orientation of the participants and—within limits, it is true—a meshing together of their activity. As with any face-to-face interaction, there is much chance for communication and its feedback through a wide variety of signs, for the damping and surging of response, and for the emergence of homeostatic-like controls. As soon as the ride gets underway, there is a circulation of feeling among the participants and an "involvement contour" may emerge, with collective shifts in the intensity, quality, and objects of involvement. Every ride, then, can be fruitfully viewed as an instance or run of a somewhat closed self-realized system. And this is so even though we know that this episode of reality is tied in with the day's activity at the merry-go-round, the state of the amusement park as a whole, the park season, and the community from which the riders come, just as we know that, for the man who runs the merry-go-round, a single ride may appear as a hardly distinguishable part of a day's work.

Some of the concepts introduced earlier regarding positions and roles can be applied, *mutatis mutandis,* to situated activity circuits. Certainly in the case of the merry-go-round there is role differentiation: those who ride; those who watch; and those who run the machine. Further, a role in such a system does imply an image of self, even a well-rounded one. For the merry-go-round rider, for example, the self awaiting is one that entails a child's portion of bravery and muscular control, a child's portion of manliness, and often a child's title. So, too, we know that children can become attached to such a role, since some will scream when finally taken off their horses. Further, some concepts, such as function, can be applied to a situated circuit of activity better perhaps than anywhere else, since here at least we deal with a clear-cut, well-bounded, concrete system.

The application of other role concepts to situated activity systems must be more carefully considered. To what, for example, can a child commit himself in becoming a rider? In coming to the amusement park, the child may be foregoing another kind of amusement that day. In paying his dime, he is committing some measure of purchasing power, but even for him perhaps no great amount. And once the machine starts, he may have some commitment to finishing the ride, as a person piloting a plane has a commitment to stay with his task until a landing is made. But, in the main, a rider's commitment is small. He can, for example, easily arrange to take on the role or divest himself of it.

The role of merry-go-round operator might constitute a greater commitment, since this role is not only performed regularly but also is likely to be enacted by a regular performer. In following his present line of work, the operator may well have automatically excluded himself from the recruitment channels leading to other kinds of jobs. The money he can make on the job, further, may be committed to the upkeep of his domestic establishment, and his budget may have been planned on the basis of his continuing to operate the concession. Relative to the individuals who ride his steeds, then, he is committed to his position and locked into it.

But this is a loose way of talking, derived from traditional role analysis. If the operator is employed by the amusement park, then he is committed to performing some job in connection with the organization. Within the organization's formal setting, however, he may, in fact, change his situated role, managing the candy and popcorn concession one day and the merry-go-round the next—and on some days even both. Although these changes entail a radical shift in the tasks he performs and in the intimate system of situated activity in which these tasks fit, he may find little change in his situation in life. Even where he owns the concession and has invested all his money in the merry-go-round, he need not be committed to the role of operator but merely to hiring someone to perform the role whose hire he can afford to pay.

The point about looking at situated activity systems, however, is not that some traditional role concepts can be applied in this situational setting, but that the complexities of concrete conduct can be examined instead of by-passed. Where the social content of a situated system faithfully expresses in miniature the structure of the broader social organization in which it is located, then little change in the traditional role analysis is necessary; situated roles would merely be our means of sampling, say, occupational or institutional role. But where a discrepancy is found, we would be in a position to show proper respect for it.

The Problem of Expression

With this preliminary review and revision of role concepts, and the introduction of the notion of situated activity systems, we can begin to look at the special concern of this paper, the issue of expression. I must backtrack a little at first, however, before proceeding with expression on merry-go-rounds and other situated systems.

I have already reviewed the assumption that when an individual makes an appearance in a given position, he will be the person that the position allows and obliges him to be and will continue to be this person during role enactment. The performer will attempt to make the expressions that occur consistent with the identity imputed to him; he will feel compelled to control and police the expressions that occur. Performance will, therefore, be able to express identity. But we need only state that doing is being to become aware of apparent exceptions, which, furthermore, arise at different points, each throwing light on a different source of instability in the presumed expressiveness of role.

One issue is that roles may not only be *played* but also *played at*, as when children, stage actors, and other kinds of cutups mimic a role for the avowed purpose of make-believe; here, surely, doing is not being. But this is easy to deal with. A movie star who plays at being a doctor is not in the role of doctor but in the role of actor; and this latter role, we are told, he is likely to take quite seriously. The work of his role is to portray a doctor, but the work is only incidental; his actual role is no more make-believe than that of a real doctor—merely better paid. Part of the confusion here, perhaps, has been that actors do not have a right to keep amateurs from playing at being actors in amateur theatricals, a fact that helps give the whole trade a bad name.

A professional actor differs from a child in the degree of perseverance and perfection the professional must manifest in the role he simulates. Professional and child are similar, however, in making no continued effort to convince any audience that performer and performed character are the same, and they are similarly embarrassed when this over-belief occurs. Both are to be contrasted with actors employed in one version or another of the cloak-and-dagger business. These desperate performers are caught exactly between illusion and reality, and must lead one audience to accept the role portrait as real, even while assuring another audience that the actor in no way is convincing himself.

Further, under certain rare and colorful circumstances, a man who first appears, say, to be a surgeon, accepting others' acceptance of him in this role, may in fact be a knowing imposter, knowing of radical grounds that others do not know they have for not accepting him. And in addition to this classic kind of misrepresentation, there is the situation in which individual may, against his will, be temporarily misidentified by others who have accepted the wrong cues regarding him. It is a sad fact that a Negro intern or resident in a predominantly white hospital is likely to acquire experience in telling patients and visitors that he cannot see to minor requests because he is not an attendant.

Whether an individual plays a role or plays at it, we can expect that the mechanics of putting it on will typically expose him as being out of character at certain regular junctures. Thus, while a person may studiously stay *in role* while in the staging area of its performance, he may nonetheless *break role* or go out of role when he thinks that no one or no one important can see him. Even a performer of one of our most splendid roles, such as a surgeon, may allow himself to "go out of play"—to stare vacantly, pick his nose, or comb his hair, all in a manner unbecoming a surgeon—just before he enters the operating room or just after he leaves it. But again, it is just these expressive incongruities that role analysis allows us to perceive and account for.

Furthermore, students these days are increasingly examining "role dissensus," in connection with the plurality of cultural and group affiliations which differentially impinge upon persons present in a role to one another (see Gross *et al.*, 1958; and Gouldner, 1957). Thus, some surgeons are more alive than others to the opinion of patients, others to the opinion of their colleagues, and still others to the view that the hospital management has of them. Each of these audiences is likely to have a somewhat different view of ideal standards of performance; what is one man's ideal for role performance may to another seem almost infraction.

I want to add a point that is insufficiently appreciated. Before a set of task-like activities can become an identity-providing role, these activities must be clothed in a moral performance of some kind. Mere efficient enactment is not enough to provide the identity; activities must be built up socially and made something of. Although this role formation or social capitalization of jobs seems the usual practice in urban life, it is by no means universal. There are, for example, ancient inbred island communities of Britain where kinship and fellow-islander status is so fundamental that a native who is employed in a local shop to sell to members of the community is unlikely to build this work activity into a stance to be taken to customers. Such clerks take the point of view of the other not only in manner, as in the case of urban sellers, but also in spirit, the other in this case being treated not as a customer but as a kinsman, as a neighbor, or as a friend. Often, no variation can be observed in tone or manner as the clerk weaves personal gossipy conversation in amongst the words of advice he offers as to which of the local shops (not just his own) sells which product at the most advantageous price. Here, the richness of communal life entails an impoverishment of the self-defining aspects of occupational roles: required tasks are done, but they are scarcely allowed to form the base for the development of a special loyalty and a special orientation to the world.[1] Here doing is not being. The person who is the salesman has a self, but it is not the self of a salesman. Only the manager of the store will display identification with his role, and even he appreciates that he must not throw himself too much into his calling.

The next issue concerning expression requires a more extended consideration.

Whatever an individual does and however he appears, he knowingly and unknowingly makes information available concerning the attributes that might be imputed to him and hence the categories in which he might be placed. The status symbolism in his "personal front" provides information about his group and aggregate affiliations; his treatment at the hands of others conveys a conception of him; the physical milieu itself conveys implications concerning the identity of those who are in it. Face-to-face situations, it may be added, are ones in which a great variety of sign vehicles become available, whether desired or not, and are, therefore, situations in which much information about oneself can easily become available. Face-to-face situations are, in fact, ideal projective fields that the participant cannot help but structure in a characterizing way, so that conclusions can be drawn about him, correct or incorrect, whether he wants it or not.

[1] Interestingly enough, in such communities there is often an appreciation that traditional bases for defining the self must be put aside and those of urban repute encouraged. In the Shetland Islands, where almost every man can do a surprising range of mechanical, electrical, and construction work, one may observe tacit agreements among islanders to support one of their number as a "specialist" in a skill, allowing him payment for jobs they might have done themselves. Once these specialists are established by reputation, if not by the volume and constancy of their trade, the islanders point to them with pride as evidence of the modernity of the community.

It should be appreciated that the information the situation provides about an individual who is in it need not be a direct reflection or extension of the local scene itself. By working on a charity case in a slum dwelling, a physician does not become identified with the status of his client; social dirt does not rub off on him. (The socioeconomic attributes of those who make up his office practice, however, present another problem.) Similarly, the tourist does not lose caste in appearing in an unsophisticated peasant milieu; the very presence of natives establishes him as a traveler.

The individual stands in a double relationship to attributes that are, or might be, imputed to him. Some attributes he will feel are rightfully his, others he will not; some he will be pleased and able to accept as part of his self-definition, others he will not.[2] There is some relationship between these two variables—between what is right and what is pleasing—in that the individual often feels that pleasing imputations regarding himself are in addition rightful, and unpleasing imputations are, incidentally, undeserved and illegitimate. But this happy relationship between the two variables does not always hold.

Ordinarily, the information that arises in a social situation concerning one of the participants consistently confirms for him and others a particular conception of himself which is, in addition, one that he is prepared to accept, more or less, as both right and desirable. Here, in fact, we have two basic assumptions of the role perspective—that one accepts as an identification of oneself what one is doing at the time, and that once cues have been conveyed about one's positions, the rest of the information becoming available in the situation confirms these initial cues.

But expressive consistency and acceptability are not always in fact maintained. Information incompatible with the individual's image of himself does get conveyed. In some cases, this inopportune information may give the individual more credit than he feels he could properly accept; in more cases, apparently, the troublesome information undercuts the individual's self-image. Some of this self-threatening information may be valid, referring to facts which the individual wishes would not be raised concerning him. Some of the information may be invalid, implying an unwarranted image of himself that he ought not to have to accept.

In any case, it should be clear that the individual cannot completely control the flow of events in a social situation and hence cannot completely control the information about himself that becomes available in the situation. Even the best run interactions throw up events that are expressively somewhat inconsistent with effective claims regarding self. Men trip, forget names, wear slightly inappropriate clothes, attempt to buy a too-small amount of some commodity, fail to score well in a game, arrive a few minutes late for an appointment,

[2] Psychiatrically, this is sometimes referred to as a difference between ego-syntonic and ego-alien.

become a trifle overheated in argument, fail to finish a task quite on time. In all these cases, a momentary discrepancy arises between what the individual anticipated being and what events imply he is.

Whether a social situation goes smoothly or whether expressions occur that are in discord with a participant's sense of who and what he is, we might expect—according to the usual deterministic implications of role analysis—that he will fatalistically accept the information that becomes available concerning him. Yet when we get close to the moment-to-moment conduct of the individual we find that he does not remain passive in the face of the potential meanings that are generated regarding him, but, so far as he can, actively participates in sustaining a definition of the situation that is stable and consistent with his image of himself.

Perhaps the simplest example of this "control of implications" response is the "explanation." Here, the individual volunteers information which is designed to alter radically the information that has been, or otherwise will be, generated in the situations. Another is that of the "apology," through which the individual begs not to be judged in the way that appears likely, implying that his own standards are offended by his act and that therefore some part of him, at least, cannot be characterized by the unseemly action.[3] A display of righteous indignation has the same effect, but it is the other who is cast in a bad light instead of a split-off portion of oneself. Similarly, by introducing an unserious style, the individual can project the claim that nothing happening at the moment to him or through him should be taken as a direct reflection of him, but rather of the person-in-situation that he is mimicking. Thus, there is in our society a special tone of voice and facial posture through which "baby talk" is conveyed at strategic moments, for example when a second helping is requested by an individual who does not want to appear to be intemperate.

Explanations, apologies, and joking are all ways in which the individual makes a plea for disqualifying some of the expressive features of the situation as sources of definitions of himself. Since these maneuvers are often accepted by the others present, we must see that the individual's responsibility for the self-expressive implications of the events around him has definite limits.

Role Distance

The occurrence of explanations and apologies as limitations on the expressiveness of role leads us to look again at what goes on in concrete face-to-face activity. I return to our situated example, the merry-go-round.

A merry-go-round horse is a thing of some size, some height, and

---

[3] Explanations and apologies are, of course, often combined into the "excuse" through which both restructuring information and self-abasement are introduced at the same time. (See the treatment in Jackson Toby, 1952.)

some movement; and while the track is never wet, it can be very noisy. American middle-class two-year-olds often find the prospect too much for them. They fight their parents at the last moment to avoid being strapped into a context in which it had been hoped they would prove to be little men. Sometimes they become frantic halfway through the ride, and the machine must be stopped so that they can be removed.

Here we have one of the classic possibilities of life. Participation in any circuit of face-to-face activity requires the participant to keep command of himself, both as a person capable of executing physical movements and as one capable of receiving and transmitting communications. A flustered failure to maintain either kind of role poise makes the system as a whole suffer. Every participant, therefore, has the function of maintaining his own poise, and one or more participants are likely to have the specialized function of modulating activity so as to safeguard the poise of the others. In many situated systems, of course, all contingencies are managed without such threats arising. However, there is no such system in which these troubles might not occur, and some systems, such as those in a surgery ward, presumably provide an especially good opportunity to study these contingencies.

Just as a rider may be disqualified during the ride because he proves to be unable to handle riding, so a rider will be removed from his saddle at the very beginning of the ride because he does not have a ticket or because, in the absence of his parents, he makes management fear for his safety. There is an obvious distinction, then, between qualifications required for permission to attempt a role and attributes required for performing suitably once the role has been acquired.

At three and four, the task of riding a wooden horse is still a challenge, but apparently a manageable one, inflating the rider to his full extent with demonstrations of capacity. Parents need no longer ride alongside to protect their youngsters. The rider throws himself into the role in a serious way, playing it with verve and an admitted engagement of all his faculties. Passing his parents at each turn, the rider carefully lets go one of his hands and grimly waves a smile or a kiss —this, incidentally, being an example of an act that is a typical part of the role but hardly an obligatory feature of it. Here, then, doing is being, and what was designated as a "playing at" is stamped with serious realization.

Just as "flustering" is a classic possibility in all situated systems, so also is the earnest way these youngsters of three or four ride their horses. Three matters seem to be involved: an admitted or expressed attachment to the role; a demonstration of qualifications and capacities for performing it; an active *engagement* or spontaneous involvement in the role activity at hand, that is, a visible investment of attention and muscular effort. Where these three features are present, I will use the term *embracement*. To embrace a role is to disappear completely into the virtual self available in the situation, to be fully seen in terms of the image, and to confirm expressively one's acceptance of it. To embrace a role is to be embraced by it. Particularly good illustrations of full embracement can be seen in persons in certain occupations: team managers during baseball games; traffic policemen at intersections during rush hours; landing signal officers who wave in planes landing on the decks of aircraft carriers; in fact, any one occupying a directing role where the performer must guide others by means of gestural signs.[4]

An individual may affect the embracing of a role in order to conceal a lack of attachment to it, just as he may affect a visible disdain for a role, thrice refusing the kingly crown, in order to defend himself against the psychological dangers of his actual attachment to it. Certainly an individual may be attached to a role and fail to be able to embrace it, as when a child proves to have no ticket or to be unable to hang on.

Returning to the merry-go-round, we see that at five years of age the situation is transformed, especially for boys. To be a merry-go-round horse rider is now apparently not enough, and this fact must be demonstrated out of dutiful regard for one's own character. Parents are not likely to be allowed to ride along, and the strap for preventing falls is often disdained. One rider may keep time to the music by clapping his feet or a hand against the horse, an early sign of utter control. Another may make a wary stab at standing on the saddle or changing horses without touching the platform. Still another may hold on to the post with one hand and lean back as far as possible while looking up to the sky in a challenge to dizziness. Irreverence begins, and the horse may be held on to by his wooden ear or his tail. The child says by his actions: "Whatever I am, I'm not just someone who can barely manage to stay on a wooden horse." Note that what the rider is apologizing for is not some minor untoward event that has cropped up during the interaction, but the whole role. The image of him that is generated for him by the routine entailed in his mere participation—his virtual self in the context—is an image from which he apparently withdraws by *actively* manipulating the situation. Whether this skittish behavior is intentional or unintentional, sincere or affected, correctly appreciated by others present or not, it does constitute a wedge between the individual and his role, between doing and being. This "effectively" expressed pointed separateness between the individual and his putative role I shall call *role distance*. A shorthand is involved here: the individual is actually denying not the role but the virtual self that is implied in the role for all accepting performers.

In any case, the term role distance is not meant to refer to all behavior that does not directly contribute to the task core of a given role but only to those behaviors that are seen by someone present

[4] Here, as elsewhere, I am indebted to Gregory Stone.

as relevant to assessing the actor's attachment to his particular role and relevant in such a way as to suggest that the actor possibly has some measure of disaffection from, and resistance against, the role. Thus, for example, a four-year-old halfway through a triumphant performance as merry-go-round rider may sometimes go out of play, dropping from his face and manner any confirmation of his virtual self, yet may indulge in this break in role without apparent intent, the lapse reflecting more on his capacity to sustain any role than on his feelings about the present one. Nor can it be called role distance if the child rebels and totally rejects role, stomping off in a huff, for the special facts about self that can be conveyed by holding a role off a little are precisely the ones that cannot be conveyed by throwing the role over.

At seven and eight, the child not only dissociates himself self-consciously from the kind of horseman a merry-go-round allows him to be but also finds that many of the devices that younger people use for this are now beneath him. He rides no-hands, gleefully chooses a tiger or a frog for a steed, clasps hands with a mounted friend across the aisle. He tests limits, and his antics may bring negative sanction from the adult in charge of the machine. And he is still young enough to show distance by handling the task with bored, nonchalant competence, a candy bar languidly held in one hand.

At eleven and twelve, maleness for boys has become a real responsibility, and no easy means of role distance seems to be available on merry-go-rounds. It is necessary to stay away or to exert creative acts of distancy, as when a boy jokingly treats his wooden horse as if it were a racing one: he jogs himself up and down, leans far over the neck of the horse, drives his heels mercilessly into its flanks, and uses the reins for a lash to get more speed, brutally reining in the horse when the ride is over. He is just old enough to achieve role distance by defining the whole undertaking as a lark, a situation for mockery.

Adults who choose to ride a merry-go-round display adult techniques of role distance. One adult rider makes a joke of tightening the safety belt around him; another crosses his arms, giving popcorn with his left hand to the person on his right and a coke with his right hand to the person on his left. A young lady riding sidesaddle tinkles out, "It's cold," and calls to her watching boy friend's boy friend, "Come on, don't be chicken." A dating couple riding adjacent horses holds hands to bring sentiment, not daring, to the situation. Two double-dating couples employ their own techniques: the male in front sits backwards and takes a picture of the other male rider taking a picture of him. And, of course, some adults, riding close by their threatened two-and-a-half-year-old, wear a face that carefully demonstrates that they do not perceive the ride as an event in itself, their only present interest being their child.

And finally there is the adult who runs the machine and takes the tickets. Here, often, can be found a fine flowering of role distance. Not only does he show that the ride itself is not—as a ride—an event

to him, but he also gets off and on and around the moving platform
with a grace and ease that can only be displayed by safely taking what
for children and even adults would be chances.

Some general points can be made about merry-go-round role distance. First, while the management of a merry-go-round horse in our
culture soon ceases to be a challenging "developmental task," the task
of expressing that it is not continues for a long time to be a challenge
and remains a felt necessity. A full twist must be made in the iron law
of etiquette: the act through which one can afford to try to fit into
the situation is an act that can be styled to show that one is somewhat
out of place. One enters the situation to the degree that one can
demonstrate that one does not belong.

A second general point about role distance is that immediate audiences figure very directly in the display of role distance. Merry-go-
round horsemen are very ingenuous and may frankly wait for each
time they pass their waiting friends before playing through their gestures of role distance. Moreover, if persons above the age of twelve
or so are to trust themselves to making a lark of it, they almost need
to have a friend along on the next horse, since persons who are "together" seem to be able to hold off the socially defining force of the
environment much more than a person alone.

A final point: two different means of establishing role distance seem
to be found. In one case the individual tries to isolate himself as much
as possible from the contamination of the situation, as when an adult
riding along to guard his child makes an effort to be completely stiff,
affectless, and preoccupied. In the other case the individual coopera-
tively projects a childish self, meeting the situation more than halfway, but then withdraws from this castoff self by a little gesture
signifying that the joking has gone far enough. In either case the individual can slip the skin the situation would clothe him in.

A summary of concepts is now in order. I have tried to distinguish
among three easily confused ideas: *commitment*, *attachment*, and *embracement*.[5] It is to be noted that these sociological terms are of a
different order from that of *engagement*, a psychobiological process
that a cat or a dog can display more beautifully than man. Finally, the
term *role distance* was introduced to refer to actions which effectively
convey some disdainful detachment of the performer from a role he
is performing.

Role Distance and Serious Activity

The role of merry-go-round rider can be regularly performed at any
amusement park but hardly by a regular performer. After a few years
each of us "outgrows" the role and can only perform it as an occasional thing and as an occasion for the display of much role distance.

[5] A somewhat different and more differentiated analysis may be found in G. P.
Stone, 1959.

As an example, then, merry-go-round riding is not a very serious one; furthermore, it is somewhat misleading, since it implies that role distance is displayed in connection with roles no adult can take seriously.

Actually, we deal with a more general phenomenon, with roles that categories of individuals find it unwise to embrace. Even a short step away from merry-go-rounds shows this. Take, for example, six lower-middle-class high-school girls, not of the horsy set, taking a vacation in a national park and deciding to "do" horseback riding on one of their mornings. As long as they come to the riding stable in self-supporting numbers, they can nicely illustrate distance from a role that persons of another social class and region might take seriously all their lives. The six I observed came in clothing patently not designed as a consolidation of the horsewoman role: pedal pushers, cotton leotards, ballet-type flats, frilly blouses. One girl, having been allotted the tallest horse, made a mock scene of declining to get on because of the height, demanding to be allowed to go home. When she did get on, she called her horse "Daddy-O," diverting her conversation from her friends to her horse. During the ride, one girl pretended to post while the horse walked, partly in mockery of a person not in their party who was posting. Another girl leaned over the neck of her horse and shouted racing cries, again while the horse was locked in a walking file of other horses. She also slipped her right foot out of the stirrup and brought it over the saddle, making a joke of her affectation of riding sidesaddle and expressing that both positions were much alike to her—both equally unfamiliar and uncongenial; at the same time she tested the limits of the wrangler's permissiveness. Passing under low branches, the girls made a point of making a point of this by pulling off branches, waving them like flags, then feeding them to their horses. Evidences of the excretory capacities of the steeds were greeted with merriment and loud respect. During the latter part of the two-hour ride, two of the girls became visibly bored, dropped the reins over the saddlehorn, let their hands fall limply to their sides, and gave up all pretense at being in role.

Again we can detect some general facts about role distance. We can see that a role that some persons take seriously most of their lives may be one that others will never take seriously at any age. We see that participation with a group of one's similars can lend strength to the show of role distance and to one's willingness to express it. In the presence of age-peers elegantly attired for riding and skilled at it, the girls I observed might falter in displaying role distance, feeling hostile, resentful, and unconfident. Presumably, if one of these girls were alone with thoroughgoing horsewomen she would be even less prone to flourish this kind of distance. We can suspect, then, that role distance will have defensive functions. By manifesting role distance, the girls give themselves some elbow room in which to maneuver. "We are not to be judged by this incompetence," they say. Should they make a bad showing, they are in a position to dodge the reflection it could cast on them. Whatever their showing, they avoid having to be humbled before those who are socially placed to make a much better showing. By exposing themselves in a guise to which they have no serious claim, they leave themselves in full control of shortcomings they take seriously.

While horse trails and children's playgrounds provide fine places for studying repertoires of role distance, we need not look to situations that are so close to being unserious, situations where it is difficult to distinguish role playing from playing at. We know, for example, that tasks that might be embraced by a housewife or maid may be tackled by the man of the house with carefully expressed clumsiness and with self-mockery. Perhaps it should be noted that similar out-of-character situations can easily be created experimentally by asking subjects to perform tasks that are inappropriate to persons of their kind.

The published literature on some of our occupational byways provides serious material on role distance. Psychoanalysts, for example, who have told us so much about the contingencies of a particular trade (even when not telling us all we might want to know about their patients), provide interesting data on role distance in connection with "resistance" on the part of the patient. Resistance here takes the form of the patient refusing to provide relevant associations or refusing to allow the therapist to function solely as a "therapist." From the therapist's view of the patient's motivation, then, resistance expresses some rejection of the constraints of one's role as patient:

> Up to this point I found myself, as the doctor, comfortably installed in my explicit instrumental role; the role assignment given me by the patient appeared to be concerned with her "problem." The system of roles was complementary and apparently well integrated. The next moment, however, the patient initiated a new role assignment. She asked me if I had seen a recent performance of "Don Juan in Hell" from *Man and Superman*. The question seemed a simple enough request for information regarding my playgoing habits. But since I did not know what role I was being invited to take, and because I suspected that behind whatever explicit role this might turn out to be there lurked a more important implicit one, I did not answer the question. The patient paused for a moment, and then, perceiving that I would not answer the question, she continued. . . .
>
> In continuing after the pause, the patient delivered a highly perceptive account of Shaw's intention in the Don Juan interlude, of the actors' interpretations, and of her reactions. The account was so long that I finally interrupted to ask if she knew why she wanted to tell all this. At the point of interruption I had become aware that my new role was an expressive one—to play the appreciative audience to her role as a gifted art and drama critic. (Spiegel, 1954.)

The therapist then goes on to explain that had he merely fallen in with the patient's maneuver to keep herself at a distance from the role of patient he would have had to pass up "the opportunity to get more information regarding the hidden, implicit role buried in this transaction and thus to learn more about her motivation for shifting out of her initial instrumental role in which she had started the interview" (Spiegel, 1954). The therapist could have added that to ask the patient why she felt it necessary to run on so is a classic therapist's ploy to put the patient in her place, back in role.

Situated roles that place an individual in an occupational setting he feels is beneath him are bound to give rise to much role distance. A good example is provided by Isaac Rosenfeld in a reminiscence about a summer job as a barker at Coney Island. The writer begins his description by telling of his return after many years, seeing someone else handling his old job:

> He was sneering, just as I used to do in the old days, and no doubt for the same reason: because the summer was hot, and the work hard, sweaty and irritating, stretching over long hours for poor pay. It was absolutely indispensable, now as it was then, to separate oneself from the job—one had to have a little ledge to stand on all to himself; otherwise perish. I used to pitch this ledge very high. The higher I stood, the greater my contempt, and the more precious the moments of freedom I won for myself by this trick of balancing above the crowd. I remembered how I used to mix T. S. Eliot with my spiel (in those days there was hardly anyone in Freshman English who did not know a good deal of *The Waste Land* by heart): "Step right up ladies and gentlemen mingling memory with desire for the greatest thrill show on earth only a dime the tenth part of a dollar will bring you to Carthage then I come burning burning burning O Lord thou pluckest me out ten cents!" (Rosenfeld, 1953:219.)

Some of the most appealing data on role distance come from situations where a subordinate must take orders or suggestions and must go along with the situation as defined by superordinates. At such times, we often find that although the subordinate is careful not to threaten those who are, in a sense, in charge of the situation, he may be just as careful to inject some expression to show, for any who care to see, that he is not capitulating completely to the work arrangement in which he finds himself.[6] Sullenness, muttering, irony, joking, and sarcasm may all allow one to show that something of oneself lies outside the constraints of the moment and outside the role within whose jurisdiction the moment occurs.

Given these various examples of role distance, I want to go on to argue that this conduct is something that falls between role obligations on one hand and actual role performance on the other. This gap has

[6] Some excellent illustrations of this may be found in Tom Burns, 1953, a paper to which I am very much indebted. A good illustration from army life is provided in William Styron's novel *The Long March*, in connection with a captain's minor remonstrances against orders issued by his colonel.

always caused trouble for sociologists. Often, they try to ignore it. Faced with it, they sometimes despair and turn from their own direction of analysis; they look to the biography of the performer and try to find in his history some particularistic explanation of events, or they rely on psychology, alluding to the fact that in addition to playing the formal themes of his role, the individual always behaves personally and spontaneously, phrasing the standard obligations in a way that has a special psychological fit for him.

The concept of role distance provides a *sociological* means of dealing with one type of divergence between obligation and actual performance. First, we know that often distance is not introduced on an individual basis but can be predicted on the grounds of the performer's gross age-sex characteristics. Role distance is a part (but, of course, only one part) of *typical* role, and this routinized sociological feature should not escape us merely because role distance is not part of the normative framework of role. Secondly, that which one is careful to point out one is not, or not merely, necessarily has a directing and intimate influence on one's conduct, especially since the means for expressing this disaffection must be carved out of the standard materials available in the situation.

We arrive, then, at a broadened sociological way of looking at the trappings of a social role. A set of visible qualifications and known certifications, along with a social setting well designed as a showplace, provides the individual with something more than an opportunity to play his role self to the hilt, for this scene is just what he needs to create a clear impression of what he chooses not to lay claim to. The more extensive the trappings of a role, the more opportunity to display role distance. Personal front and social setting provide precisely the field an individual needs to cut a figure in—a figure that romps, sulks, glides, or is indifferent.

References

BURNS, TOM
   1953   "Friends, Enemies and the Polite Fiction." *American Sociological Review*
           18:654–62.
GOULDNER, A. W.
   1957   "Cosmopolitans and Locals: Toward an Analysis of Latent Social Roles
           —I." *Administrative Science Quarterly* 2:281–306.
GROSS, NEAL, WARD MASON, and ALEXANDER McEACHERN
   1958   *Explorations in Role Analysis.* New York: John Wiley & Sons.
ROSENFELD, ISAAC
   1953   "Coney Island Revisited." In WILLIAM PHILLIPS and PHILIP RAHV, eds.,
           Modern Writing. New York: Avon.
SPIEGEL, J. P.
   1954   "The Social Roles of Doctor and Patient in Psychoanalysis and Psychotherapy." *Psychiatry* 17:372–73.

STONE, G. P.
    1959   "Clothing and Social Relations: A Study of Appearance in the Context
            of Community Life." Unpublished Ph.D. dissertation, Department
            of Sociology, University of Chicago.
STYRON, WILLIAM
    1952   *The Long March.* New York: Modern Library.
TOBY, JACKSON
    1952   "Some Variables in Role Conflict Analysis." *Social Forces* 30:323–37.

III. Getting Together: Sociability and Solidarity

III. Getting Together:
Sociability and Solidarity

Human beings are unique in that they are simultaneously actors and observers of the actions of others and themselves. People are rarely able to avoid monitoring their own behavior and that of others. What George Herbert Mead, a founding father of sociology, called "taking the role of the other" is necessary for engaging in interaction with others. Indeed, we really cannot "know" other people except by assuming in our own minds, or in fantasy, that we are in their social position. This very human trait is no better demonstrated than on occasions when discussions of serious interests are put aside or are regarded as inappropriate. Parties and other festive events may not be considered places for furthering one's self-interest, but they certainly demand that we remain alert to our fortunes. Given that little is at stake materially, why do the guests energetically engage in face-to-face interaction, as if the very life of society depended on it?

Social competence is still very much the focus of interest at parties. On such occasions one is expected to make small talk—something for its own sake, something to be continued in order to maintain continuity. There are rules of irrelevance here as well as on other, more instrumental occasions: At a party, it is considered bad taste to introduce discussions of the interaction itself, particularly the lack of it. When people do so at a party, a pall is cast: The assembled guests are supposed to be able to keep things going, and an open discussion of how dull or otherwise unpleasant the party is clearly reveals their failure.

People display competence, showing support for the occasion, in numerous ways—by knowing what is acceptable and making appropriate entries and exits, by participating in ceremonial activities such as drinking, by wearing the right clothes. People also support occasions by talking about deviant acts—the disruptive incidents, the boners and gaffes made at parties past—and by identifying others who have not established their right to be there, such as "gate crashers" and "party poopers."

Negative displays, such as talking critically about the occasion, can produce solidarity between individual guests. Rebellious and conspiratorial behavior can establish bonds that go beyond the occasion itself. Other party members, regarding it as a threat to the occasion when

141

people get too tight with each other instead of just getting "tight," sometimes try to break up such goings on. Going up to someone and saying, "Don't you hate mixers?" as Sandy does in the film *Carnal Knowledge*, may be a tired opener, but it permits the other either to punish the person for failure to uphold the spirit of the occasion or to reward him for daring irreverence. Play is fun, but one still has to beware of the risks; one still has to be good at it. Knowing how and when to break the rules is something one learns on sociable occasions, when social solidarity is rarely at stake and one breaks the rules in order to establish ties with others. Moreover, displays of this kind are less threatening to the group than is similar behavior by individuals. Not being able to enlist the cooperation of another in one's doings is often a condemnation of the act as one of madness, as when Morgan, in the film of that name, breaks up his ex-wife's wedding by appearing in a gorilla costume. In contrast, Benjamin, in *The Graduate*, is able to get away with his highjinks because his girl goes along with them.

Sociability may provide a respite from a person's instrumental activities but not from his obligations to others present at the encounter. Sherri Cavan's work on social behavior in public drinking places demonstrates how complex social interaction can be. Louis A. Zurcher's article on card-playing demonstrates how people who have assumed an ephemeral role are nonetheless not excused from being fully engaged in it. People who participate in games are obliged to appear to be spontaneously involved. It is interesting that, although etiquette manuals abound, as do books on how to play games better, little has been published on the place of manners in games. Perhaps this is so because the requisite appearance of spontaneity precludes its systematic literary discussion. Once it is known that people owe their "spontaneity" to being prepared rather than to the occasion, they may well become suspect.

One way to establish individuality is by being capable of easeful interaction. A way of confirming the identity of others is by giving them something that represents the image one has of them. In his essay on the social psychology of the gift, Barry Schwartz examines the ways in which social solidarity may be maintained, modified, or dissolved through the act of giving. Moreover, group boundaries and members' loyalties are often made visible by gifts, or even by their absence.

1. Bar Sociability *

SHERRI CAVAN

Public drinking places are "open regions": those who are present
have the right to engage others, acquainted or not, in conversational
interaction and the duty to accept the overtures of sociability proffered
to them.[1] While many, and perhaps the majority, of conventional
settings customarily limit the extent of contact among strangers,
sociability is the most general rule in the public drinking place.
Although the bar is typically populated primarily by strangers, interaction is available to all those who choose to enter.

The physical door through which one enters a drinking establishment is a symbolic door as well, for those who come through it declare
by entering that unless they put forth evidence to the contrary, they
will be open for conversation with unacquainted others for the duration
of their stay. Whatever their age, sex or apparent position, their biographical blemishes or physical stigmas, all who enter are immediately
vested with the status of an open person,[2] open both in having the right
to make contact with the others present and the general obligation of
being open to others who may contact them. To decline the status of
being open, to demand that one remain uncontacted requires work of a
particular kind, for the assumption that one will not be contacted by
another without good reason is unfounded within the bar. Those who
desire to avoid the overtures of others must be able to distinguish
themselves from the others present, for the general rule of civil inattention (Goffman, 1963:84;95) is held in abeyance, and not only idle

* Reprinted from Sherri Cavan, *Liquor License* (Chicago, Aldine Publishing Co.,
1966); copyright © 1966 by Sherri Cavan. Reprinted by permission of the author
and Aldine-Atherton, Inc.

[1] Erving Goffman (1963:131–32). This goes beyond the obligation not to snub
the other, requiring that those approached be open to a more protracted interaction.

[2] This is to say, available for interaction with anyone else present. Goffman
(1963: 125–26) says of the old and the very young, who are sometimes defined as
open persons, that they "seem to be considered so meager in sacred value that it
may be thought their members have nothing to lose through face engagement and
hence can be engaged at will." Given the moral repute of the public drinking
place, such might be applicable to the bar patron as well.

glances at other patrons but also idle glances at features and fixtures of the establishment all convey one's openness. There are no protective goods, no newspapers, letters and books to serve as an alternative form of involvement.[3] If such props are used, they may themselves serve as grounds for initial overtures of sociability.

> A middle-aged woman was sitting by herself, thumbing through a large book of Steinberg cartoons. A man sitting at the other end of the bar came over, asked her what she was looking at and then joined her.[4]

Not infrequently, what would pass for civil inattention in other settings is taken as an invitation for interaction in the bar. Thus in most cases entering patrons are either completely ignored, remaining entirely unacknowledged by those already present, or they are gazed at in such a way as to be extended an invitation to join or at least to respond to the gazer.

In most establishments in San Francisco, the physical bar structure forms the center of social gravity, and it is here that the greatest amount of contact occurs between strangers on the premises. Thus one solution to the problem of setting oneself apart from the sociability of the establishment is to avoid the bar itself and sit at the tables and booths available for just this purpose. But it is rare to find solitary individuals seated at tables and booths. In most instances it is couples or larger groups desiring to remain self-contained who utilize the seating facilities away from the bar. Those solitary individuals who do locate themselves away from the bar are generally assumed to be waiting for someone, and they often give such a reason for their choice of seating.

> There were about ten empty stools at the bar; one couple and a number of larger groups were seated at the tables and booths. A solitary male entered, stood by the door for a moment, and then went to sit at one of the vacant tables. When the cocktail waitress came over to him he said in a very audible voice, "Oh, I might as well order while I wait."
>
> I had been sitting at one of the tables by myself for about a half hour when the cocktail waitress came over to me in a rather matter-of-fact manner and asked, "Are you waiting for Jack Wilson?"

The solitary individual who desires to remain alone for the duration of his stay will ordinarily seat himself at the bar, like those who are more open for interaction, but he will sit in a particular posture. Unlike those who are open for interaction, the solitary drinker typically minimizes the amount of physical space he takes up at the bar. He will sit with his forearms either resting on the edge of the bar, or flat on the bar before him, his upper torso hunched slightly forward over the bar, with all of his drinking accoutrements (drink, cigarettes, change, ash-

---

[3] See Goffman (1963:138–39) on the use of such devices in open regions.

[4] Quoted materials, unless otherwise cited, are excerpts from field notes.

tray, and the like) contained within the area before him. The area delimited by the inner sides of his arms defines his visual focus as well, for transitory eye contact is not defined as civil inattention in the public drinking place; if the solitary patron is caught in eye contact by another, his whole posture may be discredited. While eye contact is not a necessary prelude to an encounter in the public drinking place, it is sufficient to discredit the display that is used to decline the status of being open.

The encounters begun among the unacquainted in public drinking places, like those in any other setting, have variable careers. They may remain momentary interchanges, or may develop into something more, perhaps even into a lifelong relationship which transcends the setting itself. But most remain momentary interchanges. The corollary to the rule that no patron is a priori exempt from overtures of sociability on the part of any other patron is the rule that no patron is a priori committed to an encounter with any other patron. Just as it requires active work for patrons to decline the definition of being open for interaction, so too does it require active work for them to maintain an encounter once it has begun.

Most encounters between unacquainted patrons begin with a "remark," a brief, casual statement which, while it is directed to alter by ego, requires no verbal response from alter. These remarks are usually commentaries on the present scene which carry with them the option of either a verbal counter-remark or a gestural acknowledgment that the first remark has been put forth. The choice of response which alter makes to ego's remark is taken to indicate whether an encounter of more than momentary duration can be expected between them there and then. If alter replies verbally, an exchange of interchanges, and hence an encounter of more than momentary duration, will have begun; for while alter has an option in his choice of response to ego's original remark, ego, once he has put himself forth by his first remark as one seeking an encounter, has no similar option with respect to alter's counter-remark. He is expected to reply to it verbally. But after ego's verbal reply to alter's counter-remark, the extent of the encounter between them is variable. All other things being equal, the encounter may be terminated by either ego or alter at any time after this third statement has passed between them.

If, on the other hand, alter merely responds to ego's remark with a nod, a glance, or a tentative smile, the response will be taken by ego to indicate alter's reluctance to engage in any prolonged encounter between them at that time. But alter's gestural response to ego's remarks does not carry with it alter's absolution from any further remarks directed to him by ego. After a period of grace, and if the two remain within communication distance,[5] ego may direct another remark to alter without fear that he will be characterized by alter as

[5] This is equivalent to about three bar stools.

"pushy." Thus it is possible for an entire afternoon or evening to be composed of such partial encounters of remarks and gestural responses between two patrons, for alter, by his presence in the public drinking place, has forfeited any claim to an order which would provide him with a basis for indignation in the face of continued remarks directed to him by ego.[6]

While remarks are statements directed specifically to another within communication distance, bar encounters between the unacquainted may also begin by "declaractions." Declaractions are quite like remarks in content, but they are made to the collectivity at large rather than to any specific patron. Frequently, declaractions have the appearance of being made to the bartender, but they are typically made when the distance between the person making the declaraction and the bartender exceeds the customary communication distance. Hence the declaraction must be made in a loud and clear voice which is audible to all.

Like remarks, declaractions are used for the initiation of encounters. However, since they are made to the collectivity at large, they require no response from any specific patron. Unlike the remark, they can be completely ignored and do not require a gestural response even from those in the immediate vicinity of the person making the declaraction. In part because they do not require or elicit any response (unless an encounter is to develop from one patron's declaraction), they are generally one-shot attempts. Once a patron has made a declaraction, usually he will not make another unless a verbal response is forthcoming.

Terminations

No matter who initiates an encounter, either person may terminate it at any time, unless one participant has lessened the physical distance between himself and the other or has been made the recipient of a gift drink. The general rule that either participant may terminate may thus make those present more amenable to entering an encounter in the first place, insofar as withdrawal cannot easily be construed as an offense to either participant. (See Goffman, 1953:161.)

Since the public drinking place is defined as an area where all present are mutually open, anyone has the right to initiate contact with anyone else and those so contacted are obliged to accept such contact. The patterns of social distance which are predicated upon and in return support a hierarchal order of statuses are legitimately ignored. Whatever statuses of regard or disregard patrons might claim or be accorded outside the setting are effectively held in abeyance for the duration of their stay, making everyone present the social equal of everyone else and

---

[6] In some respects, many of the features of participant accessibility which are present in the public drinking place are present on the ocean liner as well—but not all. Apparently those on the ship still maintain a general right to be absolved from contact with others. *Cf.* Amy Vanderbilt, 1960:667–68.

absolving all of the necessity of paying deference to any apparent social position.

At the same time, little deference need be paid to any pre-existing relationships. The majority of patrons are strangers who are not merely unacquainted but are not likely to become acquainted outside the bar. Their lives generally have little overlap beyond their mutual presence in the immediate setting. But even for those whose lives outside the public drinking place are tangential or interrelated, their mutual openness, by divesting them of social position in relation to each other, abridges any relationships that might exist. Consequently, participation in bar encounters is not predicated on any claims or considerations associated with pre-existing positions or relationships that require showing an interest where no interest exists. There is, as it were, no effective pre-existing commitment to require maintenance of an encounter beyond the point of waning interest. Hence there are no proprieties that automatically allocate to one participant or another control over the termination of an ongoing encounter.[7]

Occasionally, encounters in public drinking places are terminated in ceremonial fashion, similar to the ceremonial terminations of encounters outside the bar. Patrons whose interest in the encounter has waned, or who must leave because their future time is committed to some other activity or setting, may await an appropriate moment—a moment which allows the other to ratify the impending termination—and then say, "Well, it's been nice talking to you. I have to leave now. Hope to see you again," and leave the premises with a final nod and a smile to the other. But more frequently encounters in public drinking places are terminated by much less explicit leave-taking ceremonies, whether or not the participants may be leaving the premises.

Generally, this leave-taking is not accompanied by any verbal statements. For example, if a patron is leaving the premises or changing his location within the establishment, the termination of an ongoing encounter may be signified only by the patron gathering up his possessions from the bar (change money, cigarettes, matches, etc.). Such activity is usually understood by the other to mean that the encounter has come to an end, although nothing may have been said before the activity started and nothing may be said afterward. Talk simply ceases when the collection of goods and possessions begins. He who is about to move may offer the other a curt nod as he gets up, but this is not obligatory and frequently not possible. Typically, the other will become involved in some activity such as finishing his drink, lighting a cigarette, or instigating an encounter with another, permitting ego's departure to occur silently and unobtrusively. However, unless one verbally declares before he physically moves that he will socially return (as, for example, saying, "I'm just going to the bathroom," or "I only want to get a pack

[7] Where hierarchal statuses are effective, the superordinate usually controls the termination procedures. Cf. Pear, 1939:57.

of cigarettes"), even temporary departures are conventionally read as having effectively terminated the encounter.[8] Once the other has returned to the spatial proximity the two share, any further talk between them requires the same ceremonial opening that began the initial conversation.

While bar encounters are most frequently terminated by spatial separation, they may be ended by nothing more than mutual silence. As a practical problem, such termination silence is often difficult to distinguish from a conversation lull. Both have the same form—moments of mutual silence which exist within ongoing encounters. This is particularly true for patrons seated along the bar, since encounters begun between patrons seated side by side may involve only sporadic eye contact, if any. The absence of sustained eye contact precludes any decisive termination by means of discontinuing such contact. Becoming involved with one's drink or toying with a glass or ashtray is equally ambiguous, for such activities are frequently used to smooth over routine conversational lulls as well. Thus both conversation lulls and actual terminal silences pose a question for the participants: Is an encounter between them still in progress? There is nothing to indicate whether the quietness shows a loss of interest in the topic under discussion or a loss of interest in the encounter as such.

The solution is usually to treat all moments of mutual silence in ongoing encounters as termination points, a solution which generates the peculiar tenor of bar conversation. As noted before, the termination of one encounter does not preclude the instigation of another with a given patron as long as he remains within conversational distance. After a period of grace, either patron has the option of putting forth a new remark as a means of beginning a new encounter. But since conversation lulls are typically treated as if they were termination points, the interaction between two patrons in a public drinking place, whether it represents one continuous encounter or a series of sequential encounters, routinely has the patterns of remark/ counter-remark/ interchange/ silence/ remark/ counter-remark/ etc. Silences are thus treated as if the other participant had physically departed and another patron were now in his place, that is, as if a totally new encounter had begun.

This characteristic form of bar encounters affects their substantive content as well. Since remarks are the most casual and general of statements, the topics of discussion they generate are equally casual and general. The typical topics (such as the weather, spectator sports, popular music and gossip) require little beyond personal interest to sustain them and have little, if any, consequential import for the daily lives of the discussants. Even topics which could be treated on a less casual and more specific level customarily remain general. Bar talk is

[8] Goffman (1953:162) notes that informal encounters frequently are ended by such spatial separation of the participants, and if they are not ended by such means, at least their ending is confirmed.

essentially small talk, as the following excerpts of bar conversations overheard and engaged in attest:[9]

Three men talked mainly of two men at the far end of the bar playing
poker dice—specifically, how long they had been playing.
    A man and a couple talked for almost fifteen minutes about the
rain and about rain in various communities in which they had lived.
    A woman talked to me for over a half hour on the care, feeding,
personalities, and problems of her four cats.
    The bartender told me about some of the records on the juke box.
(This occurred on a number of occasions in a number of establishments.)
    A woman told us about the comic strip "Peanuts."
    Two men talked about football for almost an hour.
    A man talked to me about how crowded the bar was. (This again
on a number of occasions and in a number of establishments.) [10]

In part, the inconsequential character of the topics of conversations
held in public drinking places ensues from the problem of locating
subjects on which verbal engagements can take place with total
strangers. In the absence of prior information about matters of mutual
interest or knowledge, the more innocuous the topic, the greater the
probability it can serve as a vehicle for talk. The small talk of acquaintances can cover a broader range of subject matter because areas of
mutuality have already been staked out. The small talk of strangers
often revolves around the present scene or current events because these
are among the few areas where there is some probability of mutual
interest or knowledge.

The absence of pre-existing commitments predisposes encounters in
public drinking places to short lives. The mutual openness of bar patrons
also characterizes their encounters and this also shortens the life span
of such interactions. Bar encounters are granted little or no conventional
closure,[11] and just as individuals are defined as open to contact, so are
their encounters defined as open to the participation of others. This is
particularly true of encounters between patron and bartender and
between patrons along the bar, but it is not uncommon to find en-

[9] See Bronislaw Malinowski (n.d.) on "phatic" communication. Erving Goffman
has suggested that the character of such bar conversation might be better described
as "tiny talk."

[10] In a study of English pubs, a frequency distribution of the topics of 157 conversations overheard in a variety of establishments found pubs and drinking the
most frequent single topic (18 per cent) and only 22 per cent of the conversations
revolved around such consequential matters as jobs, money, and war. In the same
study, a similar count made by B. D. Nicholson was quoted in which 37 per cent
of the conversations were on the topic of sports and 33 per cent on serious matters
(money, politics, religion). Mass Observation, 1943:186–87.

[11] By "conventional closure" is meant, in Goffman's terms, "some obligation and
some effort on the part of both participants and bystanders to act as if the engagement were physically cut off from the rest of the situation." (1963:156.)

counters between patrons standing or seated away from the bar also treated as if there were nothing private about them.

> Four of us had moved to one of the booths, where we sat chatting about the music on the juke box, old movies, and a variety of other miscellaneous subjects. During this time, one of the patrons seated at the next booth, a patron passing by from the bar on his way to the bathroom, and two patrons standing behind the booths entered into the conversation for a moment or two, occasionally starting a separate encounter with one of us as well.
>
> P.C. and I had sat down at one of the tables where we could watch the proceedings around the bar. Some of the patrons had organized a limbo line, using the pool cue, and one of the men came over to our table and asked if we wanted to join in. We declined and he went on to say, "Yeah, it's fun to watch the monkeys." A little later one of the other male patrons came over to the table and asked if I would dance with him. Afterward the first man came back to the table, put his arm around me, and began telling us that he was out celebrating tonight.

In the absence of conventional closure, the maintenance of any specific encounter as an ongoing state of talk between a given number of designatable participants becomes problematic. The number of participants in a single encounter can be increased by others who were previously engaged in separate encounters, because the events occurring in one encounter can properly be treated as legitimate stimuli for the invasion and co-mingling by the participants of other encounters. This is often the case when such subjects as sports are under discussion, although any topic can provide grounds for the entrance of others and few topics, if any, are treated as too personal for others to enter.

Sometimes one participant will move from one encounter to another, linking the participants of each into a single encounter. New arrivals who may be acquainted with one or more participants in each group may have the same effect, even though those with whom they are acquainted may not know one another. The bartender is also instrumental in bringing conversational groups together.

> There were nine persons in groups of two and three and singles. A Negro man came in, sat down, and began tapping a coin on the bar. Finally he called to the bartender, who said, "I'm down here serving three people [which he wasn't] and you come in and start that." The Negro man got up and stalked out of the bar. When he left, the bartender said to those present in a general kind of way, "Was that a regular customer?" Everyone laughed and smiled at one another; a few people exchanged remarks with others with whom they had not been talking and then went back to their original encounters.

Occasionally non-patrons will cause two or more previously separate ongoing encounters to become one larger encounter, as in the following example:

A group of three men and the bartender were talking at one end of the bar, and a second group of two men, separated by one bar stool from the first group, were similarly engaged. The beat patrolman came in and stood directly behind the empty stool between the two groups. He said something indistinguishable to the bartender and then turned to the larger group, who had the dice boxes in front of them, and said, "Oh, boy, I see you guys are gambling." Then he started telling them about a recent event at the bar across the street, an establishment apparently of little esteem in the eyes of the patrons of the present place. At this point the second group joined in. After the patrolman left, the bartender left, and the two groups continued talking (on various subjects) for about twenty minutes more and then returned to their separate encounters.

A variety of incidents, scenes, and out-of-the-ordinary events may generate a focus of attention for some or all of the patrons, bringing them momentarily or for a longer time into a single encounter that may either temporarily or permanently dissolve the boundaries of separate, ongoing encounters.

A patron came in with a dog. He told the bartender that the dog had followed him for three or four blocks. After a few minutes he started buying pieces of beef jerky for the dog, making the dog beg before he would give the meat to him. The dog became the focus of attention, and for a little while there was a general discussion among everyone in the bar on the merits of various kinds of dogs.

There were six or seven people sitting around the piano bar (two groups of twos and the rest singles), who seemed to be enjoying the entertainer's playing and singing. After a while one of the patrons at the bar became louder and louder and then began to sing along with the entertainer in such a way that the latter was completely drowned out. Finally the entertainer stood up at the piano and said, "The singer doesn't appreciate having his lines stepped on." This did little to daunt the patron at the bar, but it did result in a conversation among all those at the piano bar, which lasted for about three or four minutes.

A midget had come in and sat down at the bar next to Ruth (a woman in her mid-fifties). He kept looking at her with adoring eyes and every so often would lick his lips or make puckering, kiss-like gestures toward her. Ruth finally got up and left and a few minutes later the midget left. At this time there were five separate groups of patrons, in twos and threes and some alone, spaced along about three-quarters of the physical bar. About five minutes after she left, Ruth returned, very, very angry, and declared, ostensibly to the bartender but in a voice loud enough for everyone to hear, "Oh, I could have hit him. The nerve of him!" After Ruth's declaration there was a good deal of laughter and conversation within the groups, but once she left the bar again, comments such as "She should take what she can get" and "At her age she should be flattered" were made between groups. Then Alice said, "He offered her ten dollars. If that had been me, I would have kicked him and run." By this time all the patrons in the bar were engaged in one large conversation, first about commercial sex and then about other topics. The large encounter continued to contain everyone who remained until about ten minutes after closing time.

When large encounters bring together patrons previously in separate, smaller encounters, sometimes the separate encounters are never resumed, as in the example above. But the participants of the larger encounter may also realign themselves with one another, and when the larger encounter subsequently breaks down into smaller, separate units, these smaller encounters may contain new participants.

In addition to participant drift, ongoing encounters may be altered by participant confiscation. An uninvited participant entering conventional encounters may excuse his intrusion with a ritual preface ("Excuse me, but . . ."), which carries the tacit promise that the newcomer will leave the encounter as he found it. Ongoing encounters in public drinking places, being defined as open to all, do not require any ritual preface from those who enter. Rather, uninvited participants may join without ceremony and may well appropriate one or more of the participants for some other encounter, since the absence of conventional boundaries implies that there is little impropriety associated with such activity.

In summary, the rules governing behavior in public drinking places that facilitate conversation between strangers at the same time hinder the maintenance of encounters between the unacquainted once they have begun. The definition of "open person" accorded to all who enter abridges the deferential order that serves to allocate control and the procedure of terminating encounters, and the definition of encounters as accessible to all holds in abeyance expectations of conventional closure which serve to delimit who is or is not a participant of any given encounter. Thus, while sociability is available to all in the public drinking place, there is little to guarantee that encounters between the unacquainted, once begun, will proceed in a neat and orderly fashion. Rather, from the onset their career is problematic, subject to a variety of contingencies that make them always tentative and often superficial.

The tentative and superficial character of bar conversations is further reinforced by a general expectation that any encounter occurring in a public drinking place will be circumscribed in time and space. One of the general features of bar encounters is that their existence need never be recognized again at another time or in another place. Regardless of the nature of the encounter—whether it was merely a momentary interchange or whether it extended over an entire evening, whether it consisted of no more than an idle chat or whether it consisted of gaming, dancing, or treating as well—in the establishment, or in the same establishment at some other time, the participants are not obliged to recognize one another in any way or make any indication that some form of mutual activity existed between them on a prior occasion. Like spies in alien territory, once out of a bar encounter the participants typically refrain from showing any recognition of the other (Goffman, 1963:113).

Annie and Frank, to whom we had talked a few times at the bar across the street, were seated two stools away. Neither made any indication that they recognized us.

Bill and Al, with whom I had spent about two hours at a bar down the street only a few days previously and who had, on the last occasion, bought me a couple of drinks, were present, standing about four feet from where I was sitting. Neither made any indication they had ever seen me before.

Nick, who had introduced himself to me and with whom I had danced one night, was here, but said nothing to me, nor did he "apparently" recognize me.

Dave, with whom we had spent most of the evening talking the last time we were here, came in with another fellow. They sat down one stool away from us, but Dave gave no indication that he recognized us.

Henry, with whom I had been talking on and off for almost an hour at a bar next door earlier in the evening and who, before he left, had offered a general invitation to my husband and me to "come and have dinner at my place some time" was seated by the door as we entered the bar. He made no indication that he had ever seen me before, much less that he had extended a dinner invitation to us.

Cuts of this kind are taboo in other settings (Goffman, 1963:114–15).

If a new encounter begins between bar patrons who had been engaged in another encounter at some previous time, recognition of that earlier encounter may be expressed. However, the existence of an earlier encounter conventionally carries no greater right to initiate a new encounter in the bar setting than the right already established by the bar patron's openness. And it carries no right whatever to initiate an encounter outside the bar setting.

There may be, in any establishment, a core of regulars whose continual presence in the setting may result in their eventual recognition of each other. But even among such groups, failure to acknowledge the other is neither uncommon nor an impropriety, as the following example indicates:

A group of three or four men and the late-duty bartender were sitting at the far end of the bar, talking. A man came in alone, sat down about three stools away from the group, and ordered. He began his drink, apparently paying no heed to the group at the end of the bar. After about five or ten minutes the late-duty bartender called down to him, saying, "Hey, Fred, aren't you even going to say hello," and the rest of the group laughed at the bartender's statement.

Even where an acquaintance relationship exists for two patrons outside the bar setting, their mutual presence in the public drinking place need not necessarily be acknowledged.

Stan, whom I had met a few times at Morrie's house as well as at another bar, made no sign that he saw me in the bar, either when he came in or when he left, although I was looking right at him.

Whether persons who are acquainted outside the bar will or will not acknowledge one another may be a consequence of the nature of their relationship. Those who fall into the category of "mere" or "casual" acquaintances are apparently less likely to acknowledge others in the bar than are those who consider one another "good friends." This, of course, does not contradict the statement that the openness of patrons in the public drinking place abridges hierarchal relationships that exist outside the setting, inasmuch as those whose relationships are denoted as "friendships" characteristically treat one another on an equalitarian basis in the first place.

Often social acknowledgment will be proffered to those known outside the bar when the one instigating the action is leaving and his impending exit prohibits more than a fleeting nod or perhaps a handshake. The following example comes from a popular bar located in the vicinity of the civic center that draws the majority of its patrons from those who work in the numerous offices in the area.

> Two men and one woman were sitting at one of the tables near the door. They were apparently known to about five or six men who were present, for when these other patrons were leaving they would pause by the table momentarily and nod or shake hands with the two men and then go on through the door. None of these men paid any apparent attention to the group before they were leaving, however, in spite of the fact that the table at which the group was sitting was entirely visible to anyone present.

Thus, as a result of the assumption that the bar is unserious—that it is time out from consequential life—conversations, encounters and acquaintanceships take on a particular flavor. They are in effect trivialized in a way that might appear dangerous or undesirable in more serious settings.

References

GOFFMAN, ERVING
    1963 *Behavior in Public Places*. New York: Free Press.
    1953 "Communication Conduct in an Island Community." Unpublished Ph.D. dissertation, University of Chicago.
MALINOWSKI, BRONISLAW
    n.d. In Supplement I, C. K. OGDEN and I. A. RICHARDS, *The Meaning of Meaning*. New York: Harcourt, Brace.
Mass Observation
    1943 *The Pub and the People*. London: Victor Gollancz.
PEAR, T. H.
    1939 *The Psychology of Conversation*. London: Thomas Nelson & Sons.
VANDERBILT, AMY
    1960 *New Complete Book of Etiquette*. Garden City: Doubleday.

2. The "Friendly" Poker Game: A Study of an Ephemeral Role*

LOUIS A. ZURCHER, JR.[1]

Games, forms of play with consensually validated sets of rules, assist in the socialization and personality formation of the individual. The structure and dynamics of various games often reflect specific traits, values, expectations, and kinds of social control within a given culture. For adults, games may maintain existing societal forms, or resolve perceived conflicts and threats in the social world (cf. Caillois, 1961; Erikson, 1950; Huizinga, 1955; Piaget, 1951; Robbins, 1955; Strauss, 1956; Sutton-Smith and Roberts, 1963).

Card playing apparently continues to be a favorite American game. Though recent statistics are not available, an American Institute of Public Opinion poll (1948), with a national sample, revealed that 56 percent of the respondents played cards either regularly or occasionally, and 19 percent preferred poker. There have been several studies of gamblers, gambling, and gaming behavior (cf. Bergler, 1957; Herman, 1967a; Edwards, 1955), but few studies which seek to determine the social-psychological functions of card playing (cf. Crespi, 1956), and fewer such studies of poker playing (cf. Lukacs, 1963; Martinez and LaFranci, 1969) despite the fact that poker and many of its terms are prominent in our culture. There is no previous study, to the author's knowledge, of the "friendly game" of poker, that regularly scheduled game "among the boys" held alternately in one of their houses for relatively low stakes.

The participants of the friendly game are not gamblers in the social-problem sense of the word. Their game is not part of a commercial enterprise, yet they are drawn together regularly, take their participation

* Reprinted from *Social Forces*, Vol. 49 (Dec., 1970), pp. 173–86. Reprinted by permission of The University of North Carolina Press.

[1] The author expresses his appreciation to William Key, William Bruce Cameron, Erving Goffman and James Henslin, and to Frank Bean, Ivan Belknap, Richard Curtis, Russell Curtis, Robert Cushing, Dale McLemore, and Susan Lee Zurcher for their helpful comments. For the opportunity to have known and interacted with the poker group members, and for the insights they generously offered during interviews, the author is profoundly grateful.

seriously, and usually thoroughly enjoy themselves. What social-psycho-logical functions does the friendly game serve for the participants? What is its attraction? What aspects of society-at-large are reflected in its dynamics?

The structure and some of the social-psychological functions of a friendly game were observed by a participant, yielding an analytical ethnography of the poker group and highlighting the theoretical con-cept "ephemeral role." An ephemeral role is a temporary or ancillary position-related behavior pattern *chosen* by the enactor to satisfy social-psychological needs incompletely satisfied by the more dominant and lasting roles he regularly must enact in everyday life positions.[2]

Procedure

For twelve months the author attended the twice-monthly friendly game of a long-established poker group. He was a "complete participa-tor" in Gold's (1958) classification. That is, he played and the other players did not know they were being observed. No notes were taken during the game, nor were any recording devices used. Though such techniques would have enhanced reliability, they may have disrupted the game. The author did, however, outline his observations immediately following adjournment of the session, and dictated a narrative based on the outline within eight hours.

Recreation, and not detached research was the primary reason for the author's joining the friendly game. However, after the first session he felt that the social dynamics of the game and the manifest benefits of participation for the players were important to record and analyze.

The day after his last game (the day before his departure to a job in another state), the author conducted semistructured individual inter-views with all of the regular players concerning their reasons for play-ing, criteria for selecting new players, socialization processes, group rituals, and group argot.

The Players

The seven "core" players who attended almost every game during the period of observation were all college educated, married, professional men: a lawyer, a college coach, a high school coach, an engineer, a sociologist, a social-psychologist (the author), and an insurance broker. Four had been playing poker together for over ten years, and two others for over five years. They ranged in ages from early thirties to late forties, and all were in the middle, salaried, socioeconomic bracket. Four had been reared and educated in the midwestern city (population 125,000) where the game took place, and where all of the players presently resided. When the friendly game first formed, the players had

[2] For an earlier definition and example of the concept, see Zurcher (1968).

been associated with a small local college. Three of the current players still were employed by the college, each in a separate department. A second common characteristic of the founding members and four of the current members was experience in coaching scholastic athletic teams.

Since three core players, because of job transfers or time conflicts, were going to leave the group, members were actively recruiting "new men." Those new men invited during the course of the observation included, after the author: an accountant, a rancher, a sports writer, a high school teacher, and a purchasing agent. The author had been brought into the group by the sociologist, who was a co-worker at a local psychiatric research facility.

The Setting and Structure of the Game

The games were held twice monthly, between 7:30 P.M. and 12:00 P.M. on Monday nights, in rotation at each of the core player's homes. One of the players hosted the game in a den; the others in dining rooms, kitchens, or spare rooms. Three had purchased commercially produced, green felt covered, poker tables; the others used whatever large table was available. The playing table was surrounded by smaller tables containing ashtrays, and bowls of chips and pretzels. Hot coffee and soft drinks were available throughout the game, but no alcoholic beverages were allowed during the game. Then, after the completion of the "last deal around the table," which started at 12:00 P.M., the hosting player was responsible for a meal of hors d'oeuvres, sandwiches, and desserts.

The evening's leisure was divided into three major components: (1) the informal discussion while waiting for all the players to arrive and the poker chips to be distributed; (2) the game itself; (3) the meal following the game. During the game it was understood that there were to be no "outside" interruptions. There were no radios or television sets playing, no wives serving beverages, no children looking over shoulders. The atmosphere was quite relaxed and the dress casual (although on occasion a member arrived in suit and tie following a business meeting). There was no apparent seating preference around the table except that if there was an empty chair, it generally would be next to a new man.

At the beginning of the game each player purchased $3.00 worth of chips (blue, 25 cents; red, 10 cents; white, 5 cents). One had the option to buy additional chips at any time, although frequently cash was introduced in place of chips. The host player was responsible for being the banker, and also for dragging a dime or so out of each pot to defray the cost of the post-game meal. The betting limit was established at 25 cents, with a three-raise limit. Drawing "light" (borrowing money) from the pot or purchasing chips by check was tolerated.

The general rules of poker were closely followed, but the games played under "dealer's choice" were more varied than in a commercial poker setting. Use of the joker or naming of wild cards was forbidden. Often the "draw" and "stud" games were dealt with the stipulation that the high hand split with the low hand, or the high hand split with the low spade. Rarely, low ball (where low hand wins) was played. Each player seemed to have one or two favorite games which he dealt regularly and which were called "his" games.

Becoming a Member: Selection and Role Socialization

The criteria by which a new man was judged for membership revealed much about the group dynamics and functions. The core players, when being interviewed by the author, reflected about these criteria:

> A fellow coming into the game almost must feel like he's walking into a closed group, because we've been playing together for quite a while. I guess some newcomers leave the game sometimes feeling 'will they ever ask me back again' or 'I don't want to play with that bunch of thieves again.' Sometimes we have fellows join us who we decide we don't want to come back. In particular, we don't like people who slow up the game, or bad players who get wiped out. They have to be capable of playing with the other players, or we don't want them.
>
> In our game the group is the thing. We invite people in who we think are nice persons, and who we can be friends with. That's the important thing. But he has to be more than a nice person. He has to be able to play poker with the rest of us. It's no fun to sandbag a sucker! So to get invited to sit in regularly, we've got to like the person, and he's got to know what he's doing so that he adds to the game and doesn't subtract from it. The group has to be kept in balance. One dud can throw the whole thing out of focus. Another thing, too. In our group, he has to be able to take a lot of teasing, and maybe give out some too. We have a good time teasing each other.

The new man therefore had to be friendly and experienced enough to learn, compete, and to maintain the pace and stability of the game.

Lukacs (1963:58) has observed that "there are a thousand unwritten rules in poker, and continuous social standards and codes of behavior." The new man, as a prerequisite to invitation was expected to know the basic rules and etiquette of poker. He was to be socialized, however, in accordance with the group's idiosyncratic expectations. He was to learn the local rules of the game, the style and tempo of play, and the patterned interactions. In other words, he was not going to be taught how to play poker, but how to be a member of this poker group.

Many of the socialization messages were verbal instructions from the core members, particularly with regard to betting rules, games allowed, quitting time, and borrowing money. Other socialization messages were more subtle, though no less forceful. The player who slowed the pace of the game might hear the drum of fingers on the green felt or an annoyed clearing of the throat. The player who talked too lengthily about a topic unessential to the game might be reminded that it was his deal, or his turn to bet.

The new man would be strongly reinforced for behavior that conformed to the group's expectations by verbal compliment, camaraderie, or a simple but effective "now you've got it!" One new man, for example, unwittingly disrupted the group's unwritten strategy, that of killing large raises from a strong hand by exhausting the three-raise limit with nickel bets. Three of the core players immediately made pleasant comments about the "lack of insurance" in that particular hand. They did not directly admonish the new man for not having enacted his part of the "insurance." When on a later occasion he did carry out the strategy, he was immediately reinforced by a hearty, "good play!" from two core players.

At no point during the entire period of observation did any of the core players show overt anger at a new man's violation of group expectations. They did on a few occasions invoke what appeared to be their most severe sanction, an absence of response cutting the errant player momentarily from group interaction. When, for example, a new man challenged a dealing core player's choice of game, the dealer dealt and the rest continued to play their cards as if the new man had not said a word. On another occasion, when a new man angrily threw down his cards in disgust, two of the core players quietly gathered them up, handed them to the dealer, and there was otherwise a total absence of response.[3] If someone suggested a game be played which was not in the group's repertoire, he would be met with a lack of enthusiasm that was more crushing than any verbal negation could have been.

One of the core players commented about the "silent communication that takes place" within the group:

> We've been playing together for so long that we can read each other's expressions for the opinions that we have about something. If one of the fellows who's new or who is just sitting in for the night does something out of line, there's a quick and silent communication that takes place, and almost simultaneously we know what to do about it. We tease him or we give him instruction or something.

Sometimes the core players united in humorously expressed sanctions of a player's behavior. One new player had committed the cardinal sin of criticizing the play of core members. He had also lectured on the "right way to play poker." As if on cue, a core player deliberately checked his bet and, when the bet came around to him again, laughingly announced he was going to raise (an act which actually was forbidden by the group, as the bettor knew). The new man exploded: "You can't do that! You can't check and then raise! What kind of a game is this!

---

[3] See Goffman (1956) for a description of emotionally "flooding out" from group interaction.

Where did you learn to play poker!" A second core member with straight face replied, "We always do that! We do some strange things in our group!" A third added, "Yes, sometimes we allow ourselves to take back our discards if we think they can improve our hand." A fourth added, "Well, but we have to match the pot first!"

Shortly thereafter, when the man won his first pot, a core member again with straight face asked for 25 percent of the pot to put into the kitty, since "it is a custom that you always donate one-fourth of your first pot in this game." The new man, who was not asked to return, was effectively excluded from the group interaction, even though he was present for the remainder of the evening.

One core player told how novices were covertly appraised:

It's hard to put your finger on it, but there's a secret evaluation of a new player during the game. You know, we look at each other, and seem to be able to come to a conclusion about whether or not we want him to come back and play with us again, even before the game is over. Sometimes we talk about the player after the game, or during the week if we see each other before the next game. But most of the time we know even before that.

Of six new men, including the author, invited to "sit in for a night" three were asked to return. Each of these had manifested during their first night, behavior which corresponded to group expectations and which was openly reinforced. In two cases, the new men at the end of the session were welcomed to "our group" and told where the game would be held two weeks hence. The third man was informed by telephone after some of the core members had "talked it over," and agreed to invite him back. When core members felt unsure about inviting a new man back, or when they were certain that they did not want to invite him back, there was no post-game discussion of the next meeting.

A new man who was being accepted could be observed increasingly identifying himself as a member. During the early hours of the game he would ask questions about specific rules that "you fellows have." In the later hours he might phrase his questions differently, asking what "we" do in certain situations.

The core players clearly seemed to enjoy instructing a new man, overtly and covertly, about their expectations. In fact, his receptivity to those socialization messages was a key criterion for acceptance. A core player expressed how he felt about the socialization process:

I think there is a certain enjoyment in teaching the rules of our game to people that can learn them. It's a kind of pride. Maybe it's a simple pride, but it's still a matter of pride to be able to show other people how to play in our game, when you know all the rules, but they don't.

Once accepted as a core member the individual retained that status even if circumstances precluded his regular participation. This was clearly illustrated when three core members terminated regular attendance. The author was present when the first member announced he was being transferred to a job in another state. The players were eating their post-game meal, when he said:

> I may as well tell you fellows this before you find out from somewhere else. I won't be able to play anymore because I got orders to go to Wisconsin. I hate to tell you this, because I hate to leave my contacts here with all my friends, and especially I hate to leave the poker club.

The group was silent for several seconds, and a few players stopped eating. Finally, one said, sadly, "That's too bad." Several inquiries were made about the specifics of his transfer, and players commented that he would be missed. One added that "the gang won't be the same without you." They talked briefly about the "breaking up of the group," and discussed the importance of starting to recruit new men for permanent positions. As they left, they warmly said goodbye to the departing member, and several of them earnestly asked him to "get in touch" whenever he visited the city. "Remember," encouraged one, "there will always be a chair open for you in the game." The offer of "an open chair" was similarly made to two core members who subsequently had to terminate regular attendance; one of them has played while in town at the time of a scheduled session.

A returning core member was not immune from socialization, however. During the author's participation one returned to "sit in for a night" after an absence of two years. Throughout the evening he inadvertently violated some of the group norms. He started to bet beyond the limit, and he began to deal a game not in the repertoire. One of the core members smilingly reminded him of the norms, and said, "You've been away so long you've forgotten our standing rules." The visitor was gently being resocialized.

Benefits of Membership: Satisfactions from the Ephemeral Role

Participation in the friendly game seemed to provide the individual with several rewarding social-psychological experiences, including opportunities for scripted competition; self- and situation control; event brokerage; normative deception and aggression; micro-institutionalizing; and retrospective conquest.

SCRIPTED COMPETITION: "KNOCKING HEADS"

The criteria for acceptance as a core member included one's ability to "hold his own" in the game. He was not to be "easy" or a "pigeon," but rather should be able to "put up a fight" and maintain the "balance" of the play. The new man was expected to be a competitor, to have "guts" and not be a "feather merchant."

Zola (1964) has pointed out that the importance and relevance of competition to gambling varies with the social context in which it occurs. Competition among the players seemed to be a carefully scripted and central dynamic in the friendly game. Competition involved money, but more importantly accomplishments of skill, daring, and bluffing, as two core players indicated:

> We cut each other's throats while the game is going on. We forget about it after the game, but it's that very competitive part of the game that I enjoy so much. Maybe it's a carry-over from my sports days, but I just like to compete. There aren't many places anymore where I can really get eye to eye with someone and 'knock heads.' A hand starts and you try to get other players to drop out. Then there's just two or three of you left, and you really start putting the pressure on. You can really slug it out, but it's only a game, and you forget about it when you leave the table.
>
> It's sort of like when you were a kid, and you were testing yourself all the time. Poker is like the good old days; you get a chance to test yourself.

Several other observers have reported that competition in gambling, whether against others or "the system," provides individuals with opportunities to demonstrate self-reliance, independence, and decision-making abilities which for some reason or other are unavailable to them in their major life roles (cf. Herman, 1967b; Bloch, 1951; Crespi, 1956; Goffman, 1967). All of the core players were employed in bureaucracies. It may have been that their jobs made impossible the kind of competition, the kind of "testing" that they desired—particularly in the case of those members who had histories of athletic competition. Within the friendly game they could carefully and normatively script for themselves satisfactory and safe competitive experiences.

SELF- AND SITUATION CONTROL: "SHOWING SKILL"

Each of the players was expected to possess considerable skill in dealing, betting, playing his hand, and bluffing. A player who noticeably showed skill was pleased with his accomplishment, whether or not he won the hand. Core members rewarded his demonstration of skill with compliments and verbal recounting ("instant replay") of the action.

Skill was closely related to competition, as illustrated by the following:

> I like to keep a mental file about the way people play. I like to think about how a person acts when he has something, and how I might act myself when I have something, and try and change that periodically. I think about how someone played a hand last time, and then try to figure out what he has by the way he's playing this time. You decide how to play your hand by the way you see others playing. That's the real skill in the game.

It's a beautiful thing to see a guy play a hand of poker well. It's better, of course, if you are the one who's doing it, but it's still nice to watch somebody else make a good bet, play his cards right, and then win. I don't like to lose, but if I've got to lose, I'd much rather lose to someone who's showing some skill in the game than to somebody who just steps into it.

Crespi (1956) pointed out that "skill players of necessity play frequently and by preference with others who are also highly skilled," and that they "seek to demonstrate their mastery of the necessary skills and, if possible, their skill superiority." Zola (1964:255) concurred when he observed in the horse parlor that "the handicapper gains and retains prestige not because of monetary profits or preponderance of winners, but because he demonstrates some techniques of skill enabling him to select winners or at least come close."

Skill, as it appeared in the friendly game, seemed also to be related closely to control over other players, over self (e.g., "poker face"; resisting temptations to bet or draw cards impulsively), and to a large extent over luck. Lukacs (1963:57) considered "the uniqueness of poker to consist of its being a game of chance where the element of chance itself is subordinated to psychological factors, and where it is not so much fate as human beings who decide." Zola (1964:260) extrapolated this interpretation to gambling in general, and felt that it "occasionally allows bettors to beat the system through rational means, and thus permits them to demonstrate to themselves and their associates that they can exercise control, and for a brief moment that they can control their fate . . . (it) denies the vagaries of life and gives men a chance to regulate it." Skill in this sense indeed has a rational character, but also seems to have a kind of magical quality.

EVENT BROKERAGE: "FEELING THE ACTION"

The poker group did not tolerate disruption of the "pace" of the game. Some players commented about the rapid series of "thrills" that were strung together in a night's playing—the thrill of the "chance" and the "risk." Gambling, according to Bloch (1915:217–18), allows the player to "escape from the routine and boredom of modern industrial life in which the sense of creation and instinctive work-manship has been lost. Taking a chance destroys routine and hence is pleasurable." Bergler (1957:117) wrote of the "mysterious tension" that is "one of the pivotal factors in deciphering the psychology of gambling . . . This tension is a mixture, part pleasurable, part painful. It is comparable to no other known sensation." Goffman (1967:155; 185) saw gambling as being most thrilling when it requires "intense and sustained exercising of relevant capacity," and when, as "action," "squaring off, determination, disclosure and settlement occur over a period of long enough time to be contained within a continuous stretch of attention and experience." Each hand of poker met the criteria for "action" and the requirement for "intensive and sustained exercising of relevant capacities" (skill and competitiveness). Central to this process was the opportunity for the player to make decisions concerning his participation in the play, decisions which were perceived to influence the outcome of his "action." Herman (1967b:101) wrote that the function of money, in the context of the gambling institution, is primarily to reify the decision-making process, establishing "the fact of a decisive act" and "verifying the involvement of the bettor in the action."

Both Goffman and Herman, in their discussions of "action" and "decision-making," referred to commercial gambling establishments. However, these factors, particularly as they relate to the stimulation of players and their experiencing of "thrill," were clearly manifested in the friendly game. A core member explained, when the author first joined, "We don't eat sandwiches and things like that during the game, and we don't shoot the bull, because it causes a break in the action." Another remarked, "It's like a new game every hand. There's a new dealer, you get a new set of cards, and it's a whole new ball game. You get your new cards dealt to you and you've got to think all over again what you are going to do with this hand." Each player was a broker of events potentially thrilling to himself and his colleagues.

NORMATIVE DECEPTION AND AGGRESSION: "YOU'RE A LIAR!"

To "bluff" in poker is to attempt by a pattern of betting, physical cues, and playing the cards to deceive other players about the quality of your hand. In poker the bluff is

> not only occasional but constant, not secondary but primary. Like certain other games of chance, poker is played not primarily with cards but with money; unlike other games the money stakes in poker represent not only our idea of the value of cards, but our idea of what the other player's idea of the value of cards might be (Lukacs, 1963:57).

Goffman (1961:38–39) observed that, "assessing a possible bluff is a formal part of the game of poker, the player being advised to examine his opponents' minor and presumably uncalculated expressive behavior."

Bluffing is related to the dynamics of competition, skill, decision-making, and action. Each player attempts to "fake out" the others. By giving the appearance that the cards randomly dealt to him are really something other than what they appear to be, he tries symbolically to control fate. With each succeeding hand the player must decide whether to try to "run one by" or to "play them straight."

Shortly after the author joined the group, he was shown a cartoon sketch of the players that one had drawn. The drawing caricatured the core members at play. They were addressing one another, and strikingly every comment referred to self, others, or the whole group "lying."

In the friendly game, to "lie" or "speed" meant to bluff, and the performance of this act, successful or not, brought great pleasure to all, as indicated by the following interview responses:

> I really enjoy slipping one by the other guys . . . Putting one over on them—that's *really* a great feeling. I get a kick out of that.
> I like the teasing that goes on in the game. You can say things there to people that you couldn't say elsewhere. I tell one of the other players he's a damned liar, for example, and he might take offense at that under other circumstances. But here it's almost a form of endearment. You'll say something to the rest like 'nobody here is telling the truth. Everybody is a phony.' Well, some of the guys may hit you on the head with something if you said that anywhere else.

To be called a "liar" or to be accused of speeding was a compliment, a sign that one could engage in the intense personal interaction that bluffing stimulated. The game, and particularly the bluff, established the kind of "focused gathering" that Goffman (1961:17–18) described as providing "a heightened and mutual relevance of acts; an eye to eye ecological huddle" quite generative of a gratifying "we rationale."

Core members often discussed their ability to catch one another "speeding," and the cues that would give fellow players away:

> When he puts a big stack of chips on his cards like that, I know he's bluffing. . . . When he puffs his pipe like that, he's trying to speed. . . . He's got that funny look in his eye. . . . When he says, 'I don't know why I'm doing this' or 'I must be stupid to stay in this,' you better look out.

Lukacs (1963:57) commented, "Since the important thing to poker is not the cards but the betting, not the value of the player's hands but the player's psychology, as one gets to know the habits, the quirks, the tendencies, the strengths, the weaknesses of the other players, the play becomes increasingly interesting."

To be caught speeding and then teased as a liar seemed to be a *rite de passage* for a new man. On his first night, a new player was caught attempting to bluff and lost to a better hand. The men burst into laughter, and a core player loudly commented, "Now you're a member of this thieving group! You've been caught lying! Trying to speed, huh? Now you're one of us!" The new man was asked to return for subsequent sessions.[4]

On the other hand, not to have the capacity or inclination to bluff, or to be considered "honest," was flatly an insult. A new man in exasperation asked during his first and only night why it was that everyone dropped out whenever he initiated a bet or a raise. A core player shook his head and responded, "because you are too honest."

[4] The "liar" in the poker group seems honorifically similar to the "handicapper" in horse playing (cf. Zola, 1964:255).

This was said unsmilingly, and was based upon the new man's tendency to bet only when he had cards to validate the size of his bet. He was not inclined to bluff or lie. He was *too* predictable. One didn't have to read subtle cues or study the pattern of his play in order to approximate whether or not he was speeding or "for real." Potentially, he was a "pigeon" who would destroy the group "action."

Ironically, a player had to be caught bluffing if others were to know that he was a "speeder." Once caught and appropriately teased, he established his potential for speeding and further stimulated the intense personal interaction, competition, and opportunity for cue-reading skill that generated from the bluff. In essence, the speeder contributed to the uncertainty in the game and to cognitive imbalance for the players. The resolution of this uncertainty and cognitive imbalance seemed to be pleasurable and thus rewarding.

When a core player was caught in a particularly gross bluff, there were comments from others about historically memorable "lies," and the former culprit, if present, was again teased for his attempt. Usually someone would add, "Well, that's a time we caught him. Nobody knows how many times his lying is successful!" The uncalled winner does not have to show his hand in poker, so players are never really certain when he was bluffing. A common poker strategy used occasionally in the group is deliberately to be caught bluffing so that on subsequent occasions the relation between betting and hand strength is less clear.

The lie can also be interpreted as an opportunity to engage safely in behavior which might be considered "deviant" according to norms outside the friendly game.[5] "Honesty" became a negative attribute and "dishonesty" became a positive attribute. A fellow player could be called a liar and he would laugh. To have called him such in public would probably have invited anger. Within the game, delimited aggression and deception were normative and functional.

MICRO-INSTITUTIONALIZING: "ALMOST A LAW"

Ritual, magic, and tradition, complexly interrelated, have often been described as central components in human play. That component complex is present in poker, and was dramatically apparent in the friendly game. In addition to the more explicit rules governing play discussed above, there were instances of at least implicit "rules of irrelevance." According to Goffman (1961:19–21), rules of irrelevance are an important aspect of focused interactions. They strengthen idiosyncratic norms and the cohesion and "separateness" by declaring irrelevant certain characteristics of the participants or setting which may have considerable saliency in the world "outside."

[5] For a relevant treatment of group norms for deviance, see Erikson (1962).

In the friendly game, even though a player's occupational status may have had some influence in his being invited that status became irrelevant. The author was, for example, asked by a new man what his occupation was. Before he could answer, a core player laughingly but nonetheless forcefully exclaimed, "Right now he's a poker player, and it's his deal!"

Although all the core players were married, family roles were also deemed irrelevant. One might talk about family problems or items of mutual interest in the "socializing" before the game began or during the meal after the game but certainly not in the game. The mere presence of wives or children was prohibited, and even the thought of allowing wives to play was, as one core player summarized it, "horrible!" Another commented, "My son would like to come and watch us, but I won't let him. It's kind of an invasion of privacy, and you don't want *people* to be butting in at times like that."

During the game virtually all topics of conversation not appropriate to the action were deemed irrelevant. "My wife asked me what we talk about when we play cards," observed a core player. "I tell her we don't talk about anything, we play cards. She can't understand that, because they gossip when they play bridge. But they aren't really playing a game then." On one occasion a core player worriedly interjected, "My God, how about this war in Viet Nam!" The others were silent for a few seconds, then one answered, "Whose deal is it?" The player who had commented about the war continued his statements, and quickly was interrupted by another who somewhat sternly though not angrily advised, "I didn't come here to hear you give a speech. I came here to play poker. I could give a speech myself you know." "Who will sell me some chips," inquired another, and the game continued.

Along with the accepted and expected verbal interactions of teasing and "game talk," the players enjoyed, indeed institutionalized, a core member's occasional references to the sagacity of his grandfather as a poker player. Whenever he was facing a particularly difficult decision, he would lean back in his chair, puff on a cigar (all but one of the players smoked either pipes or cigars during the game), and reflectively comment, "Well, my grandfather used to say," (for example) "never throw good money after bad." Often other players would make similar statements when they were faced with problem situations. The "grandfather" quotes had reference to betting, bluffing, soundness of decision, or competition. The content of the messages might accurately be described, as suggested by an interviewee, as "a poker player's Poor Richard's Almanac." The quotes seemed to be an important mechanism for bringing into the friendly game, as a lesson of a wise, "pioneer" man, considerations of the Protestant Ethic. The advice of grandfather was often cited to new men, thus serving a socialization function.

The verbal rituals, rules of irrelevance, and various behavioral taboos seemed to support valued group dynamics. The no-alcohol rule, for example, was adopted early in the group's history when an inebriated player had disrupted the pace. Similarly, the no-eating rule was inaugurated when players were observed to drop cards, or get them sticky. A number of specific games or methods of playing split-pot games were outlawed because they had in the past caused anger among players.

Although the players stressed the use of skill, particularly as a manifestation of control over fate, they also invoked what Malinowski (1948:38; 88) called "practical magic," primarily in an attempt to control the flow of cards or to change their luck. They would, for example, talk to the deck, urging it to give them good cards; rap the table with their knuckles just before receiving a card; slowly "squeeze out" a hand dealt to them, particularly after having drawn another card or cards, in order to "change the spots"; make a "fancy cut" as a luck changer; bet a hand "on the come" or "like you had them," as a means of guaranteeing getting the card or cards desired; deal a different game in order to "cool off" or "heat up" the deck; get up and stretch, or get a cup of coffee, in order to "change the way the money is flowing on the table"; stack their chips in a "lucky" way. On one occasion a player reached over and disordered another's chips, laughingly saying, "That should change your luck! You're winning too much!" [5]

The most striking example of magical behavior within the friendly game was the clearly understood and always followed rule that a player must bet fifteen cents, no more and no less, on the first face-up ace he received in a hand. It was agreed that if one did not follow this rule he would "insult the ace" and would inevitably lose. No one seemed to know where the "rule" originated, but all followed it and made a point of instructing new men to do likewise. Three members specifically referred to the fifteen-cent rule when interviewed about "specific rules." "I don't know why we do that," commented one, "but that's our precious ritual. I do remember one time I forgot to bet in that way, and by God I lost!" The second member thought betting fifteen cents on the ace was "a funny rule, but still a rule." The third man referred to the fifteen-cent bet as "almost a law. It's stupid, I guess, but it makes the game more fun." In this case, the magic served not only the function of insuring against possible loss but also as another contributor to group cohesion. It may have been a "stupid" law, but it was "our" law.

The meal following the game might be considered a ritual feast. The strict poker rules and interactions were loosened, and the players discussed various topics deemed inappropriate during the game itself.

[5] For a fascinating discussion of such behavior among craps shooters, see Henslin (1967).

Retrospective Conquest: "If I Had Only . . ."

In the friendly game, winners necessitate losers. Unlike forms of betting games in which the participants play against the "house," not every player in poker can win.

The most a member could win or lose was approximately $30.00. Generally, there was one "big winner," one "big loser," and the rest were distributed in between. One core player was a "big winner" more often than the others, but not enough to disrupt the balance of the group. There was no consistent "big loser." All of the members were in approximately the same income bracket, and thus winning or losing $30.00 had a similar impact upon them. Goffman (1961:69) pointed out that if betting is low relative to the financial capacities of the players, interest may be lacking in the game and they may not take it seriously. If conversely players feel that betting is too high then interest may be "strangled" by concern for the money they could lose. The core members understood the impact of someone who "couldn't afford to lose" or "didn't care about losing." In their view the former "makes you feel guilty if you win," and the latter "is no challenge, because if he's not really losing anything, you're not really winning anything." It was important that the financial conditions of the players be such that they maintained the dynamic equilibrium of the group.

The players knew that someone had to lose and inevitably at times it would be themselves. All agreed it was better to win than lose, but losing was not a disgrace so long as one did so through no lack of skill. For the member who had "played well" but nonetheless ended up a loser at the end of the evening the group offered and accepted several rationalizations, most commonly sympathizing about a plague of "second-best hands." This meant that the loser had played his cards well, "knocked heads" to the very end, and then come up with a slightly inferior hand. In essence, the cards were being blamed for his loss. It was no fault of his, because he "played well." When a player of this quality lost, luck was the culprit. But, when he won, it was by virtue of his skill; luck had nothing to do with it.

The core members looked with disfavor upon anyone who won by luck alone. A skillful player might invest some money early in a hand, but should not consistently "ride the hand out" hoping subsequently to be dealt some good cards. He should assess the odds, appraise through observation of cues and actions the quality of others hands, and if evidence warranted he should decide to drop out and take his temporary loss.

Those who had lost a hand were often seen to "relive" the play. They would utter such statements as: "I figured that you . . ."; "If I hadn't thrown away those . . ."; "All I needed was another spade and . . ."; "I thought you had three of a kind because you were betting . . ." Zola (1964:256) observed this phenomenon, which he called "the hedge," in the horse parlor, and described it as a means of maintaining some status even when losing. The loser would give a series of reasons why he lost, and how he wouldn't have if he had done some minor thing differently.

Goffman (1967:247) pointed out instances where in competitive interactions "both parties can emerge with honor and good character affirmed." This opportunity was clearly provided in the friendly game for those players who would "knock heads." There was potential in that situation for a "good winner" and one or more "good losers."

If a core player clearly had made a blunder, he would be teased by the others. Often the blunderer, in defense, would narrate a blunder historical for the group, whether made by himself or some other player. "Remember the time when Joe bet like crazy on his low hand because he thought the game was high-low split, and it was a high hand take all!" Considerable detail would be shared about the nature of the epic mistake. The current blunderer effectively would have anchored his own current error on a point somewhere less gross than a historical one. The core players appreciated and were comforted by the fact that all of them made mistakes. As one interviewee pointed out, "Nobody likes to play poker against a machine."

The player who had lost despite his skill might choose some other form of rationalization. He might consider the evening to have been "cheap entertainment," or "the cost of some lessons in poker." He might indicate that it was "his turn to lose tonight," or he had "let the host win." Nobody ever really complained about losing (although frustration was expressed concerning "second-best hands"). "I have more fun *losing* in this group," commented a core member, "than I do *winning* at roulette, or something like that."

The amount of money won or lost was discussed only in the most off-hand manner. Specific figures were seldom mentioned, only estimates given, and then only sporadically and without pattern by different players. A core member reflected,

> At the end of the evening the game is over. Who cares how much you win or lose on one evening because each of us wins or loses, and it balances it out. It's each hand during the game that counts, and whether you win or lose that hand. The overall thing doesn't mean as much.

The money, out of the context of group interaction, seemed unimportant.

Conclusions: The Ephemeral Role

The core members perceived themselves to be in a "different world" when they were playing. The friendly game, with its idiosyncratic roles, norms, rituals and rules of irrelevance, maintained clearly established boundaries. New men were selected carefully, and anyone or anything that disrupted the group dynamics or reduced the satisfactions experienced was eliminated or avoided. The players testified to their awareness that the poker group was "separate" from their other, broader, day-to-day social relationships:

> I look forward every other Monday to getting away from it all. I can do that when I'm playing poker with the guys. I forget about my job, and other problems that I have, and I can just sort of get lost in the game.
> It's a chance to get away from our wives and families. Every man needs a chance to get away from that once in awhile.
> When that first card hits the table, it's like we're on an island, you know, all to ourselves. Nobody bothers us. You're your own man! I miss it whenever we have to cancel a game for some reason or another.

In this sense, the friendly game seemed, as did Zola's (1964:248–49) horse parlor, to allow the players to effect "disassociation from ordinary utilitarian activities."

Goffman (1961:36; 67–68) described a "gaming encounter" as having social participants deeply involved in a focused interaction, and as such has "a metaphorical membrane around it." When the core players had all arrived, they formed the metaphorical membrane, and the friendly game became "a little cosmos of its own" (Riezler, 1941:505). Within the group boundaries, each member enacted the "ephemeral role" of core member, providing him the opportunity for scripted competition, self- and other-control, event brokerage, normative deception and aggression, micro-institutionalizing, and retrospective conquest. More specifically it provided him with the following opportunities for satisfaction: to share in the establishing and/or maintaining of a personally relevant group structure and interaction pattern; to compete vigorously but safely with equals; to bluff, tease, or otherwise "one-up" equals; to demonstrate and be admired for skill in betting and playing; to become deeply involved in intense but controlled personal interaction; to read, analyze, and utilize cues emitted from other players; to control and become immersed in action, including a series of thrills and the exhilaration of "pace"; to enjoy the fellowship of a chosen and mutually developed primary group; to exert control over self, others and luck or fate; to capture or relive some of the competencies and freedoms of youth; to reaffirm one's masculinity; to enjoy legitimized deviancy; to implement, in rapid succession, a great number of significant decisions; to declare as irrelevant, norms and roles which society-at-large deems mandatory in favor of idiosyncratic group norms and roles; and to escape the routine and "ordinary" social dynamics of everyday life.

The core member appeared to enter and leave the metaphorical membrane and ephemeral role through two buffer zones structured into the friendly game. The first buffer zone was the pre-game socializing period during which players waited and discussed various topics until all had arrived. The transition from everyday social interaction to the contrived interaction in the game, the "easing" into the ephemeral role, was facilitated by this short delay. Players who had arrived late and thus missed the socializing period were heard to comment, for example, "give me a second to shift gears," or "let me put on my poker hat."

The other buffer zone, the meal after the game, served a similar function. The players then were behaving as members of any other group sitting down to have a snack together. The topics of conversation were unrestricted, and only rarely and briefly were any comments made concerning the game itself. During that period of the evening, the players were being "eased back" into their day-to-day complex of social roles.

Those who could not make the transition into the ephemeral role were disruptive to the group. This happened on only two occasions observed by the author. The first occasion involved a new man whose home had some months before been destroyed by a severe tornado. Shortly before the game had begun a tornado watch had been announced for the area; the sky was heavy with clouds and the wind was noticeably increasing. The new man kept looking over his shoulder and out of the window, rose several times to walk to the front porch and look up at the sky, and twice dropped out of the game to phone his wife. A core player commented, in an uncriticizing manner, "Your mind is wandering, isn't it." The distracted man commented that since he was "so nervous" it might be a "good idea" for him to go home. The group quickly agreed with him, and he left. A minute or so later a core player announced, "Okay, let's settle down and play some poker," and the game went on.

In the second incident, a core player seemed to be distracted throughout the game. He told short jokes, talked about "irrelevant" topics, and generally slowed down the pace. "What the hell's the matter with you!" inquired another. "Why are you so talkative tonight?" The reasons for his behavior were not clear until later, during the meal, when he announced that he was being moved to another area and would no longer be able to participate. He apparently had found it difficult to enact fully the ephemeral role, since he realized he would no longer be part of the friendly game. His distraction by the world "out there" had distracted the other players. As Goffman (1957) observed, in a gaming encounter "the perception that one participant is not spontaneously involved in the mutual activity can weaken for others their own involvement in the encounter and their own belief in the reality of the world it describes."

Core member of the friendly game is only one example of an ephemeral role. Other examples might include such diverse behavioral patterns as LSD "tripper," encounter "grouper," adulterer, volunteer work crew member (Zurcher, 1968), vacationer, weekend fisherman, or whatever is intense and intermittent and defined in contrast to one's day-to-day social world. Hopefully, we may see more systematic and comparative studies showing why people choose to develop or enact specific ephemeral roles, the satisfactions they gain, and the relation between ephemeral roles and major "life" roles.

References

American Institute of Public Opinion
  1948 "The Quarter's Polls." *Public Opinion Quarterly* 12 (Spring):146–76.
BERGLER, E.
  1957 *The Psychology of Gambling.* New York: Hill & Wang.
BLOCH, H. A.
  1951 "The Sociology of Gambling." *American Journal of Sociology* 57 (November):215–21.
CAILLOIS, R.
  1961 *Man, Play and Games.* New York: Free Press.
CRESPI, I.
  1956 "The Social Significance of Card Playing as a Leisure Time Activity." *American Sociological Review* 21 (December):717–21.
EDWARDS, W.
  1955 "The Prediction of Decisions Among Bets." *Journal of Experimental Psychology* 50 (September):201–14.
ERIKSON, E.
  1950 *Childhood and Society.* New York: Norton.
ERIKSON, K.
  1962 "Notes on the Sociology of Deviance." *Social Problems* 9 (Spring):307–14.
GOFFMAN, E.
  1967 *Interaction Ritual.* Chicago: Aldine.
  1961 *Encounters: Two Studies in the Sociology of Interaction.* Indianapolis: Bobbs-Merrill.
  1957 "Alienation from Interaction." *Human Relations* 10 (February):47–60.
  1956 "Embarrassment and Social Organization." *American Journal of Sociology* 62 (November):264–71.
GOLD, R.
  1958 "Roles in Sociological Field Observation." *Social Forces* 36 (March):217–23.
HENSLIN, J. M.
  1967 "Craps and Magic." *American Journal of Sociology* 73 (November):316–30.
HERMAN, R. D. (ed.)
  1967a *Gambling.* New York: Harper & Row.
  1967b "Gambling as Work: A Sociological Study of the Race Track." In R. D. HERMAN, ed., *Gambling.* New York: Harper & Row, pp. 87–104.
HUIZINGA, J.
  1955 *Homo Ludens, The Play Element in Culture.* Boston: Beacon Press.
LUKACS, J.
  1963 "Poker and American Character." *Horizon* 5 (November):56–62.

MALINOWSKI, B.
  1948 *Magic, Science and Religion.* New York: Doubleday.
MARTINEZ, T. M., and R. LAFRANCI
  1969 "Why People Play Poker." *Trans-action* 6 (July-August):30–35; 52.
PIAGET, J.
  1951 *Play, Dreams and Imitations in Childhood.* New York: Norton.
RIEZLER, K.
  1941 "Play and Seriousness." *The Journal of Philosophy* 38 (September):
        505–17.
ROBBINS, F. G.
  1955 *The Sociology of Play, Recreation and Leisure Time.* Dubuque: Brown.
STRAUSS, A.
  1956 *The Social Psychology of George Herbert Mead.* Chicago: University of
        Chicago Press.
SUTTON-SMITH, B., and J. M. ROBERTS
  1963 "Game Involvement in Adults." *Journal of Social Psychology* 60 (First
        Half):15–30.
ZOLA, I. K.
  1964 "Observations on Gambling in a Lower Class Setting." In H. BECKER,
        ed., *The Other Side.* New York: Free Press, pp. 247–60.
ZURCHER, L. A.
  1968 "Social Psychological Functions of Ephemeral Roles." *Human Organiza-
        tion* 27 (Winter):281–97.

3. The Social Psychology
of the Gift*

BARRY SCHWARTZ

The Gift as a Generator of Identity

Differential emphasis has been placed upon form and content in social analysis. Simmel's discussion of "sociability" is perhaps the most radical statement on form in social life, for it is with regard to this mode of sociation that content is asserted to be of no consequence (Simmel, 1950:40–55). Goffman expresses a similar idea, the "Rule of Irrelevance," in his essay "Fun in Games." The content of the game, as that of sociability, must be "self-sufficient" or irrelevant to the relationship between players in non-game encounters (Goffman, 1961:19). This is especially true of the gift, over whose contents an excessive display of pleasure or displeasure would affront the giver, violate the Rule of Irrelevance, and take the entire encounter out of the sphere of "pure" sociability.

The rules of self-sufficiency or irrelevance must not be understood to imply that the contents of things can be stripped of their meanings. Thus, despite the principle which subordinates the content or quality of the gift to its significance as a token of the social relationship itself, it is clear that the presentation of a gift is an imposition of identity.

Gifts are one of the ways in which the pictures that others have of us in their minds are transmitted. This point is seen in recurrent controversies over the prevalence of "war toys" on American gift lists. And the function of "masculine" and "feminine" gifts relative to sexual identification is clear enough. By the giving of different types of "masculine" gifts, for example, the mother and father express their image of the child as "a little soldier" or "a little chemist or engineer." Doubtlessly, an analysis of the gift-buying habits of parents would be a significant contribution to our knowledge of socialization. One important aspect of such an investigation would surely focus upon the increasing popularity of educational toys, the bisexual distribution

* Reprinted from *American Journal of Sociology*, Vol. 73 (1967), pp. 1–11. Copyright 1967 by The University of Chicago. Reprinted by permission of The University of Chicago Press and the author.

of which may contribute to and reflect the lessening differentiation of American sex roles.

The gift as an imposition of identity is well seen in its burlesqued form, the "Office Pollyanna," the ideal type of which obtains when gift recipients are chosen at random and presented with inexpensive items which make comical or witty reference to that part of their personal makeup which, in the eyes of the giver, is most worthy of exaggeration.

If gift giving socializes and serves as a generator of identity, it becomes necessary to acknowledge the existence of gifts which facilitate or impede maturation. One way in which upwardly mobile parents cause anxiety in their children is to provide gifts for which they are not yet ready—or even gifts whose level they have long ago outgrown. In this light, regressive possibilities exist on both sides of every gift-giving relationship. What has been implied here is that gift giving plays a role in status maintenance and locomotion. This is illustrated best in the "rites of passage" which gifts normally accompany. In such instances, they not only serve the recipient (e.g., a newlywed) as tools with which to betray more easily his or her former self but symbolize as well the social support necessary for such a betrayal.

The Giver

The gift imposes an identity upon the giver as well as the receiver. On the one hand, gifts, as we noted, are frequently given which are consonant with the character of the recipient; yet, such gifts reveal an important secret: the idea which the recipient evokes in the imagination of the giver. This point enables us to appose to Cooley's recognition of the social looking glass an additional source of self-concept: this is our "ideas of others"—which, when made public, are self-defining. Indeed, gift giving is a way of free associating about the recipient in his presence and sometimes in the presence of others. This principle is recognized by the maker of a last will who is obliged to distribute benefits among two or more persons. The identity he thereby generates for himself is perhaps the most important of a long career of identity pronouncements, for it is his last—and is unalterable.

The act of giving is self-defining in a more direct way. Men tend to confirm their own identity by presenting it to others in objectified form. An extreme instance of this type of self-presentation is the display of masculinity through the giving of gift cigars following the birth of a child. Emerson, in fact, has suggested that this tendency toward self-objectification be made explicit (and in so doing provides insight into that which the new father's gift cigar symbolizes):

> The only gift is a portion of thyself. . . . Therefore the poet brings his poem; the shepherd, his lamb; the farmer, corn; the miner, a gem; the sailor, coral and shells; the painter, his picture; the girl, a hand-

kerchief of her own sewing. This is right and pleasing, for it restores society in so far to its primary basis, when a man's biography is conveyed in a gift. (Emerson, 1936:358.)

It is common knowledge that men present themselves publicly by the conspicuous presentation of gifts. Generous contributions to charity have always been a source of prestige in the United States. This is especially true when such gestures are made by individuals rather than corporations, and has been carried to an extreme by the members of movie society, for whom giving is an aspect of public relations. But professional fund raisers recognize this tendency in general society as well and therefore provide "I Gave" stickers which are generally affixed to the front door as certification of the family's willingness and ability to give away wealth. The charity potlatch is an important mode of the public presentation of self.

In middle- and upper-class society, the wife is a ceremonial consumer of goods, for decency "requires the wife to consume some goods conspicuously for the reputability of the household and its head." (Veblen, 1934:83. See also pp. 84, 149.) Thus, the husband elaborates his identity by the bestowal of gifts upon the wife, who becomes the public exponent of his selfhood. Children, furthermore, are more and more assuming the role of family status representatives as the adult female moves from the social to the economic sphere. The gift presentation of automobiles and other expensive items to children and teenagers testifies to this drift. Of course, the negative side of an excessive giving-receiving ratio in favor of the parents consists of a denial to the child of those rewards to selfhood which accompany the giving of gifts, the chief of which is an image of oneself as a source of gratification to others.

This leads into the interesting area of the giving of gifts to oneself. This is normally spoken of in terms of "self-indulgence," opposition to which, stripped to its essentials, represents an unwillingness on the part of the ego to strike a bargain with the id. This inflexibility is dangerous when other people (as sources of satisfaction) are not available, for it makes adjustment to hostile or impersonal environments unlikely. Deprived of material demonstrations of recognition from others, the internalization of such disregard can only be avoided by the utilization of oneself as a source of pleasure. The "self-gratifier" is an interesting product of the non-intimate community who, despite his pervasiveness, has received little attention from the social sciences. This is the person who, without significant affectional bonds, somehow makes it through life in one piece. He creates his own (emotional) "nutrition" and survives.

Gift Rejection

Earlier, in our treatment of the gift as an imposition of identity, it was suggested that the acceptance of a present is in fact an acceptance of the giver's ideas as to what one's desires and needs are. Consequently, to accept a gift is to accept (at least in part) an identity, and to reject a gift is to reject a definition of oneself. It follows that the receipt of gifts from two incompatible persons or groups raises questions as to the real sources of one's identification.

At another extreme are found outright rejections of gifts with a conscious view to affirming the selfhood whose status an acceptance would threaten. A radical illustration from Ruth Benedict makes this type of reaction clear in our minds:

> Throw Away invited the clan of his friend to a feast of salmon berries and carelessly served the grease and berries in canoes that had not been cleaned sufficiently to do them honor. Fast Runner chose to take this as a gross insult. He refused the food, lying down with his black bear blanket drawn over his face, and all his relatives, seeing he was displeased, followed his example. (Benedict, 1960:175–76.)

The covering of the face suggests that Fast Runner is defending himself against the disparaging definitions of his selfhood which the dirty canoes imply. And from the standpoint of the giver of the rejected gift, we see an immediate world that has somehow lost its dependability. As Helen M. Lynd notes, the giver trusts himself to "a situation that is not there" and is thereby forced to cope with the dilemma of shame.

Gift Exchange: Control and Subordination

Lévi-Strauss has written that "goods are not only economic commodities but vehicles and instruments for realities of another order: influence, power, sympathy, status, emotion; and the skillful game of exchange consists of a complex totality of maneuvers, conscious or unconscious, in order to gain security and to fortify one's self against risks incurred through alliances and rivalry." [1] In other words, the regulation of one's bonds to others is very much part of the matter of the exchange of goods. Similarly, Homans and Malinowski have convincingly argued that men are less constrained in their actions by separate controlling activities and institutions than by obligations which they incur in reference to one another (Homans, 1960:284–92; Malinowski, 1959:58; 59). Furthermore, it is generally true that men maintain ascendancy by regulating the indebtedness of others to them. An exaggerated instance of this is described in Korn and McCorkle's essay on prison socialization:

> Once an inmate has accepted any material symbol of service it is understood that the donor of these gifts has thereby established personal

[1] Claude Lévi-Strauss, 1965:76. Similarly, Michael Polanyi is quoted by Norman Brown: "He [man] does not act so as to safeguard his individual interest in the possession of material goods; he acts so as to safeguard his social standing, his social claims, his social assets" (Brown, 1959:262).

rights over the receiver. The extreme degree to which these mutual aid usages have been made dependent to power struggles is illustrated by the custom of forcing other inmates to accept cigarettes. . . . Aggressive inmates will go to extraordinary lengths to place gifts in the cells of inmates they have selected for personal domination. These intended victims, in order to escape the threatened bondage, must find the owner and insist that the gifts be taken back. (Korn and McCorkle, 1954.)

The principle of reciprocity, then, may be used as a tool in the aspiration for and protection of status and control. William F. Whyte, for instance, notes that the leader takes care not to fall into debt to his followers but to insure, on the contrary, that the benefits he renders unto others are never fully repaid (Whyte, 1964:258). Parents are especially aware of the fact that the child pays the cost of social inferiority when he accepts a gift from them and fails to reciprocate. "What is more," notes Homans, "he may, in becoming an inferior, become also a subordinate: the only way he can pay his debt may be to accept the orders of the giver." (Homans, 1961:319.) This principle is perhaps nowhere better seen than through the character of Santa Claus, the greatest of all gift givers, whose powers of surveillance and ability to grant and withhold benefits are annually exploited by parents as instruments of control over their children.

Santa Claus should not be taken lightly by the sociologist for, as we have seen, he plays an important role with respect to social control.[2] It must also be noticed that he is not only a Christian but a Caucasian—and a blue-eyed Nordic one at that. This has particular significance for the non-Christian and non-Caucasian. That little Jewish boys and girls, for example, must depend upon a blue-eyed Christian for their gifts may lead to many hypotheses concerning the role of the myth in general and of St. Nicholas in particular with respect to ethnic dominance. Most Jewish parents are very aware of Santa's great seductive powers and of his ability to confound the developmental problem of ethnic identification. Therefore, the existence of Santa Claus is sometimes denied straightaway, and in his stead the hero of the Jewish holiday of Hanukkah, Judas Maccabee, is placed. But there is no contest: first of all, Judas is not a gift giver and as such is due neither promises of loyalty nor obedience. Further, there is no connection between the Hanukkah gift and the Maccabees. It is little wonder that Jewish children feel themselves shortchanged in December, for Hanukkah is indeed an imitation Christmas—and the very existence of imitation implies a dominant object and an inferior one. The Hanukkah gift, moreover, lacks the sociological quality of the Christmas present. The former, often given in the form of cash or Hanukkah *gelt*, merely (in Simmelian terms) "expresses the general element contained in all exchangeable objects, that is, their exchange value, it is

[2] For a general discussion of the social role of Santa Claus, see James H. Barnett (1954). See also Warren O. Hagstrom (1966).

incapable of expressing the individual element in them." (Simmel, 1950:390–91.) By contrast, the concrete Christmas present, especially chosen in terms of the personality of giver and receiver, is more specifically reflective of and incorporable into their respective life systems. To this extent, the giver of Hanukkah *gelt* inevitably surrenders to the recipient a measure of control because money, unlike a particular commodity, does not presume a certain life system: it may be used in any way and thus becomes a more flexible instrument of the possessor's volition.

Incidentally, the above point, it seems, is relevant to the area of public assistance, where there has been some debate about whether benefits to the needy should be given in the form of cash or goods. Social workers are more prone to argue in favor of the former alternative, often on the basis of its implications for the psychological autonomy of the recipient. Opponents of this policy argue that the presentation of money severely limits the welfare department's band of control, for cash may be spent on disapproved commodities. Its abstractness dissolves the authority of the giver, which is inherent in concrete items.

Gift Giving as an Unfriendly Act

Once a connection is made between gift exchange and social control, it becomes necessary to explore the possibility of unfriendliness as a component of gift giving. One need not look far before ample evidence for such a possibility is found. Lowell's assertion that "a gift without the giver is bare" implies that sincere affection is not a necessary correlate of gift presentation. But the popular warning, "Never look a gift horse in the mouth," is an even more direct acknowledgment of gifts as expressions of hostility. And the practical joke is an instance of man's need to give gifts which hurt or embarrass the recipient: "hot" chewing gum, cigars that blow up, gift-wrapped boxes containing a replica of a portion of feces, etc., are all purchased with a view to the direct or indirect satisfaction of this need.

The very nature of the gift exchange provides a condition for unfriendliness. Although gift giving is itself rewarding (in ways to be later described), it is accompanied by obvious deprivation as well, for the giver presents to another that which could have been employed for self-gratification. While he may receive a gift in return, there is certainly some loss of personal control over income and output of goods and money. The recipient in this light becomes a depriver about whom various degrees of ambivalence may emerge.

But the most obvious instance of hostility in gift exchange is found in the potlatch, which has as an essential aim the degradation of the recipient. Among the Arapesh, for example, a *buanyin* or exchange partner is assigned in early male adolescence. It is the duty of the *buanyins*, writes Mead, to insult one another continually and to try to outdo one another in gift exchange (Mead, 1962:34–35). But it is the

Kwakiutl who carry this practice to its extreme. Here, the boy who receives his first gift selects another person to receive a gift from him. "When the time came for repayment if he had not doubled the original gift to return as interest, he was shamed and demoted, and his rival's prestige correspondingly enhanced." (Benedict, 1960:169.)

Benedict describes the phenomenon at greater length:

> The whole economic system of the Northwest Coast was bent to the service of this obsession. There were two means by which a chief could achieve the victory he sought. One was by shaming his rival by presenting him with more property than he could return with the required interest. The other was by destroying property. In both cases the offering called for return, though in the first case the giver's wealth was augmented and in the second he stripped himself of goods. The consequences of the two methods seem to us at the opposite poles. To the Kwakiutl they were merely complementary means of subduing a rival, and the highest glory of life was the act of complete destruction. It was a challenge, exactly like the selling of a copper, and it was always done in opposition to a rival who must then, in order to save himself from shame, destroy an equal amount of valuable goods. (Benedict, 1960:172.)

Marcel Mauss was rightly struck by the similarity between the potlatch and conspicuous spending in the twentieth century (Mauss, 1954:4). He neglected, however, to indicate that it was Veblen who had done the most extensive study of "conspicuous waste" in his *Theory of the Leisure Class*. The goals of such waste are essentially those directing the Kwakiutl: extravagant provision of commodities is made with a view to shaming the consumers, especially those who openly compete with the host in such matters as feasts, balls, and other social events (Veblen, 1934:75).

One expresses unfriendliness through gift giving by breaking the rule of approximate reciprocity (returning a gift in near, but not exact, value of that received). Returning "tit for tat" transforms the relation into an economic one and expresses a refusal to play the role of grateful recipient. This offense represents a desire to end the relationship or at least define it on an impersonal, non-sentimental level. An exact return, then, is essentially a refusal to *accept* a "token of regard," which is to Mauss, "the equivalent of a declaration of war; it is a refusal of friendship and intercourse." (Mauss, 1954:11.)

Both gift giver and receiver evaluate presents according to some frame of reference. A giver may therefore express contempt for the recipient by purchasing for him an inferior gift (in comparison with his gifts to others). Thus unfriendliness is shown by the mere invocation of a frame of reference. This mechanism, of course, is what enables the last will and testament to become partly an instrument for the expression of hostility.

We might also mention the object-derogation ritual by means of which the gift to be presented is "cursed." This ritual is reserved especially for those occasions where a presentation of a token of regard is mandatory. Thus children, in relaying a Christmas gift from their parents to the teacher, will feign a spit upon the package—or suggest its use as toilet paper, with an indecent gesture. Such rituals have as their purpose the "contamination" of the item with unfriendly sentiment. The ritual yields its fruit when the teacher accepts the contaminated gift with pleasure and thanks. On the other hand, the recipient may be aware of the contempt of the giver and, though obliged to accept the gift, may prevent contamination by destroying it, failing to use it, forgetting about it, etc.

Gifts may reflect unfriendliness in at least two final ways. First, the gold watch presented at retirement is normally more representative of a feeling of good riddance than of recognition for achievement; it is indeed a gilded "pink slip." Lastly, psychoanalytic theories of symbolism suggest that death wishes may be expressed in such gift objects as electric trains, satin blankets, ships, and other vehicles which take "long journeys." Inasmuch as such theories are valid, the popularity of electric trains as Christmas gifts has enormous implications.

Unfriendliness in the Recipient

What has been said about unfriendliness in gift giving should not draw attention away from hostility in the receiver. Ralph Waldo Emerson reminds us of this point in his essay:

> The law of benefits is a difficult channel, which requires careful sailing. . . . We wish to be self sustained. We do not quite forgive a giver. The hand that feeds us is in some danger of being bitten. We can receive anything from love, for that is a way of receiving it from ourselves; but not from *anyone* who assumes to bestow. We sometimes hate the meat which we eat, because there seems something of degrading dependence in living by it. (Emerson, 1936:359.)

Emerson here suggests that an understanding or meaningful analysis of gift exchange requires a knowledge of the relationship between giver and receiver.

Status Anxiety

The possibility of unfriendliness in the gift exchange is recognized by most people. This is best supported by reference once again to popular slogans and proverbs which warn against being deceived by the gift. Translated sociologically, there is a general awareness that gift givers and receivers do not always believe in the role they are playing: the thought behind the gift may run anywhere from cynicism to sincerity. Insofar as persons employ one another as "social looking glasses," this variability in role sincerity gives rise to an uncertainty which may be called "status anxiety." Yet, it might also be suggested that the cynical giver (or the cynical role player, in general) is himself plagued by two sources of discomfort: there exists both the fear of "being found out" and a degree of guilt over the insincerity itself. When ambivalence reaches a certain point, the *compulsive* gift giver emerges who protects himself from both guilt and the unmasking anxiety by ritualistic presentations. In general, then, the ritual of gift exchange is not understandable by its anxiety-reducing qualities alone; it is itself a generator of anxiety, for if it is not properly executed, the public front of sincerity is likely to be jeopardized.

Awards

Gifts as ceremonial tokens of regard may be distributed analytically into two overlapping categories: those presented in recognition of status and those presented in recognition of achievement. In the former grouping are found Christmas, birthday, and anniversary gifts, Mother's Day and Father's Day presents, and so forth. We find the purest forms of the achievement gift in prizes, trophies, etc. Mixed forms involve achievement gifts for persons of a certain (usually kinship) status, for example, graduation presents.

It is important, however, to note that status gifts are often presented *publicly* as achievement gifts. Lévi-Strauss, for example, writes, "The refinement of selection [of Christmas cards], their outstanding designs, their price, the quantity sent or received, give evidence (ritually exhibited on the mantlepiece during the week of celebration), of the recipient's social bonds and the degree of his prestige." (Lévi-Strauss, 1965:77.) Thus status and achievement gifts share a characteristic which provides insight into one of their more important properties: both are objectifications of past or present social relationships. The ceremonial display of such objectifications is a powerful tendency in social life: persons invariably seek to make known their social bonds in daily encounters. Veblen suggests that in advanced societies this tendency "develops into a system of rank titles, degrees and insignia, typical examples of which are heraldic devices, medals and honorary decorations." (Veblen, 1934:44.) The presentation of self, then, is often made with symbols of one's connections to others. And gifts represent the purest forms of such symbols. These may of course be displayed with such elaboration and ostentation as to bring down the displeasure of the audience. Thus, the gift diamond, automobile, or other trophies must be displayed tactfully and with a certain degree of humility.

Gift Exchange: Reciprocity and Distributive Justice

Gift exchange is governed by the norm of reciprocity. The degree to which this norm has been fulfilled in a given exchange of gifts may be stated in terms of distributive justice, which obtains when social rewards are proportional to costs and to investments. The concept of distributive justice is important in itself for it leads to interesting and non-obvious statements about human behavior. The principle tells us, for example, that a gift giver will experience discomfort if reciprocity fails to occur; but the idea that over-reciprocation will produce disturbance in the original giver is more interesting and leads into the area of undeserved rewards, to which shame, according to Helen M. Lynd, is connected.[3] The use of a reward (often in the form of a gift) *as a punishment* is a device employed by many sets of contemporary "love-oriented" parents and may be subsumed under the general category of "shaming techniques," which consist of three separate operations: (1) the provision for the child of an unfavorable derogation-praise ratio, (2) the presentation of a gift, and (3) a verbal declaration of the lack of commensurability between the child's merit and the gift he has received. ("Daddy and mommy are giving you a present even though you've been a bad boy!") Shame is therefore doubly established by a statement of one's knowledge of another's sins and the giving of a reward despite them.

Distributive justice is particularly interesting in view of the rule which prohibits an equal-return "payment" in gift exchange. This suggests that every gift-exchanging dyad (or larger group) is characterized by a certain "balance of debt" which must never be brought into equilibrium, for a perfect level of distributive justice is typical of the economic rather than the social exchange relationship. It has, in fact, already been suggested that the greater the correspondence in value between gift received and gift returned, the less the sentimental component in the relationship is likely to be. But this proposition needs to be qualified by our noting that an absence or inadequate amount of reciprocity is not at all functional for the intimate relationship. There exists, then, a band—between complete and incomplete or inadequate reciprocity—within which the giver of the return gift must locate its value.

The continuing balance of debt—now in favor of one member, now in favor of the other—insures that the relationship between the two continue, for gratitude will always constitute a part of the bond linking them. Gouldner, in this connection, considered gift exchange as a "starting mechanism" for social relationships (Gouldner, 1960). Simmel likened the phenomenon to "inertia" in his essay on "Faithfulness and Gratitude":

An action between men may be engendered by love or greed of gain, obedience or hatred, sociability or lust for domination alone, but this action usually does not exhaust the creative mood which, on the contrary,

[3] Helen M. Lynd (1958:34). For a discussion of this topic in terms of balance theory, see C. Norman Alexander, Jr., and Richard L. Simpson (1964). Homans's rule of distributive justice is stated in his *Social Behavior* 1961:75.

somehow lives on in the sociological situation it has produced. Gratitude is definitely such a continuance. . . . If every grateful action, which lingers on from good turns received in the past, were suddenly eliminated, society (at least as we know it) would break apart. (Simmel, 1950:389.)

It must be noted that gratitude binds not only the living, but connects the living and the dead as well. The will is an institutionalization of such a connection. Inherited benefits, insofar as they cannot be reciprocated, generate eternal indebtedness and thereby link together present and past. Thus the absence of a sense of family tradition among the poor is due not only to familial instability, for example, "serial monogamy," but to a lack of willable commodities, that is, gratitude imperatives.

Simmel makes another important observation which implies that every gift-exchanging dyad is characterized by a moral dominance of one member over another. This has to do with the initiation of benefit exchange:

Once we have received something good from another person, once he has preceded us with his action, we no longer can make up for it completely, no matter how much our return gift or service may objectively or legally surpass his own. The reason is that his gift, because it was first, has a voluntary character which no return gift can have. For, to return the benefit we are obliged ethically; we operate under a coercion which, though neither social nor legal but moral, is still a coercion. The first gift is given in full spontaneity; it has a freedom without any duty, even without the duty of gratitude. (Simmel, 1950:392.)

Following the same line of thought leads us to observe the tendency for initial aggression to be opposed with a disproportional amount of hostility, for the original aggressive act contains the decisive element of freedom. The object of the initial attack justifies his own retaliation, no matter how superior or devastating it may be, by simply noting the voluntary character of the original hostility. It is perhaps for this reason that vengeance is restrained in ancient (*lex talionis*) and modern law— and in moral interdictions as well. ("Vengeance is mine, saith the Lord.")

In order to draw our discussion on obligation balance to its logical completion, we are required to note that, while a gift exchange of items of nearly equal value generates gratitude, which binds the relation long after the exchange has actually taken place, an absence of reciprocity will inject into the bond an element of hostility that will be equally persistent. Simmel, then, failed to recognize the negative consequences of the norm of reciprocity, which prescribe vengeance, or at least grudge, for harm done, just as their counterparts call for reimbursement and gratitude for benefits received. It is, in this regard, worth noting that man could not altogether cease to show vengeance without ceasing to show gratitude as well, for both reflect and depend upon the internalized imperative of reciprocity.

Suspense and Social Exchange

We have just completed a discussion of that quality of gift exchange which provides a social relationship with inertia, in the form of gratitude or grudge. It remains to point out that the gift has a binding effect upon the relation before it is actually given and received. The growing cohesion of two potential exchanges, for example, obviously results from mutual expectation of a gift. Now, mutual expectation is reflective of an important fact about social life; that is, its easy predictability: the institutionalization of social action provides for this. But the substance of social life is as unpredictable as its form is certain—and this property of social exchange saves us from the tedium of perfect knowledge.

Without suspense, the entire tone of the gift exchange is altered—and with it, the relationship, which is correspondingly deprived of its mystery and surprise. Gifts are hidden or kept secret for the sake of the giver as well as the receiver for, as noted, the recipient's reaction to the present is crucial to the giver.

Suspense is most prevalent in childhood, since gifts differ greatly from year to year as a result of maturation. In contrast, the adult's status is more stable, and the types of gifts he recieves will normally follow a set pattern.

Suspense and Insulation

Although suspense develops gradually, it ends abruptly when the unknown gift is revealed. Therefore, if suspense were the only constituent of the impending gift exchange, its consummation would immediately plunge the exchange partners into boredom. To some degree, this is general throughout society, as the "after-Christmas letdown" testifies. However, gift exchange is insulated by other less suspense-producing events, for example, the feast and church services, family get-togethers, leisure-time activities, etc., which immediately follow the exchange. Through such insulating devices the post-exchange "letdown" is cushioned. It is implied here, of course, that persons participating in the feasts, reunions, and whatnot be *outside* the circle of gift exchanges.

The foregoing account of insulation is a specific instance of the more general principle that a certain degree of group incohesion is functional for its preservation as far as the non-integration of its parts prevents an externally imposed shock from permeating its entire system (Gouldner, 1959:253). Thus, while each exchange circle experiences the "after-Christmas letdown" individually, the shock is irrelevant to their coming together for feasting and sociability; thereby the distant circles provide for one another the support which the constituents of a single system would fail to give by force of their integration.

It therefore becomes meaningless to speak, as Gouldner does, of need satisfaction being related to the degree of dependence of one object upon another (Gouldner, 1959:254), for our discussion has shown this notion to be too static for social analysis. It is clear that members of a social circle may be resourceful to one another up to a certain point in time, after which they must turn from each other to other circles for support or gratification. This has been shown to be the case in Christmas gift exchange, and, if space permitted, other examples could be cited. Our time, however, would be more profitably employed by noting that the process we have just described is subsumable under the property of "autonomy toleration," which provides for the system's periodic setting free of its members to find "rescue persons" outside its own boundaries and thus to remind its members of its own mortality and replaceability.[4] The check on a group's encompassing tendencies is institutionalized in conventional society by such mechanisms as the wife's and husband's "night out" for cards or bowling, or the more extended "trips home" and "camping expeditions." Gift exchange with persons outside of the immediate social circle is an especially important instance of this use and maintenance of outsiders as resource persons.

Group Boundaries, Deviance and Guilt

Those to whom we give gifts are in some way different from those to whom no token of regard is given. The gift exchange, then, is a way of dramatizing group boundaries. As Arensberg and Kimball point out, it is also a mode in which a child learns to adopt requisite behavior and sentiments toward those with whom others in his family are bound:

> Thus the Irish child very early meets his mother's and father's brothers and sisters; he runs errands and receives small gifts from them; as soon as he is able he carries presents. . . . At various times of crisis in his career, such as First Communion, Confirmation, and marriage, he receives gifts from them which signalize the intimacy between him and them. (Arensberg and Kimball, 1940;81.)

Moreover, when a single present is offered to a plurality, for example, a married or engaged couple, or a family, there is a heightening of awareness (on both sides) of their existence as a team.

Before going on it should be noted that the boundary-maintaining

[4] I owe the idea of "autonomy tolerance" to Dr. Otto Pollack, who presented the concept in his lectures.

functions which have just been noted are opposed by the property of autonomy tolerance. There is a constant tension between these poles—which underlies the fact that every social circle is characterized by a certain (quantifiable) ratio of intragroup-extragroup benefit exchanges. Put differently, gift exchange influences group boundaries by clarifying them; and the more group boundaries are defined, the greater the favorability of intragroup over extragroup exchange. This effect, however, is limited by the property of autonomy tolerance. Out of this tension, perhaps, emerges an exchange ratio equilibrium.

Social rankings are also reflected in and maintained by the gift, for the allocation of presents, in terms of quantity or quality, is normally co-ordinate with the social rank of the considered recipients. The obligation to present gifts, then, brings people into comparison who would ordinarily not be contrasted with one another.

Importantly, the gift-giving ritual helps to maintain social stability insofar as it enables members to cope with their own consciences. If the group provided no means of atonement for sins, it would surely disintegrate, for the shame that its very existence would call forth within each member would make that existence intolerable. The gift, then, is an important tool for the mending of deviations. Norman Brown, for example, has suggested that "giving is self-sacrificial; self-sacrifice is self-punishment." (Brown, 1959:266.) Thus, man "gives because he wants to lose." (Brown, 1959:265.) In this sense, asserts Brown, reciprocity in gift exchange implies that "social organization is a structure of shared guilt . . . a symbolic mutual confession of guilt." (Brown, 1959:269.) And one of the functions of God is to structure the human need for self-sacrifice (Brown, 1959:265).

Although we may disagree with Brown in his implication that gift exchange is "nothing but" an expression of guilt, we must agree that guilt may be an important component of many exchanges, and add that the strengthening of the social bond is a consequence of the *sacrificial gift*. Mauss and Hubert, in this connection write:

> At the same time they find in sacrifice the means of redressing equilibriums that have been upset: by expiation they redeem themselves from social obloquy, the consequence, and re-enter the community. . . . The social norm is thus maintained without danger to themselves, without diminution for the group. (Hubert and Mauss, 1964:102–3.)

The authors might have noted that most deviations are undetected by the group—and this ignorance, if not carried to an extreme, is functional for its continuation. (See Moore and Tumin, 1949.) From this point of view an important latent function of sacrifice is the provision of atonement for *unseen* deviations.

References

ALEXANDER, C. NORMAN, JR., and RICHARD L. SIMPSON
    1964 "Balance Theory and Distributive Justice." *Sociological Inquiry* 34 (Spring):182–92.
ARENSBERG, CONRAD M., and SOLON T. KIMBALL
    1940 *Family and Community in Ireland.* Cambridge: Harvard University Press.
BARNETT, JAMES H.
    1954 *The American Christmas.* New York: Macmillan.
BENEDICT, RUTH
    1960 *Patterns of Culture.* New York: Mentor Books.
BROWN, NORMAN
    1959 *Life Against Death.* New York: Random House.
EMERSON, RALPH WALDO
    1936 "Gifts." In *Emerson's Essays.* Philadelphia: Spencer Press.
GOFFMAN, ERVING
    1961 "Fun in Games." In *Encounters.* New York: Bobbs-Merrill.
GOULDNER, ALVIN
    1960 "The Norm of Reciprocity: A Preliminary Statement." *American Sociological Review* 25 (April):176–77.
    1959 "Reciprocity and Autonomy in Functional Theory." In LLEWELLYN GROSS, ed., *Symposium on Sociological Theory.* Evanston: Row, Peterson.
HAGSTROM, WARREN O.
    1966 "What Is the Meaning of Santa Claus?" *American Sociologist* 1 (November):248–52.
HOMANS, GEORGE C.
    1961 *Social Behavior: Its Elementary Forms.* New York: Harcourt, Brace & World.
    1960 *The Human Group.* New York: Harcourt, Brace & World.
HUBERT, HENRI, and MARCEL MAUSS
    1964 *Sacrifice: Its Nature and Function.* Chicago: University of Chicago Press.
KORN, RICHARD, and LLOYD W. McCORKLE
    1954 "Resocialization Within Walls." *Annals of the American Academy of Political and Social Science* 293 (May):90.
LÉVI-STRAUSS, CLAUDE
    1965 "The Principle of Reciprocity." In LEWIS A. COSER and BERNARD ROSENBERG, eds., *Sociological Theory.* New York: Macmillan.
LYND, HELEN M.
    1958 *On Shame and the Search for Identity.* New York: Harcourt, Brace.
MALINOWSKI, BRONISLAW
    1959 *Crime and Custom in Savage Society.* Paterson: Littlefield, Adams.
MAUSS, MARCEL
    1954 *The Gift.* London: Cohen and West.
MEAD, MARGARET
    1962 *Sex and Temperament.* New York: New American Library.
MOORE, W. E., and M. M. TUMIN
    1949 "Some Social Functions of Ignorance." *American Sociological Review* 14 (December):787–95.

SIMMEL, GEORG

    1950   "Sociability" and "Faithfulness and Gratitude." In KURT WOLFF, ed.,
          The Sociology of Georg Simmel. New York: Free Press.

VEBLEN, THORSTEIN

    1934   *The Theory of the Leisure Class*. New York: Modern Library.

WHYTE, WILLIAM F.

    1964   *Street Corner Society*. Chicago: University of Chicago Press.

IV. Keeping Together, Staying Apart: Social Control

IV. Keeping Together, Staying Apart: Social Control

Social control—how members of society keep one another in line—is an insufficiently studied subject in modern sociology. This perspective on social life is based on many sound assumptions, the main one being that we all do during the course of a day many things that we would prefer not to do. Perhaps so many sociologists study deviance (and so large an audience exists for writings in this area) because of the pleasure of examining what others dare to do and the satisfaction of discovering—and of telling the conforming members of society—that the disrespectable elements do not have that much fun. Demonstrating the hardships involved in being a criminal, a prostitute, a homosexual, or a vagrant may in itself be a form of social control; that is, it sets the deviant apart from one's own kind and reaffirms the rules for conforming members of society.

Social control operates on less formal, less literary and scholastic, levels as well. When people get together and talk about their absent friends, when they ridicule rivals, or when they use sarcasm to bring a potentially rebellious member of their group back into line, they are practicing social control. People who seek to enforce the rules for members or to draw the boundaries separating members from nonmembers have to maintain a very delicate balance. When the method used is inappropriate, perhaps too strong for the transgression noted, one runs the risk of crystallizing the deviance into an alternative standard of behavior. On the other hand, inaction or a weak response may lead to more serious breaches of expected behavior. The use of inappropriate forms of social control may be regarded by others as in itself a violation of the rules. Currently, laws concerning victimless crimes, such as homosexuality, drug use, and prostitution, are considered by many to be major sources of criminal behavior, for the legitimacy of other laws is called into question when these laws are enforced.

Avoiding the use of one social form or another conveys that an unnamed but real relationship exists between people. Edward Sagarin presents us with an example of how the forms of address, what we call each other, regulate relationships that fall between the formal and specific and the informal and diffuse. Most often, people will carefully avoid presumptions of familiarity and equality by skirting the use of both given and family names. A no-name relationship develops, which permits a limited mutuality. Perhaps a new social vocabulary is in order to match the new informality, much as there are now informal but clearly designed "party clothes" to wear to certain festivities.

Sometimes social forms are created to keep potential combatants or potential allies apart. A great deal of social control takes the form of the maintenance of formality and coordination. There may be potential for conflict between people who are not fully aware of each other's intentions. Janey Levine, Ann Vinson, and Deborah Wood discuss the behavior of commuters on subway trains in big cities. Although breaking the rules by identifying oneself as an interested commuter may have its interesting and even hilarious moments, it may also result in never getting to one's destination. Just as there are rules of the road that coordinate interaction between drivers of cars, so there are rules that are taken for granted and generally complied with for people who ride public conveyances. Often, when commuting, we do not know that the rules exist until they are violated.

Finally, Sasha R. Weitman provides a provocative discussion of how intimate behavior is protected and regulated when it is prevented from occurring in public places. One implication of his essay is that social control may be necessary to preserve the individual's identity and the nature of emotional bonds as well as to keep people in line. Certainly, here is an opportunity for reflection about some of the more rewarding activities of human beings.

1. Etiquette, Embarrassment, and Forms of Address

EDWARD SAGARIN *

Forms of address are an important part of everyday conversation. They express not only the status of the person being addressed but also the recognition by the speaker of that status and of the relationships between the participants (Brown and Ford, 1961). When any one of these three elements is in doubt in the mind of the speaker, or when he wishes to express the doubt even when he does not himself feel it (this latter, a rarer occurrence), alternative roads are open. These involve avoidance of the encounter, avoidance of the addressing situation, waiting for cues, or use of one form or another accompanied by stress. Such situations will arise particularly when one of the participants is attempting to produce an impression of a status that is not recognized by the other, when there is a failure to have clear-cut institutionalized roles governing the status, when a change of status is occurring or has occurred, when two (or on occasion even more) simultaneous reciprocal roles are held by the speaker and the one he is addressing, or when there is a conflict between the speaker and the addressee over their definition of the statuses they occupy. Furthermore, both deference and degradation are expressed through forms of address, but these cannot always be inferred from the form used; rather, they must frequently be taken in context, in order to determine the meaning of the particular form for the speaker, the impression that he sought to give, and the impression obtained by the listener.

In English, particularly in American English, this is complicated by several factors and simplified by others. It is complicated by the habit of frequently using a proper name during the most casual discussion. That this is almost unavoidable when speaking about one, or when calling him, is clear, but the usage in direct conversation is a matter of linguistic habit, not born of necessity. For example, the person in the next room will be called: "John, will you come here a minute?" If there are several people in that room, there is no

---

* This article has not been published previously.

substitute for the use of the name *John* or *Mr. Smith*. If there is only one person in that room, it would be possible, but by linguistic habitude awkward, to just call out, "Will you come here a minute?" However, even when two people are having an ordinary conversation, sitting with each other only, and no ambiguity could arise from the failure to use the name, it crops into the conversation "naturally," so to speak—that is, almost without conscious control. I asked students to make a studied effort to avoid any such name or form of address in a dyadic conversation, and, of seven students, six reported that they found it very uncomfortable. One reported:

> I was talking to my mother, and I just found myself saying *Ma*, and realized it was coming out of my mouth every other word. [Every other word?] No, every other sentence. I just couldn't talk to her without saying *Ma*. [Do you think you could learn to?] It would take a lot of training. Why bother?

From another:

> I was with this friend of mine, Joe, and we were on our way to a double date, sitting in the car; he was driving. Every time I said *Joe*, I caught myself, and, for about one or two sentences, I wouldn't say it. Finally, I told him about the experiment, and he tried to join in. But we couldn't talk to each other. Maybe, if we got used to it, we might be able to do it.

This practice of using a name during a conversation has probably increased as first names and nicknames have come to replace the more formal *Mr., Miss, Mrs.* (and now *Ms.*). In a conversation with several couples present, I noticed that all of them were either using a first name or a substitute term, such as *fellow, guy, dear, honey*, and others. In French, young people often address one another as *mon vieux*, for example.

On the other hand, English does not require that a person choose between a familiar and a formal mode of address in the second-person pronoun (as is done in almost all Germanic languages, in the Romance tongues, and in many languages outside the Indo-European family, such as Mandarin). *You* can be used not only when speaking to one person or several but when speaking to stranger, superior, intimate friend, child, or animal. Many of the ambiguities in choosing a form of address in English are a matter of expression of the degree of formality or familiarity in the relationship, and what is determined by the shift from *Mr.* or *Professor* to *John* or *Jack* may be a replication in English of the shift from *vous* to *tu* in French,[1] a matter that has been investigated by Brown and Gilman (1960).

---

[1] In the 1930's, there was a popular song in France on this theme, which expressed the fantasy of a youth dreaming that he and his girlfriend can start addressing each other as *tu* instead of using the formal *vous*. The song went: *Nous nous disons vous, dans nos rendezvous, mais dans mes rêves, je vous dis tu, non, ce n'est pas défendu: Tout est permis dans les rêves!*

Some role relationships are drawn with such lack of ambiguity that there is no possibility of choice in form of address. This occurs particularly when, in a superordinate-subordinate situation, the form of address is utilized as a symbolic expression of the recognition of the inequality. One such institutionalized form is the use of *sir* in the American military; another, the use of *Your Honor* in court. Note that, in the military, a commissioned officer cannot be answered with the simple "Yes"; this is as unacceptable as to say "Yes, John," or "Yes, I will." The *sir* is a mandatory appendage; it serves as a constant reminder that the relationship is one of inequality. In court, the judge is referred to as *His Honor* and addressed as *Your Honor*, but this does not require endless repetition. Seated higher than the attorneys and other participants in the trial proceedings, he will make decisions on the procedure and sometimes on the outcome of the conflict, but there is usually no battle of wills in which he must impress his authority upon others. Thus, *sir* becomes demeaning to the speaker rather than respectful to the addressee, whereas *Your Honor* is an expression of respect for the judge that does not demean or "put down" the speaker.

These are highly institutionalized roles that offer little possibility for flexibility and misunderstanding. The same is not true in other instances, either because the relationship is undergoing change or has ambiguity built into it or because the social customs are themselves changing. Instances of the following situations will be discussed in this paper: (1) when people have two simultaneous but different relationships, each of which would call for a different form of address, as with a nurse who is also a wife, or a colleague who is also a nephew; (2) when there is a changing relationship, as when a former professor has developed an attitude of friendship with his student or when the latter has begun to see his professor as a colleague; (3) when the institutions are themselves ambiguous, as with mother-in-law and father-in-law; and (4) in the changing scene, as when the young and often bearded professor who is not much older than his students, and frequently even younger, is led by the developing college atmosphere to be seen as a friend and buddy as well as a professor.

Two Relationships Simultaneously Sustained

Although sociological literature has focused a great deal on role conflict, there is relatively little on dyadic reciprocal roles in which ego and alter are, at the same time and in the same space, related to one another in more than one way. The two relationships may require different forms of address; sometimes this is rather important when within earshot of others.

In a situation devoid of conflict, ambiguity, and overlapping roles, the major contrast, as Brown and Ford (1961) point out, is between the use of first name only and last name preceded by a title, with such variations as titles without names, multiple names, and last names alone. It is when one role calls for one choice while another role calls for a different choice that interactive problems arise.

The wife (or other intimate relative or close friend) who is also a nurse exemplifies this duality very clearly. As wife, she calls the man by his first name, or by some form of endearment; for a nurse, this would be inappropriate, because it would fail to impress all others with the impersonal, efficient, and scientific nature of nurses and their tasks. In those branches of the medical or paramedical professions in which the practitioner is not an M.D. but has some other degree entitling him to the sobriquet of *Doctor* (as a dentist, osteopath, clinical psychologist, for example), this can assume even greater importance, because the M.D. is not in need of a constant reinforcement of his image as a doctor. He is *the* doctor, and all other doctors are such in a peripheral sense that must be impressed upon their patients.

A nurse who is the wife (or other intimate associate) of the doctor may conceal this from the patients. In the presence of others, on the telephone, and even alone with him, in the office, she calls him *Doctor*; at all other times, he becomes *Jim* or *honey*. In the third person, she would never find it difficult to say, "Doctor Jones will see you in just a minute," and the use of the first name in that context would be unthinkable. An even greater degree of impersonality, and probably a clearer instance of rank elevation, would be signified if she said, "The doctor will see you in a few minutes."

When the people in the office know of her relationship to the doctor, they find this quite acceptable. They hear her call to her husband, "Doctor Jones, can you come to the telephone?" and do not find it bewildering or hypocritical that she uses this form of address. They know she is speaking in her capacity as nurse, addressing him in his capacity as doctor, and they are reassured by the speech that they are not in his living room or kitchen but in an office in which their medical needs will be taken care of not only by him but by other personnel.

For her, the problem is to switch the first names on and off when speaking to him or about him. At the table, with the children, or in bed, he is no longer *Doctor Jones*. Women in this situation tell me that they do not slip, that the right word comes easily and naturally. One nurse who is the cousin of the physician says that she hardly ever has occasion to use a first name socially. However, when I asked her to take note of the social occurrences, she reported that she was avoiding any name at all, just speaking to him directly, and, in speaking about him, was able to pick up the cues of the words being used by others. Thus, in family circles, when others spoke about *Howard*, she could take it from there, as if the thread had been extended to her, but, among actual or potential patients, when they talked of *Doctor So-and-So*, she would pick up the word *Doctor*.[2]

In a college situation that I learned about, a young man came to teach in the same department as his uncle. He had previously always called the man *Uncle Joe*. He found this to be embarrassing because others were often present or might overhear, and he soon fell into the habit of saying *Joe*, just as the other members of the department did. However, when he took this home, he found considerable resentment from other family members, who interpreted the familiarity as disrespectful. Nevertheless, the switch from *Joe-with-Uncle* to *Joe-alone* was uncomfortable, and the school situation prevailed. He would thus find himself with brothers, wife, and others all referring to *Uncle Joe* or calling the man by that name while he had dropped the *Uncle* part. To avoid embarrassment, he likewise avoided any form of address except in school.[3]

Terms of Respect and Terms of Degradation

In an era when people who know one another for only a brief period of time use the first name or a nickname as the form of address, one is likely to interpret such a means of speech as a sign of friendliness. Nevertheless, it can also be a sign of disrespect and degradation, a dehumanization derived from unwillingness to confer the status of humanity and adulthood on the other. In the United States, the use of a first name in addressing a black person was traditionally just such a symbol of degradation. He or she was still a child, in the minds of the speaker, and was not entitled to be addressed as *Mr.*, *Miss*, or *Mrs.* In courts, there were historic fights over this issue, when witnesses refused to speak unless addressed in a respectful manner. Further, cross-examining attorneys would use the demeaning first name or nickname in order to impress upon the judge and jury the unreliability, childishness, and unworthiness of a black witness. However, the attorneys for the side for which the black was appearing would also use the first name, not only because it was a custom that they dared not break but also because they wanted to say to the judge and jury

---

[2] Gold (1952) points out that the use of the identification by occupation, instead of name, can be demeaning, if the occupation is a low-status one, such as janitor. This is sometimes overcome by attempting to switch the name and thereby upgrade the occupation. Thus, to call the person a super, instead of a janitor, might be more acceptable. If it is an honorific to address a person as *Doctor*, *Professor*, or even *Doc*, what Gold is describing might well be called an antihonorific.

[3] A variation on this is described by Robert J. Kelly (private communication). A number of people are introduced at a gathering, each by first and last name—Bob Jones, Jim Jackson, and the like—until one is introduced as Dr. White. Kelly suggests that the host provide everyone with a tacit instruction as to what he can appropriately call each other person. Not only is Dr. White given his title, but his first name is missing, compelling the others to use his title, unless they choose avoidance or inquire about the missing first name.

that, despite the fact that they had a black man as a witness, they did not want to be sullied by the notion that they believed in racial equality.

Gunnar Myrdal (1944:611) describes the importance of the form of address in expressing racial attitudes:

> The conversation [between whites and Negroes in the South] is even more regimented in *form* than in content. The Negro is expected to address the white person by the title of "Mr.," "Mrs.," or "Miss." The old slavery title of "Master" disappeared during Reconstruction entirely and was replaced by "Boss" or sometimes "Cap" or "Cap'n." From his side, the white man addresses the Negro by his first name, no matter if they hardly know each other, or by the epithets "boy," "uncle," "elder," "aunty," or the like. If he wishes to show a little respect without going beyond the etiquette, he uses the exaggerated titles of "doctor," "lawyer," "professor," or other occupational titles, even though the term is not properly applicable. . . . That there has been a slight tendency for this pattern to break down is shown by the use of the Negro's last name without title in many recent business relations. Too, a few salesmen will actually call Negroes by their titles of "Mr.," "Mrs.," and "Miss" in order to gain them as customers. [Italics in original.]

On which one might comment, "Anything for monetary gain—even racial equality!"

Charles S. Johnson (1941:277) also emphasizes the significance of forms of address in racial etiquette in the rural South, where Negroes always had to use *Mr.* and *Mrs.* when addressing whites, a form of speech that was reciprocated in some counties but not in others, and Myrdal reports that reciprocation took place in private. It was acceptable to be courteous, provided one's peers did not know about it.

It is pointed out by Thomas O. Beidelman (1963) that the first name here replaces the informal pronoun as an expression of familiarity without affection. In a crosscultural study, he found that the informal pronoun (the equivalent of the obsolete *thou*) was used when addressing children, friends, members of the immediate family, and also when one wished to insult or to denote absence of respect (all analogous to use of first name in American English). Such a term was used, he wrote,

> . . . to servants, vagrants, prostitutes, beggars, prisoners, or members of minority groups. A French informant states that he was instructed to address Negro Senegalese troops by the informal. Germans in the Nazi regime called Jews by this form. . . . The informal is also used in a personal insult and always in anger.

Thus, intimate pronouns, Beidelman contends (and I would add, first names in English), may have a double-edged meaning of affection and condemnation, "for it is precisely those persons who know one best who are most able to know one's faults and vulnerabilities." I would suggest, rather, that, when intimacy is devoid of affection, it is intrusion, disrespect, insult, and condemnation. Further, it is demeaning to speak to an adult as if he were a child, but it is not demeaning to speak in the same manner to a child.

As a result of the struggle to command respect and to have this symbolized by such terms as *Mr.*, middle-class blacks were reluctant to embrace the first-name movement that spread through America earlier in this century. I have found in offices where only blacks were working, particularly if they had white-collar and professional occupations, that they were addressing each other as *Mr.* long after this habit had been abandoned by whites.

Thus, the same term can express friendship or a rebuff of friendship; it can express affectionate familiarity or contemptuous familiarity; it can indicate equality or inequality. This depends on the total context, both social and linguistic, and this, in turn, depends on the meanings imputed to the speaker by the other or others. This is a sort of verbal looking-glass self: A's image of self is affected by the meanings that A attributes to B with regard to B's image of A. In this gamesmanship, A seeks to manipulate B, but B, in turn, must anticipate the meanings that A (as well as others) will attribute to himself (B) in the choice of the form of address, and the power situation compels B to make choices pleasing or displeasing to A.

Changing Relationships Reflected in Changing Forms of Address

Earlier, I discussed dual and conflicting status relationships simultaneously held. When a status relationship changes, the form of address may have to be altered to reflect the new situation, provided the old and new relationships each called for different modes of speech. Sometimes this is gradual: A fellow starts by calling his date by her first name and then continues, soon thereafter, by slipping into what Schneider and Homans (1955) call "terms of endearment," such as *honey, sweetheart, sweetie pie, doll,* or *darling*. Rebuff is unlikely if the change in statuses has been reciprocal, and this reciprocity is noted in the shift to new forms of address from both sides.

Formerly, an analogous situation frequently developed as people became acquainted and went from *Mr.* to first name. Today, *Mr.* has almost entirely dropped out of usage in informal relations. Even in formal ones, such as those involved in a business luncheon, *Mr.* barely survives the first few minutes. "The use of the given-name," wrote H. L. Mencken (1947:275), "was popularized by Rotary, the members of which so address one another, and no doubt was also fostered by the advent of the Hon. James A. Farley, whose greeting to all comers was 'Call me Jim.'" Thus, the hail-fellow-well-met, backslapping greeter, who has been a stereotype in American fraternal associations and veterans' organizations, among others, spread throughout the

United States, and his spirit was expressed by the use of first names.

In a footnote, Mencken quotes from the Dayton, Ohio, *News*, of January 5, 1934, as follows: "Members of the United States Senate largely address each other, in private at least, by their first names. The President of the United States, to hundreds of his friends, is simply *Frank*." But this was true not only of forms of address but also in talking about the President. It is difficult to imagine the newspapers, during World War I, talking about Woodrow or Woody, though they did occasionally refer to the commander-in-chief as WW. It is an indication not only of the general disaffection of youth with the establishment but also of the degree to which informality in address is normative that young people so often talked about the President since 1970 as Dick, Dickie, and, more disparagingly, Tricky Dick.

Just how the first name came to be so widely used in the United States, and what cultural meanings this may imply, is not clear. It may represent equality and the relaxation of restrictive role demands; it may also represent informality and friendliness. These are not all of the same cloth. It would appear to me that the use of a single term of address, by almost everyone and to almost everyone, is an expression of pseudohomogeneity and of pseudoclasslessness. It is as if one wishes to project an image of equality precisely because the reality is absent. It is a characteristic described by Wheelis (1958); Riesman (1953:37) uses the term "pseudo-personalized," as in: "For the other-directed types political events are likewise experienced through a screen of words by which the events are habitually atomized and personalized—or pseudo-personalized." There is not so much an informality as a superficiality to a relationship in which *everyone* is a friend, a first name, a *honey* or *darling*. Again from Riesman (1953:94):

> Etiquette can be at the same time a means of approaching people and of staying clear of them. For some, etiquette may be a matter of little emotional weight—an easy behavioral cloak; for others the ordering of human relations through etiquette can become highly charged emotionally—an evidence of characterological compulsiveness. But in either case etiquette is concerned not with encounters between individuals as such but with encounters between them as representatives of their carefully graded social roles.

Nevertheless, *Mr.* survives, not only for the moment of introduction, and for journalistic, courtroom, and other uses, and in records and on envelopes (where the omission has a bareness that appears somewhat insulting, unless the letter is being sent to a child), but also as a form of direct address where informality is avoided and, sometimes (in addition), superordination is being expressed. An example of both of these is to be found in the college and sometimes the high school or elementary school classroom. In the latter, the male teacher is almost always addressed as *Mr.* by the children, and sometimes this form prevails in relationships with parents, colleagues, and superiors. In the college classroom, there is a wider variety of choices: *Mr.* is usually discarded if a doctorate has been earned. If that is not the case, it can still be dropped in favor of *Professor* (even when that title is not technically available). There are some occasions in college in which, in addition to *Mr.* (or one of the feminine analogues), *Doctor*, and *Professor*, the first name is used, particularly if the teacher is young and is not anxious to express his authoritative position by the affirmation of status differentiation through the form of address.

There is likewise a range of choices for the college teacher in talking to the student; he can use *Mr.*, *Miss*, occasionally *Mrs.*, and now *Ms.*; use the last name without any modifier; combine these last two forms by dropping the *Mr.* for males but keeping the *Miss* for females; or shift to first names. If he has invited and encouraged the students to first-name him, he is expected to first-name them, but, if he first-names them, this does not give the student the right to reciprocate. The leadership in going from formality to informality is in the hands of the person in the superordinate position.

A professor-student relationship is sometimes simultaneously a collegial one, with the professor as the senior colleague and hence still in the superordinate position, or it may shift from professor-student to full collegial, or even to one of friends on a peer-group type basis, sweethearts, lovers, roommates, or spouses. These shifts demand corresponding changes in the form of address, with *Professor* or *Doctor* being dropped in favor of the first name. Because, however, the first name had been in use by the professor for some time, possibly from the beginning of the relationship, there cannot be a superordinate shift to act as a cue that the subordinate one would be welcome. Uneasiness often punctuates this interim scene. It may be allayed by the professor's expressing his wish to be addressed by his first name: "Why don't you just call me Bill, like everyone does around here?" and this may mark a sudden shift with success.

Failing this, there may be a deliberate avoidance of any form of address. On the telephone, this is particularly noticeable: "Hello, this is Howie," instead of "Hello, Jim" or "Hello, Professor Brown."

It would appear that the new relationship is preferable to the old, and hence the formerly subordinate person would want to affirm his status of equality by using the term that expresses it. Why hesitate? Is it because of fear of rebuff? This is unlikely. Perhaps the interim period is one of discomfort and uncertainty and there is a greater security in the former system. However, the invitation to equality must come from the superordinate status holder if there is an expectation that friendship and affection will be present in the new equal-status relationship. In a political situation where there is inequality, the demand for its abolition can and almost always does arise from the subordinates, because the new equality statuses being sought involve not primary-group, affectional relationships but impersonal and often antiaffectional ones. Brown and Ford (1961) refer to the superordinate as the pacesetter "not in linguistic address alone but in all acts that increase intimacy." I would agree with this if the linguistic address is meant to connote intimacy, but, if it is meant to correct nonreciprocity and hence connote equality, the subordinate can and usually does assume the pacesetter role. Put another way, if the dyadic relationship is isolated and is no more than impersonal, the higher-status figure initiates change; if it is part of a social scene, and any alteration is to become a constitutive element of social change, the lower-status figure acts as pacesetter. In the former instance, change is by invitation; in the latter, by demand.

A relationship between two people, one of whom is subordinate to the other, if it calls for nonreciprocal forms of address, may be based on rank position of age, or one status may be higher than the other. These two elements may conflict. Brown and Ford (1961) found that, in such an instance, the occupational or other status was the determinant of the form of address. Thus, an older janitor uses *Mr.* in speaking to a younger landlord or employer, but the latter first-names the former.

A change in relationship, when it has not been accomplished through a formal ceremony (a wedding, for example), may involve considerable strain, precisely because it takes place so gradually. One must recognize the verbal and nonverbal cues, the invitations and the rebuffs, and pick up the thread at exactly the right moment. An informal, non-institutionalized ceremony may be involved, and the avoidance of the ceremony is at stake. Because the lower-status person may have the burden of initiating the change, he must be able to perceive the moment when approval is indicated, though it remains tacit. The other, the superordinate, must ratify the change; if this ratification is not forthcoming, it may be difficult for the lower-status person to retreat and bring the relationship to the point where it had been before the false step.

All of this may be a matter of the risks being greater than the rewards.

Lack of Institutionalized Roles

When there is no consensus on the institutionalized roles, and when the ambiguities may lead to a variety of choices of forms of address, the situation becomes particularly anxiety-provoking. This is exemplified by the mode of address to one's parents-in-law, particularly to one's mother-in-law.

Who is the mother-in-law? She is not *Mother* (and hence not *Ma, Mamma, Mom,* or some such), not only because the American kinship system does not provide that she become this but also because that word is reserved for one person, unlike such terms as *Uncle, Aunt, Grandma,* or *Doctor,* which can apply to entire classes or groups. There is only one person who can be *Ma* or *Mamma,* with a special case in the instance of a stepmother, where the word *Ma* is meant to express that one accepts the new person as a replacement for the old.

A young man or woman is usually still in the dating period when relationships with the people who will eventually become in-laws are commenced. The older people are either *Mr.* or *Mrs.* (perhaps the new morality will bring *Miss* into this arena, though that has not yet occurred); sometimes, in the light of the common usage of first names, the mother and father become *Lilly* or *Mac* to the youth, but this is probably rare: The relationship usually begins on a *Mr. Miller* or a *Mrs. Jones* basis.

It appears that the shift to a new role comes suddenly. There is a ceremony at a given time and place, and the daughter's boyfriend becomes the son-in-law. This is not in actuality as sudden as the *rite de passage* of a wedding would have us believe. All the people concerned have drifted into a frame of mind where they will be anticipating the new statuses; one can say that the statuses come gradually to be occupied in all but the most legal and formal senses. The ceremony gives a stamp of official recognition to a relationship that is not entirely novel for the participants.

Tradition would seem to demand that the parents prefer to be called *Mom* and *Dad*, or some synonym, by the newly acquired in-law, but the latter recalls that the word is reserved for one person and finds it difficult to articulate it for any other. Sometimes a separation is used: One says *Dad* to his father and *Pop* to his father-in-law, for example. Sometimes the form of address used by the spouse is adopted; because it is used by the spouse, it will also be used by oneself as if one were speaking through the spouse. Actually, it is an expression of the fact that, lacking an institutionalized form of address for someone accepting (even enthusiastically) the person as an in-law, one must improvise with an unacceptable and possibly an uncomfortable form of speech.

The growth of first-naming and the spread of first-name informalities during this century in the United States, with young people so often calling others by first names or nicknames, have provided a means for handling this difficult problem for the son- or daughter-in-law. It is often done with discomfort, and sometimes haltingly, as if to offer a cue and to await a response.

As in other situations of ambiguity, evasion may come to the rescue, but this is not a physical avoidance, as is the mother-in-law avoidance described by anthropologists; it is merely a verbal one of the address form. The youth goes in front of his in-law and looks directly at him or her before speaking, or he may even decide not to say a certain thing or not to ask a certain question, so as to be able to avoid using the word *Mom* or *Joan.* Schneider and Homans (1955) point out that evasion, as well as deliberate drift from one form of address to another, is often used not only by the son- and daughter-in-law but also by the son and daughter, who rarely confine themselves to a single term and express a variety of moods by specific choices on given occasions. The choice may be avoidance, but it remains a choice.

Avoidance, like deviance, can provide highly cohesive functions, for it can be a manner in which people manipulate a situation in order to keep intact an ongoing relationship. The charge of social incompetence, boorishness, or violation of a rule of etiquette is avoided when one employs a strategy of not using any form of address at all. It may be that the relationship is sufficiently important to the person that it is its disruption that is being avoided.

To return to the child-in-law: The ambiguity is sometimes resolved when the young couple have had children, by adopting *Grandma* and *Grandpa* as forms of address. This generally begins in the presence of the child and loses any absurdity that it would inherently contain because the speaker is not addressing his or her grandparent, and because it is a validation of a valued relationship, that of being a grandparent. Having used this as the form of speech on many occasions, one begins to slip into using it even in the absence of the grand-children.

Conclusion

Verbal interaction requires various forms of address. They range from honorifics to nicknames, from expressions of respect to those that are demeaning. The choice of word differs with social-class, occupational, ethnic, and other variables and must be studied in each of these contexts. No choice is haphazard and devoid of meaning. In using one term rather than another, or by avoiding the use of a term entirely, one not only follows the social conventions governing such action but also reveals the nature of that relationship as one wants the other (or others) to see it. Uneasiness and ambiguity result from failure to have institutionalized roles, from simultaneous occupation of two or more status relationships, or from shifts from one type of relationship calling for a given form of address to another that calls for a different form.

Whether one says *Jim*, *Doctor*, or *hey*, the choice is meaningful and often fraught with difficulties. Interaction is a gamble, Goffman says, and verbal interaction is both a reflection of a relationship and a force in its development.

References

BEIDELMAN, THOMAS O.
    1963 "Terms of Address as Clues to Social Relationships." ALVIN W. GOULDNER and HELEN P. GOULDNER, eds., *Modern Sociology: An Introduction to the Study of Human Interaction.* New York: Harcourt Brace & World.

BROWN, ROGER, and MARGUERITE FORD
1961 "Address in American English." *Journal of Abnormal and Social Psychology* 62(2): 375–85.
BROWN, ROGER, and A. GILMAN
1960 "The Pronouns of Power and Solidarity." In T. SEBEOK, ed., *Style in Language*. New York: John Wiley & Sons.
GOLD, RAY
1952 "Janitors Versus Tenants: A Status-Income Dilemma." *American Journal of Sociology* 57: 486–93.
JOHNSON, CHARLES S.
1941 *Growing up in the Black Belt: Negro Youth in the Rural South*. Washington, D.C.: American Council on Education.
MENCKEN, H. L.
1947 *The American Language*. New York: Knopf, 4th ed.
MYRDAL, GUNNAR
1944 *An American Dilemma*. New York: Harper.
RIESMAN, DAVID (with NATHAN GLAZER and REUEL DENNEY)
1953 *The Lonely Crowd*. Garden City: Doubleday.
SCHNEIDER, DAVID M., and GEORGE C. HOMANS
1955 "Kinship Terminology and the American Kinship System." *American Anthropologist* 57 (December): 1194–1208. Reprinted in NORMAN W. BELL and EZRA F. VOGEL, eds., *A Modern Introduction to the Family*. Glencoe: Free Press, 1960.
WHEELIS, ALLEN
1958 *The Quest for Identity*. New York: W. W. Norton.

2. *Subway Behavior* *

JANEY LEVINE, ANN VINSON, AND DEBORAH WOOD

Subway behavior is regulated by certain societal rules and regulations that serve to protect personal rights and to sustain proper social distance between unacquainted people who are temporarily placed together in unfocused and focused interaction. This trivial occasion gives rise to many rules pertaining to larger social gatherings, particularly those focusing on a specific issue. For this reason, we can study the larger problems of social order by focusing on these small units, these interludes of everyday life. Subway riding demonstrates, for example, the ways in which we generally afford "civil inattention" to others in one's immediate presence and, in turn, the others' acceptance of complete absorption in "subordinate" involvements by ourselves. Despite this closeness of contact and the mutual vulnerability of the passengers, little focused interaction occurs, few people are accosted, and few friendships arise. How these things *do not take place* is the problem for discussion here.

This essay will examine several of the social regulations that are arrived at and maintained by riders in subways, the various mechanisms employed to sustain them, and the rewards and costs, in the form of social sanctions, incurred by travelers in their daily use of the subways. The rules, we maintain, can be best discovered and confirmed by examining and even committing infractions and improprieties against the socially accepted behavior of riders. The conclusions drawn in this essay are based on actual observations of behavior in the Boston and New York City subways. The participant observers in this project, although basically intent upon classifying actual behavior, on several occasions deliberately broke the informal regulations existing in subways in order to ascertain what reactions, if any, would occur among the passengers and what kinds of behavior would restore civil inattention and complete absorption in subordinate involvements.

In most cases, the people entering a subway car do not have similar focuses of activity, because their usual activities have been temporarily suspended and their main involvement is passively riding to their

* This essay, previously unpublished, appears here by permission of the authors.

destinations—hardly a demanding task for someone who knows the way or has repeated the trip almost daily for several years. Indeed, one way in which competence in the role of rider is exhibited is to sit with closed eyes or actually go to sleep and then jump up at the precise moment the train comes to the stop where one wants to get off.

Passengers immediately feel the threat of potential "unwanted" face engagements with strangers by virtue of their copresence. When a person enters a car in which there are many empty seats in various places, two conflicting considerations may influence that person's selection of a seat, both of which are aimed at reducing the threat of exposure and accessibility to others, particularly if the rider is a woman. The first consideration concerns the newcomer's discomfort at being "on stage" in front of other riders as he stands and walks among them; he feels compelled to take the nearest vacant seat so that he can discreetly slip in among the mass of seated passengers. This desire to shift attention from himself is indicative of the general desire of most subway travelers to conceal from each other information about their personal identities, often accomplished by concealing the means they have of expressing themselves; by not using their bodies, particularly those parts that are most often used to communicate with other people, such as the eyes, hands, and voice, they permit little information to be transmitted and interpreted as an invitation to others to begin an encounter. Unlike the model who walks down an aisle through spectators seated at a fashion show, the subway rider is giving a nonshow, communicating to others that he does not wish to be communicated with.

A second consideration of the newcomer in the subway car concerns whom he will sit beside or between; an act of this kind involves a choice, but the actor cannot reveal that his preferences warrant that others might consider this an invitation to others to begin an encounter. In our observations, we found that, should there be a large section of empty seats close to the door through which the person passes, he will sit there and thereby avoid having to choose whom to sit by. In so doing, the rider conceals the fact that he is choosing to avoid potential interaction. If there is a large empty section at the other end of the car, however, the newcomer will usually not parade himself in front of the strange and potentially dangerous gazes of onlooking faces. Like the person entering a car containing no large and free section of seats, he is forced to decide whom he will sit next to, a decision he may later regret having made.

Accordingly, we were able to form some general conclusions from our observations about who sits next to whom. Newcomers usually look for seated people who appear self-contained, that is, who are sitting squarely in their seats and either directing their attention to newspapers or books or concealing any interest in their surroundings with blank faces. When choosing among different but equally uninvolved riders, people tend to sit down next to others of the same sex.

The least desirable people chosen as "seatmates" seem to be older, shabbily dressed people and people apparently lacking in self-control, sprawled in their seats and looking as if they are not going anywhere.

When seated, people usually assume inconspicuous behavior—sitting squarely, at first turning neither left nor right, and maintaining expressionless faces. Faces are often immediately buried in newspapers and books that the riders appear to carry specifically for reading at this time; sometimes passengers may be indulging in various forms of autoinvolvements, especially daydreaming. People without books or papers, once they have established themselves as being nonthreatening to others by some parallel but innocuous behavior upon first sitting down, may begin to stare at fellow passengers, alternating fleeting or blank stares with an innocent staring off into space. These stares and glances at fellows are quite restricted and concealed and are made so because they are not to be interpreted as invitations to others to begin an encounter; they are the behavioral components of what Goffman (1963:84) has termed "civil inattention," occurring when "one gives to another enough visual notice to demonstrate that one appreciates that the other is present (and that one admits openly to having seen him), while at the next moment withdrawing one's attention from him so as to express that he does not constitute a target of special curiosity or design." Such expressions permit others to infer about this rider "that he has no reason to suspect the intentions of the others, to be hostile to them, or wish to avoid them." Such are the properties of the face and body that this communication can go on without a word being exchanged.

Yet a minimal verbal comunication can be carried on between these accidental companions or those who do indeed know each other, despite the loud noises that the train makes when in motion; moreover, civil inattention is continuously afforded to such conversants by the strangers surrounding them, permitting some animated conversations to be sustained. Despite the borders that arise around two or more people when a conversation begins on a subway train, the immediately surrounding passengers usually become absorbed in the speakers as a side involvement of their own, finding it very difficult to avoid listening in such close quarters. Although the listeners may try to maintain an unattached front by blankly glancing elsewhere, this usually conceals that their attention has been drawn into the ongoing conversation; for, when voice levels drop or when the train makes exceptional noises, the listeners' heads move toward the conversation to improve their tracking capacities.

Displays of visual inattention are limited in subways to the advertising that is placed there, which takes advantage of the limited scene and the effort of riders to display civil inattention to their fellow passengers. Travel above ground reduces the problem of avoiding prolonged staring and too close attention to others through the convenient distractions provided by the outside scenery. Sometimes these efforts backfire, as when a persistent person knows that the other is looking at something outside of the vehicle and makes a casual comment about it, providing the beginnings of an encounter. Indeed, the blank-face expressions of most riders have their deterring effect because they cannot be the basis of an encounter without calling direct attention to it, rather than to the object of the gaze; in such cases, the person who seeks to initiate conversation would begin it with an insult that could only be answered in kind or with icy silence.

Those who subtly satisfy their curiosity toward the many new and interesting faces around them withhold any reactions that might reveal that they are curious and also how they feel toward these new objects of their attention. In such an atmosphere, where revealing facial expressions are discouraged, verbal interaction is difficult to initiate. In Goffman's view of this ongoing drama, the passengers deny their accessibility, for accessibility is double-edged: It can be very helpful for strangers to relate information that one does not have; yet, in normal situations, a stranger's speaking demands that one acknowledge him and thus creates a bond between speaker and listener that, in turn, poses a threat.

In general, some people are more open to interaction than others, usually because of the innocuous qualities that we can attribute to them. Middle-aged housewives of matronly build, who are neat in appearance and are usually carrying shopping bundles, are one such type. For instance, they often indicate a readiness for conversation not by speaking directly to their fellow riders but by commenting about the heat or the weight of their bundles or talking on some other broad plane. In so doing, they can protect themselves against a rebuff by claiming that they did not intend that these remarks be given a response. Moreover, they can demonstrate by word as well as appearance that they are no threat to anyone: They can ignore the rule about the inaccessibility of those around them because they offer no threat to others and others would certainly regard them as unthreatening. They show by age, stature, attire, and demeanor that there are no sexual innuendos intended in their remarks. The role that they have accepted, that of housewife and mother, holds little power to threaten anyone, and their overcompliance with the rules of deportment indicates an over-all passivity.

Another interesting exception to the civil inattention rule is found in the behavior that riders display when young children are present. The majority of people, because they feel that children are a permissible outlet for their attention, are less careful in directing their curiosity toward them than toward adults. One is permitted to stare at a child longer than at an adult. In turn, the child's stare is often greeted by a smile rather than a sign of discomfort; the passenger, by smiling, shows that he is not threatened by this violation of face-to-face interaction and even returns the openness shown him.

Even when morally spurred to approach a stranger and aid or warn him in the presence of some danger, people feel reluctant to threaten themselves or infringe on another's rights. Such a failure to give aid or warning was witnessed on one occasion: On a seat near one of the doors was a large puddle of water. A woman entered through the door, and, in accord with our previous hypothesis, chose to sit there because of its isolation from other passengers. As she began to sit, a young man sitting across from her seemed ready to warn her of the water, but, after a moment of indecision, he elected to remain silent. She sat uncomfortably in the water while everyone tried to avoid acknowledging what had just happened. It was a few moments before she moved to another seat, acting as if nothing had happened. Perhaps her hesitation indicated that she feared moving because she might be regarded with suspicion by people toward whom she was moving for no apparent reason.

The respect accorded to fellow passengers via civil inattention can go too far, as the last illustration suggests. Yet it takes an interesting form in the taboo against physical contact, a reminder of the kind of situation in which one is participating. Physical contact usually connotes intimacy between people, and, on the subways, people move as far away from each other as possible, if and when the opportunity arises. In the event that there are cramped seating accommodations, one must be careful that any physical contact does not exceed the boundaries of an accidental touching of the person next to him. Once, when riding on a car having no empty seats, an observer held onto a pole that was also being grasped by an older man. When the train jerked, her hand touched his, and both quickly pulled their hands away while simultaneously and self-consciously apologizing to each other; this was followed by both parties' deliberately turning their backs to each other, a way of restoring mutual civil inattention and limiting vulnerability to interaction.

These rules of close, face-to-face interaction enable people to avoid unnecessary encounters and to hide their emotions. In urban environments, where so much interaction or potential interaction takes place, this may be a necessity in order to get through the day and limit the moral claims that every other might make upon you. Yet such efforts at concealment of emotions make us feel isolated and defensive during subway travel, producing an emergent atmosphere of hostility among passengers. As a result, each rider is not only upholding the rules when he looks out for himself, but he also expects others to look out for themselves in the same way. This was evidenced by a general slackening of manners and courtesy, on the part of many passengers, regardless of social class, who were observed pushing to get seats and, once having secured them, rarely offering them to disabled or frailer persons. On one occasion, a young man did get up to offer his seat to an old woman nearby; however, she was not anticipating such treatment, and, before she realized the significance of the gesture, another man had taken the seat. One might conclude from this incident that an act of grace cannot take place unless it is recognized as such by a respectful audience; in this case there were no such witnesses.

On another occasion, one observer, who was sitting beside a well-dressed middle-aged woman, purposely violated the rights of accessibility in order to validate this hypothesis on subway behavior. After some time beside the passenger, who had not acknowledged the presence of her "seatmate" in any way, the observer took out a silk slip from her shopping bag and quickly asked the woman what she thought about the quality of the slip. The woman was so shocked that she responded by hitting the observer with a large pocketbook. Although this rider's response to a direct violation of the rules of accessibility was somewhat exaggerated and violent, her reaction was still a plausible one. The observer had broken the code of conduct requiring passengers on subways to refrain from verbal contacts, and had opened herself up more than was ordinarily allowed in polite public encounters (except for emergency or informative verbalizations). Surely, the choice of a lady's slip as opposed to a box of nondescript stationery allowed for the possibility of the overture to be regarded as a sexual threat as well as a communicative one. Nevertheless, the rules concerning conduct are there precisely to prevent one's vulnerability to be taken advantage of, sexually or otherwise.

The isolation imposed upon subway riders by their acceptance of the code of conduct delineated above can have far more serious consequences than just a loosening of good manners. One observer was seated with two shopping bags at her feet, and she remained in the same seat with approximately the same people around her for a good length of time. An older man, who had had no bundles when he had entered the subway car and who had sat beside her for several stops, casually picked up one of her bags and began to walk off at the next stop. Although most people were able to see and to realize what was happening, no one offered her any assistance, and she was forced to recover the shopping bag for herself. The newspapers of New York and Boston are filled with eyewitness accounts of passengers who were beaten or mugged and who received no aid from their fellow riders, indicating the extreme defensiveness and unwillingness to get involved that this code of conduct encourages.

The social interaction taboos that force people into becoming uninvolved observers in order to protect themselves are structured very differently during the rush hours. People may fit into two broad categories during these times: (1) the aggressive types (the pushers and the shovers) and (2) the passive resisters (those people who are resigned to their immediate fate but determined to take it with a smile or with indifference). The possibility of surreptitious staring at people, or being stared at, is greatly diminished because the distance between travelers is reduced considerably, necessitating stricter adherence to civil inattention. Thus, the closer together people are, the more they must get immersed in subordinate involvements; yet the ones that are immediately available to them, each other, are mainly out of bounds. Accordingly, the physical taboos are also temporarily altered during the rush hour; yet they are enforced more strictly and overtly. There is no longer a choice of open spaces, and the overcrowded conditions arbitrarily place each person in close contact with many others, making any act of touching not ordinarily a personal advance toward any one individual. It requires special recognition of unnecessary closeness during these hours to claim that one is being violated in this way and special willingness to withstand the accusation of being a hysterical person if one makes a scene by accusing another of taking advantage of the physical closeness of the riders during rush hour. To move away is not easy under these circumstances, and overt efforts to get someone to stop touching brings attention to oneself as well as to the culprit, opening oneself up for encounters with others.

One incident of such sexual significance occurred during a rush hour when the observer was standing in a corner of the train, unable to move because of the crowd around her. A large man managed to squeeze beside her and began swaying to his own time rather than to that of the normal movements of the subway car. He continued to press himself and the observer into the corner, making it difficult for her to afford civil inattention to his obvious intentions. The observer tried to elbow the man, but he remained fixed and unrelenting. It was obvious that he was intent upon taking advantage of the situation and violating her territorial rights by blatantly ignoring the unwritten code of polite distance. Moreover, he knew full well that the rules could not be enforced by others or by the victim under these circumstances without creating a scene, thereby turning an effort to get from one place to another by rapid transit into an episode of great importance.

Despite the problems that are presented to the rider during rush hour, there remains the full knowledge of all involved that they share the common fate of little people trying to get to or from work or shopping. As a result, people often seem more relaxed and approachable. While holding many bundles and standing in a crowded car, an observer was having some trouble maintaining her balance. A little old man, who was well dressed and appeared "grandfatherly," saw her dilemma and smilingly advised her how to "ride the crowd" in the car and better maintain her balance. When a seat was eventually vacated near the man, he signaled for her to sit down; when she finally left the subway car, he said good-bye. In a less crowded subway train, at a different time, the observer would probably have felt terribly threatened by this man, for his comments would have been gratuitous; yet, under these circumstances, she found his actions quite permissible.

Rules that exist on subways are often violated by groups or individuals, serving either to unite the subway passengers against the violators or to allow the violators certain privileges they normally could not obtain by adhering to proper riding behavior. Several occurrences were observed that pointed to the fact that infractions of normal behavioral codes, either by a group of people or by an individual, seemed to threaten a large number of passengers (as opposed to less noticeable and isolated threats against single individuals). In such instances subway riders banded together and temporarily focused their attention on the violators, providing in this way the final ingredients of a public incident. During one ride, the train made a stop at a point in Boston's Chinatown district. Prior to this stop, many of the passengers had been situated together for a rather long time but had not acknowledged each other except by affording civil inattention. A large group of Chinese women entered the car, found no vacant seats, and were forced to stand. Rather than disperse throughout the car, they cluttered around the first available pole and began to chatter excitedly in Chinese about some apparently humorous event that the remainder of the passengers could not comprehend. These animated Chinese women attracted the attention of everyone on the subway, and those viewing them openly displayed their amazement, without attempting to conceal their reaction. In turn, the Chinese passengers acknowledged their fellow travelers with smiles and nods, breaking down the usual subway comportment of isolation and defensiveness.

Still another case of unification of typically uncommunicative passengers was evident during a night ride through an undesirable area of Boston. An inebriated man with a bulky cast on his arm staggered into the car and dumped himself into the nearest vacant seat. Probably because of his drunken state, he did not look to the left or right, as is commonly done by oncoming riders; certainly, he did not display any attempt to conceal his drunkenness and lack of self-control from those already present. When he had determined where he was, he loudly insisted that those riders around him autograph his cast. As a result of this sociable drunk's efforts at communication, the typical social distance maintained between passengers was quickly broken down; because he sought out several people in his request, rather than just one person, the passengers moved out of the area as a group, while exchanging comments and looks of disgust among themselves, producing a solidarity in the face of this minor danger.

Finally, while riding the subway during rush hours, one observer noticed a car fairly vacant of people. Yet, upon entering the car, she encountered a large group of seemingly normal children, probably on their way to school. Upon closer investigation, it became apparent that these children were using hand motions to communicate with each other and were deaf and dumb. Other passengers who entered the car would promptly leave upon viewing this strange group of children rapidly moving their hands and communicating magnificently amid the din of the subway. These children, who shared a defect and a mode of communication, banded together, imposing a threat upon nondefective passengers.

Sometimes, when the rules are deliberately violated as a way of extending an invitation to begin an encounter and make the ride more interesting by striking up a conversation with a fellow rider, the overture is misunderstood and claims are made that go beyond the bounds of sociability for its own sake. One observer entered the head car of a train accompanied by a young male friend. The young man stood before the front window and pretended to drive the train. A shabbily dressed old man, upon observing the young man's carefree and open behavior, engaged him in conversation and the two became mutually accessible. As the conversation progressed, however, the observer noticed that, though the man was talking to her friend, his eyes were intently fixed on her own legs. After a few moments the old man asked the observer's friend to instruct her to move her legs apart. This request, a gross infraction of the rules of subway riding, occurred primarily because the young man had broken the rules of verbal contact by giving signals indicating that he was open for engagement. When the old man responded to the signals and was reinforced in turn by further conversation, he felt that he was free to extend his demand for accessibility to the young lady.

In conclusion, we have found that regulations regarding behavior in subways aim primarily at protecting unacquainted individuals from accessibility to each other during periods of suspension of main involvement, or when main involvements are passive. It should be noted that, in similar situations, as in the waiting rooms of doctors or dentists, the proprietors provide seating arrangements that are unconducive to eye contact between patients and to the beginnings of face engagements, as well as reading material that permits the establishment of subordinate involvements as a means to keep people apart and protected from each other. In the subways, in contrast, people are more on their own, and protection is afforded by particular seating arrangements, the affording of civil inattention, involvement shields to maintain distance that are brought with the passenger, and taboos against physical contact. Only during exceptionally unpleasant times, such as during a rush hour or when passengers feel threatened by rule violators, will subway travelers ignore the rules, compromise their defenses, and help each other avoid the dangers of riding underground.

Reference

GOFFMAN, ERVING
1963 *Behavior in Public Places*. New York: Free Press.

3. Intimacies: Notes Toward a Theory of Social Inclusion and Exclusion[*][1]

SASHA R. WEITMAN[1]

> Les amoureux qui s'bécottent sur les bancs publics,
> Bancs publics, bancs publics,
> En s'foutant pas mal du r'gard oblique
> Des passants honnêtes
> Les amoureux qui s'bécottent sur les bancs publics,
> Bancs publics, bancs publics,
> En s'disant des "Je t'aime" pathétiqu's
> Ont des p'tit's gueul's bien sympathiqu's.
>
> GEORGES BRASSENS
> (from the song "Bancs Publics")

By definition, intimacies are acts of affection in which people engage comfortably in private but not in public. From the standpoint of the collectivity, they may also be defined as those acts of affection whose practice is tolerated, or is at least considered tolerable, in private but not in public.[2] The question to be considered here is why acts of

[*] This article was previously published in English in Archives Européennes de Sociologie, Vol. 11 (1970), pp. 348–67. This first publication in the United States is by permission of the author.

[1] My thanks go to a number of people who have taken time out to read and to comment on an earlier version of this paper, in particular Randall Collins, Lewis Coser, Emmanuel Marx, Merton Hyman, Dan O'Neil, Philip Slater, Arthur Stinchcombe, Eugene Weinstein, and Kurt Wolff. My thanks go also to the few anthropologists (less than 20 per cent) who responded to the one-page questionnaire I sent them, especially Dorothy Billings, Annemarie de Waal Malefijt, Ruth Useem, and Roy Wagner.

[2] By "in public" I mean in front of others—or, to be a little more precise, in the presence of people whose participation is limited to what Schachtel (1949) calls the "distance senses," seeing and hearing. It should also be noted at the outset that not all intimacies, as they are here defined, are "sexual" in the ordinary sense of this term. Thus, the carefree, affectionate horseplay between parents and children, between siblings, between close friends, between members of a solidary ethnic or regional subgroup, or even between a person and his pet animal can also qualify as intimacies, in so far as such affections tend to be given freer and fuller expression in private than in public places.

affection are everywhere morally distinguished into these two classes: the class of those considered intimate and whose expression is, as a rule, inhibited in public places, and the residual class of those considered decent and proper enough to be openly practiced.

This is a comparatively trivial problem as problems go, but it does raise some intriguing questions. Furthermore, its solution suggests, as I hope to show, a potentially useful set of insights into the meaning and function of some of our most familiar mores and customs.

I

Typically, this question elicits one or the other of the following two immediate responses: The first sounds like an explanation and states that the reluctance of people to engage in intimacies in full view of the public is nothing but a conditioned inhibition; the second response, which is a factual criticism rather than a proposed explanation, states that the reluctance to act intimately in public may be true of some societies but certainly is not equally true of them all. It is thus common knowledge that certain acts of affection (such as kissing), considered intimate and therefore refrained from in public expression in certain societies (like Japan), are often perfectly acceptable and commonplace in others (like France).

Both these points may be granted. The former in particular may be disposed of at once, if only because it is little more than a harmless truism, roughly on a par with the well-known (though probably apocryphal) explanation by medieval scholastics that the reason poppy seeds make you sleepy is that they possess soporific properties.[3] As for the second point, it too may safely be granted because the existence of crosscultural variations in the specific acts that are felt to be intimate does not really challenge the proposition here under consideration, which is that such a distinction, *regardless of the specific activities to which it refers,* is nevertheless a universal feature of all societies. What could call into question the validity of this proposition would be the documented existence of a substantial number of societies, or even of stable groupings within them, where this type of moral distinction and segregation of affectionate activities is completely absent. As far as I have been able to learn, however, this kind of distinction and segregation is to be found in *all* societies, even among Indian tribes of the Brazilian highlands such as the Kaingáng (see Henry, 1941), which

[3] Clearly, to explain that people behave in X manner because they have been so conditioned does not explain anything. All it does is make us reiterate our question: Why are they being so conditioned? As for the further clarification that they are so conditioned because they are under the empire of cultural norm X', that does not advance us either. On the contrary, because it only leads us to rephrase the original (and, I believe, scientifically more fruitful) question, "Why behavior pattern X?" to the narrower, more problematic question, "Why cultural norm X'?"

are, from the sexual standpoint, among the most voracious, un-restrained, and promiscuous known to ethnography.[4]

A third response commonly elicited by this problem states that intimacies as I have defined them belong to the more general category of *private activities*. These, in turn, are given a dramaturgical explanation: They are explained by reference to the need of individual actors to maintain control over the impressions they make on others. Thus, niches of privacy provide the actor not only with the necessary "backstage" (Goffman, 1956b:112–34) in which freely to rehearse for his public performances but also with the no less indispensable haven in which he can occasionally give himself up to such all-absorbing activities as love-making (hence intimacies) *without regard to the impressions he might involuntarily emit in the course of such activities.*

This explanation is not without its sizable grain of truth; yet it is not quite satisfactory, because it accounts for only half of the phenomenon under consideration. The other half, in fact, would even seem to contradict it. In effect, the dramaturgical explanation accounts for why those who themselves wish to engage in intimacies favor such privatization of their effusions, but it fails to explain why the spectacle of such activities should be offensive and upsetting to *others*, that is, to those who witness them but do not partake in them. After all, what is so upsetting about people expressing their love and affection for one another? Or, even if we grant for argument's sake that the body posturations and vocal exclamations characteristic of intimacies are demeaning, still: Why should anyone become upset at others for making fools of themselves? It would even seem, on the basis of the logic on which the dramaturgical explanation is built, that exactly the opposite should be expected, namely, that those who come upon a couple "caught in a compromising position" would be positively *elated* rather than upset by their discovery, because the resultant status loss by the indiscreet couple represents a corresponding status gain for the discoverers. In other words, according to the logic underlying the dramaturgical thesis, those who chance on a public display of intimacies would be expected to behave like *paparazzi*, or even like blackmailers,

[4] Two comments are necessary at this point. The first is that what I affirm to be a matter of fact—namely, the universality of this distinction between, and segregation of, high- and low-intensity acts of affection—is perhaps more an assumption of fact than a *bona fide* matter of fact. This assumption, which the reader is asked to accept for the sake of the argument I am about to develop, is based on a broad though unsystematic survey of anthropological monographs and on direct oral as well as written replies by a sample of over fifty anthropologists who have done field work among non-Western peoples. Second, the fact that in a number of societies intimacies are, on certain occasions (for example, during rites of defloration, rites of marriage) ceremonially performed in full view of the public does not constitute, I believe, a disconfirmation of my general proposition—no more than the existence of public executions constitutes disproof of the prohibition against intragroup killing.

whereas in point of fact many of them appear to be genuinely offended, even outraged, by that kind of spectacle.

II

The explanation I should like to propose here is that the fundamental reason for this universal tendency on the part of human beings to hide in order to give rein to their intense affections is out of a deep (although usually inarticulate) recognition that one unmistakable meaning of intimacies to those who witness them but are not privileged to partake in them is that they are excluded from the bond of affection being cultivated in their presence. One reason, then, though not necessarily the only one, or even necessarily a conscious reason, for this tendency to inhibit the impulse to engage in intimacies in the presence of others is out of deference to them, out of consideration for their sensitivities, and, more specifically, *in order to spare them the experience of feeling excluded as total strangers*, even if they are total strangers.

If there is some truth to this explanation, we should expect to find the unabashed public display of intimacies to be most prevalent, paradoxically enough, in precisely those societies where people are least considerate of the feelings of others. In fact, one should even be prepared to witness the most torrid public displays of love and affection in those societies where people are positively *nastiest* to one another. That, I propose, may be precisely the reason why, among the Western nations, embracing in public, kissing in public, and fondling in public are most prominent in France.[5] That is why, in the United

[5] Again a number of caveats are in order. First of all, by "nastiness" I mean (without, I believe, stretching ordinary usage too far) the tendency deliberately to act in such a way toward others as to make them feel keenly demeaned and excluded. Second, concerning the French, I do not believe that the nastiness I attribute to them is but a figment of my imagination, or of my own nastiness. It was, after all, France that begot the philosopher who bequeathed on us this dramatic definition of Hell: *L'enfer, c'est les autres* ("Hell is other people"). It was France also that begot sadism—and by sadism I refer not to the moral aberration as such but to the fully articulated philosophy of living that flourishes to this day in intellectually respectable French *avant-garde* circles (see Bataille, 1962). And, on a much more mundane, though no less significant, level, it is about their treatment at the hands of the French rather than of any other people in Europe that foreign tourists seem to complain the most. Not so long ago, in fact (*New York Times*, 1965), France's government became so concerned that it launched (without, of course, any success) an utterly preposterous campaign aimed at mollifying Frenchmen's conduct toward foreign tourists. The campaign consisted of providing every incoming tourist with a book of "smile checks" to reward especially cooperative and courteous *gendarmes*, chambermaids, taxi-drivers, bellhops, train conductors, café waiters, and so forth. (By the end of the year, the government promised, those with the most checks would win a free trip to Tahiti, the West Indies, or the United States.) I should also add, concerning this unflattering characterization of the French, lest it be foolishly attributed to Francophobia on my part, (1) that I regard this nastiness as but one aspect of an enormously complex and multifaceted

States, they appear to be far more in evidence in New York City than in any other large city (New York being to the United States roughly what France is to the Western world and what Paris is to France). That may also be why, in general, such displays seem more prominent in large metropolitan centers than in small towns; [6] why they appear more prevalent among bohemians than among conventional people; among the young than among the middle-aged; among tourists (and especially among soldiers on furlough in occupied countries) than among the natives. In all these examples, what distinguishes the members of the former category from those of the latter is that they are less imbued with—or, depending on your point of view, less burdened by—a sense of social responsibility toward the members of the surrounding community. I am suggesting that, as a general phenomenon, the public indulgence in intimacies is probably not most fruitfully understood as the product of a generalized lack of inhibitions, or even as part of a generalized defiance of prevailing standards of proper demeanor. Rather, it is most fruitfully understood as a product of a general mentality for which only the French, significantly enough, have a special and remarkably appropriate expression, *le je-m'en-*

---

people who are in several respects among the most charming, attractive, and remarkable in the West and (2) that I tend to attribute this nastiness of theirs not— it should go without saying—to their genetic make-up but to a peculiarity of their national political structure. Specifically, I think this nastiness is at least partly attributable to their centuries-old experience of being essentially *an administered rather than a self-governing nation.* The tendency in an administered society is for people to feel relatively little need for one another because essential public services and collective decisions are generated not by free association but by the organs of the state. This absence of significant constraints to cooperate leads progressively to the dissipation from the population of the spirit of cooperation and the spirit of social responsibility. Such a state of affairs has been further compounded in France's particular case by the *divide et impera* manner in which the central government has traditionally ruled the country, especially during the three centuries usually referred to as the *ancien régime* (Tocqueville, 1955; Weitman, 1968). These two factors, the lack of necessity to cooperate and the divisive style of national leadership, may account in large part for the proverbial nastiness, cliquishness, and snobbism of the French, toward one another no less than toward outsiders. For a hilarious essay, incidentally, on this general subject, see Mark Twain's "The French and the Comanches" (1879), a selection from a larger work written, we are informed, "as a study in comparative anthropology" devoted to showing that, appearances notwithstanding, the French really are every bit "as advanced as any other semi-civilized nation."

[6] One might want to explain this difference in public demeanor by pointing to the differential degrees of *anonymity* in large and small localities. But the anonymity of a community, unlike its geographical location and climatic properties, is not an externally given characteristic. Rather, it is nothing but a variant (albeit a collectively sanctioned variant) of the more general phenomena of social irresponsibility and unconcern to which I shall allude shortly. In effect, what else do we mean when we say of a setting that it is "anonymous" if it is not that, in it, people feel free to disregard some of the most elementary rules of sociability, and thereby temporarily to define and treat one another as nonpersons? (The concept of the nonperson is introduced in Goffman, 1956b:151–53.)

foutisme—roughly translatable as "don't-give-a-damnism"—by which is denoted a spirit of deliberate indifference, of social irresponsibility, and of unconcern with a vengeance.

To summarize: Acts of intimacy, whatever specific shape and content they may take in different societies, are of course best understood first and foremost as acts of gratification of one's affections. When, however, they are practiced in public, they become in addition an open declaration and demonstration of the bond of love between the people involved, and therefore, and just as explicitly, they also signify the exclusion from that bond of all those who are only witnesses to it.[7] Public intimacies, then, are best understood not only as acts of gratification of the love between two people but also as gestures of exclusion unequivocally (even if unintentionally) communicated to all those present.

III

It is perhaps just this type of harsh exclusion of others that is avoided through the taboo on incest. Were incestuous bonds permitted, the integrity and solidarity of the familial group would be fundamentally threatened. The formation of permanent dyadic relationships and their unrestrained indulgence in the passionate affections occasionally generated by such relationships would *ipso facto* make the remaining members of the family feel brutally excluded, that is, would make them feel like nonmembers. That is why, it seems to me, husband and wife tend to treat each other modestly, in some societies even formally, before their children. That is why they avoid being overly intimate and absorbed in one another in front of them, why they seclude themselves to make love behind closed doors in their bedroom [8] (where presumably they cannot be seen or heard), and why they do

[7] Let me only mention in passing that this gross and superficial distinction between witnesses and participants raises one of the most complex, exciting, and profound questions in sociological theory, the question of how much and what kind of involvement (that is, visual, oral, tactile, proxemic, and so forth) in collective activities constitute group membership. It is because he fails to appreciate the sociological significance of this fundamental question that Marshall McLuhan (1964: Part One, *passim*) is led to make the extravagant claim that, through television, humanity is presently being "retribalized" on a global scale.

[8] For a splendid historical account of the postmedieval evolution of norms of adult modesty in the presence of children in Western societies, and of how these norms came to be expressed and enforced through the interior design of homes and even through the ecology of cities, see Philippe Ariès (1962). Also relevant here is the custom in polygamous societies for the husband not to sleep with any of his wives and concubines in the presence of the others. Either each of his spouses has her own dwelling, in which case the husband visits and sleeps with each one separately, or else all the women live together in one dwelling (for example, in a harem), in which case the husband sends for one of them at a time and sleeps with her in his own quarters, also in seclusion from the others.

so at night under the cover of darkness (when, presumably, the children are fast asleep). Nevertheless, however, it would be foolish to assume that children are thereby not being excluded, or that they are not made to feel excluded in certain respects—in some highly meaningful respects, in fact—from the special relationship that binds their parents together. What happens instead is that children become gradually, almost imperceptibly, and very delicately conditioned to sense and eventually to understand that, while they belong to the family group, their membership in it is more peripheral than that of their parents. Gradually, they are conditioned to accept that their membership rights are only temporary, to be enjoyed only until they have grown enough and have acquired the necessary strength and skills to fend for themselves in the outside, and eventually to found their own family groups, in which each of them along with his or her mate will, in turn, become the central and permanent members.

A second implication is that it complements (and complicates) the classic hypothesis of the Oedipal complex. In effect, what I have been suggesting is that the young child, in addition to having to inhibit his carnal love for the parent of the opposite gender, is at the same time subtly yet irresistibly being conditioned by *both* his parents to the realization that he does not completely and permanently belong to the familial group in the same way they do. So, I submit that, if repression of love in this situation must take place, it is not only the love the child has for the parent of the opposite gender that must be repressed but also, and no less significantly, the love he has for both of his parents. That is, the child must also repress the wish to be a permanent, full-fledged member of the family group. And, by the same token, if repression of hatred in this situation must take place, then it is not just the child's hatred of the parent of the same gender that has to be repressed but also his hatred of both his parents for gradually excluding him from the family circle. (For a related argument, see Slater, 1961.)

IV

If I understand Claude Lévi-Strauss (1969) correctly, he maintains, following in this respect Marcel Mauss (1967), that social bonds—and, indeed, the whole of social life properly so designated—are created and perpetuated by repeated acts of generosity, by sacrificial acts. The most spectacular illustration of this proposition is provided by the *potlatch* of the Indians of northwestern America—those Indians of Alaska and of the Vancouver region whom Lévi-Strauss describes as evincing "a genius and exceptional temperament in their treatment of the fundamental themes of a primitive culture." But, he is quick to add, we, too, continually reaffirm, re-enact, and reillustrate in myriad little ways the profound truth of this general proposition. We do this, for example, when we send holiday presents to our relatives, when we send greeting cards to our neighbors and acquaintances, when we invite friends into our homes and treat them to extraordinary meals, when we socialize our earnings in the form of taxes and voluntary donations, and, above all else, when we raise our own children (particularly our daughters) so that others may profit from their labor and so that others may enjoy them as friends, lovers, and spouses.

What I said earlier about intimacies bears, I believe, a direct relationship to this general phenomenon. In effect, the prohibition against the public display of intimate affections resembles the taboo on incest, as well as the imperative disapproval of unrestrained exhibitions of extreme happiness in public places. The latent sentiment on which these and other such taboos and proscriptions are based is what may be called a "socialist" sentiment. This sentiment, the dynamics and potency of which are as a rule far better understood and appreciated by those who lead men than by those who study them, is embodied in the principle that excess good fortune ought to be socialized, that the larger community should be allowed to share in it also. The failure to heed this muffled yet extraordinarily powerful demand for inclusion is liable to arouse collective indignation, anger, and punitive retaliation. As Lévi-Strauss put it with regard to the commission of incest, "The violent reaction of the community is the reaction of a community wronged." To which I would only add that this reaction is so automatic, so passionate, and potentially so devastating not because *any* social norm has been broken but, rather, because the particular norm that has been violated happens to be the norm against gratuitous acts of social exclusion. Or, to be a little more precise, the norm that has been violated is the norm against acts that make others *feel* excluded, the significant nuance here being —sociological "realists" of the orthodox Marxian variety notwithstanding—that men become furiously aroused more by the ostentatious display of acts of social exclusion than by the existence *per se* of such acts.[9] In the case of intimacies, therefore, the community appears grudgingly to recognize the right of every member to indulge in exclusive affectionate relationships, but what it expects from him on such occasions—in fact, what it demands from him—is that he totally refrain from parading his great pleasure and good fortune in the

[9] Marx and Engels themselves subscribed to the absolute deprivation theory of revolution as well as to the relative deprivation theory of revolution, though they espoused the former in 1848 and the latter in 1849 (see Davies, 1962:5–6). The absolute deprivation theory, it should be noted, is perfectly consonant with their over-all materialist interpretation of history, while the relative deprivation theory, being explicitly sociopsychological and noneconomic (as is made extremely clear by the passage citied in Davies, 1962:5), is thoroughly at odds with that type of interpretation. Whether Marx and Engels realized this contradiction I do not know. But, by espousing the relative deprivation theory, they were in effect joining the ranks of those "reactionaries" who, like Alexis de Tocqueville (1955), maintained that revolution was more the product of a state of mind than of a state of the economy. (It would seem, therefore, that science, too, makes strange bedfellows.)

presence of others, so as to spare them the vivid reminder of the relative misery of their own lot. Hence the moral distinction between high- and low-intensity acts of affection, and the impassioned insistence that the former be scheduled in time and be segregated in space in such a manner as to be completely insulated from view and from hearing.[10]

V

The interpretation of intimacies being advanced here is based on a partial theory of human conduct that, though still at a very rudimentary stage of elaboration, might as well be made explicit now.

Proposition One of this theory is that human passions, particularly the social passions (that is, the passions whose objects of consummation are other people), tend to be aroused by, and in their turn tend to give rise to, processes of social inclusion and exclusion. Let me define the principal terms of this proposition before proceeding to elaborate it.

Passions are here defined as sentiments that distinguish themselves by their extraordinary intensity, their automaticity, their capacity to overwhelm, and their escalatory propensities. The extraordinary intensity of passionate sentiments is what prompted Emile Durkheim (1933) to refer to them as *des états forts de la conscience*—potent mental states. Under their spell, men have a tendency to behave, to paraphrase Pascal's famous aphorism, as though the heart followed reasons that reason cannot follow. Passions are aroused automatically, which is to say that a deftly administered flattery, insult, or caress will activate them at once and in force, even against the recipient's better judgment. (It is this type of *sui generis* dynamism that Durkheim [1933:139] tried unfelicitously to convey through the adjective "mechanical.") Once

---

[10] Here ends the discussion of the phenomenon of intimacies proper. Before proceeding to the more general theory under which it is subsumed, I should say that the explanation advanced here is not the only one available. There are currently at least two other sociological explanations of this phenomenon—one by Goffman (1963), the other by Slater (1963)—that are at least as interesting and compelling as mine. Goffman treats public intimacies ("mutual involvements") as particular instances of the broader category of challenges to the "moral order of situated activities," whereas Slater treats them as cases of "social regression," that is, of libidinal withdrawal from larger collectivities and their ongoing enterprises. I do not present these explanations here, because their authors, both of whom are exceedingly literate, have already done so much better than I ever could. Nor do I argue here the merits and demerits of their respective explanations relative to mine, because to do so at this, after all, highly abstract and speculative stage would bear little scientific fruit. Much more than theoretical polemics, what is needed now is the accumulation of a body of detailed documentary evidence on critical social processes (such as intimacies) that public opinion (understandably enough) considers too trivial, too private, or too dangerous to deserve our finest scientific efforts. It is only on the basis of such evidence that we shall ever be able to assess the relative merits of competing interpretative schemes such as the inclusion-exclusion paradigm presented here, Goffman's normative order perspective, Slater's psychoanalytical model, and the currently popular paradigm of gain-motivated transactions.

passions have been activated, the urge for their expression or consummation is so overwhelming that they are likely to monopolize one's thoughts, to take command over one's mental faculties, and, on occasion, even to assume control over one's overt actions—hence the common and invidious designation of behavior carried out under their empire as "irrational behavior." [11] Passions, finally, and the social passions in particular, distinguish themselves by their escalatory propensities, by which I mean that, when people feeling them are provoked to action, the magnitude of the response the passions tend to call forth is not equivalent to that of the stimulus but is much larger. It is thus that a casual remark by A prompts B to riposte with a nasty insult, which so stings A that he, in turn, cannot contain himself and slaps B across the face, which triggers such a rage in B that he assaults A with "intent to do great bodily harm," as the lawbooks put it, and so on and so forth.

Passions, I said, tend to be aroused in the context of acts of social inclusion or of social exclusion. By *acts of social inclusion* are here understood those activities whereby a person or group communicates to another person or group one or more of the following messages:

What I am/have/do, you too may be/may have/may do.

The best of what I have is not good enough for you.

You are more worthy/more attractive than you have been credited with being.

Let us join together and form a new entity, more integral and self-sufficient than either of us is without the other.

Processes of social inclusion consist of more or less complex sequences of mutual penetration and incorporation and are variously expressed in such familiar social activities as flirting, complimenting or flattering, honoring, introducing, initiating or debuting, exchanging gifts or secrets, promoting or electing for high office, taking into one's confidence, dancing together, hosting, eating together, playing together, corresponding, caressing, making love or sleeping together, singing, marching, traveling or vacationing together, marrying, living together, and so forth. One thing all these activities have in common is that they make people —or, rather, they are designed to make people—feel as though they have free and privileged access to certain highly valued social activities.

Conversely, the expression *acts of social exclusion* is used to denote the myriad ways and means that people throughout the ages have devised to make other people feel as though they have no access, or

[11] Passions have but one aim: Their own exhaustion (Durkheim, 1933: Book 1, Ch. 2). Or, as Lewis Coser (1956:49) puts it, they provoke conflicts (which he calls "nonrealistic") that "are not occasioned by the rival ends of the antagonists, but by the need for tension release of at least one of them."

at best have only very restricted access, to these highly valued activities. More specifically, they consist of acts that communicate one or several of the following meanings:

What I am/have/do, you are not and may not be/do not and may not have/cannot and may not do.

What is good enough for me is too good for you.

You are less worthy/attractive than you and others think.

Go away/I am leaving you: I am better off without you/with someone else.

Among the most common and least subtle of these processes of exclusion is, on the one hand, the entire gamut of *acts of expulsion*, such as demotion, dismissal, ceremonial degradation, execution, humiliation, excommunication, exile, imprisonment, mutilation, insult, defamation, and commitment. And, on the other hand, there is the equally variegated collection of *acts of obstruction to entrance*, as expressed, for example, in the withholding of appropriate keys or passwords; in the erection of walls, fences, barricades, and the display of signs that say things like "Private Property," "Beware of Dog," "No Loitering," "Trespassers Will Be Prosecuted"; in the posting at entrances of border guards, policemen, immigration and customs officials, dogs, automatic alarm systems, bouncers, and concierges; in the imposition of age, citizenship, and other formal entrance requirements; and so on and so forth *ad nauseam*.

Having defined the terms of Proposition One, let me return to it and make it a little more explicit. What this proposition maintains is that two of the fundamental kinds of processes through which the social passions are aroused are the processes of social inclusion and those of social exclusion. More specifically, what I am suggesting is that *processes of social inclusion tend to activate the associative passions* —which might also be called the "passions of social attraction," the "sympathetic passions," or the "anthropophilic passions," under which are here subsumed, among others, such emotions as erotic love, filial and parental love, loyalty, friendship, patriotism, and fraternity. *Processes of social exclusion, on the other hand, tend to arouse the dissociative passions*—that is, the types of passions that could also be called the "passions of social rejection," the "antipathetic passions," or the "passions of hostility," all of which refer to such emotions as contempt, detestation, repugnance, spite, hatred, alienation, resentment, envy, and jealousy.[12]

[12] I should not like to create or to leave the impression here that I have actually *defined* acts of social inclusion and exclusion. All I have done is offer various examples of what I mean by these terms, which is a considerably easier task than to provide them with the kind of conceptual definition that will prove scientifically fruitful.

We now come to Proposition Two of the theory, which derives from the observation that acts of social inclusion and acts of social exclusion are as inseparable as the two faces of a coin. More precisely, what Proposition Two proposes is that *the very same activities that are, to those privileged to partake in them, unambiguous acts of social inclusion are at the same time liable to represent to those who are not so privileged equally unambiguous acts of social exclusion.* Thus, whenever colleague A invites colleague B for supper, he thereby runs the risk, unless he takes adequate precautions, of alienating his other colleagues C, D, and E. Likewise, our love for our own woman is so absorbing and so exclusive that we are thereby depriving other, equally meritorious women of our love.[13] (The same, incidentally, can be said of our relationship to our children.) When we bestow a medal on a soldier, we are thereby choosing not to bestow that medal on other soldiers, who may think themselves equally brave and deserving. When we elect a candidate for office, we are thereby automatically rejecting his opponents. When we single out a friend and take him into our confidence, we are thereby deliberately choosing not to confide in our other friends.[14] This particular property, which seems to be unique and distinctive in acts of social inclusion, may be referred to as the intrinsic *ambivalence of human bonds.*[15]

We now have all the elements needed to derive our third and last proposition. Because acts of social inclusion may also be acts of social exclusion (according to Proposition Two) and because these are liable

[13] By the same token, I suppose, we are thereby also preventing other men—not quite as meritorious as we, to be sure, but almost as meritorious—from claiming a share of our own woman's love.

[14] Proposition Two may strike the reader as highly overstated. Various examples of acts of inclusion may come to his mind that do not on their faces appear to also represent acts of exclusion. The reader may conceivably be right: Proposition Two may indeed turn out in the end to have been overstated. But, before I agree to such a conclusion, I would argue, first, that a pointed analysis of acts of inclusion would reveal in most instances that just about all such acts of inclusion are exclusive in one form or another, to some degree or another. Thus, even the most universalistic of the proselytizing religions (especially Christianity and Islam) require of their new members that they undergo a formal conversion, which consists usually of reneging on membership in their previous religious group and taking an oath of allegiance to their new faith (see Solomon, 1965). Second, I would argue that, if so many acts of inclusion are indeed commonly carried out without provoking the antipathies of the excluded, it is only because the actual manner and context in which such acts of social inclusion usually take place are richly endowed with various and sundry palliative devices, most of which (like walls, for example) we take so much for granted as to be virtually blind to them, and all of which serve essentially the same function: to avoid creating "hard feelings" among those who have been left out. This theme is elaborated on in the next section.

[15] Not to be confused with the psychoanalytic concept of "ambivalence," which refers to a psychological (that is, intrapsychic) phenomenon. What the notion of "ambi-valence" used here refers to is a sociological phenomenon, namely, the property of certain objects or events to have significance [X] to members of set A and at the same time the very opposite significance [-X] to those of set B.

to kindle and to fan the meanest and most destructive of human passions (according to Proposition One), Proposition Three is now advanced to suggest that acts of love in particular and *acts of social inclusion in general are potentially just as provocative of hostile retaliation as are "naked" acts of social exclusion.* Acts of social inclusion are therefore potentially dangerous. They can be dangerous, first of all, to insiders (that is, those included) in so far as they run the risk of being assaulted and injured by outsiders (that is, those excluded). Second, they can be dangerous to outsiders because any assault on insiders may well provoke, given the escalatory propensities of the passions, a much more devastating retaliatory blow by the insiders and their allies. Finally, acts of social inclusion can also be dangerous to the larger community because the ever widening circle of conflict they are liable to produce risks disrupting ongoing cooperative activities of major importance, as well as jeopardizing the chances of future cooperative activities on which the collectivity's welfare, prosperity, and security might depend.[16]

VI

With this last proposition I have reached at long last the point at which my argument must either wander off into absurdity or else pay off with sociologically meaningful insights and propositions. I say wander off into absurdity because, if my theory is correct—if, in other words, simple acts of love and solidarity are really as fraught with perils as I have made them seem—then the next claims I might perhaps be expected to make are that the human species as we know it is unviable and that the fearsome combat of all against all is bound sooner or later to stop—indeed that it should have stopped a long time ago—if only because of a lack of live combatants left to carry it on.

While I am not prepared to make quite such a claim, I am prepared to suggest on the basis of the theory that *it is precisely because of the explosive potential of acts of social inclusion and exclusion that societies everywhere and at all times have developed an extraordinarily dense network of measures designed to prevent such acts from occurring and to bring them under control if and when they do occur.* The types of mechanisms involved so pervade and structure life as we live it from day to day, and are so intimately and profoundly enmeshed in even the most elemental of our habits, that social scientists—to say nothing of ordinary laymen—rarely think of seriously questioning their *raisons d'être*. Neither our familiarity with these patterns of conduct, however, nor their presumptive dismissal by public opinion as trivial represents good grounds for ignoring their existence, taking them for granted, or discounting their sociological significance. Quite to the contrary, in fact, as used to be unmistakably recognized decades ago by

[16] This is especially true of such socially contagious collectivities as the segmentary-lineage societies. (See discussion by Fallers, 1963.)

Sumner, Durkheim, Simmel, and Freud and is now gradually being rediscovered in contemporary American sociology (see, for example, Slater [1963], Goffman [1963], Blau [1964], and Garfinkel [1967]) under the combined impact of current events, psychoanalysis, anthropology, and ethology.[17]

What I shall attempt to do, therefore, in the remaining pages of this essay is to demonstrate, or rather to illustrate, how this theory provides what may be the organizing principle, the explanatory master key to a host of seemingly disparate customs, habits, norms, mores, laws, and institutions, all of which are seen here as mechanisms designed to achieve essentially the same broad functional objective: to prevent, by various containment strategies, exclusive activities from provoking destructive outbursts of passionate hostilities.

There are, first of all, the various mechanisms of *privatization*, by which I mean essentially the same thing Merton (1957:114) and R. Coser (1961) mean by the "insulation from observability of behavior," which consist simply of the removal of certain activities from the perceptual range of those not invited to partake in them. The phenomenon of *intimacies*, the analysis of which occupied the first pages of this paper and led me to where I am, is a clear instance of a set of activities that are, in one way or another, universally privatized. The *clothing* of nudity—or rather of what are believed to be erogenous zones—represents another obvious instance of privatization. (It is interesting to note in this regard that it was in France that the bikini was first introduced—around 1950, I believe—and that it has been widely used there ever since by men as well as women, whereas the more modest and considerate people of Great Britain and the United States have only recently begun to wear bikinis. In fact only women wear them in the United States; men there are still too shy to do so.)

Privacy, I should emphasize, is ordinarily thought of as the right of a person against the encroachment of society. As it has been analyzed in this paper, it is that, to be sure, but, more significantly perhaps, it is also *society's right*, that is to say, *the right of others* not to have to be subjected to the sights and sounds of desirable experiences that they have not been invited to share. In short, walls, fences, curtains, venetian blinds, doors, and, generally, all the partitions erected to ensure privacy are just as necessary for those outside as they are for those inside. (For a different interpretation, see Schwartz, 1968.)

The second category of mechanism is that of *compensatory inclusion*. These are the numerous little ways by which we occasionally include people into our lives to make up, to compensate for our

[17] It was not a sociologist but a "behavior physiologist," Konrad Lorenz (1963:79), who, basing his ideas on naturalistic studies of ducks, fish, geese, and the like, declared on the subject of "good" manners that "we do not, as a rule, realize either their function of inhibiting aggression or that of forming a bond. Yet it is they that effect what sociologists call 'group cohesion.' "

deliberate and systematic exclusion of others, even our friends, relatives, and colleagues, from the inside of our homes. To this end, *rituals of hospitality* have evolved that command (1) that we invite them into our home from time to time, (2) that on such occasions we treat them extraordinarily well, that is, substantially better than we would ordinarily treat our own selves at home, and (3) that we assure them before their departure, though we may not mean one word of it, that our home is open to them any time they wish to come by. Another, no less striking compensatory inclusion mechanism is the one embodied in the *rituals of salutation*. Chance encounters between acquaintances are punctuated by more or less elaborate greeting rituals, which may include (depending on the culture, social occasion, and statuses involved) such varied gestures as bowing, curtsying, kneeling, smiling, hat tipping, glove doffing, handshaking, hand kissing, cheek pinching, mouth kissing, shoulder gripping, bear-hugging, back patting, ass slapping, even ball grabbing, nose rubbing, joking, querying about one another's health, about close relatives, about business fortunes, and so forth, after which comes the entire gamut of departure rituals: again, handshakes, kisses, smiles, expressions of pleasure for having met, "good-bye," "*shalom*," "*adieu*," "take it easy," "best regards to everyone," and so forth.

Like the rituals of hopitality, the rituals of salutation can be regarded as acts of temporary inclusion, during which people who are otherwise relatively indifferent to one another take time out, out of a sense of *humanité oblige*, of ordinary social generosity, to acknowledge each other's existence, to express interest in one another, to honor one another, to wish the best to one another—in brief, to become *familiar* with one another. (For a somewhat different interpretation of deference gestures, see Goffman [1956a].) It seems to me that the various gift-giving and donation rituals on the occasion of holidays also belong to this class of compensatory mechanisms of inclusion.

There is still another class of compensatory inclusion mechanisms, which differ from the ones above in that they belong to the realm of beliefs rather than of rituals. Most evident among these is *transcendental religion*—the "opium of the people"—especially those religions that propound the Myth of Heaven and Hell, the myth that those who are excluded in this miserable world stand a good chance of being the included (the "Elect") in the next world, which is, after all, the only important world because it is the world of Eternal Life. The Myth of Reincarnation has a similar sociological meaning. So does, to some extent, the secular Myth of Revolution. And so does the Jewish Myth of the Messiah and of the Chosen People, and the Christian credo that "Blessed Are the Meek for They Shall Inherit the Earth," and the democratic Myth of Universal Equality, as expressed for example in the Horatio Alger myth that, with hard work, perseverance, and a little bit of luck *everyone* in America has a fighting chance to become as rich as Croesus.

Closely related to these compensatory inclusion myths is the interesting subset of those that consist of the *glorification of the excluded*. It is thus that, in many modern societies, the lower and working classes—by definition the most excluded people in the society—have occasionally been glorified as the "real people" (*Le Peuple, Il Popolo*), as representing the marrow and essence of the nation, the finest it has to offer. Similarly, there has sometimes been a tendency to glorify, or at least to romanticize, though more ambivalently than in the case of the lower classes, such excluded categories of the population as bandits (nowadays guerrillas) hiding in the mountains, madmen confined to asylums, Jews in ghettos, gypsies, blacks, Indians, hustlers, bohemians, and so forth.

The third broad category of passion-containment mechanisms consists of *norms against nastiness*, that is, against gratuitous acts of exclusion, particularly when the acts are overt. Norms of this type are so numerous, so varied, and so commonplace that I shall mention only one of them here, the norm—in some societies it has the strength of a taboo—against the uttering of curses and insults. What is interesting about curses and insults is, first, that they are verbal stimuli whose one and only purpose is deliberately to provoke in others what I called earlier the antipathetic passions and, second, that an analysis of these stimuli reveals that most of them consist of symbolic acts of exclusion. Thus, "To hell with you!" exiles you to a very unpleasant place, and "son of a bitch!" excludes you (as well as your mother) from the species *Homo sapiens* and reclassifies you as a mere canine.

Fourth, there are the numerous *safety-valve* mechanisms, which have long since been recognized by sociologists (see, for example, L. Coser, 1956:32–48). These comprise, first of all, such *role-reversal holidays and gatherings* as Purim, Halloween, Queen-for-a-Day, wife-swapping parties, and the like, through which those who are ordinarily excluded become included while those who are ordinarily included are excluded, and during which the former are accordingly licensed to behave with impunity for a limited period of time, usually a day or less. Second, there are the great *equal-access festivals*, such as the annual *bals masqués* (masquerade parties), Mardi gras, orgies, carnivals, and bacchanalia, in all of which the norm is for people who are ordinarily accessible to only a very few to become accessible to the many. Festivals of this sort have been known to last anywhere from one night to several days. Third, there are various *devices of hostility redirection*. the function of which is not so much the abatement of hostile reaction to exclusion as its distraction from the actual *agents provocateurs* and its redirection toward targets on which it can be more safely dissipated. Three such hostility-redirection devices are (1) *competitive games*, for instance, participation in sports, which provide one with the chance to exclude others from the rewards of triumph; (2) *dramatic spectacles*, whether athletic, theatrical, literary, pictorial, plastic, or cinematographic, the function of many of which is deliberately to arouse the emotions

under relatively controlled conditions and allow them to be vented for
brief stretches of time—the optimum duration for such cathartic
exercises in Western societies ranges between one and a half and three
hours—while at all times maintaining control over the spectators'
overt behavior and keeping their passions focused on the symbolic
representations of good and evil, rather than on good and evil as
they operate on that other, larger dramatic stage in which all of us are
actors; and (3) *scapegoating*, a device that provides the masses of the
excluded with the twin opportunities to do some excluding of their
own and at the same time justify this cruelty by blaming all their
miseries on their victims.[18] *Paranoidism*, that is, the deeply ingrained
tendency to perceive sinister conspiracies behind every unexplained
contrariety of some importance, is also characteristic of the system-
atically excluded and may be seen as a relatively benign form of
scapegoating.

Fifth are the passion-framing mechanisms—the mechanisms of
institutionalization—which consist of the imposition by the collectivity
of standardized molds on the kinds of passional outbreaks whose
incidence and prevalence are so great as to be generally accepted as
virtually ineradicable. Outbreaks of heterosexual love are thus ritualized

[18] Jews, as everyone knows, have been the all-time favorite scapegoats of
European societies. The principal reason for the Jews' extraordinary knack for
eliciting the vilest hostilities against themselves is not their religion *per se* or their
alleged historic role as Christ-killers, to say nothing of the other fantastic crimes
attributed to them. Rather, their principal "crime" has been, and to this day
continues to be, that they impress others as forming *relatively exclusive communities*—a "state within the state," as some of their more sophisticated detractors
have been fond of saying. (This expression, incidentally, is said to have been coined
by Richelieu in reference to Protestants, not to Jews.) Jews are viewed as exclusive—
and, therefore, sociologically speaking, they *are* exclusive: They speak their own
dialect; they follow their own customs; they worship their own God without any
attempt at proselytizing their religion (that is, without any attempt at inviting
others to join). They are also exclusive in that they are endogamous, in that they
have great pride in themselves as a nation, and in that they appear to be always
ready to assist one another in times of hardship, without regard to the national
and geographical boundaries separating them from their brethren. In short, and this
is the only reason for this lengthy digression, the tragic fate of the Jewish nation
in exile illustrates, more tellingly than any other historical example I can think of,
the profound perils of social solidarity (see Proposition Three of the theory). This
is the terrible predicament that has plagued and haunted the Jewish people for
centuries and that triggered the rise of the Zionist movement as a self-conscious
and deliberate effort to, if you will, "privatize" Judaism by gathering the scattered fragments of the Jewish nation and *erecting solid walls around it*—walls
that not only should provide Jews with a fighting chance to repel the on-
slaughts of anti-Semites but should also contribute substantially to the removal
of the root causes of anti-Semitism itself. (I might add, therefore, that the hope,
which is widely cherished in America, even among Jews, that ignorance is the root
cause of anti-Semitism, and, therefore, that only the spread of education can stamp
it out once and for all, is as naïve and futile as would be the homologous belief
that ignorance is at the root of jealousy and that only a better education can
becalm the murderous passions of the cuckold.)

into dating and courtship, formalized into engagement, and legally framed into marriage. (For a marvelously Pirandellian exposition of this process of societal intervention, see Slater, 1963:351–56.) Similarly, grave cases of antagonism and hostility are hurriedly pressured into the formal harness of duels, jousts, blood feuds, or legal suits, all of which serve essentially not only to localize the incipient conflict and prevent it from spreading to other parties but also (and no less importantly) to pump out of it, via the insistence on rigid adherence to ritual procedures, much of the emotional fuel that helped to ignite the conflict in the first place. This double aim is achieved, interestingly enough, not by entirely insulating the two antagonists but by fetching a third ("outside") party and involving him in the conflict. To be acceptable to the antagonists as well as effective in resolving their conflict, this third party must be viewed not only as impartial but also as *emotionally neutral*. Each antagonist, in vying for the third party's support, must therefore defuse his appeals of their passional content and base them on general principles acceptable to all. (The classic treatment of the sociological significance of the third party is in Simmel, 1950:140–69; for a more recent elaboration of this theme, see Caplow, 1968.) The proliferation of specialized conflict-mediating agencies such as arbitration panels, government-appointed mediators, courts of law (civil as well as criminal), and parliamentary bodies constitutes one of the hallmarks of the modern rational society.

Sixth and last of the mechanisms of passion containment examined in this essay are those that aim at the *devaluation* of the passions. In spite of being the most innocuous, or, rather, precisely because they are the most innocuous, these are probably the most reliable and effective of all the mechanisms considered. They consist of all the linguistic, cognitive, and normative devices whereby inclusion-exclusion activities, as well as the passions they arouse and through which they themselves are brought into being, are morally denigrated and intellectually trivialized as "childish," "in poor taste," "degrading," "immature," and "ugly." It is thus that the most obvious stimulants and technics of love tend to be publicly ignored, as though by some tacit gentlemen's agreement, and that the mere mention of them in public, to say nothing of their actual exposure, is nervously and impatiently dismissed. The ban on them in our culture has been so powerful, in fact, that they are not even legitimate subjects on the agenda of the academic social sciences, on the presumptive grounds that they are, as topics, insignificant at best and vulgar, frivolous, and pornographic at worst. The same applies, though to a substantially lesser degree, to the arts and letters, which prompted Freud (1962:30) to puzzle over the fact that "the genitals themselves, the sight of which is always exciting, are nevertheless hardly ever judged to be beautiful; the quality of beauty seems, instead, to attach to certain secondary sexual characters." (For an interesting elaboration of this theme, see Comfort, 1962:Ch. 5.)

As for the exclusive activities that arouse the antipathetic passions, as well as for these passions themselves, a similar fate befalls them. The man who has been insulted, assailed, and spat upon by a fellow group member is immediately surrounded and soothed by his friends and subjected to repeated and insistent advice not to make "a mountain out of a molehill," not to "stoop" to the other man's level, not to "get into the gutter" with him. In a word, he is enjoined to realize that the spittle on his face is not so much his problem as it is the other man's. Restraints of this type are, it is true, particularly potent in contemporary middle-class social circles, but they do, nevertheless, seem to operate to one degree or another in all societies.

VII

The six types of passion-containment mechanisms presented above are by no means intended as a systematic typology or an exhaustive catalogue. Such a typology and catalogue are yet to be constructed. Rather, the six types and their subtypes have been presented mainly to dramatize some of the main contentions of this essay, which are

1. The organized activities of men depend on the effective curbing of their passions, particularly their aggressive passions.
2. Typically, passions of this sort are provoked by acts of exclusion.
3. Because it is neither possible nor even desirable to root out altogether acts of exclusion, societies everywhere and at all times have devised innumerable mechanisms to prevent or at least control the passions that such exclusive acts are liable to provoke.

What I should like to suggest by way of a conclusion is, first, that this vast profusion of mechanisms of passion containment constitutes the better part of what are ordinarily referred to as the "norms of civility"— that rich complex of "gestures which we sometimes call empty [but which] are perhaps the fullest things of all." (Goffman 1955a:497.) Expressed differently, this means that one of the essential functions performed by civility is to hold man's irascible nature in check. Second, therefore, I should like to propose that, if such is indeed one of the critical functions of civility and of the other mechanisms catalogued in the preceding section, then we might expect such mechanisms to be most developed under conditions in which acts of social exclusion are liable to occur with greatest frequency.

One such condition is that of *crowding*. Where people live at some physical distance from one another, as in rural areas, the likelihood of their being offended again and again by the inclusive-exclusive activities of their neighbors is not great, for the simple reason that their neighbors are usually out of the range of their perception. In urban settlements, however, where (by definition) people live in close proximity to one another, the likelihood of their being subjected to inclusive-exclusive activities is much greater. It should, therefore, come as no surprise that it is precisely in the context of cities that many of the mechanisms of passion containment should have found their most varied, most elaborate, and most differentiated expression. Thus, typically, cities have been characterized as the "cradles" of (1) *norms of civility* (the obvious etymological connection is anything but fortuitous); (2) *modern democracy*, that is, the systematic extension of rights of inclusion to the excluded; (3) *transcendental religion*; (4) the institutions of *privacy*; (5) ideals of *rationality* (which implicitly or explicitly condemn passional behavior); (6) the *dramatic arts and spectacles*; and so forth.

Durkheim (1933) argued that crowding had caused modern urban agglomerations to develop a division of labor, which, in turn, constitutes the source par excellence of the sentiments of solidarity through which such societies are held together. What is being suggested here is that, though the division of labor may indeed constitute such a source of cohesion, the dense network of norms of civility, institutions of privacy, and so forth discussed in this chapter constitutes an equally significant, or perhaps an even more significant, source of cohesion in urban agglomerations and, in general, in most highly crowded societies.

References

ARIÈS, PHILIPPE
    1962   *Centuries of Childhood: A Social History of Family Life.* Translated by ROBERT BALDICK. New York: Knopf.
BATAILLE, GEORGES
    1962   *Death and Sensuality: A Study of Eroticism and the Taboo.* New York: Walker.
BLAU, PETER
    1964   *Exchange and Power in Social Life.* New York: John Wiley & Sons.
CAPLOW, THEODORE
    1968   *Two Against One: Coalitions in Triads.* Englewood Cliffs: Prentice-Hall.
COMFORT, ALEX
    1962   *Darwin and the Naked Lady: Discursive Essays on Biology and Art.* New York: Braziller.
COSER, LEWIS A.
    1956   *The Functions of Social Conflict.* Glencoe: Free Press.
COSER, ROSE LAUB
    1961   "Insulation from Observability and Types of Social Conformity." *American Sociological Review* 26 (February):28–39.
DAVIES, JAMES C.
    1962   "Toward a Theory of Revolution." *American Sociological Review* 27 (February):5–19.
DURKHEIM, EMILE
    1933   *The Division of Labor in Society.* New York: Macmillan.

FALLERS, LLOYD A.
  1963 "Political Sociology and the Anthropological Study of African Societies."
        Reprinted in REINHARD BENDIX, ed., *State and Society: A Reader in*
        Comparative Political Sociology. Boston: Little, Brown, 1968.
FREUD, SIGMUND
  1930 *Civilization and Its Discontents.* Edited and translated by JAMES
        STRACHEY. New York: Norton, 1962.
GARFINKEL, HAROLD
  1967 *Studies in Ethnomethodology.* Englewood Cliffs: Prentice-Hall.
GOFFMAN, ERVING
  1963 *Behavior in Public Places: Notes on the Social Organization of Gather-*
        ings. New York: Free Press.
  1956a "The Nature of Deference and Demeanor." *American Anthropologist*
         58 (June):473-502.
  1956b *The Presentation of Self in Everyday Life.* Revised and expanded edi-
         tion. New York: Doubleday Anchor Books, 1959.
HENRY, JULES
  1941 *Jungle People: A Kaingáng Tribe of the Highlands of Brazil.* New York:
        J. J. Augustine.
LÉVI-STRAUSS, CLAUDE
  1969 *The Elementary Structures of Kinship.* Boston: Beacon.
LORENZ, KONRAD
  1966 *On Aggression.* Translated by MARJORIE KERR WILSON. New York:
        Harcourt, Brace & World.
McLUHAN, MARSHALL
  1964 *Understanding Media: The Extensions of Man.* New York, Toronto,
        London: McGraw-Hill.
MAUSS, MARCEL
  1967 *The Gift: Forms and Functions of Exchange in Archaic Societies.* Trans-
        lated by IAN CUNNISON. New York: Norton.
MERTON, ROBERT K.
  1957 "The Role-Set." *British Journal of Sociology* 8 (June):106-20.
New York Times
  1965 "Paris Opens Drive and Contest to Win Courtesy for Tourists.'
        April 7:45.
SCHACHTEL, ERNEST G.
  1949 "On Memory and Childhood Amnesia." *Psychiatry* 10:1-26.
SCHWARTZ, BARRY
  1968 "The Social Psychology of Privacy." *American Journal of Sociology* 73
        (May):741-52.
SIMMEL, GEORG
  1950 *The Sociology of Georg Simmel.* Translated, edited, and introduced by
        KURT H. WOLFF. Glencoe: Free Press.
SLATER, PHILIP
  1963 "On Social Regression." *American Sociological Review* 28 (June):339-
        64.
  1961 "Toward a Dualistic Theory of Identification." *Merrill-Palmer Quarterly*
        of Behavior and Development 7:113-26.
SOLOMON, VICTOR
  1965 *A Handbook of Conversions to the Religions of the World.* New York:
        Stravon Educational Press.

TOCQUEVILLE, ALEXIS DE
1955   *The Old Regime and the Revolution.* Translated by STUART GILBERT. New York: Doubleday.

TWAIN, MARK
1879   Fragment from manuscript "A Tramp Abroad." In BERNARD DE VOTO, ed., *Mark Twain's Letters from the Earth.* New York: Harper & Row, 1962; pp. 181–89.

WEITMAN, SASHA REINHARD
1968   "Bureaucracy, Democracy, and the French Revolution." Unpublished Ph.D. dissertation. St. Louis: Washington University.

V. Ways of Doing Things: Institutions and Organizations

V. Ways of Doing Things:
Institutions and Organizations

Institutions and organizations provide the settings for many of the obvious and ordinary routines of daily life. Accomplishing things on a large scale is always done in a social context, where the judgments and evaluations of others—supervisors, colleagues, clients, customers, patients, staff—are always considered during the process. One may regard these relationships as far more abstract than more intimate associations because exchange is the nexus of the relationships, as far more precise because a specific set of techniques is involved, and as far more elaborate because there is a complex division of labor. Yet, in these relationships, people are still engaged in interactions, the outcomes of which can either reinforce or call into question these organizational arrangements. As each participant seeks to gain control over the situation, any moment can produce consequences that might threaten the organization's continued existence.

One of the important common-sense notions we have about institutions and organizations is that technical standards of evaluation prevail. However, working for others means that some subjective criteria of evaluation also will be imposed on the performance of a task; working with others means that standards indigenous to the work team or occupational community will emerge and be sustained, independent of what supervisors or outsiders say. Thus, the risk of failure is based not merely on inability to meet some objective standard of performance: The style of working becomes important when significant others are watching. Ways of convincing others that one is working hard are sometimes created; ways of alleviating stress introduce rituals to rational organizations; ways of restricting productivity to preserve a group's integrity come into being when standards are arbitrarily imposed. Indeed, making the response of their various publics manageable is one of the central activities of all those with fixed assignments in organizations.

Institutions not only get things done; they are regarded as the *right* ways to get certain necessary tasks accomplished. Once an institution gains a monopoly over a set of tasks, it is expected that all members of society will recognize that it possesses knowledge concerning the one best way of accomplishing these tasks. Once the legitimacy of an institution is acknowledged in this way, competitive methods of performing are treated with suspicion, potential clients are prevented from using these services freely, potential recruits are prevented from learning how to provide them. Needless to say, institutions seek to acquire, maintain, and extend control over important tasks. The professions routinely handle other people's emergencies, dominating the relationship with clients and with subordinate occupational groups; they have gained control over their work environment and the requirements of entry to their fields; they have established ways of categorizing the problematic in daily life and have established routine procedures for dealing with it. The professions have convinced the society at large that they have special skills in dealing with the uncertain.

The selections in this section examine ways in which performers of various occupational roles deal with the contingencies that arise in their work, despite their establishment of some routine certainties in their working day. William Foote Whyte examines the task-related and integrative problems of restaurant work in his famous study of the management of conflict in a small institution. Ray Gold observes some of the complexities of "class warfare" in face-to-face situations: the conflicts between janitors and tenants in apartment buildings. He locates some of the strains produced in performers of jobs that have low prestige but relatively high economic rewards. Gold also describes the ways in which janitors receive support from their peers in dealing with tenants who regard them as lower in class than themselves because of the "dirty" nature of their job. Joan P. Emerson analyzes how doctors and nurses tell patients in hospitals some of the details of their cases and their prospects for recovery, using humor to convey some potentially distressing and disruptive information.

Finally, we end this book with a selection from Erving Goffman's brilliant *The Presentation of Self in Everyday Life* on the "team" nature of work, the generic life of all institutions or establishments. Despite the commonly expressed attitude "I only work here," a collective effort is required to sustain a definition of the situation commensurate with one's self-regard and that of the institution. A person's expressions of self require situations for their appearance and cooperation with others who seek to find outlets for their self-expressions as well. Thus, we cannot create and sustain a certain self without permitting others to do the same. Every occasion requires activity in this direction, usually based on the cooperation available from others in interaction. When people come into one another's presence, they seek to present themselves as best they can, but they can only do so with the help of others. A team effort is required. But a team is a grouping constituted on the basis of a periodic series of interactions rather than on the basis of sharing a similar location in the social structure or ties of friendship or blood. A team, then, is based more on covert and tacit intimacy in performance than on affection. The study of institutions clearly reveals the social nature of human beings: We must be with and for others in order to be ourselves. The study of institutions also reveals the human nature of society: It is made and remade again and again out of the activity of men.

1. The Social Structure
of the Restaurant *

WILLIAM FOOTE WHYTE

While research has provided a large and rapidly growing fund of knowl-edge concerning the social organization of a factory, studies of other industrial and business structures are only beginning. Sociologists who are concerned with working out the comparative structures of economic organizations must therefore look beyond as well as into the factory. This paper represents one effort in that direction. It grows out of a fourteen-month study of restaurants.[1] We do not claim to have studied a representative sample of restaurants. In an industry having so many types of operations and sizes of units, such a task would have taken years. We did aim to find out, at least in a general way, what sort of structure a restaurant is and what human problems are found within it.

Here I shall present a schematic picture of the findings as they bear upon problems of social structure. I am also using the discussion of re-search findings to illustrate certain points of theory and methodology in studies of social structures. Discussions of theory and methodology, divorced from the research data upon which the theory and methods are to be used, are generally fruitless. In a brief paper, discussion of our research findings must necessarily be sketchy, but that will provide a basis for at least tentative conclusions.

* Reprinted from *American Journal of Sociology*, Vol. 54 (1949), pp. 302–10. Copyright 1949 by The University of Chicago. Reprinted by permission of The University of Chicago Press and the author.
[1] The research was financed by the National Restaurant Association. The field work was done by Margaret Chandler, Edith Lentz, John Schaefer, and William Whyte. We made interview or participant-observation studies of twelve restaurants in Chicago and did some brief interviewing outside Chicago. From one to four months was spent upon each Chicago restaurant. In Whyte (1948), I report the study in detail. Since the book is primarily addressed to restaurant operators and supervisors, the sociological frame of reference given here does not duplicate the more detailed publication.

Characteristics of the Restaurant

The restaurant is a combination production and service unit. It differs from the factory, which is solely a production unit, and also from the retail store, which is solely a service unit.

The restaurant operator produces a perishable product for immediate sale. Success requires a delicate adjustment of supply to demand and skilful coordination of production with service. The production and service tie-up not only makes for difficult human problems of coordinating action but adds a new dimension to the structure of the organization: the customer-employee relationship.

The contrast between factory and restaurant can be illustrated by this simple diagram, representing the direction of orders in the two structures.[2]

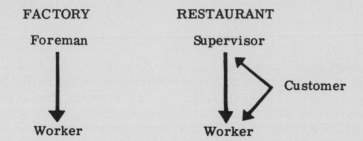

The problems of coordination and customer relations are relatively simple in the small restaurant, but they become much more difficult as the organization grows. This may be illustrated structurally in terms of five stages of growth.[3]

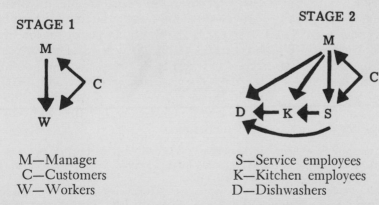

STAGE 1

STAGE 2

M—Manager
C—Customers
W—Workers

S—Service employees
K—Kitchen employees
D—Dishwashers

[2] This is, of course, an oversimplified picture, for many factory workers interact also with inspectors, engineers, time-study men, etc., but the frequency of such interaction does not compare with that which we observe between customers and waiters or waitresses in a restaurant.

[3] I am indebted to Donald Wray for the particular structural approach presented here.

In the first stage, we have a small restaurant where the owner and several other employees dispense short orders over the counter. There is little division of labor. The owner and employees serve together as cooks, countermen, and dishwashers.

In the second stage, the business is still characterized by the informality and flexibility of its relationships. The boss knows most customers and all his employees on a personal basis. There is no need for formal controls and elaborate paper work. Still, the organization has grown in complexity as it has grown in size. The volume of business is such that it becomes necessary to divide the work, and we have dishwashers and kitchen employees, as well as those who wait on the customers. Now the problems of co-ordination begin to grow also, but the organization is still small enough so that the owner-manager can observe directly a large part of its activities and step in to straighten out friction or inefficiency.

As the business continues to expand, it requires a still more complex organization as well as larger quarters. No longer able to supervise all activities directly, the owner-manager hires a service supervisor, a food production supervisor, and places one of his employees in charge of the dishroom as a working supervisor. He also employs a checker to total checks for his waitresses and see that the food is served in correct portions and style.

STAGE 3

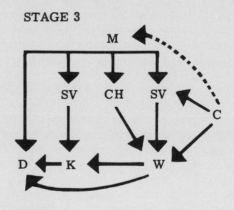

M—Manager   W—Waitress
SV—Supervisor   K—Kitchen worker
CH—Checker   D—Dishwasher
C—Customer

In time, the owner-manager finds that he can accommodate a larger number of customers if he takes one more step in the division of labor. Up to now the cooks have been serving the food to the waitresses. When these functions are divided, both cooking and serving can proceed more

STAGE 4

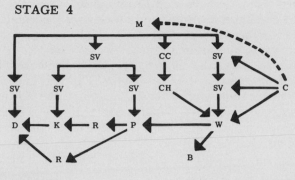

M—Manager
SV—Supervisor
CH—Checker
CC—Cost control supervisor
C—Customer
W—Waitress

B—Bartender
P—Pantry worker
K—Kitchen worker
R—Runner
D—Dishwasher

efficiently. Therefore, he sets up a service pantry apart from the kitchen. The cooks now concentrate on cooking, the runners carry food from kitchen to pantry and carry orders from pantry to kitchen, and the pantry girls serve the waitresses over the counter. This adds two more groups (pantry girls and runners) to be supervised, and, to cope with this and the larger scale of operation, the owner adds another level of supervision, so that there are two supervisors between himself and the workers. Somewhere along the line of development, perhaps he begins serving drinks and adds bartenders to his organization.

Stage 5 need not be diagrammed here, for it does not necessarily involve any structural changes in the individual unit. Here several units are tied together into a chain, and one or more levels of authority are set up in a main office above the individual unit structures.[4]

This expansion process magnifies old problems and gives rise to new ones. They may be considered under three headings: administration, the customer relationship, and the flow of work. Whenever we lengthen the hierarchy, adding new levels of authority to separate top executive from workers, the problem of administration becomes more complex. However, this is true for any organization, and therefore these problems of hierarchy need not be given special attention in an article on restaurants.

The particular problem of the large restaurant is to tie together its line of authority with the relations that arise along the flow of work. In the first instance, this involves the customer relationship, for here is where the flow of work begins. The handling of the customer relation-

[4] The structural changes arising with union organization are beyond the scope of this article. They are discussed in Whyte (1948) in the chapter "The Role of Union Organization."

ship is crucial for the adjustment of the restaurant personnel, and a large part of that problem can be stated in strictly quantitative inter-action terms: Who originates action for whom and how often? In a large and busy restaurant a waitress may take orders from fifty to one hundred customers a day (and perhaps several times for each meal) in addition to the orders (much less frequent) she receives from her supervisor. When we add to this the problem of adjusting to service pantry workers, bartenders, and perhaps checkers, we can readily see the possibilities of emotional tension—and, in our study, we did see a num-ber of girls break down and cry under the strain.

Our findings suggested that emotional tension could be related directly to this quantitative interaction picture. The skillful waitress, who maintained her emotional equilibrium, did not simply respond to the initiative of customers. In various obvious and subtle ways she took the play away from customers, got them responding to her, and fitted them into the pattern of her work. She was also more aggressive than the emotionally insecure in originating action for other waitresses, ser-vice pantry people, and supervisor.

While in the rush hour the waitress works under a good deal of tension at best, the supervisor can either add to or relieve it. Here again we can speak in quantitative terms. In one restaurant we observed a change in dining-room management when a supervisor who was still skilful in originating action for customers (thus taking pressure off waitresses) and who responded frequently to the initiation of waitresses was replaced by a supervisor who had less skill in controlling customers and who originated for the girls much more frequently and seldom responded to them. (Of the new supervisor, the waitresses would say, "She's always finding something to criticize"; "She's never around when we need her"; "She's always telling you; she doesn't care what you have to say"; etc.) This change was followed by evidences of increased ner-vous tension, especially among the less experienced waitresses, and finally by a series of waitress resignations.

Here we see that the customer-waitress, waitress-supervisor, waitress-service-pantry-worker relationships are interdependent parts of a social system. Changes in one part of the system will necessarily lead to changes in other parts. Furthermore, if the people involved in the system are to maintain their emotional balance, there must be some sort of compensatory activity to meet large interactional changes. For example, when waitresses are subject to a large increase in the origina-tions of customers (at the peak of rush hours), the supervisor allows them to originate action for her with increasing frequency and dimin-ishes the frequency with which she gives them orders. This is, in fact, the sort of behavior we have observed among supervisors who enjoy the closest co-operation with waitresses, as reported by the waitresses.

The customer relationship is, of course, only one point along the flow of work which brings orders from dining-room to kitchen and food from kitchen to dining-room. In a large restaurant operating on several floors, this is a long chain which may break down at any point, thus leading to emotional explosions in all quarters. The orders may go from waitress to pantry girl and then, as the pantry girl runs low in supplies, from pantry girl to pantry supplyman, from pantry supplyman to kitchen supplyman, and from kitchen supplyman to cook. And the food comes back along the same route in opposite direction. Where drinks are served, the bar must be tied in with this flow of work, but there the chain is short and the problem less complex.

We have here a social system whose parts are interdependent in a highly sensitive manner. Thus the emotional tension experienced by waitresses is readily transmitted, link by link, all the way to the kitchen.

I have already noted how a skilful dining-room supervisor may help to relieve the tension on the entire system at its point of origin. Here we may consider other factors which affect the relations among employees along the flow of work: status, sex relations, and layout and equipment.

I would propose the hypothesis that relations among individuals along the flow of work will run more smoothly when those of higher status are in a position to originate for those of lower status in the organization and, conversely, that frictions will be observed more often when lower-status individuals seek to originate for those of higher status. (This is, of course, by no means a complete explanation of the friction or adjustment we observe.)

While more data are needed on this point, we made certain observations which tend to bear out the hypothesis. For example, in one kitchen we observed supplymen seeking to originate action (in getting food supplies) for cooks who were older, of greater seniority, more highly skilled, and much higher paid. This relationship was one of the sore points of the organization. Still, we discovered that there had been one supplyman who got along well with the cooks. When we got his story, we found that he had related himself to the cooks quite differently from the other supplymen. He sought to avoid calling orders to the cooks and instead just asked them to call him when a certain item was ready. In this way, he allowed them to increase the frequency of their origination for him, and, according to all accounts, he got better co-operation and service from the cooks than any other supplyman.

Much the same point is involved in the relations between the sexes. In our society most men grow up to be comfortable in a relationship in which they originate for women and to be uneasy, if not more seriously disturbed, when the originations go in the other direction. It is therefore a matter of some consequence how the sexes are distributed along the flow of work. On this question we gave particular attention to the dining-room–service pantry and dining-room–bar relationships.

In the dining-room–pantry situation there are four possible types of relationship by sex: waiter-counterman, waiter-pantry girl, waitress-pantry girl, and waitress-counterman. We are not able to give much attention to the first two types, but we did make intensive studies of two restaurants illustrating the third and fourth types. Ideally, for scientific purposes, we would want to hold everything else constant except for these sex differences. We had no such laboratory, but the two restaurants were nevertheless closely comparable. They were both large, busy establishments, operating on several floors, and serving the same price range of food in the same section of the city.

Perhaps the chief differences were found in the dining-room–pantry relationship itself. In restaurant A, waitresses gave their orders orally to the pantry girls. On the main serving floor of restaurant B, waitresses wrote out slips which they placed on the spindles on top of a warming compartment separating them from the countermen. The men picked off the order slips, filled them, and put the plates in the compartment where the waitresses picked them up. In most cases there was no direct face-to-face interaction between waitresess and countermen, and, indeed, the warming compartment was so high that only the taller waitresses could see over its top.

These differences were not unrelated to the problems of sex in the flow of work. One of the countermen in restaurant B told us that, in all his years' experience, he had never before worked in such a wonderful place. Most workers who express such sentiments talk about their relations with their superiors or with fellow-employees on the same job or perhaps about wages, but this man had nothing to say about any of those subjects. He would discuss only the barrier that protected him from the waitresses. He described earlier experiences in other restaurants where there had been no such barrier and let us know that to be left out in the open where all the girls could call their orders in was an ordeal to which no man should be subjected. In such places, he said, there was constant wrangling.

This seems to check with experience in the industry. While we observed frictions arising between waitresses and pantry girls, such a relationship can at least be maintained with relative stability. On the other hand, it is difficult to prevent blowups between countermen and waitresses when the girls call their orders in. Most restaurants consciously or unconsciously interpose certain barriers to cut down waitress origination of action for countermen. It may be a warming compartment as in this case, or, as we observed in another restaurant, there was a man pantry supervisor who collected the order slips from the waitresses as they came in and passed them out to the countermen. There are a variety of ways of meeting the problem, but they all seem to involve this principle of social insulation.

The rule that all orders must be written also serves to cut down on interaction between waitresses and countermen, but this in itself is not always enough to eliminate friction. Where there is no physical barrier there can be trouble unless the men who are on the receiving end of the orders work out their own system of getting out from under. Such systems we observed at one bar and at one of the serving counters in restaurant B. The counter in this case was only waist high. While the girls wrote out their orders, they were also able to try to spur the men on orally, and there was much pulling and hauling on this point both at the bar and at the pantry counter.

The men who did not get along in this relationship played a waiting game. That is, when the girls seemed to be putting on special pressure for speed, they would very obviously slow down or else even turn away from the bar or counter and not go back to work until the offending waitresses just left their order slips and stepped away themselves. Thus they originated action for the waitresses. While this defensive maneuver provided the men with some emotional satisfaction, it slowed down the service, increased the frustrations of the waitresses, and thus built up tensions, to be released in larger explosions later.

One bartender and one counterman not only enjoyed their work but were considered by waitresses to be highly efficient and pleasant to deal with. Both of them had independently worked out the same system of handling the job when the rush hour got under way. Instead of handling each order slip in turn as it was handed to them (thus responding to each individual waitress), they would collect several slips that came in at about the same time, lay them out on the counter before them, and fill the orders in whatever order seemed most efficient. For example, the bartender would go through the slips to see how many "martinis," "old fashioneds," and so on were required. Then he would make up all the "martinis" at once before he went on to the next drink.

When the work was done this way, the girl first in was not necessarily first out with her tray, but the system was so efficient that it speeded up the work on the average, and the girls were content to profit this way in the long run. The men described the system to us simply in terms of efficiency; but note that, in organizing their jobs, they had changed quantitatively the relations they had with the waitresses. Instead of responding to each waitress, they were originating action for the girls (filling their orders as the men saw fit and sending them out when the men were ready).

Along with our consideration of layout and equipment in the flow of work, we should give attention to the communication system. Where the restaurant operates on one floor, the relations at each step in the flow can be worked out on a face-to-face basis. There may be friction, but there is also the possibility of working out many problems on a friendly, informal basis.

When a restaurant operates on two or more floors, as many large ones do, face-to-face interaction must be supplemented by mechanical means of communication. We saw three such mechanical means substituted for direct interaction, and each one had its difficulties.

People can try to co-ordinate their activities through the house telephone. Without facial expressions and gestures, there is a real loss of understanding, for we do not generally respond solely to people's voices. Still, this might serve reasonably well, if the connection between kitchen and pantry could be kept constantly open. At least in the one restaurant where we gave this subject special attention, that solution was out of the question, as one call from kitchen to pantry tied up the whole house phone system and nobody could call the manager, the cashier, or anybody else on this system as long as another call was being made. Consequently, the telephone could be used only to supplement other mechanical aids (in this case, the teleautograph).

The public address system has the advantage over the telephone that it can be used all the time, but it has the great disadvantage of being a very noisy instrument. Busy kitchens and service pantries are noisy places at best, so that the addition of a public address system might be most unwelcome. We do not yet know enough of the effect of noise upon the human nervous system to evaluate the instrument from this point of view, but we should recognize the obvious fact that surrounding noise affects the ability of people to communicate with each other and becomes therefore a problem in human relations.

The teleautograph makes no noise and can be used at all times, yet it has its own disadvantages. Here we have an instrument in the service pantry and one in the kitchen. As the pantry supplyman writes his order, it appears simultaneously on the kitchen teleautograph. The kitchen's replies are transmitted upstairs in the same way. The machine records faithfully, but it does not solve the problem of meaning in interaction. We may pass over the problem of illegibility of handwriting, although we have seen that cause serious difficulties. The more interesting problem is this: How urgent is an order?

When the rush hour comes along, with customers pushing waitresses, waitresses pushing pantry girls, and pantry girls pushing supplymen, the supplyman is on the end of the line so far as face-to-face interaction is concerned, and he is likely to get nervous and excited. He may then put in a larger order than he will actually use or write "Rush" above many of his orders. If he overorders, the leftovers come back to the kitchen at the end of the meal, and the kitchen supplymen and cooks learn thus that the pantry supplyman did not really know how much he needed. They take this into account in interpreting his future orders. And, when everything is marked "Rush," the kitchen supplymen cannot tell the difference between the urgent and not so urgent ones. Thus the word becomes meaningless, and communication deteriorates. Stuck in this impasse, the pantry supplyman may abandon his machine and dash down to the kitchen to try to snatch the order himself. The kitchen people will block this move whenever they can, so, more often, the pantry supplyman appeals to his supervisor. In the heat of the rush hour, we have seen pantry supervisors running up and down stairs, trying to get orders, trying to find out what is holding up things in the kitchen. Since they have supervisor status, the kitchen workers do not resist them openly, but the invasion of an upstairs supervisor tends to disrupt relations in the kitchen. It adds to the pressures there, for it comes as an emergency that lets everybody know that the organization is not functioning smoothly.

It is not the function of this article to work out possible solutions to this problem of communication. I am concerned here with pointing out a significant new area for sociological investigation: the effects on human relations of various mechanical systems of communication. It is difficult enough to coordinate an organization in which the key people in the supervisory hierarchy are in direct face-to-face relations. It is a much more difficult problem (and one as yet little understood) when the co-ordination must be achieved in large measure through mechanical communication systems.

Implications for Theory and Methodology

In presenting our observations on the restaurant industry, I have discussed formal structure, quantitative measures of interaction, symbols in relations to interaction, attitudes and interaction, and layout and equipment (including mechanical systems of communication). Data of these categories must be fitted together. The uses of each type of data may be summarized here.

1. *Formal structure.*—We have ample data to show that the formal structure (the official allocation of positions) does not *determine* the pattern of human relations in an organization. Nevertheless, it does set certain limits upon the shape of that pattern. Thus, to analyze the human problems of a restaurant, it is necessary to outline its structure in terms of length of hierarchy, divisions into departments, and flow of work (as done in the five stages above).

2. *Quantitative measures of interaction.*—Within the limits set by the formal structure, the relations among members of the organization may fall into a variety of patterns, each of which is subject to change.

The pattern we observe we call the *social system.* A social system is made up of *interdependent* parts. The parts are the *relations* of individuals in their various positions to each other. This is simply a first description of a social system, but there are important theoretical and practical conclusions which flow from it.

The relations of individuals to one another are subject to *measurement,* sufficient to allow them to be compared and classified. We can, for example, count the number of times that a waitress originates action for her customers compared with the number of times they originate it for her in a given period and observe how often she originates action for her supervisor and how often the supervisor does so for her, and so on, through the other relations in the system. So far, mathematically precise measurements of interaction have only been made in laboratory situations involving interviewer and interviewee. (Chapple, 1940; Chapple and Coon, 1941: Ch. 1–4, esp.; Chapple and Lindemann, 1942.) Nevertheless, in the present state of our knowledge, we can get, through interviewing and observation, quantitative data which, though only approximate, are sufficiently accurate to allow us to predict the course of developments or explain how certain problems have arisen and point the way to their possible solution.

As the terms are used here, *interaction, origination,* and *response* are abstractions without content. That is, they are indices which have no reference to either the symbols used or the subjective reactions felt by the interacting individuals. Such measures do not, of course, tell us all it is useful to know of human relations. Indeed, many students will think it absurd to believe that any useful data can come from abstractions which leave out the "content" of human relations. To them I can only say that science is, in part, a process of abstraction, which always seems to take us away from the "real world." The value of such abstractions can be determined only by testing them in research to see whether they enable us better to control and predict social events.

Since the social system is made up of *interdependent relations,* it follows that a change in one part of the system necessarily has repercussions in other parts of the system. For example, a change in origin-response ratio between waitresses and supervisor necessarily affects the waitress-customer and waitress–service-pantry-girl relations, and changes in those parts lead to other changes in the system. Therefore, in order to study the social system or to deal with it effectively, it is necessary to discover the *pattern* of relations existing at a given time and to observe changes within that pattern. The nature of the interdependence of the parts of the system can be discovered only through observing how a change in Part A is followed by change in Part B, is followed by change in Part C, etc. Therefore, social systems must be studied *through time.* A static picture of the social structure of an organization is of little value. Science requires that we develop methods of study and tools of analysis to deal with constantly changing relations.

3. *Symbols in relation to interaction.*—We cannot be content simply with quantitative descriptions of interaction. We need to know why A responds to B in one situation and not in another or why A responds to B and not to C. In part, this is a matter of habituation, for we respond to the people we are accustomed to responding to and in the sorts of situations to which we are accustomed. But we must go beyond that to explain the development of new patterns and changes in old patterns of interaction.

We observe that individuals respond to certain symbols in interaction. I have discussed here status and sex as symbols affecting interaction (the problems of the originating from below or action for high status individual or by woman for man).

I have noted some problems in language symbols in the discussion of mechanical means of communication. That leaves the whole field of symbols in face-to-face interaction untouched, so that it represents only the barest beginning of an attempted formulation of the relations between symbols of communication and interaction.

Especially in economic institutions, it is important to examine the bearing of *economic symbols* (see Whyte, 1950), on interaction, but this is a large subject and can only be mentioned here.

As we analyze social systems, symbols should always be seen in terms of their effects upon interaction. They are *incentives* or *inhibitors* to interaction with specific people in certain social situations. Thus, to put it in practical terms, the manager of an organization will find it useful to know both the pattern of interaction which will bring about harmonious relations and also how to use symbols so as to achieve that pattern.

4. *Attitudes and interaction.*—Changes in relations of individuals to one another are accompanied by changes in their *attitudes* toward one another and toward their organizations. In recent years we have developed excellent methods for attitude measurement, but the measurement in itself never tells us how the attitudes come about. The whole experience of our research program leads us to believe that the dynamics of attitude formation and change can best be worked out as we correlate attitudes with human relations in the organizations we study.

5. *Layout and equipment.*—Here the sociologist is not directly concerned with the problems of the mechanical or industrial engineer. He does not undertake to say which machine or which arrangement of work space and machines will be most productively efficient. However, he cannot help but observe that, for example, the height of the barrier between waitresses and countermen or the nature of the mechanical communication system [has] important effects upon human relations. Only as these effects are observed do the physical conditions come in for sociological analysis. (Of course, human relations have a bearing upon efficiency, but the sociologist, if he tackles the problem of efficiency, uses types of data and schemes of analysis quite different from those used by the engineer.)

A few years ago there was a great debate raging: statistics versus the case study. That debate is no longer waged publicly, but it still troubles many of us. On the one hand, we see that an individual case study, skilfully analyzed, yields interesting insights—but not scientific knowledge. On the other hand, we find that nearly all statistical work in sociology has dealt with the characteristics of aggregates: How much of a given phenomenon is to be found in a given population? Such an approach does not tell us anything about the relations among the individuals making up that population. And yet, if we are to believe the textbooks, the relations among individuals, the *group* life they lead, are the very heart of sociology.

So let us have more individual case studies, but let us also place the individual in the social systems in which he participates and note how his attitudes and goals change with changes in the relations he experiences. And let us have more quantitative work, but let us at last bring it to bear upon the heart of sociology, measuring the relations among individuals in their organizations.

References

CHAPPLE, ELIOT D., with the collaboration of CONRAD M. ARENSBERG
  1940 *Measuring Human Relations: An Introduction to the Study of the Interaction of Individuals.* Genetic Psychology Monographs No. 22. Provincetown: Journal Press.
CHAPPLE, ELIOT D., and CARLETON S. COON
  1941 *Principles of Anthropology.* New York: Henry Holt.
CHAPPLE, ELIOT D., and ERICH LINDEMANN
  1942 "Clinical Implications of Measurement of Interaction Rates in Psychiatric Interviews." *Applied Anthropology* 1, No. 2 (January–March): 1–12.
WHYTE, WILLIAM FOOTE
  1950 "Framework for the Analysis of Industrial Relations." *Industrial and Labor Relations Review* 3 (April):393–401.
  1948 *Human Relations in the Restaurant Industry.* New York: McGraw-Hill.

2. Janitors Versus Tenants:
A Status-Income Dilemma *

RAY GOLD

There is some kind of status relationship between the worker and the person served in almost any occupation where the two meet and interact. For example, when the salesperson and the customer meet, each brings to bear on the other valuations by which the other's status category can be tentatively ascertained. This tentative status designation enables each to make a rough judgment as to how to act toward the other person and as to how he thinks the other person will act toward him. If their association is resumed, their initial judgments strongly influence the character of their subsequent interactions. If they are separated by wide barriers of social distance, they may carry on an almost formal salesperson-customer relationship for years. Or their respective status judgments may be such that the status barriers are gradually penetrated. In any case, the status relationship between them is always present, unless it is resolved into an absolute equalitarian relationship. Likewise, in the case of the physician and his patients, the plumber and his customers, the minister and his parishioners, and in others, there is a status relationship of which both parties are more or less aware and which influences the pattern of their interactions. Such being the case, the nature and form of these status relationships can and should be studied wherever they occur.

The present example, which concerns the apartment-building janitor and his tenants, is a case study in such status relationships. The form these relationships have taken is that of a marked dilemma of status and income.

Status and Income

The status-income dilemma may be expected to occur in two situations. One is that in which an individual earns too little to pay for the

* Reprinted from *American Journal of Sociology*, Vol. 57 (1952), pp. 486–93. Copyright 1952 by The University of Chicago. Reprinted by permission of The University of Chicago Press and the author.

goods and services generally associated with his other social characteristics. The other is that in which he earns enough to pay for goods
and services generally associated not with *his* other social characteristics
but with those of members of higher social classes. When an individual
in the first dilemma meets and interacts almost daily on a rather
personal level with one in the second as, respectively, in the case of the
tenant [1] and the apartment-building janitor, they develop an association
whose form and content are of sociological interest.

The data in this article are based entirely upon interviews with
janitors.[2] What results is a penetrating view of the janitor's conceptions
of tenants and of his interpretations of their conceptions of him. Thus,
we obtain an intimate understanding of the janitor's view of how he
and tenants spar to resolve their respective dilemmas. Although many
of the tenants may not be so sensitive as the janitor to this contest,
it is safe to assume that, through his untiring efforts to play the
game with his rules, the tenants are aware that he is agitating to change
their traditional patterns of interaction.

In the early part of this century, before janitors in Chicago were
unionized, they catered to virtually every whim of their employers and
tenants in order to establish job security. Since they have become
unionized, their duties have been greatly delimited, their wages increased, and their privileges extended to include a rent-free basement
apartment in one of the larger buildings which they service. At present,
they are required to fire the furnace to provide heat and hot water
for the tenants, to remove the tenants' garbage regularly, to make minor
emergency repairs, and to keep the building and grounds clean.

Having a history, the janitor also has a reputation. The tenant-
public seems to look upon him as an ignorant, lazy, and dirty occupational misfit. There has developed a general belief that, if a man
cannot do anything else successfully, he can always become a janitor.
This stereotype has been perpetuated by the public because of a
number of beliefs, principally the following: (1) many janitors are
foreign-born and therefore strange and suspicious; (2) the janitor is
always seen wearing dirty clothes, so the tenants seem to feel that he
habitually disregards cleanliness; (3) the janitor lives in the basement,
which symbolizes his low status; and (4) the janitor removes the tenants' garbage, a duty which subserves him to them. It is because
the public has singled out these features in their view of the janitor
that his ascribed status has been lowly. In the public's view it seems
that the janitor merely is a very low-class person doing menial work
for the tenants.

[1] The term "tenant" herein refers to the housewife, as the janitor seldom comes
in contact with the man of the house.

[2] Thirty-seven janitors were interviewed by the author during the fall of 1949
and winter of 1949–50. The interviews were open-ended, averaging about two and
one-half hours in length. A verbatim record of the interview proceedings was kept.
A complete report and discussion of interfindings is in Gold (1950).

It is true that the performance of janitorial duties requires neither lengthy training nor a high order of mechanical or technical skills. However, the nature of the janitor's situation has led him to play roles and incorporate self-conceptions which frequently overshadow those which others expect of a combination caretaker and handy man. Because he does not work under direct supervision and can plan his work to suit himself, he feels that he is his own boss: he, alone, is in charge of the building and responsible for the safety of the tenants. After becoming proficient at making repairs for tenants, he magnifies his handy-man role into that of a master mechanic. Combining these two roles, he then sees himself as an entrepreneur who runs a cash business of attending to the tenants' service needs.

These roles, together with others which stem from the work situation, contradict the public's stereotyped view of the janitor. Being sensitive to these social conceptions, the janitor strives to gain the tenants' acceptance as a person who has risen above the disreputable fellow these conceptions describe. Toward this end he not only plays the role of a respectable, dignified human being but of one who has a very substantial income (about $385 per month in Chicago). In this setting it is evident that the janitor's social relationships with the tenants are of crucial importance to him. These relationships are pervaded by his persistent disowning of his unhappy occupational heritage and the justification of his claim to middle-class status.

So important are social relationships with the tenants that the janitor defines success in terms of them. As many janitors have pointed out:

> The most important thing about a janitor's work is that you have to know how to deal with people. Then, when you show the tenants that you have a clean character and are respectable, you can train them to be good tenants, that's what's really important in being a success.

Because the janitor attempts to realize his self when interacting with his tenants, his efforts to train them are actually channeled toward the establishment of relationships which support, rather than oppose, his self-conceptions. The "good" tenants support his self-conceptions; the "bad" tenants oppose them.

It will be well now to examine the nature of these social relationships to determine how they give rise to the personal and social dilemmas which comprise the central theme of this discussion.

The janitor believes that, in general, tenants hold him in low esteem. Even the most friendly tenants maintain some social distance between the janitor and themselves. Tenants, generally, overlook his qualifications as an individual and see him only as a member of a low-status group. In their view he is merely an occupational type.[3] The most militant proponents of this view are the "bad" tenants.

[3] R. E. Park (1926): "Why is it that to the average American all Chinese like all Negroes look alike? It is because the individual man is concealed behind the racial type. The individual is there to be sure, but we do not meet him."

There are two characteristics of a special group of "bad" tenants which are apposite to this presentation. These characteristics, jealousy and resentment, are descriptive of only those tenants who are embittered by the janitor's economic prowess. They are people whose incomes are usually below, but sometimes slightly above, the janitor's income. The janitor often refers to these tenants as "fourflushers." They live on the brink of bankruptcy, and he knows it.[4] Status symbols are very important to them. Unlike the janitor, they apparently strain their budgets to improve the appearance of their persons and their apartments. When they see the janitor's new car or television aerial, their idea of high-status symbols, it is almost more than they can bear. It violates their sense of social justice. In consequence of his high income, the janitor can acquire things which these tenants may interpret as a threat to the established social order.

The janitor's new car, parked conspicuously in front of the building, serves constantly to remind tenants of his pecuniary power. It draws the most criticism from the jealous tenants. Commenting on the tensions thereby engendered, Janitor No. 35 remarked:

> There is a certain amount of jealousy when janitors try to better themselves. A whole lot are jealous because the janitor makes more than they do. But they don't consider the time a janitor puts in. When I got my Dodge two years ago somebody said, "Huh, look at that fellow. He must be making the money or he wouldn't be buying a new car." I know one party, they think a janitor should be in working clothes all the time. Just because a janitor likes to go out in an auto and they don't have any, there is that feeling between janitor and the tenant, that's for sure.

Some of these fourflushers do own an automobile. But if the janitor's car is bigger and newer than theirs, they are extremely mortified. Janitor No. 33 experienced the wrath of such people:

> About a third of the tenants are very pleasant about it when they see my car, but the rest say, "Holy cripe, the janitor got a new car!" The same majority is the ones you are in trouble with all the time. They say, "How is the 'nigger' with the big car?" meaning I am a "nigger" because I got a Buick and my car is bigger than theirs.

The janitor finds that the jealous tenants are impossible to accommodate. They do not want to be accommodated by him. "No matter what you do," protested Janitor No. 14, "they squawk." Their animosity

---

[4] In the boiler-room the janitor sorts out the noncombustible garbage from the combustible garbage, the former to be removed by a scavenger and the latter to be burned by him in the furnace. In the course of these sorting and burning operations he wittingly or unwittingly comes across letters and other things which serve to identify the different bundles or other forms of garbage accumulation. Thus, each of the tenants is readily identified by her garbage. What the garbage reveals about the tenant over a period of time enables the janitor to make intimate judgments about her.

seems to know no bounds. They deliberately attempt to create trouble for the janitor by complaining about him to his employer.

Besides complaining about him, these tenants reveal their resentment of the janitor's mobility efforts by making nasty remarks to him. This was shown very clearly in a conversation with Janitor No. 12 and his wife:

> JANITOR: When we got our 10 per cent raise a short time ago, the tenants didn't like it. You see how nice this [first-floor] apartment looks. Well, there ain't another apartment in the building that's decorated as nice as this. I had all those cabinets in the kitchen tore out and got new ones put in. That brick glass and ventilator in the transom opening—I had it done. Tenants didn't like to see me do all that. They resent it.
>
> INTERVIEWER: How do they show their resentment?
>
> WIFE: Mostly by making snotty remarks. One woman told us that we shouldn't live in such a nice apartment on the first floor, that we should live in a hole [basement apartment] like other janitors. Then they are sarcastic in a lot of other ways. They just don't like to see us have a nice apartment and a new car. I guess they'd rather see us live like rats.

The basement apartment is symbolic of the janitor's subservient status. If he can arrange with his employer to obtain a first-floor apartment, there is nothing that the jealous tenants can do to stop him. They can only try to make life miserable for him.

Jealous tenants disdainfully address him as "Janitor," rather than using his given name. It is bad enough, from his standpoint, that all other tenants address him by his given name, thereby indicating his historically servile status. But these resentful tenants go further. They call him by his occupational name. Symbolically, their use of this "dirty" name means that they want their relationship with him to be as impersonal as possible. They want the janitor to be aware of the great social distance which he would dare to bridge. Janitor No. 4 commented on this form of address:

> JANITOR: The bad ones squawk as long as they live. No matter what you do they squawk. They're the ones that don't call you by your name. They're a lower class of people, but they try to make you feel even lower than them.
>
> INTERVIEWER: Why do they call you "Janitor"?
>
> JANITOR: It's either out of stupidity or to make you think you are a slave to them—an underdog. Janitors get the same crap all over the city, I know.

These fourflushers who address him as "Janitor" are unalterably opposed to his efforts to better himself. The longer they live in the building, the worse their relationships with him become. This point was brought out by Janitor No. 4:

Boy, I'll tell you about one thing that happened to me last Christmas morning. This woman rings my bell when I'm out and gives an envelope to my wife to give to me. I passed by the back windows here a little while later and looked in like I always do to wave at the kid, and my wife called me in because she thought there must be a present in the envelope. So I went in and opened it up and there was a note inside that said, "I'll be home today so please keep the heat up." I was so mad I coulda booted her ass right over the fence if she was there. That's how the tenants get when they been living here too long. Most of them think they own the building, and you should do just what they want.

As Janitor No. 4 insisted, the fourflushers' unthinking demands for personal service, their utter disregard for the janitor's integrity and authority, and their possessiveness toward the building increase with their length of residence. The building becomes more and more like "home" to them, the longer they live there. "They can't afford to have a home and servants of their own," observed Janitor No. 18, "so they try to treat the janitor as their servant." They like to think of him as a mobile part of the building, always at their beck and call. Still, the deep-seated animosities between these tenants and the janitor preclude any mutually satisfactory adjustment of their respective roles. Through the years they continue to be jealous and resentful of him. Meanwhile, he continues to resent their uncooperativeness and disrespect. The building becomes as much "home" to him as it does to them. But there is something about "home" that can never be remedied. From the standpoint of these fourflushers, that something is the janitor. From the janitor's point of view, that something is the fourflushers.

Turning now from janitors whose tenants have incomes that are marginal to theirs to janitors whose tenants are plainly well-to-do, it is evident that there is a remarkable contrast in janitor-tenant relationships. The following conversation with Janitor No. 26 will serve as an introduction to this contrast:

> INTERVIEWER: Some fellows have told me that many of their tenants resent their getting a new car or a television set. Have you ever come up against that?
> JANITOR: That class of people don't live here, of course. The class of people you're talking about are making two hundred a month, don't have a car, and are lucky they're living. Yeah, I've met up with them. . . . People here aren't jealous if you got a new car. People here feel you have to have a car, like bread and butter.

Tenants whose incomes are clearly higher than the janitor's have no cause to be jealous of him. They do not compete with him for symbols of pecuniary power. There is more prestige attached to having an engineer in the building than to having a janitor, so they call him "the engineer." These people obviously do not have the status-income problems of the fourflushers who contemptuously address him as

"Janitor." Clearly, then, tenants who are well-to-do have no need to make demands. As Janitor No. 17, many of whose tenants have incomes marginal to his, so penetratingly observed:

> The people that don't have anything put up the biggest front and squawk a lot. The people who got it don't need any attention. I'd rather work for rich tenants. The ones we got here are middle ones. Those tenants that sing don't have a right to. . . . Some few tenants just got here from the Negro district. They were stuck there until they could find a place to move to. Man, they're real glad to be here. They don't give me no trouble at all.

Demonstrating remarkable insight, Janitor No. 17 pointed out that the "rich" tenants do not feel that they need attention from the janitor; that the "refugee" (like the poor) tenants feel that they are in no position to make demands; and that the fourflushers or "middle" (probably lower-middle) tenants are the most troublesome.

When a janitor works for many years in a building occupied by well-to-do tenants, it is not unusual that a genuinely warm relationship develops between him and these tenants. They probably come to see him as an old family employee, while he believes that he has been accepted for himself. As Janitor No. 26 asserted, "They feel they're no better than me—I'm no better than them, and they always invite me in for coffee or something like that." There is no problem in sharing identification of "home." The building is undisputedly "home" to both the janitor and the "rich" tenants, because they most probably view their relationship with him as a status accommodation, which he interprets as an equalitarian relationship.

In the next section the status-income dilemma is illustrated in terms of the janitor's professional behavior and outlook, which are in marked contrast with the tenants' lack of respect for him.

Professional Behavior and Professional Attitudes

It is likely that in every low-status occupation, where the worker associates with the customer, the workers meet with certain customer-oriented situations in which they typically behave in accordance with standards that people have traditionally called "professional." These low-status workers certainly do not label themselves "professionals," nor do others so label them. Yet, there is ample evidence that some of their behavior is ethically comparable to the behavior exhibited by members of the so-called "professions." R. E. Park, some twenty-six years ago, made similar observations of the tendency of even the lowest status occupations to become quasi-professions in some respects:

> In the city every vocation, even that of a beggar, tends to assume the character of a profession and the discipline which success in any vocation imposes, together with the associations that it enforces, emphasizes this

tendency—the tendency, namely, not merely to specialize, but to rationalize one's occupation and to develop a specific and conscious technique for carrying it on. [Park, 1925:14.]

While it is true that the janitor's self-conceptions are instrumental in forming the superstructure of his professional behavior, the foundation of such conduct is formed primarily out of situational requisites. This being the case, his status-income dilemma is intensified, because he is frequently called upon to act in a professional manner toward the disrespectful tenants. Thus, whether mainly out of choice (expression of self-conceptions) or out of necessity (fulfillment of situational requisites), the relationship between janitor and tenant sometimes assumes the character of that between professional and client.

The nature of the janitor's work leads him to find out a great deal about the personal lives of his tenants. He meets with many situations which force him to decide how much and to whom he should tell what he knows about them. Generally, he exercises scrupulous care in the handling of this intimate knowledge, as he considers himself to be intrusted with it in confidence.

The janitor gets some of his information from sources other than the tenants themselves. When he acts as an informant (e.g., for insurance checkers), he finds out a great deal about their personal affairs. One tenant tells him about another. The garbage reveals much about them. From these sources he acquires information of a very confidential nature.

The janitor also gets information directly from the tenants. They confide in him not only about illnesses but also about personal problems. As Janitor No. 20 remarked, "Some of them stop you and think they have to tell you if they got a toothache."

How the janitor dispenses his intimate knowledge about tenants was related by Janitor No. 32:

If tenants want to know what's going on, they come to me about it. You hear and see a lot of things in your time. There are even times when you are requested to keep quiet. And there are times when you have to answer—for FBI and insurance inspectors. You can't tell them everything, either, you know. See and not see; hear and not hear—that's the best policy.

Like the bartender and the barber, whose ascribed occupational status beclouds the fact that they frequently share their customers' personal secrets, the janitor is placed in problematical situations requiring some kind of ethical rules. When it is understood that occupational problems which accrue from the same kinds of situations are basically the same without respect to status, then the similar receipt of confidences by the janitor, the lawyer, or the bartender becomes clear. These workers are, in this instance, in the kind of situation which requires them to protect the customer's personal secrets. Whether the disposition of these secrets involves as little as remaining silent or as much as stretching the truth, the workers protect their relationship with the customer by protecting his confidences. Likewise, in other given kinds of work situations which require the solution of ethical problems, the worker-customer relationship becomes overly complicated unless the worker makes and observes appropriate rules. Such ethical rules are not simply a matter of honorable self-conceptions or formalized professional codes. They are fundamentally a matter of situational requirements, irrespective of personal and occupational status.

Another area in which professional behavior is found concerns the janitor's relationships with overamorous tenants. Janitor No. 12 described what he considers to be the proper procedure for easing gracefully out of such a delicate predicament:

> Another thing about janitors—lots of women try to get you up in apartment just "to talk" or for some phony excuse. When you walk in they are on couch, ask you to sit down, and that means only one thing. When that happens to me and I begin to sweat, I know I better leave. Thing is not to refuse them so they get embarrassed, so I act dumb. I excuse myself and say I forgot about water running some place which I must shut off right away. It's hard to do, but it's best.

One can easily imagine hearing the bishop advise the young minister or the elderly doctor instruct the young doctor in a similar vein. The minister and the doctor must be prepared to meet such situations in a like fashion. The janitor instructs tenants to call him for repairs only during daylight hours, except for what he considers to be genuine emergencies. In the same way, the physician teaches his patients to call him only during office hours, except for a bona fide emergency. Some janitors recognize the similarity to doctors' problems. As Janitor No. 19 observed:

> Did you ever stop to think that we have a lot in common with doctors? I used to meet them in the halls at all hours of the night. We'd kid each other about making emergency calls at all hours of the night and never getting through with work.

Not only the janitor and the physician but others who deal routinely with customers' emergencies have problems of the same kind.

Yet another cluster of work situations wherein the janitor exhibits professional behavior concerns those occasions when he is called upon to do mechanical work for the tenants. The most clear-cut evidence of professional behavior in this area was submitted by Janitor No. 11.

> Some of the repair work the tenant is responsible for and I'm supposed to charge for it. Well, if I replace some glass that costs me three and a half dollars, I may charge the tenant a half dollar or two dollars more

for my labor, depending on how much she can afford. If it's a little thing and the tenant isn't well off, I won't charge her anything for it if she's supposed to pay.

The janitor's practice of charging for repairs on the basis of the customer's ability to pay is a high standard of service—quite in the tradition of the medical profession—and he knows it.

The Dilemma

The janitor's professional behavior, together with his substantial income, contradicts what he believes are his tenants' conceptions of him. His struggle to gain their respect is a struggle for status. His high standards of conduct constitute a way of favorably influencing their estimation of his worth. Still, he finds that tenants regard him as hardly more than *a janitor*. He strongly resents their failure properly to recognize him, particularly in the case of the fourflushers. As Janitor No. 18 bitterly remarked:

> They're the kind that are very important. They think you're a fireman— should drop everything and run to them. They adopt a superior attitude: "I'm the tenant and you're the janitor." Like the East and the West in that saying. Confidentially, a lot of us janitors could buy out most tenants. They put on airs and try to be bossy.

The janitor has a higher income than many of the tenants; yet, the latter "adopt a superior attitude." So he does considerable soul-searching to seek a satisfactory explanation of his relatively low status. The conversation which we had with Janitor No. 28 is in point:

> INTERVIEWER: What things are janitors touchy about?
> JANITOR: A lot of tenants figure he's just a goddamn janitor, a servant. Here [with "rich" tenants] it's not so bad. You say something to them and they [the "bad" tenants] say, "Hell, you're nothing but a janitor." Or when you're talking to even a working man and you tell him you're a janitor, he smiles—you know, people think there's nothing lower than a janitor. You get that feeling that they're looking down on you, because you're working for them. I know I feel that way sometimes. During the depression I was making better than most, so what the hell. It's good earned money.
> INTERVIEWER: Well, why do you say you get that feeling that they are looking down on you? Why do you feel so sensitive?
> JANITOR: In different places you hear people talk janitor this and janitor that, and they say they'd never be a goddamn janitor. So you think people here must say and think the same, but not to you. It makes you feel funny sometimes.

It is noteworthy that Janitor No. 28 does not reject his idea of the tenants' definition of a janitor. For that matter, virtually no other janitor does so either. To explain this, it is necessary to understand how the janitor relates himself to other janitors in terms of the occupational title.

The individual janitor strongly identifies himself with the name "janitor," despite his belief that tenants look down on janitors. Their view does not annoy him very much because he, too, looks down on *other* janitors. He feels that he is different from and better than other janitors. So, when tenants (nonjanitors) speak disparagingly of janitors, he does not resent it because of the group solidarity in the occupation, for, in reality, there is little such solidarity. Rather he resents it because his self-conceptions are so involved in the name "janitor" and because the tenants fail to recognize his individual worth. Thus, when a janitor (No. 8) proudly states, "Tenants never treated *me* like a janitor," there is no doubt that he agrees with their definition of janitor but that he, by virtue of being singularly superior to other janitors, has been treated in accordance with his conception of himself.

This attitude of "different and better" may be characteristic of the members of any occupation (or other group) whose public reputation is one of censorious stereotypes. This attitude implies that the individual member agrees that most of his colleagues do have the characteristics attributed to them by the public. The interesting question is: Why does the member agree with the public? The study of janitors suggests that the answer is likely to be in terms of (1) the nature of the member's association with his colleagues (he probably knows only a few of the "better" ones) and (2) the status relationship between the member and the portion of the public he associates with in his work.

Although the individual janitor capably defends himself from the public's conceptions of janitors, he still must perform tasks which preclude advance to a higher occupational, hence social, status. The janitorial reputation refers to the members' personal characteristics and work habits. Closely related to, but distinguishable from, these alleged personal traits are readily verified features of janitoring which involve dirty work (e.g., shoveling coal and removing garbage). Work is dirty when society defines it as such, that is, when society defines it as being necessary but undesirable or even repugnant. Middle-class people seem consciously to avoid such tasks. They apparently realize that the kind of work one does is often more important than one's income when it comes to getting established as a member of the middle class. Yet, in a materialistic society certain costly things, like a new automobile and a television set, become symbolic of high status, even to them. This accounts for the dilemma of the fourflushers.

But what about members of occupations which require the performance of dirty tasks? It seems that, like members of the janitorial occupation, they have the financial but lack the occupational qualifications for acceptance by the middle class. Speaking on this dilemma, Janitor No. 35 argued:

A lot think they're better than the janitor because he has to take down their trash. Still the janitor makes more money. I believe the janitor *should* be making a lot more money than white-collar workers. After all, a janitor has a whole lot of responsibility and long hours.

Janitor No. 35, in summarizing the status-income dilemma, is painfully aware that tenants look down on the janitor. Their trash, the garbage, is undoubtedly the biggest single element in the janitor's continued low status. The removal of garbage is dirty work, incompatible with middle-class status. It causes the janitor to subserve the tenants, all of his individual attributes notwithstanding. The garbage symbolizes the dilemmas of the janitor-tenant relationship.

Conclusion

This account of the status-income dilemma suggests that, since high-prestige and high-income occupations are frequently distinguishable from one another, the *kind* of work a person does is a crucially qualifying factor in so far as his status possibilities are concerned. Viewed another way, the trend toward professionalization of occupations becomes an effort either to bring status recognition into line with high income or to bring income into line with high-status recognition. The janitor-tenant relationship has been graphically presented to call attention to a dilemma which is so prevalent that it is apt to be overlooked.

References

GOLD, RAY
     1950   "The Chicago Flat Janitor." Unpublished M.A. thesis, Department of Sociology, University of Chicago.
PARK, R. E.
     1926   "Behind Our Masks." *Survey Graphic* 56 (May):136.
     1925   "Suggestions for the Investigation of Human Behavior in the Urban Environment." In R. E. PARK, ed., *The City*. Chicago: University of Chicago Press.

3. Negotiating the Serious Import of Humor*

JOAN P. EMERSON

Negotiations to Address Taboo Topics

Joking provides a useful channel for covert communication on taboo topics.[1] Normally a person is not held responsible for what he does in jest to the same degree that he would be for a serious gesture. Humor, as an aside from the main discourse, need not be taken into account in subsequent interaction. It need not become part of the history of the encounter, or be used for the continuous reassessment of the nature and worth of each participant, or be built into the meaning of subsequent acts. For the very reason that humor officially does not "count," persons are induced to risk messages that might be unacceptable if stated seriously. In a general hospital, for instance, where staff and patients take for granted that matters related to death, staff competence, and indignities to patients will be discussed circumspectly or avoided, many joking references to these topics are found.[2]

Sometimes a topic of covert communication introduced through humor emerges into the open. One person makes a joke and the second person, acknowledging that the first person intended a joke, responds with a serious comment on the content of the joke as though the first person had spoken seriously. By including a taboo topic in this way, the parties are negotiating a private agreement to suspend a

* From *Sociometry*, Vol. 32 (June, 1969), pp. 169–81. Reprinted by permission of the American Sociological Association and the author.
1 "When two teams establish an official working consensus as a guarantee for safe social interaction, we may usually detect an unofficial line of communication which each team directs at the other. This unofficial communication may be carried on by innuendo, mimicked accents, well-placed jokes, significant pauses, veiled hints, purposeful kidding, expressive overtones, and many other sign practices." (Goffman, 1959:190.)
2 The hospital incidents cited in this paper come from a study of spontaneous wisecracks and pleasantries on two wards of a general hospital. (See Emerson, 1963.)

general guideline of the institutional setting (cf. Berger and Luck-man, 1966).

The prevailing practice in a hospital, for example, is to exclude certain topics from staff-patient encounters. Since the staff has the upper hand, most of these taboos are designed for their convenience. The prohibitions assist the staff in concentrating on technical matters and avoiding the human, emotional side of the patient. But at times a staff member may want to make a concession to a patient or a patient may demand concessions to which he is not officially entitled. At such times the particular parties involved may negotiate to suspend the guidelines and conduct their encounter in a fashion which could be labeled deviant were the guidelines in force. One way they may proceed is to transpose a taboo topic from humor to the serious conversation.

Negotiations about humor, then, may be regarded as bargaining to make unofficial arrangements about taboo topics. Two main issues pervade such negotiations. How much license may be taken under the guise of humor? While it is understood that persons have some leeway in joking about topics which they could not introduce in serious discourse, the line between acceptable and unacceptable content is ambiguous. So it must be negotiated in each particular exchange. Anyone making a joke cannot be sure that the other will find his move acceptable and anyone listening to a joke may find he is offended.

How will responsibility for circumventing the guidelines be allocated? Each party tries to forestall the other's possible move to reinstate the guidelines by claiming: were the guidelines reinstated, you, and not I, would be held responsible for rule violations. The transposer threatens the joker with responsibility for a joke which exceeds the bounds of decorum; the joker threatens the transposer with responsibility for introducing a taboo topic into the conversation (on negotiating responsibility, see Scott and Lyman, 1968; Scheff, 1968).

In the transitions considered in this paper, the transposer acknowledges the joke, but evidently takes the topic so seriously that he does not want to leave it in the joking realm. Before turning to such transactions, I will mention briefly a related interchange in which the joker fails to have his gesture accepted as a joke. Here also a covert topic is brought into the open, but inadvertently and not as the result of a negotiated agreement.

A person using the joking medium for covert communication must indicate simultaneously that he intends humor and hint that his message should be taken into account. If the listener will not accept his gesture as a joke, he becomes responsible for matters of dubious content. For example, during the early period of the Nazi regime in Germany (1933–1938), a series of cabaret entertainers were arrested for their wisecracks and mimicry of Hitler and his regime. At the time of the stage performances the entertainers and their audiences did not see themselves as engaged in a political crime, yet the subsequent arrests placed the performances in that light. That the concentration of power resulted in rather one-sided negotiations only highlights the fact that the meaning of one's action does not rest with oneself alone.

Failure to have a gesture accepted as a joke seems most likely when the joker underestimates the listener's sensitivity to the topic. The listener may find the topic too emotionally charged and the reference too blatant to be ignored in the main discourse. But failure ultimately depends on the relationship between the parties: the more power the joker has, the more obligations the listener owes to him, and the higher the price of sanctioning the joke, the more likely is the joker to have his claim validated. Other contributing factors are acknowledgment of the joker as a person who has the right to joke, appropriateness of joking in the situation, and the extent to which the joke has been delivered with cues indicating humor.

By refusing to accept a joke, a listener inadvertently acknowledges a taboo topic. Ironically, the move is motivated by exactly the opposite aim. Yet by insisting, "This is no joke; you really mean it. I won't let you get away with it, because you know perfectly well this matter must not be discussed," a listener calls attention to the topic as potentially relevant to the serious discourse, dissolving the joker's fiction that it was not relevant. But this disagreement on interpreting the gesture disrupts the social situation, and the taboo issue is not discussed.

The significance of the transition in which humor is first acknowledged lies in the possibility of commenting on a taboo topic without a catastrophic degree of social disruption. Further significance lies in coming to an agreement to comment on taboo topics, even though this is contrary to the understandings supposedly binding on the participants. The next two sections examine negotiations to transpose a topic from a humorous to a serious framework.[3] In conclusion, these negotiations are reviewed as an instance of private agreements to suspend general guidelines.

Negotiations to Transpose the Topic

Transitions in which the listener acknowledges the joke and then comments seriously on the topic were observed to fall into two types. In the first type, the transposer, even though he has acknowledged the joke, accuses the joker of exceeding the bounds of propriety with his joke content; the transition constitutes a sanction on the joker. This pattern was observed between patients and hospital staff in the following form. A patient would imply in a joke: "I am going to die" or "I am worthless" or "The hospital and staff make me suffer." In response, the staff member would assume a professional responsibility for upholding the contrary position, apparently considering the topic too serious to remain in a joking framework. For example,

[3] The idea of a special framework for play and humor comes from Bateson (1955).

A medical student, after taking a blood specimen from a newly admitted patient, says: "Dr. Sackett will be in to see you in a little while." The patient answers: "He's already been in and then he left again. He didn't like my looks." To this jest the medical student responds seriously: "It's not that—he is very busy." [4]

The medical student tries to refute the patient's indictment of her personal appearance and let the patient know that his colleague had no personal reason for making a short visit. Because the joking framework itself is a kind of negation of the message, the medical student could have better discounted it by leaving it as a joke. By his response he dissolves the negation in which the patient has couched her remark.

But a transposer may be willing to pay this price in order to curb another's license for indirect communication by exposing the innuendoes and pinning responsibility on the insinuator. In this type of transition, an agreement is negotiated to suspend the guidelines about taboo topics, but the suspension occurs in the interest of enforcing those very guidelines. The subversive element of the move is at least partially neutralized by its conformist intent.

In the second type of transition, the transposer claims rights to which he is not entitled within the conventional definition of the situation. In contrast to the first type, the transition is definitely subversive to the guidelines. As in the following incident, a joke may serve as a trial balloon to invite a discussion of doubtful propriety (cf. Goffman, 1959:191 on "putting out feelers").

On a quiet evening a medical student wanders into the room of a twenty-six year old unmarried patient, much discussed on the ward because of an unexpected recovery from the consequences of an illegal abortion. The medical student remarks somewhat awkwardly but apparently in jest: "You have a lot of teenage magazines around here. Are you a teenager?" The patient replies with a mild sardonic humor: "Evidently in spirit." When the medical student solemnly inquires, "What do you mean by that?" the patient launches a confessional discussion about how adolescent she sees herself in believing she can get away with doing what she wants regardless of what adults say.

A wise patient waits on a doctor's pleasure before pressing for a personal discussion. Here medical student and patient banter back and forth to determine if the other is indeed willing to open a discussion. By introducing a serious discussion on a cue from a joke, the medical student takes the risk that he has misinterpreted the patient's intent. However, she accepts the transition. If the patient had responded with another light remark to "What do you mean by that?" she

---

[4] If the reader fails to appreciate the humor in this example and the following ones, he should be reminded that the impact of spontaneous levity depends on the context in which it happens.

would have indicated that she did not care to pursue the topic seriously. Had she refused the transition, the medical student would have been discountenanced by appearing stupid or insensitive for requesting a serious explanation in the midst of a bantering conversation.

The two types of transition differ in the joker's desire to transpose the topic. In the first type the joker probably does not want the transition, while in the second type he may or may not. By making the joke in the first place the joker risks a transition he may not desire, because the other may seize upon the joke as an opening. If the joker is reluctant, the transposer may use various tactics to secure his acquiescence. The transitional remark may be designed to close the topic, so that an extended discussion does not ensue. The transposer may make the transition in an ambiguous fashion so that he can gracefully decline responsibility for it if necessary. He may offer to exempt the joker from responsibility for introducing such a topic or he may blame the joker for introducing the topic. He may use the joker's cues of serious intent against him. The transposer can assume that the more the joker has implicitly acknowledged that his joking message has a serious import, the less he need fear that the joker will embarrass him by immediately denying it.

How touchy the joke content is affects the negotiation of transitions. Once included in the serious conversation, the content of a joke may in fact be too loaded not to ruffle the interaction. The bargaining parties calculate whether the transition is worth the price of contending with the concomitant awkwardness. The delicacy becomes an issue in the negotiations: one party may claim that the delicacy is manageable or would be overwhelmingly unmanageable, offer to take action to help manage it, and request that the other take action to minimize it.

The awkwardness of a deliberate transition that exposes the underlying fictions of an encounter is exemplified in the following incident.

A terminal cancer patient becomes the talk of the ward because of the enormous difficulties in contending with her. It takes four nurses to get this "baby elephant" on the bedpan. Such scenes seem ludicrous and all participants join in the mood of hilarity. On one occasion the patient abruptly stops her participation in the general merriment and pleads, "Don't laugh at me." The head nurse counters with, "You are laughing yourself." The patient then resumes the mood of hilarity: "If I'm going to die, I may as well die laughing." After a second of awkward silence, the head nurse chides her, "Who's going to die?"

The nurses are trying to give the impression that they are joining in laughter *with* the patient when actually much of their laughter is directed *at* the patient. In midstream the patient reverses her acquiescence to the nurses' pretense by disrupting the framework of humor. After such a shattering move the patient is in an awkward position to joke about death. In most hospitals it is taboo for a patient to mention his impending death to the staff unless the circumstances are exceptional and considerably more private than in the "baby elephant" example. Here the wording of the reference to death is evidently too blatant and too inappropriate in the light of the preceding exchange. The head nurse's transformation of the prospect of the patient's death into a serious context precipitates a loss of face for the patient (cf. Goffman, 1955). The patient suddenly becomes a person who does not have enough sense to keep unwelcome topics out of a lighthearted exchange of pleasantries.

Most negotiations begin with ambiguous gestures in which each tests the response of the other before committing himself to a firm line of action. Once the transposer actually makes an overt bid for a transition, the joker is constrained to accept this bid. By drawing on the prior indications that the humor has serious intent the transposer precipitates a "moment of truth" which the joker can counter only by repudiating his own line and thus risking that any future line he may offer will be discredited. Also, once one party has definitely committed himself to a line of action, the other party knows he may create a deadlock deleterious to both if he refuses to acquiesce (cf. Schelling, 1963, especially pp. 22–28). Often the joker may go along even when it may not be in his interest to do so. A joker's refusal to acknowledge a transition apparently occurs more rarely than one might expect. But should it happen, negotiations may reach a hopeless deadlock. Excerpts from newspaper dispatches tell one such story.

JOAN BAEZ MAY SUE CARTOONIST

Folksinger Joan Baez threatened yesterday to take cartoonist Al Capp to court unless he discontinues his "Joanie Phoanie" episode in the "Li'l Abner" comic strip.

Miss Baez, who arrived here [Honolulu] en route to Japan, said she had instructed her attorney to halt Capp from continuing the "Joanie Phoanie" which she believes is a caricature of herself.

Capp's comic strip Joanie is a campus idol who sings protest songs for $10,000 a concert.

Miss Baez said the satire is "vulgar and stupid," and that her lawyer is asking for a retraction in every newspaper that carries the Li'l Abner strip. . . .

She said she doesn't mind being spoofed, but objected to Capp's "taking a jab at the whole protest movement." (*San Francisco Chronicle*, January 10, 1967.)

AL CAPP'S REPLY TO JOAN BAEZ IN COMIC TIFF

Cartoonist Al Capp said yesterday that if folksinger Joan Baez can prove the character "Joanie Phoanie" in his "Li'l Abner" strip resembles her, "I feel sorry for her."

"Joanie Phoanie is a repulsive, egomaniacal, un-American non-taxpaying horror," said Capp. "I see no resemblance to Joan Baez whatsoever, but if Miss Baez wants to try to prove it, let her." (*San Francisco Chronicle*, January 11, 1967.)

Al Capp does not acknowledge that Joan Baez is the inspiration for "Joanie Phoanie" and refuses to allow her to make the transition. Capp's move leaves Joan Baez in a foolish position. The incident differs from the hospital examples in several ways which are relevant for the acknowledgment of the transition. Al Capp and Joan Baez are not encountering each other face-to-face in an ongoing social system where they can test each other's reactions by gradually moving in the direction of a transition before any irrevocable steps are taken. Further, Joan Baez makes an explicit issue of the serious intent of the caricature. If she should carry her point, Al Capp must wind up in an awkward position. Therefore, he must defeat her move. In contrast, the transposers in the hospital examples take for granted the serious intent of the humor and without making an explicit issue of it, comment on the content. Thus, the awkwardness for the joker is often circumvented and the possibility of later denying the serious intent of the humor is still open. Finally, Joan Baez wants Al Capp to assume responsibility for his act as if it had been performed seriously. In some of the hospital incidents the transposer offers to exempt the joker from official responsibility if the joker will implicitly admit that his joke has a serious intent. But Joan Baez wants to revoke Al Capp's license as a cartoonist for malpractice, as it were. Since objectionable content counts more when it is extricated from the discounting mode of humor, however, the very maneuver intended to curtail Al Capp's license and discourage future offenses serves to transform the present act into one which counts. The best he can offer her is to insist on leaving the content in a framework where it does not count.

If the joker will not agree, the transposer loses face. He may be labeled as a person with "no sense of humor" or as lacking social finesse because he misjudged the appropriate tone for the occasion. To justify sanctioning the transposer, the joker can invoke conventional understandings about conduct in social encounters which the transposer has violated. One such understanding is a general presumption that a response to an act will occur in the same framework as the act itself. If one person makes a jocular remark the other person is expected to reply lightly if he decides to take up the jocular remark at all. But the person who responds seriously to a topic presented within a joke changes the framework without explicit permission. Another understanding is that a person will not be held responsible in the serious realm for what he does in the playful realm. Otherwise, the license of the playful realm would not be possible. By transposing the topic of the joke to the serious realm, the recipient is in effect holding the jokester responsible for the implicit content of his joke. A third understanding applies to the timing of the negotiations about definitions of the framework. Customarily, the framework of an interchange is defined at the very beginning.[5] Blatant attempts at redefining the framework in retrospect are frowned upon. The definition of the framework is an important counter in the participants' struggle over control, a struggle which must be regulated by conventional understandings about the timing of definitions. The person who takes up a joking topic in a serious fashion is perpetrating a retrospective definition in defiance of this unspoken convention.

If a joker acknowledges the transition, however, he thereby gives up the opportunity to sanction the transposer, especially since he becomes an accomplice to the norm-violating act. By complying with the transposer, he may be able to claim a reciprocal favor. One such favor is protection in the transaction at hand by subsequently discounting the transition by a process of redefinition, as described in the next section.

Negotiations to Reaffirm the Opening Gesture as Humor

When a person responds seriously to the topic of a joke, he immediately opens negotiations about how the original joke is to be defined and who is responsible for introducing the topic into the serious conversation. By making it ambiguous whether he has understood that a joke was intended, the transposer leaves room for the joker later to make explicit that a joke was intended and thus partially to discount the serious discussion. After a few exchanges the joker may try in retrospect to restore the humorous definition to his remark. Two incidents which illustrate this point will be considered in detail.

A resident doctor calls a registered nurse "a nag" in jest. Soon afterward the nurse, determined to force a confrontation, approaches the doctor: "Dr. Radcliffe, I have a bone to pick with you."
 Doctor: "Well, let's do it later."
 Nurse: "No, right now. Why did you call me a nag?"
 Doctor: "Because you keep after a thing and never let it go."
 Nurse: "Is it about the same thing?"
 Doctor: "Yes."
 Nurse: "What?"
 Doctor: "That Bird machine [respirator]."
Doctor and nurse understand the reference to the respirator to stand for their prior disagreement over a nonmedical aspect of the management of a certain patient. They then proceed to air this disagreement. At the conclusion of the encounter the nurse repeats, "Why did you call me a nag?" Dr. Radcliffe claims, "I was just kidding and I'm sorry you took it seriously, but we [sic] won't call you a nag again."

Dr. Radcliffe attempts to assert his higher status to resolve a debatable

---

[5] "It would seem that an individual can more easily make a choice as to what line of treatment to demand from and extend to the others present at the beginning of an encounter than he can alter the line of treatment that is being pursued once the interaction is underway." (Goffman, 1959:11.)

matter in his own way without an open discussion wherein the nurse's views might triumph. He playfully attempts to dismiss the nurse's pressure for discussion by calling her a nag. By this tactic he inadvertently opens himself to a serious discussion because the nurse uses the joking reference to the topic as a pretext for initiating an exchange not normally permissible. By implying that the doctor has broached the topic by his joke, the nurse deliberately ignores the playful framework he has instituted. Even though the doctor verbally protests the nurse's transition, he is induced to cooperate temporarily.

It is not only the substantive issue about the patient and the respirator which is raised in this exchange. A more consequential issue is implicit: the relation between doctor and nurse. The nurse is challenging the doctor's attempt to circumvent the philosophy that a nurse's views should be taken into account in certain aspects of patient care. So the doctor has let himself in for a confrontation on the doctor-nurse relationship which presumably he would have preferred to avoid. On the other hand, although the possibilities do not materialize in this particular case, by insisting on the transition and a discussion of the topic, the nurse becomes vulnerable to a curt reminder of her proper place and constraint in future contacts with that doctor.

After collecting the advantages of transposing the doctor's joke to the serious realm, the nurse moves to reduce the cost of this maneuver. No doubt she would like to dispense with the label "nag" which has been interjected into the serious realm on her own initiative. By reintroducing the joking incident the nurse provides the doctor with an opportunity for desensitizing the joking remark about her nagging with a retrospective definition. The doctor accepts the opportunity; but he does not take the nurse entirely off the hook. He does oblige by restoring the playful definition to the label "nag," but he also alludes to the nurse's social ineptitude for misunderstanding his kidding by taking it seriously.

The underlying pattern of the second incident is parallel to that of the first.

A former patient, scheduled for experimental surgery, drops by to greet the nurses. On discovering that Miss Northrup will be on vacation during the time he will be back on the ward, and learning the date of her return, the patient says, "I'll be gone and buried by then." Miss Northrup shakes her head and says gently with a smile, yet seriously, "I don't think so." The other nurses chime in with, "Oh, don't say that, Mr. Wales" and "You're not going to die. We need you around. There are lots of things which have to be done." The patient then apologetically claims, "Oh, I was joking." The nurses say, "Oh" and the conversation goes on to something else.

The staff believed that this patient had a 50 per cent chance of surviving the operation. Yet it was not appropriate in this setting for a patient to express his fear of dying. This patient tries to circumvent this convention by making a remark without any behavioral cues of humor except its possibly outrageous content. It is not clear whether he is joking or whether this remark is a serious bid for sharing the patient's realistic fear of dying. The nurses decline to accept the ambiguous invitation. Instead, their responses chide the patient for his *faux pas* in expressing the sentiment.

To rescue what of his reputation might be salvageable, the patient tries to define his remark retrospectively as humor. But the tone of the social situation has already been shattered. If the patient's remark had been ignored or treated as a joke, the incident probably would have passed without noticeable embarrassment. The transition to the serious framework intensifies the awkwardness beyond repair. The patient's attempt to restore the *status quo ante* by claiming that he was joking emphasizes the import of his message. It is difficult to sustain the definition that merely a joke has occurred if the participants become too flustered.

Further, in contrast to the nurse-doctor example, the joker is in a weak position to allow the blame to revert to the others in the situation. The doctor's maneuver to define his remark retrospectively as a joke succeeds because his remark is more clearly marked as a joke in the first place and the nurse is more amenable to the retrospective definition. In addition, the content of the joke can be discussed in the serious realm without offending too much. But in this last example, the patient's attempt at redefinition is a failure because if the nurses accepted it, they would be in the position of having misinterpreted a remark in such a way that, uninvited, they delved into one of the most delicate areas of another person's private feelings.

These examples illustrate the process of negotiation about the allocation of responsibility in transitions. The crucial issue is: who is responsible for introducing the topic into the serious conversation? This negotiation centers around whether or not the initial remark was merely a joke or whether a message of serious import was intended. If the joker merely ventured a joke then the transposer would be responsible for introducing the topic on a serious level, perhaps against the joker's inclination. If the joker intends his remark to have serious import, then he is responsible for introducing the topic. Because the topic would not ordinarily be brought up in conversation, whoever initiates the topic may be held responsible for risking a divergence from acceptable behavior and creating chaos in the social scene.

Private Agreements to Suspend General Guidelines

Negotiations to include taboo topics by transferring joking content to a serious conversation constitute private agreements to suspend general guidelines. As the Baez-Capp exchange suggests, negotiations to suspend ordinary practices are difficult unless persons have ongoing face-to-face relations in social systems, as the persons in the hospital setting did. Such negotiations are covert and risky. Since the negotiations stand outside the ordinary framework of the encounter, the parties cannot appeal to outside authorities. What happens depends largely on the particular individuals and their relationship with each other. They may be able to make an agreement profitable to both. But in suspending the ordinary framework to arrange this agreement, each risks that the other, now free from the ordinary restrictions, will coerce an agreement disadvantageous to him. During and after this negotiation, each risks betrayal in the event that the other should reinstate the ordinary framework. Should the ordinary framework be reinstated, a participant may be assigned responsibility for actions now defined as unacceptable. That is, a person may find he has been enticed into behavior normally unacceptable on the promise that the normal standards will be suspended, only to find that the normal standards are enforced after all (cf. Cavan, 1966:238–41).

The possibility of retrospective redefinitions is what makes these negotiations so risky.[6] To have performed in retrospect the act one intended to perform, one may be obliged to enter the ensuing fray to insist that one's own definition of the act be accepted by others. Bargaining over retrospective definitions is most likely to occur when actions are relatively ambiguous and when at least one of the parties has something to gain by a favorable definition of past events. Even though the intended meaning seems clear at the time and the other person acknowledges that intended meaning, either party may subsequently move to redefine the act. Even without ambiguity, subsequent redefinition is possible because the present is more vivid than the past. With time, the implicit features of the exchange on which the validation rested slip from memory more readily than the overt act. Thus, a definition posed in the present can override memories from the past which seem to contradict it.

A person making a joke takes the risk that he will be compelled to assume responsibility for an action he did not necessarily intend if another person takes the initiative in redefining his action. Accepting an unfavorable redefinition may be preferable to engaging in the struggle required to avert redefinition. As elsewhere, retrospective negotiations in regard to humor appear to be closely linked with defining conformity to rules, specifying offers, and defending self (cf. McCaghy, 1968).

Both parties may acknowledge that retrospective negotiations are essential to resolve ambiguity. But on occasions, as in deliberate transitions of humor, what is taken as a stable situation by at least one party may be overturned by the unilateral action of the other. The unilateral move to redefine the past may lead to a bitter struggle over whether negotiations are to be opened. The first party's failure to validate the other's unilateral move and the resulting embarrassment

---

[6] The following discussion on negotiation of retrospective meaning is indebted to Garfinkel (1967).

are weapons in this struggle. The joker, for example, may feel cheated by the transposer who has acknowledged the humorous framework and then in effect immediately withdrawn his acknowledgment. On the other hand, a person who expects that he can retract his stand later and that signs of personal ineptitude may be discounted may discover that he cannot manage the retroactive negotiation after all and his tentative commitment becomes solidified against his will.

In staff-patient encounters, prohibitions against discussing certain matters clash with practical necessities or strong concerns about death, indignities, and staff competence. It is in situations where pressures for discussion and prohibitions exist simultaneously that negotiations to ignore the prohibitions are most likely to arise. When parties succeed in negotiating such agreements, they establish a presumption of trust. Not only can they trust each other in routine matters, but they share complicitly for rule violations which potentially can be extended. Thus, the contradictory pressures of social settings may encourage the formation of subgroups where an independent culture, subversive to the general culture, flourishes.

References

BATESON, GREGORY
    1955 "A Theory of Play and Fantasy." *Psychiatric Research Reports* 2 (December):39–51.
BERGER, PETER, and THOMAS LUCKMANN
    1966 *The Social Construction of Reality*. Garden City: Doubleday.
CAVAN, SHERRI
    1966 *Liquor License: An Ethnography of Bar Behavior*. Chicago: Aldine.
EMERSON, JOAN P.
    1963 "Social Functions of Humor in a Hospital Setting." Unpublished doctoral dissertation, University of California at Berkeley.
GARFINKEL, HAROLD
    1967 *Studies in Ethnomethodology*. Englewood Cliffs: Prentice-Hall.
GOFFMAN, ERVING
    1959 *The Presentation of Self in Everyday Life*. Garden City: Doubleday.
    1955 "On Face-Work: An Analysis of Ritual Elements in Social Interaction." *Psychiatry* 18 (August):213–31.
McCAGHY, CHARLES
    1968 "Drinking and Deviance Disavowal: The Case of Child Molesters." *Social Problems* 16 (Summer):43–49.
SCHEFF, THOMAS J.
    1968 "Negotiating Reality: Notes on Power in the Assessment of Responsibility." *Social Probems* 16 (Summer):3–17.
SCHELLING, THOMAS
    1963 *The Strategy of Conflict*. New York: Oxford University Press.
SCOTT, MARVIN, and STANFORD LYMAN
    1968 "Accounts." *American Sociological Review* 33 (February):46–62.

4. Teams *

ERVING GOFFMAN

In thinking about a performance it is easy to assume that the content of the presentation is merely an expressive extension of the character of the performer and to see the function of the performance in these personal terms. This is a limited view and can obscure important differences in the function of the performance for the interaction as a whole.

First, it often happens that the performance serves mainly to express the characteristics of the performer. Thus one finds that service personnel, whether in profession, bureaucracy, business, or craft, enliven their manner with movements which express proficiency and integrity, but, whatever this manner conveys about them, often its major purpose is to establish a favorable definition of their service or product. Further, we often find that the personal front of the performer is employed not so much because it allows him to present himself as he would like to appear but because his appearance and manner can do something for a scene of wider scope. It is in this light that we can understand how the sifting and sorting of urban life brings girls with good grooming and correct accent into the job of receptionist, where they can present a front for an organization as well as for themselves.

But most important of all, we commonly find that the definition of the situation projected by a particular participant is an integral part of a projection that is fostered and sustained by the intimate co-operation of more than one participant. For example, in a medical hospital the two staff internists may require the intern, as part of his training, to run through a patient's chart, giving an opinion about each recorded item. He may not appreciate that his show of relative ignorance comes in part from the staff studying up on the chart the night before; he is quite unlikely to appreciate that this impression is doubly ensured by the local team's tacit agreement allotting the work-up of half the chart to one staff person, the other half to the

* From *The Presentation of Self in Everyday Life* by Erving Goffman, copyright © 1959 by Erving Goffman. Reprinted by permission of Doubleday & Company, Inc.

second staff person.[1] This teamwork ensures a good staff showing —providing, of course, that the right internist is able to take over the catechism at the right time.

Furthermore, it is often the case that each member of such a troupe or cast of players may be required to appear in a different light if the team's over-all effect is to be satisfactory. Thus if a household is to stage a formal dinner, someone in uniform or livery will be required as part of the working team. The individual who plays this part must direct at himself the social definition of a menial. At the same time the individual taking the part of hostess must direct at herself, and foster by her appearance and manner, the social definition of someone upon whom it is natural for menials to wait. This was strikingly demonstrated in the island tourist hotel studied by the writer (hereafter called "Shetland Hotel"). There an over-all impression of middle-class service was achieved by the management, who allocated to themselves the roles of middle-class host and hostess and to their employees that of domestics—although in terms of the local class structure the girls who acted as maids were of slightly higher status than the hotel owners who employed them. When hotel guests were absent, little nonsense about a maid-mistress status difference was allowed by the maids. Another example may be taken from middle-class family life. In our society, when husband and wife appear before new friends for an evening of sociability, the wife may demonstrate more respectful subordination to the will and opinion of her husband than she may bother to show when alone with him or when with old friends. When she assumes a respectful role, he can assume a dominant one; and when each member of the marriage team plays its special role, the conjugal unit, as a unit, can sustain the impression that new audiences expect of it. Race etiquette in the South provides another example. Charles Johnson's suggestion is that when few other whites are in the region, a Negro may call his white fellow worker by his first name, but when other whites approach it is understood that mistering will be reintroduced (Johnson, 1943:137–38). Business etiquette provides a similar example:

> When outsiders are present, the touch of businesslike formality is even more important. You may call your secretary "Mary" and your partner "Joe" all day, but when a stranger comes into your office you should refer to your associates as you would expect the stranger to address them: Miss or Mr. You may have a running joke with the switchboard operator, but you let it ride when you are placing a call in an outsider's hearing. [*Esquire Etiquette*, 1953:6.]
>
> She [your secretary] wants to be called Miss or Mrs. in front of strangers; at least, she won't be flattered if your "Mary" provokes everyone else into addressing her with familiarity. [*Esquire Etiquette*, 1953:15.]

[1] Writer's unpublished study of a medical service.

I will use the term "performance team" or, in short, "team" to refer
to any set of individuals who co-operate in staging a single routine.

Until now in this report we have taken the individual's performance
as the basic point of reference and have been concerning ourselves
with two levels of fact—the individual and his performance on one
hand and the full set of participants and the interaction as a whole
on the other. For the study of certain kinds and aspects of interaction,
this perspective would seem sufficient; anything that did not fit this
framework could be handled as a resolvable complication of it. Thus
co-operation between two performers each of whom was ostensibly
involved in presenting his own special performance could be analyzed
as a type of collusion or "understanding" without altering the basic
frame of reference. However in the case-study of particular social
establishments, the co-operative activity of some of the participants
seems too important to be handled merely as a variation on a previous
theme. Whether the members of a team stage similar individual
performances or stage dissimilar performances which fit together into
a whole, an emergent team impression arises which can conveniently
be treated as a fact in its own right, as a third level of fact located
between the individual performance on one hand and the total interaction of participants on the other. It may even be said that if our
special interest is the study of impression management, of the contingencies which arise in fostering an impression, and of the techniques
for meeting these contingencies, then the team and the team-
performance may well be the best units to take as the fundamental
point of reference.[2] Given this point of reference, it is possible to
assimilate such situations as two-person interaction into the framework
by describing these situations as two-team interaction in which each
team contains only one member. (Logically speaking, one could even
say that an audience which was duly impressed by a particular social
setting in which no other persons were present would be an audience
witnessing a team-performance in which the team was one of no
members.)

The concept of team allows us to think of performances that are
given by one or more than one performer; it also covers another
case. Earlier it was suggested that a performer may be taken in by
his own act, convinced at the moment that the impression of reality
which he fosters is the one and only reality. In such cases the performer comes to be his own audience; he comes to be performer
and observer of the same show. Presumably he intracepts or incorporates
the standards he attempts to maintain in the presence of others so that
his conscience requires him to act in a socially proper way. It will have
been necessary for the individual in his performing capacity to conceal

[2] The use of the team (as opposed to the performer) as the fundamental unit
I take from Von Neumann (1947:53, especially), where bridge is analyzed as a
game between two players, each of whom in some respects has two separate individuals to do the playing.

from himself in his audience capacity the discreditable facts that he
has had to learn about the performance; in everyday terms, there will
be things he knows, or has known, that he will not be able to tell
himself. This intricate maneuver of self-delusion constantly occurs;
psychoanalysts have provided us with beautiful field data of this kind,
under the headings of repression and dissociation.[3] Perhaps here we
have a source of what has been called "self-distantiation," namely, that
process by which a person comes to feel estranged from himself.
(See Mannheim, 1956:209.)

When a performer guides his private activity in accordance with
incorporated moral standards, he may associate these standards with
a reference group of some kind, thus creating a non-present audience
for his activity. This possibility leads us to consider a further one.
The individual may privately maintain standards of behavior which
he does not personally believe in, maintaining these standards because
of a lively belief that an unseen audience is present who will punish
deviations from these standards. In other words, an individual may
be his own audience or may imagine an audience to be present. (In
all of this we see the analytical difference between the concept of a
team and that of an individual performer.) This should make us go
on to see that a team itself may stage a performance for an audience
that is not present in the flesh to witness the show. Thus, in some
mental hospitals in America, unclaimed deceased patients may be
given a relatively elaborate funeral on the hospital grounds. No doubt
this helps to ensure the maintenance of minimal civilized standards
in a setting where back-ward conditions and the general unconcern
of society can threaten these standards. In any case, on occasions
when kinfolk do not appear, the hospital minister, the hospital funeral
director, and one or two other functionaries may play out all the funeral
roles themselves and, with the dead patient now laid out, perform a
demonstration of civilized regard for the dead before no one present.

It is apparent that individuals who are members of the same team
will find themselves, by virtue of this fact, in an important relationship
to one another. Two basic components of this relationship may be cited.

First, it would seem that while a team-performance is in progress,
any member of the team has the power to give the show away or to
disrupt it by inappropriate conduct. Each teammate is forced to rely

[3] Individualistic modes of thought tend to treat processes such as self-deception
and insincerity as characterological weaknesses generated within the deep recesses
of the individual personality. It might be better to start from outside the individual
and work inward than to start inside the individual and work out. We may say
that the starting point for all that is to come later consists of the individual performer maintaining a definition of the situation before an audience. The individual
automatically becomes insincere when he adheres to the obligation of maintaining
a working consensus and participates in different routines or performs a given part
before different audiences. Self-deception can be seen as something that results
when two different roles, performer and audience, come to be compressed into
the same individual.

on the good conduct and behavior of his fellows, and they, in turn, are forced to rely on him. There is then, perforce, a bond of reciprocal dependence linking teammates to one another. When members of a team have different formal statuses and rank in a social establishment, as is often the case, then we can see that the mutual dependence created by membership in the team is likely to cut across structural or social cleavages in the establishment and thus provide a source of cohesion for the establishment. Where staff and line statuses tend to divide an organization, performance teams may tend to integrate the divisions.

Secondly, it is apparent that if members of a team must co-operate to maintain a given definition of the situation before their audience, they will hardly be in a position to maintain that particular impression before one another. Accomplices in the maintenance of a particular appearance of things, they are forced to define one another as persons "in the know," as persons before whom a particular front cannot be maintained. Teammates, then, in proportion to the frequency with which they act as a team and the number of matters that fall within impressional protectiveness, tend to be bound by rights of what might be called "familiarity." Among teammates, the privilege of familiarity —which may constitute a kind of intimacy without warmth—need not be something of an organic kind, slowly developing with the passage of time spent together, but rather a formal relationship that is automatically extended and received as soon as the individual takes a place on the team.

In suggesting that teammates tend to be related to one another by bonds of reciprocal dependence and reciprocal familiarity, we must not confuse the type of group so formed with other types, such as an informal group or clique. A teammate is someone whose dramaturgical co-operation one is dependent upon in fostering a given definition of the situation; if such a person comes to be beyond the pale of informal sanctions and insists on giving the show away or forcing it to take a particular turn, he is none the less part of the team. In fact, it is just because he is part of the team that he can cause this kind of trouble. Thus the isolate in the factory who becomes a rate-buster is none the less part of the team, even if his productive activity embarrasses the impression the other workers are attempting to foster as to what constitutes a hard day's work. As an object of friendship he may be studiously ignored, but as a threat to the team's definition of the situation, he cannot be overlooked. Similarly, a girl at a party who is flagrantly accessible may be shunned by the other girls who are present, but in certain matters she is part of their team and cannot fail to threaten the definition they are collectively maintaining that girls are difficult sexual prizes. Thus while teammates are often persons who agree informally to guide their efforts in a certain way as a means of self-protection and by doing so constitute an informal group, this informal agreement is not a criterion for defining the concept of team.

The members of an informal clique, using this term in the sense of a small number of persons who join together for informal amusements, may also constitute a team, for it is likely that they will have to co-operate in tactfully concealing their exclusiveness from some non-members while advertising it snobbishly to others. There is, however, a meaningful contrast between the concepts team and clique. In large social establishments, individuals within a given status level are thrown together by virtue of the fact that they must co-operate in maintaining a definition of the situation toward those above and below them. Thus a set of individuals who might be dissimilar in important respects, and hence desirous of maintaining social distance from one another, find they are in a relation of enforced familiarity characteristic of teammates engaged in staging a show. Often it seems that small cliques form not to further the interests of those with whom the individual stages a show but rather to protect him from an unwanted identification with them. Cliques, then, often function to protect the individual not from persons of other ranks but from persons of his own rank. Thus, while all the members of one's clique may be of the same status level, it may be crucial that not all persons of one's status level be allowed into the clique.[4]

A final comment must be added on what a team is not. Individuals may be bound together formally or informally into an action group in order to further like or collective ends by any means available to them. In so far as they co-operate in maintaining a given impression, using this device as a means of achieving their ends, they constitute what has here been called a team. But it should be made quite clear that there are many means by which an action group can achieve ends other than by dramaturgical co-operation. Other means to ends, such as force or bargaining power, may be increased or decreased by strategic manipulation of impressions, but the exercise of force or bargaining power gives to a set of individuals a source of group formation unconnected with the fact that on certain occasions the group thus formed is likely to act, dramaturgically speaking, as a team. (Similarly, an individual who is in a position of power or leadership may increase or decrease his strength by the degree to which his appearance and manner are appropriate and convincing, but it is not claimed that the dramaturgical qualities of his action necessarily or even commonly constitute the fundamental basis of his position.)

If we are to employ the concept of team as a fundamental point of reference, it will be convenient to retrace earlier steps and redefine our framework of terms in order to adjust for the use of team, rather than individual performer, as the basic unit.

It has been suggested that the object of a performer is to sustain

[4] There are, of course, many bases of clique formation. Edward Gross (1949) suggests that cliques may cross ordinary age and ethnic lines in order to bring together individuals whose work activity is not seen as a competitive reflection upon one another.

a particular definition of the situation, this representing, as it were, his claim as to what reality is. As a one-man team, with no teammates to inform of his decision, he can quickly decide which of the available stands on a matter to take and then wholeheartedly act as if his choice were the only one he could possibly have taken. And his choice of position may be nicely adjusted to his own particular situation and interests.

When we turn from a one-man team to a larger one, the character of the reality that is espoused by the team changes. Instead of a rich definition of the situation, reality may become reduced to a thin party line, for one may expect the line to be unequally congenial to the members of the team. We may expect ironic remarks by which a teammate jokingly rejects the line while seriously accepting it. On the other hand, there will be the new factor of loyalty to one's team and one's teammates to provide support for the team's line.

It seems to be generally felt that public disagreement among the members of the team not only incapacitates them for united action but also embarrasses the reality sponsored by the team. To protect this impression of reality, members of the team may be required to postpone taking public stands until the position of the team has been settled; and once the team's stand has been taken, all members may be obliged to follow it. (The question of the amount of "Soviet self-criticism" that is allowed, and from whom it is allowed, before the team's position is announced, is not here at issue.) An illustration may be taken from the civil service:

> At such committees [Cabinet Committee meetings] civil servants share in the discussions and express their views freely, subject to one qualification: they will not directly oppose their own Minister. The possibility of such open disagreement very rarely arises, and ought never to arise: in nine cases out of ten, the Minister and the civil servant who attends the committee with him have agreed beforehand what line is to be taken, and in the tenth the civil servant who disagrees with his Minister's view on a particular point will stay away from the meeting where it is to be discussed. [Dale, 1941:141.]

Another illustration may be cited from a recent study of the power structure of a small city:

> If one has been engaged in community work on any scale at all, he is impressed over and over with what might be termed the "principle of unanimity." When policy is finally formulated by the leaders in the community, there is an immediate demand on their part for strict conformity of opinion. Decisions are not usually arrived at hurriedly. There is ample time, particularly among the top leaders, for discussion of most projects before a state of action is set. This is true for community projects. When the time for discussion is past and the line is set, then unanimity is called for. Pressures are put upon dissenters, and the project is under way. [Hunter, 1953:181; see also 118 and 212.]

Open disagreement in front of the audience creates, as we say, a false note. It may be suggested that literal false notes are avoided for quite the same reasons that figurative false notes are avoided; in both cases it is a matter of sustaining a definition of the situation. This may be illustrated from a brief book on the work problems of the professional concert-artist accompanist:

> The nearest that the singer and pianist can get to an ideal performance is to do exactly what the composer wants, yet sometimes the singer will require his partner to do something which is in flat contradiction to the composer's markings. He will want an accent where there should be none, he will make a *firmata* where it is not needed, he will make a *rallentando* when it should be *a tempo*: he will be *forte* when he should be *piano*: he may sentimentalize when the mood should be *nobilmente*.
>
> The list is by no means exhausted. The singer will swear with his hand on his heart and tears in his eyes that he does and always aims to do exactly what the composer has written. It is very awkward. If he sings it one way and the pianist plays it another way the result is chaotic. Discussion may be of no avail. But what is an accompanist to do?
>
> At the performance he must *be with the singer*, but afterwards let him erase the memory of it from his mind. [Moore, 1944:60.]

However, unanimity is often not the sole requirement of the team's projection. There seems to be a general feeling that the most real and solid things in life are ones whose description individuals independently agree upon. We tend to feel that if two participants in an event decide to be as honest as they can in recounting it, then the stands they take will be acceptably similar even though they do not consult one another prior to their presentation. Intention to tell the truth presumably makes such prior consultation unnecessary. And we also tend to feel that if the two individuals wish to tell a lie or to slant the version of the event which they offer, then not only will it be necessary for them to consult with one another in order, as we say, "to get their story straight," but it will also be necessary to conceal the fact that an opportunity for such prior consultation was available to them. In other words, in staging a definition of the situation, it may be necessary for the several members of the team to be unanimous in the positions they take and secretive about the fact that these positions were not independently arrived at. (Incidentally, if the members of the team are also engaged in maintaining a show of self-respect before one another, it may be necessary for the members of the team to learn what the line is to be, and take it, without admitting to themselves and to one another the extent to which their position is not independently arrived at, but such problems carry us somewhat beyond the team-performance as the basic point of reference.) It should be noted that just as a teammate ought to wait for the official word before taking his stand, so the official word ought to be

made available to him so that he can play his part on the team and
feel a part of it. For example, in commenting on how some Chinese
merchants set the price of their goods according to the appearance
of the customer, one writer goes on to say:

> One particular result of this study of a customer is seen in the fact
> that if a person enters a store in China, and, after examining several
> articles, asks the price of any one of them, unless it is positively known
> that he has spoken to but one clerk, no answer will be made by him to
> whom the question is put until every other clerk has been asked if he
> has named a price for the article in question to the gentleman. If, as
> very rarely happens, this important precaution is neglected, the sum
> named by different clerks will almost invariably be unlike, thus showing
> that they fail to agree in their estimates of the customer. [Holcombe,
> 1895:293.]

To withhold from a teammate information about the stand his team
is taking is in fact to withhold his character from him, for without
knowing what stand he will be taking he may not be able to assert
a self to the audience. Thus, if a surgeon is to operate on a patient
referred to him by another doctor, common courtesy may oblige the
surgeon to tell the referring doctor when the operation will be and,
if the referring doctor does not appear at the operation, to telephone
him the result of the operation. By thus being "filled in," the referring
doctor can, more effectively than otherwise, present himself to the
patient's kinfolk as someone who is participating in the medical action
(Solomon, 1952:75).

I would like to add a further general fact about maintaining the
line during a performance. When a member of the team makes a
mistake in the presence of the audience, the other team members
often must suppress their immediate desire to punish and instruct
the offender until, that is, the audience is no longer present. After all,
immediate corrective sanctioning would often only disturb the interaction further and, as previously suggested, make the audience privy
to a view that ought to be reserved for teammates. Thus, in author-
itarian organizations, where a team of superordinates maintains a show
of being right every time and of possessing a united front, there is often
a strict rule that one superordinate must not show hostility or disrespect
toward any other superordinate while in the presence of a member of
the subordinate team. Army officers show consensus when before enlisted men, parents when before children,[5] managers when before
workers, nurses when before patients (Taxel, 1953), and the like. Of
course, when the subordinates are absent, open, violent criticism may

[5] An interesting dramaturgical difficulty in the family is that sex and lineal solidarity, which crosscut conjugal solidarity, make it difficult for husband and wife
to "back each other up" in a show of authority before children or a show of either
distance or familiarity with extended kin. As previously suggested, such crosscutting
lines of affiliation prevent the widening of structural cleavages.

and does occur. For example, in a recent study of the teaching profession, it was found that teachers felt that if they are to sustain an impression of professional competence and institutional authority, they must make sure that when angry parents come to the school with complaints, the principal will support the position of his staff, at least until the parents have left (Becker, 1953:134). Similarly, teachers feel strongly that their fellow teachers ought not to disagree with or contradict them in front of students. "Just let another teacher raise her eyebrow funny, just so they [the children] know, and they don't miss a thing, and their respect for you goes right away" (Becker, 1953:139). Similarly, we learn that the medical profession has a strict code of etiquette whereby a consultant in the presence of the patient and his doctor is careful never to say anything which would embarrass the impression of competence that the patient's doctor is attempting to maintain. As Hughes suggests, "The [professional] *etiquette* is a body of ritual which grows up informally to preserve, before the clients, the common front of the profession" (Hughes, 1946:273). And, of course, this kind of solidarity in the presence of subordinates also occurs when performers are in the presence of superordinates. For example, in a recent study of the police we learn that a patrolling team of two policemen, who witness each other's illegal and semi-illegal acts and who are in an excellent position to discredit each other's show of legality before the judge, possess heroic solidarity and will stick by each other's story no matter what atrocity it covers up or how little chance there is of anyone believing it (Westley, 1952: 187–96).

It is apparent that if performers are concerned with maintaining a line they will select as teammates those who can be trusted to perform properly. Thus children of the house are often excluded from performances given for guests of a domestic establishment because often children cannot be trusted to "behave" themselves, i.e., to refrain from acting in a way inconsistent with the impression that is being fostered.[6] Similarly, those who are known to become intoxicated when drink is available and who become verbose or "difficult" when this occurs constitute a performance risk, as do those who are sober but foolishly indiscreet, and those who refuse to "enter into the spirit" of the occasion and help sustain the impression that guests tacitly unite in maintaining to the host.

I have suggested that in many interaction settings some of the participants co-operate together as a team or are in a position where they are dependent upon this co-operation in order to maintain a particular definition of the situation. Now when we study concrete social establishments we often find that there will be a significant

[6] In so far as children are defined as "non-persons" they have some license to commit gauche acts without requiring the audience to take the expressive implications of these acts too seriously. However, whether treated as non-persons or not, children are in a position to disclose crucial secrets.

sense in which all the remaining participants, in their several perform-ances of response to the team-show put on before them, will them-selves constitute a team. Since each team will be playing through its routine for the other, one may speak of dramatic interaction, not dramatic action, and we can see this interaction not as a medley of as many voices as there are participants but rather as a kind of dialogue and interplay between two teams. I do not know of any general reason why interaction in natural settings usually takes the form of two-team interplay, or is resolvable into this form, instead of involving a larger number, but empirically this seems to be the case. Thus, in large social establishments, where several different status grades prevail, we find that for the duration of any particular interaction, participants of many different statuses are typically expected to align themselves temporarily into two team groupings. For example, a lieu-tenant at an Army post will find himself aligned with all the officers and opposed to all enlisted men in one situation; at other times he will find himself aligned with junior officers, presenting with them a show for the benefit of senior officers present. There are, of course, aspects of certain interactions for which a two-team model is apparently not suitable. Important elements, for example, of arbitration hearings seem to fit a three-team model, and aspects of some competitive and "social" situations suggest a multiteam model. It should also be made clear that whatever the number of teams, there will be a sense in which the interaction can be analyzed in terms of the co-operative effort of all participants to maintain a working consensus.

If we treat an interaction as a dialogue between two teams, it will sometimes be convenient to call one team the performers and to call the other team the audience or the observers, neglecting momentarily that the audience, too, will be presenting a team-performance. In some cases, as when two one-person teams interact in a public institution or in the home of a mutual friend, it may be an arbitrary choice as to which team to call the performer and which to call the audience. In many important social situations, however, the social setting in which the interaction occurs is assembled and managed by one of the teams only, and contributes in a more intimate way to the show this team puts on than to the show put on in response by the other team. A customer in a shop, a client in an office, a group of guests in the home of their hosts—these persons put on a performance and maintain a front, but the setting in which they do this is outside of their immediate control, being an integral part of the presentation made by those into whose presence they have come. In such cases, it will often be convenient to call the team which controls the setting the performing team, and to call the other team the audience. So, too, it will sometimes be convenient to label as performer the team which contributes the more activity to the interaction, or plays the more dramatically promi-nent part in it, or sets the pace and direction which both teams will follow in their interactive dialogue.

The obvious point must be stated that if the team is to sustain the impression that it is fostering, then there must be some assurance that no individual will be allowed to join both team and audience. Thus, for example, if the proprietor of a small ladies' ready-to-wear is to put a dress on sale and tell his customer that it is marked down because of soilage, or end of the season, or last of a line, etc., and conceal from her that it is really marked down because it won't sell, or is a bad color or style, and if he is to impress her by talking about a buying office in New York which he does not have or an adjustment manager who is really a salesgirl, then he must make sure that if he finds it necessary to hire an extra girl for part-time work on Saturday he does not hire one from the neighborhood who has been a customer and who will soon be one again.[7]

It is often felt that control of the setting is an advantage during interaction. In a narrow sense, this control allows a team to introduce strategic devices for determining the information the audience is able to acquire. Thus, if doctors are to prevent cancer patients from learning the identity of their disease, it will be useful to be able to scatter the cancer patients throughout the hospital so that they will not be able to learn from the identity of their ward the identity of their disorder. (The hospital staff, incidentally, may be forced to spend more time walking corridors and moving equipment because of this staging strategy than would otherwise be necessary.) Similarly, the master barber who regulates the flow of appointments by means of a scheduling book open to his public is in a position to protect his coffee break by filling a properly timed appointment with a dummy code name. A prospective customer can then see for himself that it will not be possible for him to have an appointment at that time. Another interesting use of setting and props is reported in an article on American sororities, where a description is given of how the sorority sisters, who give a tea for prospective members, are able to sort out good prospects from bad without giving the impression that guests of the house are being treated differentially:

> "Even with recommends, it's hard to remember 967 girls by just meeting them for a few minutes in a receiving line," admitted Carol. "So we've worked out this gimmick to separate the good ones from the dull characters. We have three trays for the rushees' calling cards—one for golden girls, one for look-agains, one for pots.
> "The active who is talking with the rushee at the party is supposed to escort her subtly to the appropriate tray when she's ready to leave her card," Carol continued. "The rushees never figure out what we're doing!" [Beck, 1954.]

Another illustration may be cited from the arts of hotel management. If any member of a hotel staff is suspicious of the intentions or character

[7] These illustrations are taken from George Rosenbaum (1953:86–87).

of a guest couple, a secret signal can be given to the bellboy to "throw the latch."

> This is simply a device which makes it easier for employees to keep an eye on suspected parties.
> After rooming the couple, the bellman, in closing the door behind him, pushes a tiny button on the inside of the knob handle. This turns a little tumbler inside the lock and makes a black stripe show against the circular center of the latch on the outside. It's inconspicuous enough so as not to be noticed by the guest, but maids, patrols, waiters and bellmen are all trained to watch for them . . . and to report any loud conversations or unusual occurrences which take place behind them. [Collans, with Sterling, 1954:56; ellipsis dots are the authors'.]

More broadly, control of the setting may give the controlling team a sense of security. As one student suggests concerning the pharmacist-doctor relation:

> The store is another factor. The doctor often comes to the pharmacist's store for medicine, for bits of information, for conversation. In these conversations the man behind the counter has approximately the same advantage that a standing speaker has over a sitting audience. [Weinlein, 1943:105.]

> One thing that contributes to this feeling of the independence of the pharmacist's medical practice is his store. The store is, in a sense, a part of the pharmacist. Just as Neptune is pictured as rising from the sea, while at the same time being the sea; so in the pharmaceutical ethos there is a vision of a dignified pharmacist towering above shelves and counters of bottles and equipment, while at the same time being part of their essence. [Weinlein, 1943:105–6.]

A nice literary illustration of the effects of being robbed of control over one's setting is given by Franz Kafka, in *The Trial*, where K.'s meeting with the authorities in his own boardinghouse is described:

> When he was fully dressed he had to walk, with Willem treading on his heels, through the next room, which was now empty, into the adjoining one, whose double doors were flung open. This room, as K. knew quite well, had recently been taken by a Fraulein Bürstner, a typist, who went very early to work, came home late, and with whom he had exchanged little more than few words in passing. Now the night-table beside her bed had been pushed into the middle of the floor to serve as desk, and the inspector was sitting behind it. He had crossed his legs, and one arm was resting on the back of the chair.
> . . . "Joseph K.?" asked the inspector, perhaps merely to draw K.'s distracted glance upon himself. K. nodded. "You are presumably very surprised at the events of this morning?" asked the inspector, with both hands rearranging the few things that lay on the night-table, a candle and a matchbox, a book and a pincushion, as if they were objects

which he required for his interrogation. "Certainly," said K., and he was filled with pleasure at having encountered a sensible man at last, with whom he could discuss the matter. "Certainly, I am surprised, but I am by no means very surprised." "Not very surprised?" asked the inspector, setting the candle in the middle of the table and then grouping the other things around it. "Perhaps you misunderstand me," K. hastened to add. "I mean"—here K. stopped and looked round him for a chair. "I suppose I may sit down?" he asked. "It's not usual," answered the inspector. [Kafka, 1948:14–15.]

A price must, of course, be paid for the privilege of giving a performance on one's home ground; one has the opportunity of conveying information about oneself through scenic means but no opportunity of concealing the kinds of facts that are conveyed by scenery. It is to be expected then that a potential performer may have to avoid his own stage and its controls in order to prevent an unflattering performance, and that this can involve more than the postponement of a social party because the new furniture has not yet arrived. Thus, of a slum area in London we learn that:

. . . mothers in this area, more than mothers elsewhere, prefer their children to be born in hospital. The main reason for this preference seems to be the expense of an at-home birth since proper equipment must be bought, towels for instance, and bathing basins, so that everything measures up to the standards required by the midwife. It also means the presence in the home of a strange woman, which in turn means a special cleaning out. [Spinley, 1953:45.]

When one examines a team-performance, one often finds that someone is given the right to direct and control the progress of the dramatic action. The equerry in court establishments is an example. Sometimes the individual who dominates the show in this way and is, in a sense, the director of it, plays an actual part in the performance he directs. This is illustrated for us by a novelist's view of the ministerial functions at a wedding ceremony:

The minister left the door ajar, so that they [Robert, the groom, and Lionel, the best-man] might hear their cue and enter without delay. They stood at the door like eavesdroppers. Lionel touched his pocket, felt the round outline of the ring, then put his hand on Robert's elbow. As the cue word approached, Lionel opened the door and, on cue, propelled Robert forward.

The ceremony moved without a hitch under the firm and experienced hand of the minister, who came down hard on the cues and used his eyebrows to menace the performers. The guests did not notice that Robert had a hard time getting the ring on the bride's finger; they did, however, notice that the bride's father cried overmuch and the mother not at all. But these were small things soon forgotten. [Miller, 1958:254.]

In general, the members of the team will differ in the ways and the degree to which they are allowed to direct the performance. It may be noted, incidentally, that the structural similarities of apparently diverse routines are nicely reflected in the like-mindedness that arises in directors everywhere. Whether it is a funeral, a wedding, a bridge party, a one-day sale, a hanging, or a picnic, the director may tend to see the performance in terms of whether or not it went "smoothly," "effectively," and "without a hitch," and whether or not all possible disruptive contingencies were prepared for in advance.

In many performances two important functions must be fulfilled, and if the team has a director he will often be given the special duty of fulfilling these functions.

First, the director may be given the special duty of bringing back into line any member of the team whose performance becomes unsuitable. Soothing and sanctioning are the corrective processes ordinarily involved. The role of the baseball umpire in sustaining a particular kind of reality for the fans may be taken as an illustration.

All umpires insist that players keep themselves under control, and refrain from gestures that reflect contempt for their decisions.

I certainly had blown off my share of steam as a player, and I knew there had to be a safety valve for release of the terrific tension. As an umpire I could sympathize with the players. But as an umpire I had to decide how far I could let a player go without delaying the game and without permitting him to insult, assault, or ridicule me and belittle the game. Handling trouble and men on the field was as important as calling them right—and more difficult.

It is easy for any umpire to thumb a man out of the game. It is often a much more difficult job to keep him in the game—to understand and anticipate his complaint so that a nasty rhubarb cannot develop.

I do not tolerate clowning on the field, and neither will any other umpire. Comedians belong on the stage or on television, not in baseball. A travesty or burlesque of the game can only cheapen it, and also hold the umpire up to scorn for allowing such a sketch to take place. That's why you will see the funnymen and wise guys chased as soon as they begin their routine. [Pinelli, 1953:141, 131, 139.]

Often, of course, the director will not so much have to smother improper affect as he will have to stimulate a show of proper affective involvement; "sparking the show" is the phrase sometimes employed for this task in Rotarian circles.

Secondly, the director may be given the special duty of allocating the parts in the performance and the personal front that is employed in each part, for each establishment may be seen as a place with a number of characters to dispose of to prospective performers and as an assemblage of sign-equipment or ceremonial paraphernalia to be allocated.

It is apparent that if the director corrects for improper appearances and allocates major and minor prerogatives, then other members of the team (who are likely to be concerned with the show they can put on for one another as well as with the show they can collectively stage for the audience) will have an attitude toward the director that they do not have toward their other teammates. Further, if the audience appreciates that the performance has a director, they are likely to hold him more responsible than other performers for the success of the performance. The director is likely to respond to this responsibility by making dramaturgical demands on the performance that they might not make upon themselves. This may add to the estrangement they may already feel from him. A director, hence, starting as a member of the team, may find himself slowly edged into a marginal role between audience and performers, half in and half out of both camps, a kind of go-between without the protection that go-betweens usually have. The factory foreman has been a recently discussed example.[8]

When we study a routine which requires a team of several performers for its presentation, we sometimes find that one member of the team is made the star, lead, or center of attention. We may see an extreme example of this in traditional court life, where a room full of court attendants will be arranged in the manner of a living tableau, so that the eye, starting from any point in the room will be led to the royal center of attention. The royal star of the performance may also be dressed more spectacularly and seated higher than anyone else present. An even more spectacular centering of attention may be found in the dance arrangements of large musical comedies, in which forty or fifty dancers are made to prostrate themselves around the heroine.

The extravagance of the performances found at royal appearances should not blind us to the utility of the concept of a court: courts in fact are commonly found outside of palaces, one instance being the commissaries of Hollywood production studios. While it seems abstractly true that individuals are convivially endogamous, tending to restrict informal ties to those of their own social status, still, when a social class is examined closely, one may find it to be made up of separated social sets, each set containing one and only one complement of differently placed performers. And frequently the set will form around one dominant figure who is constantly maintained as the center of attention in the center of the stage. Evelyn Waugh suggests this theme in a discussion of the British upper class:

Look back twenty-five years to the time when there was still a fairly firm aristocratic structure and the country was still divided into spheres of influence among hereditary magnates. My memory is that the grandees avoided one another unless they were closely related. They met on

[8] See, for example, Donald E. Wray (1949) and Fritz Roethlisberger (1945).

state occasions and on the racecourse. They did not frequent one another's houses. You might find almost anyone in a ducal castle —convalescent, penurious cousins, advisory experts, sycophants, gigolos and plain blackmailers. The one thing you could be sure of not finding was a concourse of other dukes. English society, it seemed to me, was a complex of tribes, each with its chief and elders and witch-doctors and braves, each with its own dialect and deity, each strongly xenophobic. [Waugh, 1956:78.]

The informal social life conducted by the staffs of our universities and other intellectual bureaucracies seems to break up in something of the same way: the cliques and factions which form the smaller parties of administrative politics form the courts of convivial life, and it is here that local heroes can safely sustain the eminence of their wit, their competence and their profundity.

In general, then one finds that those who help present a team-performance differ in the degree of dramatic dominance given each of them and that one team-routine differs from another in the extent to which differentials in dominance are given its members.

The conceptions of dramatic and directive dominance, as contrasting types of power in a performance, can be applied, *mutatis mutandis*, to an interaction as a whole, where it will be possible to point out which of the two teams has more of which of the two types of power and which performers, taking the participants of both teams all together, lead in these two regards.

Frequently, of course, the performer or team which has one kind of dominance will have the other, but this is by no means always the case. For example, during the showing of the body at a funeral home, usually the social setting and all participants, including both the bereaved team and the establishment's team, will be arranged so as to express their feelings for the deceased and their ties to him; he will be the center of the show and the dramatically dominant participant in it. However, since the bereaved are inexperienced and grief-laden, and since the star of the show must stay in character as someone who is in a deep sleep, the undertaker himself will direct the show, although he may all the while be self-effacing in the presence of the corpse or be in another room of the establishment getting ready for another showing.

It should be made clear that dramatic and directive dominance are dramaturgical terms and that performers who enjoy such dominance may not have other types of power and authority. It is common knowledge that performers who have positions of visible leadership are often merely figureheads, selected as a compromise, or as a way of neutralizing a potentially threatening position, or as a way of strategically concealing the power behind the front and hence the power behind the power behind the front. So also, [when] inexperienced or temporary incumbents are given formal authority over experienced subordinates, we often find that the formally empowered person is bribed with a part that has dramatic dominance while the subordinates tend to direct the show.

(See Riesman *et al.*, 1950:363–67.) Thus it has often been said about the British infantry in World War I that experienced working-class sergeants managed the delicate task of covertly teaching their new lieutenants to take a dramatically expressive role at the head of the platoon and to die quickly in a prominent dramatic position, as befits public-school men. The sergeants themselves took their modest place at the rear of the platoon and tended to live to train still other lieutenants.

Dramatic and directive dominance have been mentioned as two dimensions along which each place on a team can vary. By changing the point of reference a little, we can discern a third mode of variation.

In general, those who participate in the activity that occurs in a social establishment become members of a team when they co-operate together to present their activity in a particular light. However, in taking on the role of a performer, the individual need not cease to devote some of his effort to non-dramaturgical concerns, that is, to the activity itself of which the performance offers an acceptable dramatization. We may expect, then, that the individuals who perform on a particular team will differ among themselves in the way they apportion their time between mere activity and mere performance. At one extreme there will be individuals who rarely appear before the audience and are little concerned with appearances. At the other extreme are what are sometimes called "purely ceremonial roles," whose performers will be concerned with the appearance that they make, and concerned with little else. For example, both the president and the research director of a national union may spend time in the main office of the union headquarters, appearing suitably dressed and suitably spoken in order to give the union a front of respectability. However, one may find that the president also engages in making many important decisions whereas the research director may have little to do except be present in body as part of the president's retinue. Union officials conceive of such purely ceremonial roles as part of "window dressing." [9] The same division of labor can be found in domestic establishments, where something more general than task-qualities must be exhibited. The familiar theme of conspicuous consumption describes how husbands in modern society have the job of acquiring socio-economic status, and wives the job of displaying this acquisition. During somewhat earlier times, the footman provided an even more clear instance of this specialization:

> But the chief value of the footman lay in one of these [domestic] services directly. It was the efficiency with which he advertised the extent of his master's wealth. All domestics served that end, since their presence in an establishment demonstrated their master's ability to pay and maintain them in return for little or no productive work. But all were not equally effective in this respect. Those whose uncommon

[9] See Harold L. Wilensky (1953:Chap. 4). In addition to his thesis material, I am indebted to Mr. Wilensky for many suggestions.

skills and specialized training commanded a high remuneration reflected more credit upon their employers than those who were paid at lower rates; those whose duties brought them obtrusively into view more effectively suggested their master's wealth than those whose work kept them constantly out of sight. Livery servants, from the coachman down to the footboy, were among the most effective of the lot. Their routines endowed them with the highest visibility. Moreover, the livery itself emphasized their remoteness from productive labor. Their effectiveness achieved its maximum in the footman, for his routine exposed him to view more consistently than did that of any of the others. He was, in consequence, one of the most vital parts of his master's display. [Hecht, 1956:53–54.]

It may be remarked that an individual with a purely ceremonial role need not have a dramatically dominant one.

A team, then, may be defined as a set of individuals whose intimate co-operation is required if a given projected definition of the situation is to be maintained. A team is a grouping, but it is a grouping not in relation to a social structure or social organization but rather in relation to an interaction or series of interactions in which the relevant definition of the situation is maintained.

We have seen, and will see further, that if a performance is to be effective it will be likely that the extent and character of the co-operation that makes this possible will be concealed and kept secret. A team, then, has something of the character of a secret society. The audience may appreciate, of course, that all the members of the team are held together by a bond no member of the audience shares. Thus, for example, when customers enter a service establishment, they clearly appreciate that all employees are different from customers by virtue of this official role. However, the individuals who are on the staff of an establishment are not members of a team by virtue of staff status, but only by virtue of the co-operation which they maintain in order to sustain a given definition of the situation. No effort may be made in many cases to conceal who is on the staff; but they form a secret society, a team, in so far as a secret is kept as to how they are co-operating together to maintain a particular definition of the situation.

Teams may be created by individuals to aid the group they are members of, but in aiding themselves and their group in this drama-turgical way, they are acting as a team, not a group. Thus a team, as used herein, is the kind of secret society whose members may be known by non-members to constitute a society, even an exclusive one, but the society these individuals are known to constitute is not the one they constitute by virtue of acting as a team.

Since we all participate on teams we must all carry within ourselves something of the sweet guilt of conspirators. And since each team is engaged in maintaining the stability of some definitions of the situation, concealing or playing down certain facts in order to do this, we can expect the performer to live out his conspiratorial career in some furtiveness.

References

BECK, JOAN
> 1954 "What's Wrong with Sorority Rushing?" *Chicago Tribune Magazine* (January 10):20–21.

BECKER, HOWARD S.
> 1953 "The Teacher in the Authority System of the Public School." *Journal of Educational Sociology* 27 (November):128–41.

COLLANS, DEV, with STEWART STERLING
> 1954 *I Was a House Detective*. New York: Dutton.

DALE, H. E.
> 1941 *The Higher Civil Service of Great Britain*. Oxford: Oxford University Press.

Esquire Etiquette
> 1953 Philadelphia: Lippincott.

GROSS, EDWARD
> 1949 "Informal Relations and the Social Organization of Work in an Industrial Office." Unpublished Ph.D. dissertation, Department of Sociology, University of Chicago.

HECHT, J. J.
> 1956 *The Domestic Servant Class in Eighteenth-Century England*. London: Routledge & Kegan Paul.

HOLCOMBE, CHESTER
> 1895 *The Real Chinaman*. New York: Dodd, Mead.

HUGHES, E. C.
> 1946 "Institutions." In ALFRED M. LEE, ed., *New Outline of the Principles of Sociology*. New York: Barnes & Noble.

HUNTER, FLOYD
> 1953 *Community Power Structure*. Chapel Hill: University of North Carolina Press.

JOHNSON, CHARLES
> 1943 *Patterns of Negro Segregation*. New York: Harper.

KAFKA, FRANZ
> 1948 *The Trial*. New York: Knopf.

MANNHEIM, KARL
> 1956 *Essays on the Sociology of Culture*. London: Routledge & Kegan Paul.

MILLER, WARREN
> 1958 *The Sleep of Reason*. Boston: Little, Brown.

MOORE, GERALD
> 1944 *The Unashamed Accompanist*. New York: Macmillan.

NEUMANN, JOHN VON, and OSKAR MORGENSTERN
> 1947 *The Theory of Games and Economic Behaviour*. 2d ed, Princeton: Princeton University Press.

PINELLI, BABE, as told to JOE KING
> 1953 *Mr. Ump*. Philadelphia: Westminster Press.

RIESMAN, DAVID, in collaboration with REUEL DENNY and NATHAN GLAZER
    1950   "The Avocation Counselors." In *The Lonely Crowd*. New Haven: Yale
                University Press.
ROETHLISBERGER, FRITZ
    1945   "The Foreman: Master and Victim of Double Talk." *Harvard Business
                Review* 23 (Spring):285–94.
ROSENBAUM, GEORGE
    1953   "An Analysis of Personalization in Neighborhood Apparel Retailing."
                Unpublished M.A. thesis, Department of Sociology, University of
                Chicago.
SOLOMON, DAVID
    1952   "Career Contingencies of Chicago Physicians." Unpublished M.A. thesis,
                Department of Sociology, University of Chicago.
SPINLEY, B. M.
    1953   *The Deprived and the Privileged*. London: Routledge & Kegan Paul.
TAXEL, HAROLD
    1953   "Authority Structure in a Mental Hospital Ward." Unpublished M.A.
                thesis, Department of Sociology, University of Chicago.
WAUGH, EVELYN
    1956   "An Open Letter." In NANCY MITFORD, ed., *Noblesse Oblige*. London:
                Hamish Hamilton.
WEINLEIN, ANTHONY
    1943   "Pharmacy as a Profession in Wisconsin." Unpublished M.A. thesis,
                Department of Sociology, University of Chicago.
WESTLEY, WILLIAM
    1952   "The Police." Unpublished Ph.D. dissertation, Department of Sociology,
                University of Chicago.
WILENSKY, HAROLD L.
    1953   "The Staff 'Expert': A Study of the Intelligence Function in American
                Trade Unions." Unpublished Ph.D. dissertation, Department of
                Sociology, University of Chicago.
WRAY, DONALD E.
    1949   "Marginal Men of Industry: The Foreman." *American Journal of Soci-
                ology* 54 (January):298–301.